Sovereignty and Interpretation of International Norms

Carlos Fernández de Casadevante y Romani

Sovereignty and Interpretation of International Norms

Springer

Professor Carlos Fernández de Casadevante y Romani
Universidad Rey Juan Carlos
Facultad de Ciencias Jurídicas y Sociales
Paseo de los Artilleros s/n
28032 Vicálvaro (Madrid)
Spain
carlos.fernandezdecasadevante@urjc.es

The author wishes to thank Prof. John Mullen (Universidad Pontificia de Comillas, Madrid) for its work in the revision and correction of the English drafting.

Library of Congress Control Number: 2007920844

ISBN 978-3-540-68206-6 Springer Berlin Heidelberg New York

Springer is part of Springer Science+Business Media

springer.com

Production: LE-TEX Jelonek, Schmidt & Vöckler GbR, Leipzig
Cover-design: WMX Design GmbH, Heidelberg

SPIN 11949435 64/3100YL - 5 4 3 2 1 0 Printed on acid-free paper

To Virginia, Maria, Pablo,
Victoria, Irene and Clara
With love

Table of Contents

Part One:

Interpretation of International Norms: Sovereignty, Power of Discretion, Delimitation of the Discrepancy

CHAPTER I:

Sovereignty and Interpretation: A Relationship of Dependence

1 The sovereignty of the State conditions the interpretation of international norms: Discrepancy, discretion. Persistence of the problem

As we approach the beginning of the XXI century, one might think that addressing the problem of the interpretation of international norms is just another theoretical contribution to the Science of Law. Some might criticise it as being one more paper turned out by the ivory tower of the university. The problems, the practice, in other words, real life goes on outside these walls and our goal would only be another theoretical construction devoid of practical application and utility. However, the interpretation of international norms is one of the themes most closely linked to the practice of both international and domestic law. Furthermore, in the international field of law, the task of interpretation underlies the range of norms (conventional, institutional and custom), as well as the other ways of creating legal obligations (unilateral declarations), and it acquires a new dimension within the framework of the functioning of the international judicial or arbitration scenario. In this context, interpretation can be required on different occasions. This may be beforehand, as regards the declaration of acceptance of the jurisdiction of the body in question, or while exercising the judicial or arbitration function (while applying the norm to the specific case, which will acquire a variety of profiles depending on the type of norm). However, it is also required when there is a hypothetical application of the interpretation of a judgement or of the advisory opinion of the I.C.J.

So, it is evident that in the international legal order the problems linked to the interpretation of norms and the conduct of the State are neither theoretical nor trivial.

In spite of the advances made, the International Community is still a society composed mainly of sovereign States and is characterised by the decentralisation of political power.

The consequence is that sovereignty is involved both in the creation process of Law as well as in its application, despite the limits it is progressively subjected to as a result of the development of International Law as a whole and the material conditions of contemporary life. With regard to the former, the incidence of State sovereignty is clearly evident in the initial phase of the formation process of the international norm: the time when the contrasting interests of the Parties are sifted to obtain a general consensus, or even a formal international agreement. Concerning this last aspect, since the interpretation of the international norm usually occurs on the occasion of its application to a specific case. As P.M. DUPUY reminds us, one of the features of the international legal order derives from the fact that, within it, in principle, each subject has the competence, to interpret the meaning and scope of the rights and obligations he has by virtue of the international norms. This task is carried out by each State "depending on the representation of its interest in a specific situation and the distrust it has of its partners"[1].

In the initial phase, sovereignty is involved in specifying the content of the norm, with the peculiarity that, depending on the type of norm, the behaviour of the Parties or the language chosen by them is the vehicle used to express the sovereign will of the State.

In order to reach agreement, which is both the result and the instrument of international co-operation, language continues to be the fundamental tool insofar as written norms are concerned. It is through language that international rights and obligations are constructed, and these make up the written expression of the will and consent of the State.

In this regard, it would be wrong to think that States are interested in the clear determination of rights and obligations in a given situation when they act in the international field. In the majority of the cases this is not usually the case. On the contrary, the willingness of the State to be bound will be more easily achieved if there is sufficient flexibility to satisfy the proposals and counter-proposals that will give rise to the text of the agreement once these proposals have undergone a process of negotiation. In this process, the language, the terms, constitute the tools and the more general the terms in which the obligations are couched, the easier it will be to reach an agreement on the text. This fact is easy to verify in conventional international practice, especially in regard to the drafting of multilateral treaties. The other side of the coin is the difficulty encountered afterwards in practice when the time comes to determine the content of an obligation drafted in fuzzy language, which can be read at the discretion of the reader, but did make the agreement possible. Such use of very vague terms is often the price that States pay to facilitate a minimum of organised international co-operation assumed by them voluntarily and entailing progressive limitation of their sovereignty. But this vagueness of the language employed is also a source of controversy and discrepancies when the time comes to apply the norm.

---

[1] DUPUY, P.M., *Droit international public,* Dalloz, Paris1992, p. 218 et seq. Institutional norms should be added to the list of norms drawn up by this author. See also, the general treatment given by MCDOUGAL, M.S., LASSWELL, H.D., and MILLER, J.C., *The Interpretation of International Agreements*, M. NIJHOFF, Dordrecht, 1994 and LEIBIGER, M., *Die souveränitätsfreundliche Auslegung im Völkerrecht*, Frankfurt am Main, Berlin, Bern, Wien, Lang, 2005.

However, it is also true that the problems of interpretation of norms does not disappear when the obligation is drafted in clear language. In this case, the discrepancy can come about as a result of the concurrent, though divergent interpretation made by the Parties when the norm is applied to a specific case. In other words, the clarity of the norm in its initial formulation is not a guarantee of convergent interpretations at the time of application because of the discretionary competence that States have in order to interpret as a result of their sovereignty. Thus, despite the aphorism of VATTEL[2] *in claris non fiat interpretatio* clarity is not the presupposition of interpretation, but its result. The existence of divergence is sufficient to necessitate interpretation. As REMIRO points out concerning conventional norms, it will always be necessary to "determine the sense, establish the scope, clear up obscure points and ambiguity in provisions, possibly deliberately inserted by the negotiators, before applying them to specific cases"[3]. That is why SIMON speaks of the "omnipresence" of the process of interpretation which comes across more strongly in International Law than in the other branches of Law, due to the specific nature of the former.

In fact, in domestic law the extent of the lack of determination of the legal norms leading to the need for interpretation is, generally speaking, less frequent, owing both to the hierarchy of the norms and to the centralising of the essential function of interpretation in the hands of the Judge[4]. At international level, as we have already pointed out, the situation is completely different as it involves an international society characterised by the co-existence of sovereign states[5].

These problems take on a new dimension during the process of institutionalisation of the International Community which, rather than simplify these problems, makes them even more acute to the extent that obtaining agreement requires a high dose of flexibility when drafting the aspirations of the different states in a text at the risk of making the international norm unworkable. The price again entails language which is sufficiently ample to satisfy the opposing interests. As is stressed in the doctrine, the International Organisations have not replaced the

---

2 VATTEL, E., *El Derecho de Gentes o principios de la Ley Natural aplicados a la conducta y a los megocios de las naciones y de los Soberanos,* Translation by Pascual Hernández, M.M., Vol. I, Madrid. 1834, p. 474: "The first general maxim on interpretation is that *it is not licit to interpret what does not require interpretation"* (the italics are from the original).

3 REMIRO BROTONS, A., *Derecho Internacional Público. 2 Derecho de los Tratados,* Tecnos, Madrid, 1987, p. 306: Similarly VOICU, I "In order to be applied every legal norm must be interpreted, even if the proceedings are taking place *sub silentio"* (*De l'interprétation des traités internationaux,* Pedone, Paris, 1968, p. 4).

4 However, as we shall see, problems can arise concerning the interpretation of treaties by domestic judges to the extent that he may address the matter unaware of the interpretative rules proper to International Law.

5 Vid SIMON, D., *L'interprétation judiciaire des traités d'Organisations Internationales,* Pedone, Paris, 1981, p. 7.

sovereign States, but they have meant a channel for transformation as they enable greater effectiveness and provide new dimensions to the functions and scope of international legal norms. Unlike classical International Law, which was presided over by the principle of reciprocity which was involved in the creation, execution and sanction of the international legal obligations, contemporary International Law has been modified both as regards regulation and as an institutional mechanism. This regulation currently aspires to forge social reality by creating conditions of peace and by ceasing to be a Law limiting the competence between sovereign States, a Law which was "exclusively formal and procedural to become a law for regulating which defines the conduct of States as regards the satisfaction of the general interests of the International Community as a whole, that is to say, with regard to the promotion and achievement of the common good"[6] or, also of a greater or lesser group of States. Insofar as the instruments for achieving these general interests are usually the treaty and the institutional norm (both of which make up the expression of international co-operation), the use of language which is wide enough to enable a consensus on the text of the norm to be reached continues to be the means for achieving this. Consequently, the problems of interpretation do not disappear. We will have the chance to check this out in this book when we address the problems of institutional norms from the perspective of the resolutions of the United Nations General Assembly.

Moreover, within the environment of the United Nations, worrying interpretations of the Charter have been made. Recent practice in the Security Council reveals the existence of *political* interpretations of the Charter which call into question the principle of legality which ought to govern the interpretation and application of international norms. One of the most significant examples of this tendency is observed in Resolution 748 (1992) of the Security Council adopted with regard to Libya in the *Lockerbie case* by which the problem was placed within the framework of Chapter VII of the Charter. Such an interpretation does not fit in with the demands of the Charter itself. As international doctrine has pointed out the basic underlying problem in this matter is the dangerous interpretation of Chapter VII of the Charter proposed by the United States and the United Kingdom by which "the Security Council, which has been introduced into this chapter on request, can adopt any decision including those which are *para* or *contra legem* and the ICJ cannot participate or acknowledge an environment of immunity as regards the Council when it acts in order to maintain international peace and security, and convert this chapter – as SUY stated- into the *"domaine réservé"* or the "*casse gardée*" of the Council"[7]. Later on we will address this issue in depth[8].

---

6 CARRILLO SALCEDO, J.A., *El Derecho Internacional en un mundo en cambio,* Tecnos, Madrid, 1984, p. 192.

7 ANDRES SAENZ DE SANTA MARIA, M. P., "'De maximis non curat praetor'. The Security Council and the ICJ in the Lockerbie Case", *R.E.D.I.*,1992/2, p. 344.

8 See pages 185-189 of the present work.

The situation described in the preceding pages shows the relevance and the consequences that state sovereignty has in the process for the formation of international norms and in the time it is applied; characteristics which are also involved when the norm is adopted and applied within the institutions of International Organisations.

The predominant state structure of the International Community, which is also found in the structures of the International Organisations and their organic structures, together with the principle of the autonomy of the will of the parties or of the Members of the Organisation in question as a consequence of sovereignty, condition and infuse all the formation and application process of the international norms and this is obvious from the drafting of the norm and the later application which is when the necessity for interpretation arises as we have pointed out previously.

The same situation also appears regarding the customary norms and unilateral declarations but with different features. Thus, in the firsts, the difficulties become more acute as the states manifest their will and exercise their sovereignty through their conduct in practice. Consequently, this practice must be analysed in order to determine the existence of the norm in question, its content, the appropriateness of its application to the specific case and its interpretation in the event that the previous verification has been positive. In addition, there are no rules for interpretation to help those carrying out this task.

Finally, in unilateral declarations, sovereignty is expressed through the terms employed in the declaration; these terms express the will of the State as regards a situation of fact or of law. As in the previous case of the customary norms, there are no rules for the interpretation of unilateral declarations so, in accordance with the case law of the ICJ, the determination concerning whether the declaration in question produces legal effects or not must be done by interpreting the act and analysing the intention of the author of the declaration. These are some of the criteria laid down by the Court. Despite this fact, difficulties exist insofar as the institution called on to interpret the declaration in the event of controversy enjoys wide autonomy and freedom to carry out its work, and its interpretation might not coincide with the real intention of the author of the declaration. ICJ case law provides examples of this type.

Thus, it can be stated that interpretation is a problem which lies "at the heart of the application of international law"[9] but is not confined to the Law of Treaties, though it extends to the totality of international regulations[10].

---

9 SIMON, D., *L'interprétation judiciaire*, *op. cit.*, p. 6.

10 In the words of DUPUY,P.-M.: "In fact, interpretation plays an important role in the totality of international law and not only in the law of treaties because it, to a great extent, conditions its application" (*Droit international public, op. cit.*, p. 218). Consequently, the task of interpreting arises as regards conventional law, customary norms and institutional norms as well as unilateral legal acts.

At *doctrinal level* there is discussion on whether the interpretation of the norm precedes application or whether the opposite is true[11]. In our opinion, as we have stated before, the interpretation of international norms generally, though not exclusively, arises in the event of its application to a specific case. When the norm is applied to a specific case is when the controversies might arise between the Parts affected and, in fact, controversy concerning interpretation is frequent as evidenced by the examination of international judicial and arbitration case law[12]. Thus, the determination of the meaning and the scope of the norm constitute problems which delay or condition its application[13]. Therefore, if the application of the norm cannot be regulated by harmonising the range of interpretations provided by the Parties concerned, the application leads to questioning, at least, the usefulness of the norm, its operative efficacy, and even its very existence.

At a material level, this interpretation has two forms which are "in fact inseparable when a problem of application arises, therefore successive forms: establishing the general sense of the norm by abstract interpretation, seeking to fix its meaning in a particular case by specific interpretation. In the latter case, it is used together with the interpretation of the circumstances at the base of its application"[14]. However, when it is a question of customary norms both ways for interpreting appear obscure as it is first necessary to demonstrate the existence of the custom in order to interpret it and apply it to the specific case. On the other hand, the

---

11 In the presentation of its articles, the Vienna Convention of May 22, 1969 on the Law of Treaties places the application of the treaties (Part III, 2nd Section) before their interpretation (Part III, 3rd Section).

12 For example, the *case of the interpretation of the Peace Treaties with Bulgaria, Hungary and Rumania (*ICJ, *Reports 1950,* pages 65-78*); the case of the interpretation of the Agreement of March 25, 1951 between the WHO and Egypt (*ICJ, *Reports 1980,* pages 67-98*); the case regarding the arbitration Ruling of July 3, 1989 (*ICJ, *Reports 1989,* pages 53-76*); the case of the Questions of Interpretation of the Montreal Convention of 1971 as a result of the Lockerbie Air Incident (*ICJ, *Reports 1992,* pages 114-127*); the case of territorial dispute (*ICJ, *Reports 1994,* pages 6-42*).* As regards arbitration one example is the Arbitration Ruling of December 22, 1963, concerning the *case of the interpretation of the Franco-American Agreement on International Air Transport* (See on this case: COTT, J.P., "L'interprétation de l'accord franco-américain relatif au transport aérien international (Judgement Arbitral du 22 décembre 1963)", *AFDI,* 1964 pages 352-383.

13 As underlined by doctrine "the natural destiny of a legal rule is its application to social relations for which it was laid down. In order to be sure that it is applied and to what extent it is applied to a specific case, it is often necessary to previously dissipate the uncertainty and ambiguity it almost inevitably contains due to its general nature, in order to restitute its true meaning. This is the task of interpretation. It consists of unravelling the precise meaning and the content of the applicable legal rule in a determined situation" (QUOC DINH, N., DAILLIER, P. and PELLET, A. *Droit International Public,* 4th de. LGDJ, Paris 1992, p. 245). Along the same lines see VOICU, Y., *op.cit.*, p. 4).

14 SUR, S., *op. cit.*, p. 194.

way the customary norm is applied may be the basis of its interpretation through the posterior analysis of the states which are the parts involved in the application. In the event, the practice may be the element to determine the meaning and the scope of the norm. SALMON, on the other hand, considers that the interpretation and the application are concomitant, not successive, operations. This is because "when a specific case comes up against a norm whose application is to be taken into account, often the norm requires the addition of something, so that its sense be made more precise in accordance with the particular situation"[15].

But the problem of interpretation of international norms has a third aspect: the institution responsible for deciding on the controversy. Decentralisation of political power in the International Community is known to lead to the absence of obligatory international jurisdiction. Consequently, controversies regarding interpretation can only be decided by a third party if the parties in disagreement previously consent to this (which may require the previous interpretation of the agreement or the declarations of acceptance of the jurisdiction in the case of the ICJ) or if this measure is stipulated in a treaty to which they are parties. In both cases, the third party will dictate a non-authentic interpretation, as it does not proceed from the parts, but will be imposed on them as they have accepted its jurisdiction (either in general, or for this controversy or through the treaty)[16].

The analysis of international arbitration and judicial practice shows precisely that the appeal to judicial methods for solving controversies as regards interpretation is exceptional, so, except in the aforementioned circumstances or where the parts themselves are able to solve the problem through an agreed interpretation which satisfies their respective positions, which, as we have mentioned, is exceptional, the controversy will persist, and this will have its repercussions on the application of the norm.

Thus, in order to avoid such problems, in some multilateral treaties, the States stipulate that an institution be responsible for deciding on the problems regarding interpretation or its submittal to arbitration proceedings[17].

---

[15] SALMON, J., "Le fait dans l'application du droit international", *R. des C.*, t. 175 (1982-II), p. 343.

[16] The case may also arise in which the parts request the interpretation of the ruling issued regarding the controversy in question, in which case the interpretation will be authentic as it has been given by the same institution which dictated the previous one. A recent example is the Judgement pronounced by the International Court of Arbitration (Argentina/Chile) on October 13, 1995 in the *case requesting revision and interpretation in assistance submitted by Chile concerning the Judgement of October 21, 1994.*

[17] For example, the *Vienna Convention of August 23, 1978* on the succession of states regarding treaties (articles 41-45); the *Vienna Convention* on the succession of states regarding state goods, archives and debts, of April 8, 1983 (articles 42-46); the United Nations Convention of December 10, 1984 regarding the fight against torture and other cruel, inhuman or degrading treatment or punishment (article 30) and the Agreement on the prevention and punishment of the crime of genocide on December 9, 1948 (article IX).

The advantage of such treaties is undeniable since, when the States express their consent to be bound by the treaty, they automatically accept to submit to the procedure laid down therein as regards interpretation. In such cases, state sovereignty is limited voluntarily so as to decide on the issues of interpretation. But this does not mean that the express or tacit consent of the State is not decisive. What happens is that this consent "included within a tighter and complex network of international obligations and different types of conduct lacking formalisation appeared in the legal reality as relative, multiple"[18].

It can be said, on the other hand, that the attitude of the States as regards submitting their controversies on interpretation to international jurisdiction will also depend on how such jurisdiction acts concerning the problems submitted. In a way, the fact that the States tend to submit controversies on interpretation to international jurisdiction is closely related, to a greater or lesser extent to the attitude of the international judge in the sense that he confines himself to the strict interpretation or takes advantage of the chance to create Law, which at times is a mere pretext of a state dissatisfied with the decision of the judicial body. On this matter, it has been stated that the function of international jurisdiction is to interpret Law, extract the rules of custom and the general principles. But this function of interpretation, in practice, can sometimes lead to the exercise of the judge's quasi-power to dictate norms, as occurs, for example, with the case law of the European Community Court of Justice (hereinafter ECCJ) This Court "through a process which was always meant to be 'constructive' and for that very reason has given rise to spirited controversy, has completed and extensively prolonged the community law in the texts. Hence, the resistance of certain national jurisdictions"[19].

This fact is true. What happens in practice is that the creation of Law by the international judicial or arbitration organisms is closely related to the scope of jurisdiction. In fact, the examination we have carried out enables us to confirm what earlier studies on the problem of interpretation had warned of. Namely, that the creative work of the organism responsible for the interpretation is seen to be more ample in the case of organisms with obligatory jurisdiction, to which the parts are compelled to appeal in order to decide on any question of interpretation. Such is the case of the ECCJ, and in this regard, the obligatory jurisdiction laid down by the 1957 Treaty of Rome concerning interpretation has led to a considerable increase in the obligations contained in the Community Treaties and, consequently, to a reduction in the state competence and sovereignty of the Member States.

---

[18] SUR, S., *op. cit.,* p. 121.

[19] ABRAHAM, R. *Droit international, droit communitaire et droit français*, Hachette, Paris, 1989, pages 20 et seq. On the interpretation of Community Law see BREDIMAS, A. *Methods of interpretation and Community Law,* North-Holland Pub., Amsterdam, 178, CARTOU, L., "La Cour de Justice des Communautés Européenes et le droit Communitaire" in the collection *Mélanges offerts à Marcel Waline,* LGDJ, Paris, 1974, pages 163-171; CHEVALIER, R.M., "Methods and Reasoning of the European Court in its Interpretation of Community Law" *Common Market Law Review*, 1964/1965, pages 21-35.

Examples are the pronouncements of the aforementioned Court on the judicial nature of the Community and the Community regulations, as well as the principles which inspire these which are those concerning uniform, direct and immediate application, primacy, and the principle of the direct effect of the Directives.

On the contrary, in the case of organisms without compulsory jurisdiction, as is the case of the ICJ, the interpretative function, which it is granted voluntarily by the Parts which are involved in controversy over the interpretation of a particular international norm, is transformed quantitatively into a very minor incidence, though not less important, from the viewpoint of the creation of Law. Moreover, as regards the interpretation of treaties, the ICJ is restricted both by the existence of interpretative rules which it is obliged to use and by the fact that it must give reasons for its decision, which forces it to act with prudence.

Consequently, if the I.C.J. wishes to have an increasing number of States choosing it to resolve their disputes, it must be very prudent and apply international norms while not providing them with the power to expand, in order not to limit state sovereignty, a fact that could arise if the Court applies innovations to the rules existing in the different sectors of the international legal order when matters and consultations are submitted to it. Despite all this, as we will have the opportunity to confirm throughout this work, the interpretation of international norms by the I.C.J. has contributed to the development and precision of the legal system applicable in different sectors of this legal order and it has been especially innovative, for example, in the constructions it has built up on unilateral declarations, international custom and Sea Law.

The manner in which the I.C.J. acts in interpretative matters has also another dimension through the procedure of interpretation by means of advisory opinions, regulated in article 96 of the United Nations' Charter, in Chapter IV (articles 65-68) of the Statute of the Court, as well as in Title IV (articles 102-109) of its Rules.

In accordance with article 96, the following are entitled to request an advisory opinion: the General Assembly, the Security Council, as well as other organisms of the United Nations and the specialised agencies of this Organisation when they are authorised by the General Assembly[20].

---

20 In this regard, the intervention of the States is limited to the following cases: where the advisory opinion requested concerns a legal question "currently pending between two or more States" (article 102 of the Regulations of the ICJ) or when "due to collateral agreements, which do not affect the way the Courts works, the States have agreed to accept the advisory competence either as an alternative to contentious jurisdiction or where there is no contentious jurisdiction" (ROSENNE, S., *The Law and practice of the International Court of Justice*, M. Nijhoff, Dordrecht, 1993, pages 699 et seq.). This author quotes as examples the issues of *the Southwest African (vote)* and *the Southwest African Committee* in which the advisory opinion was issued without the participation of South Africa.

Regarding the objective of the advisory opinion, in article 96 of the Charter as well as in Chapter IV of the I.C.J. Rules this is stated generally as dealing with: "any legal question"[21].

Unlike the judgements pronounced by the Court in contentious issues, the advisory opinions are not binding although they do have the authority inherent to all the pronouncements of the I.C.J. as the judicial interpreter of International Law. On the other hand, in addition to the value of these advisory opinions as jurisprudence of the only international judicial organ of a universal nature, they are usually followed by resolutions of the General Assembly which, generally speaking, adopt the criterion stated by the Court. The problem then arising is that of the value or legal effects of the resolution in question, especially if it is not voted by all the States which are members of the General Assembly[22]. However, independently of this aspect, the value of the advisory opinions as interpretations of judicial questions of International Law submitted to the Court and later reaffirmed and developed in its judgements, cannot be denied[23].

In recent practice of the I.C.J. we have several examples of requests for advisory opinions. The first was posed by the WHO on May 14, 1993 concerning whether the use of nuclear weapons by a State in the course of a war or other armed conflict would constitute a breach of its obligations under International Law (including the constitution of the WHO)[24]. The second was drawn up by the General Assembly through its Resolution 49/1975 K of December 15, 1994, on the legality of the threat or use of nuclear weapons under any circumstances[25]. More recently, the request for advisory opinion drawn up by the General Assembly concerning the *Legal Consequences of the Construction of a Wall in the Occupied Palestinian Territory*[26].

---

21 In the event that the request originates in other organisms of the United Nations or specialised organisms, article 96 states precisely that it must deal with legal questions arising within the scoper of its activities. In this regard see ROSENNE, S, *The Law and Practice ..., op. cit.,* pages 698 et seq.; SINGH, N., *The role and Record of the International Court of Justice,* M.Nijhoff, Dordrecht, 1989, Szafarz, R., *The Compulsory Jurisdiction of the International Court of Justice*, M. Nijhoff, Dordrecht, 1993.

22 Concerning this issue see Chapters III and X of this work.

23 Forming the jurisprudence referred to in article 38.1 d) of the Statute of the ICJ which constitutes *auxiliary means* to determine the rules of law and which the Court must apply on deciding on the controversies submitted to it. Vid JENNINGS, R., "Le rôle et le fonctionnement de la Cour" (ICJ, *Annuaire 1991-1992* No. 46, the Hague, 1992, pages 219-227.

24 ICJ, *Reports 1993,* pages 467-468. In 1946 the General Assembly authorised the WHO to request advisory opinions from the ICJ on judicial issues arising in the framework of its activity in accordance with articles 96.2 of the Charter, 76 of the constitution of the WHO and X.2 of the agreement between the UNO and the WHO.

25 ICJ, *Reports 1995,* pages 3-4.

26 ICJ, *Reports 2003,* pages 3 et seq.

In fact, owing to the predominantly state nature of the International Community and the principle of autonomy of the will of the Parts on issuing consent, in the interpretation, as in other sectors of international regulation, the consent of the State, and therefore sovereignty, also occupies a preferential position. It is in this sense that it is said that the competence of interpretation is an attribute of state sovereignty. In other words, as far as interpretation is concerned, the sovereignty recognised to the State by International Law, implies the right of the State to appreciate and to interpret the relevant obligations and rights or those recognised as the State's by the regulation itself. This appreciation is valid "with regard to all the elements concerned in the interpretation: facts, acts or situations comprised by the Law, customary or conventional norms"[27]. So, this leads to a concurrence of interpretations proceeding from the various States involved in the problem of interpretation and this implies opposing but equal legal pretensions which have equal value. None of these interpretations is an authentic or quasi-authentic interpretation of law because they are unilateral, although they do validly establish the legal position of the State as regards the norms in question. Nevertheless, under certain conditions, especially "the tacit or non tacit consent of the other States or the intervention of a jurisdictional organism, such an interpretation can be recognised as authentic"[28].

The fact that the State has freedom to appreciate the rights and obligations recognised by International Law does not imply that this freedom is unlimited. It is modulated by the rules contained in Article 53 of the Vienna Conventions of 1969 and 1986 on the Law of Treaties and in article 103 of the United Nations Charter, as well as by the "principle of good faith" by which the discretion of the State as regards the interpretation of the norms must be checked[29].

International doctrine as well as international practice underline the fundamental nature of this principle in international relations, but recourse to this does not, in fact, prevent the persistence of the discrepancy as a consequence of the diverging interpretations of the same norm made by the Parties. What is the meaning of good faith? To what extent does this principle affect the valuation made by the State of its international obligations in the specific cases when that valuation, as occurs in practice, is made in the light of the political interests of the State in respect of that situation? Does good faith allow the Parts to undermine the interpretation? Can the interpretative rules of Articles 31 to 33 of the Vienna Conventions from 1969 and 1986 concerning international treaties guide the application of the principle of good faith as they obliged States to interpret in accordance with these rules?

---

27 SUR, S., *op. cit.*, p. 123.

28 *Ibid.*

29 Likewise the limitations arising from the attitude the Parts may adopt owing to the *reciprocity* of the obligations or as a consequence of the self-tutoring authorised by International Law (methods of counter-measures and unarmed reprisals for example).

As we can see, there are few tasks as difficult as specifying the content of this normative principle that is supposed to be always present in the behaviour of the State. We find the same difficulty while attempting to prove that the State in question at a specific time is not acting in good faith when it supports a certain interpretation of the norm. Is it possible to have a different interpretation of the same norm when this is done in good faith? What is the usefulness of this principle?

We are faced with a principle with blurred borders on which the formation as well as the application of international norms are based. The question lies in the fact that, as a consequence of the difficulty involved in specifying, the problem itself does not disappear. We are faced with a dilemma which is difficult to solve. In fact, sovereignty must be exercised in accordance with a principle which is very dependent on it and the violation of which can only be proved if the existence of bad faith can be proved.

2 The efforts to modulate the power of discretion of the State: Good faith or a principle with blurred edges

As a consequence of its nature as a general norm of international law, the *principle of good* faith plays a fundamental role in the interpretation of international norms. It was envisaged with regard to conventional norms in Articles 31 of the Vienna Conventions of 1969 and 1986 on the Law of Treaties, this principle is also present in the interpretation of other types of written norms (institutional), unwritten (custom), as well as unilateral declarations. We will go into these matters later.

Concerning doctrine as well as international jurisprudence and codification there is general agreement on the "structural" or "fundamental" character of this principle in the contemporary international legal order. It has been said that it is one of the principles expressing the fundamental values which inspire the general structure of this legal order at a specific time within its historical evolution, and so, it occupies a central place within the system as a whole[30].

This "fundamental" or "structural" character which is a result of the fact that it is expressed in the United Nations Charter and, therefore, is confined to the international obligations undertaken by virtue of the Charter[31], has been strengthened as a consequence of the higher ranking of the obligations contained in the Charter owing to what is laid down in article 103[32].

30 Cf. GONZALEZ CAMPOS, J.D., SANCHEZ RODRIGUEZ, L.I. and ANDRES, SAENZ DE SANTA MARIA, M. P., *Curso de Derecho Internacional Público*, 3rd ed. revisited, Civitas, Madrid, 2003, p. 26.

31 Thus, article 2.2 of the Charter states, "the members of the Organisation will carry out the obligations undertaken by them in good faith in accordance with this Charter in order to ensure the rights and benefits inherent to their condition of members".

32 Which states, "in the event of conflict arising between the obligations undertaken by the Members of the United Nations by virtue of this Charter and their obligations undertaken by virtue of any other international agreement, the obligations under this Charter will prevail".

Later on, this principle acquires a universal character, unlimited by the obligations undertaken under the Charter, as a consequence of Resolution 2625 (XXV), approved by the General Assembly on October 24, 1970, which contains the "Declaration on Principles of International Law concerning Friendly Relations and Co-operation among States in Accordance with the Charter of the United Nations". In the final general provision the General Assembly underlines the fundamental character of the principle by stating that,

> "The principles of the Charter incorporated into this Declaration constitute the basic principles of international law and, consequently, it urges all the States to be guided by these principles as regards their international conduct and to develop mutual relationships on the basis of strict compliance with these principles".

This conclusion is already stated in the fifth paragraph of the preamble of this Resolution when it is said that the principle of "the fulfilment in good faith of the obligations undertaken by States, in accordance with the Charter, is of the greatest importance for the maintenance of international peace and security and for the implementation of the other aims of the United Nations". The sixth paragraph adds that "the great political, economic and social changes and the scientific progress which have taken place in the world since the adoption of the Charter gives increased importance to these principles and to the need for their more effective application in the conduct of States wherever carried on".

But it is in the framework of the two last principles of this Resolution where the principle of fulfilment in good faith of the international obligations is developed to a greater extent. Firstly, in paragraph f) of the principle of sovereign equality of States, where it is said,

> "f) Each State has the duty to comply fully and in good faith with its international obligations and to live in peace with other States".

Secondly, within the framework of the principle of good faith:

> "Every State has the duty to fulfill in good faith its obligations under the generally recognized principles and rules of international law.
>
> Every State has the duty to fulfill in good faith its obligations under international agreements valid under the generally recognized principles and rules of international law"[33].

In conclusion, Resolution 2625 (XXV) universalises the principle of compliance in good faith with international obligations by extending this not only to the obligations contained in the United Nations Charter but also to those assumed by virtue of the generally acknowledged principles and norms of international law, as well as through valid international agreements.

---

[33] The first paragraph of this principle states the duty of all States to comply in good faith with the obligations assumed by virtue of the United Nations Charter and the final paragraph repeats the primacy of the obligations assumed under the Charter.

Concerning its *legal nature*, this principle has a double nature: custom and convention, custom in its origin, conventional, due to the fact that it has been included in United Nations Charter and in the Agreements on the Codification of the Treaty Law of 1969 and 1986.

On many occasions, doctrine has highlighted the fundamental character of the principle inspiring the general structure of the international system of regulations in a Society characterised by relativism and the decentralisation of political power. Thus, for example, CARREAU, who states that this principle is inherent to international society and to the stability of the legal relationships among members. In fact, "is it possible to imagine a legal system based on bad faith?"[34]

In spite of the existence of major agreement on the fundamental character of good faith, the problem persists because the question lies in the determination of its content: whether this principle is the source of a precise obligation falling on States. Actually, the difficulty lies in the definition of "good faith". While practice shows its repeated involvement in many conventional and institutional norms as well as in international jurisprudence, its exact configuration continues to be blurred. This is the reason why some wonder whether good faith does not "appear rather as a moral aspiration than a rule with its own legal content"[35]. What is its content?

These difficulties lead ZOLLER to say that in spite of the existence of a certain unanimity on the particular importance of the principle of good faith in international relations, that agreement is not so unanimous as regards its content. In fact, the concept of good faith has not been defined and the few definitions that have been attempted "call forth the ideas of sincerity, loyalty, correctness, rectitude, honesty". In this sense, efforts have focused more on the judicial consequences of the principle of good faith rather than on the definition of the concept. Consequently, the result is "the definition of the legal regime of a concept that nobody can clarify"[36].

In order to make this clarification, the maximum which has been achieved is to state that good faith "is the opposite of formalism, the rejection of the absurd, and the consecration of good sense"[37]. Any attempt to go into the matter in depth

---

[34] CARREAU, D., *Droit International,* 2nd Edition, Pedone, Paris, 1991, p. 73. Likewise CAHIER, Ph., *op.cit.,* p. 84. In Spain, for example, GONZALEZ CAMPOS, J:D:, SANCHEZ RODRIGUEZ, L. I. and ANDRES SAENZ DE SANTA MARIA, M. P., who state that Resolution 2625 "reaffirms this fundamental norm extending the duty to comply in good faith with the international obligations assumed 'under the generally acknowledged principles and rules of international law', whether these have been created by custom or by treaties" (*Curso ..., op.cit.,* p. 253).

[35] CAHIER, Ph., *op.cit.*, pages 84 and 89 et seq.

[36] ZOLLER, E., in the work of COT, J.P., and PELLET, A., already quoted, on p. 100. Cf. Also O'CONNOR, J.F., *Good Faith in International Law,* Dartmouth, Aldershot, 1991, p. 10 and KOLB, R., "La bonne foi en droit international public", *R.B.D.I.*, 1998, vol. XXXI, nº 2, pp. 661-732.

[37] ZOLLER, E., *op. cit.*, p. 100.

comes up against difficulties due to the question, What does it mean to comply with the obligations assumed by virtue of the United Nations Charter or by virtue of the generally acknowledged principles and norms of international law, or under international agreements valid under the generally acknowledged principles and rules of international law? What are the consequences of the obligation to interpret an international treaty in good faith? At this point the difficulties and doubts arise, especially in the international arena, where sovereignty takes a specific leading role as regards interpretation, both concerning the initially identical values of the unilateral interpretations issued by each State and in the absence of obligatory jurisdiction in order to decide on the problems of interpretation.

From the analysis of doctrine, what appears is the existence of an agreement about the principle of good faith as a *behavioural obligation*, implying the adoption of a determined standard of behaviour, with the difficulties deriving from this conclusion when proving its infringement. In theory, with regard to the obligations of behaviour, it is sufficient to determine that the State involved did not adopt the attitude expected of it in accordance with the obligation, in order to reach the conclusion that there has been an infringement of an international obligation. But, in practice it is not so easy to prove this unless the obligation in question has a precise content. For example, the obligation to execute a treaty or its interpretation can be hampered by the ambiguous or vague drafting of the text of the norm in question[38]. On the other hand, even in the event of *prima facie* perfectly defined specific cases, a State could defend an interpretation which protects its own interests in apparent contradiction with the written text. In this case, would it be acting in bad faith? How is bad faith demonstrated? Which body is to be appealed to? One example of this type of conduct is the argument of the United States of America justifying the trade embargo ordered on May 1, 1985 against Nicaragua by an Executive Order of the President of the United States. In its judgement, the I.C.J. declared that the direct attacks on ports, oil installations, as well as the mining of Nicaraguan ports were contrary to the1956 bilateral Treaty of Friendship, Commerce and Navigation[39]. Likewise the trade embargo which, in the opinion of the

---

[38] As QUOC DINH, N., DAILLIER, P. and PELLET, A. point out, the obligation to execute a treaty "is more difficult to determine when the conventional norms are ambiguous. Through appropriate drafting, the parties can reduce the scope of their commitments, either because their obligations are couched in sufficiently vague terms so that they can play with this ambiguity for their own benefit, or they reserve the possibility to detach themselves from the commitment under certain circumstances" (*op. cit.*, p. 213).

[39] On which he stated that "it would be difficult to imagine less appropriate acts for strengthening the bonds of peace and friendship which traditionally existed between the parts, to cite the preamble to the Treaty" (ICJ, *Reports 1986*, p. 138). A statement of the I.C.J. in the same line can be found in the case concerning *Oil Platforms* (Islamic Republic of Iran v. United States of America) (ICJ, *Reports*, 2003).

ICJ, constitutes an infringement of the obligation not to deprive the treaty of its purpose and aim[40].

If such problems arise with regard to written norms, the difficulty becomes greater in relation to customary norms because of the necessity to previously determine their existence and their content, as well as their appropriateness or not regarding the conduct in question. And this has to be done from an analysis of the conduct of the State.

In the *case of the nuclear tests* the ICJ declared that the principle of good faith was present in the creation and execution of all types of legal obligations, when it stated that "one of the basic principles governing the creation and performance of legal obligations, whatever their source, is that of good faith. Mutual trust and confidence are inherent to international cooperation, in particular in an age when this cooperation is becoming increasingly essential in many fields"[41]. However, on the Law of Treaties, the structural principle of good faith takes on a double projection: firstly, in its formation process. Then, at the time it the treaty is applied and executed. This fact was pointed out by the I.L.C. in its Draft Articles on the Law of Treaties where it stated that, "it is true that the principle of good faith is applied to all international relation, but in treaty law it is especially important and this is repeated in article 27 on the interpretation of treaties"[42].

Along similar lines, the doctrine of Public International Law states that, as in the process of formation of international norms, its application is governed, from the legal point of view, by two fundamental principles of the international legal order: good faith and equity. It adds that although good faith is not the only condition on applying the Law, it is undoubtedly the most important, without good faith an agreement between two parts is impossible, and it is absolutely necessary for the application of international customary Law"[43].

A good example of all this can be found in articles 18 and 26 of the Vienna Conventions of 1969 and 1986 on the Law of Treaties. According to article 18, the States and the International Organisations are obliged not to defeat the objective and purpose of a treaty prior to its entry into force. In this sense, they are obliged to refrain from acts which would defeat the objective and purpose of the treaty. On the basis of this Article some authors consider it as the content of the performance of a treaty in good faith, in spite of being a conception which is "perhaps too wide, therefore too vague, because it does not sufficiently characterise the other side of the coin which is bad faith. Acting in good faith should be defined as that type of act which excludes all attempts to 'defraud law', all cunning, and requires positive

---

[40] Cf. *ibid.*, p. 140. In addition, it stated that the United States "has committed acts which are contradictory to the terms" of the bilateral treaty of 1956 (*ibid.*).

[41] ICJ, *Reports 1974*, p. 268.

[42] Report on the work carried out at its 18th session. Draft Articles on Treaty Law (*ILC Yearbook,* 1996, vol. II, p. 232).

[43] GONZALEZ CAMPOS, J.D., SANCHEZ RODRIGUEZ, L.I. and ANDRES SAENZ DE SANTA MARIA, M. P., *op. cit.*, p. 253.

fidelity and loyalty to commitments. In any case, a definition is necessarily abstract; and must be clarified in practice"[44].

By virtue of Article 26, every treaty in force is binding upon the parties to it and must be performed by them in good faith. In relation to this article, the I.L.C. stated that acting in good faith and respect for the rule *pacta sunt servanda* are so intimately joined that they constitute two complementary aspects of the same principle. It added, that in the matter of interpretation of treaties, the interpretation "made in good faith and in accordance with law is absolutely necessary so that the rule *pacta sunt servanda* might have real meaning"[45].

We can conclude that we are faced with a structural or fundamental principle of international law which constitutes obligatory conduct whose content is difficult to determine and this acquires a special focus in the field of the Law on Treaties.

As we have stated above, the principle of good faith is projected over the initial as well as over the final phase of the formation process of international norms, in general, and of treaties in particular.

As regards the *initial phase*, and within this the *negotiation*, the principle of good faith is defined fundamentally by an obligation to abstain from or not to do. Thus, for example, the obligation to abstain from making the content of the negotiations public. As was pointed out by the I.C.J. in the *Case of the North Sea Continental Shelf*, during the negotiation the Parties are under "an obligation to conduct themselves in such a way that the negotiations are meaningful, which will not be the case when either of them insists upon its own position without considering any modification"[46]. Or, to put it another way, the Parts must "conduct the negotiations in such a spirit that each must in good faith pay reasonable regard to the legal rights of the other party"[47].

As ZOLLER holds, good faith required during the negotiation of a treaty "is above all a criterion of interpretation of the legal conduct of the parties, rather than a subjective quality of each of them"[48]. The point is that the divergent interpretation the parties involved might make of such conduct will, of necessity, require the

---

[44] QUOC DINH, N., DAILLIER, P. and PELLET, A., *op. cit.*, pages 212 et seq. They also add that the obligation to act in good faith persists "no matter what the uncertainties regarding the Treaty are" and the Parts "are not less bound to respect the provisions" (*ibid.).*

[45] ILC, Report on the work carried out during its 18th period of sessions. Draft Articles on the Law of Treaties, *Yearbook ILC*, 1966, vol. II, p. 240. The quotes are taken from the original. It adds that, "the interpretation in good faith follows directly from the rule *pacta sunt servanda*" (*ibid.* p. 242). In the doctrine, see, for example, GONZALEZ CAMPOS, J.D., SANCHEZ RODRIGUEZ, L.I. and ANDRES SAENZ DE SANTA MARIA, M.P., *op. cit.*, p. 253. Along the same lines, QUOC DIHN,N., DAILLIER, P. and PELLET, A, *Droit International Public, op. cit.,* p. 212; O'CONNOR, J.F. *op. cit.*, p. 124. As regards this matter, see the examples cited in the notes (39) and (40) in this work.

[46] ICJ, *Reports 1969,* p. 47.

[47] *Case of Competence in the Matter of Fishing Grounds (fondo),*(ICJ, *Reports 1974*, p. 33).

[48] ZOLLER, E. *La bonne foi en Droit International Public*, Pedone, Paris, 1977, p. 68.

intervention of a third party in order to decide if the conduct in question is in good faith or not. And it is at this point that we come up against another hurdle: States are not obliged to submit their disputes to any political or judicial mechanisms for the settlement of disputes[49]. Thus, the discrepancy as regards the interpretation and classification of this conduct may be perpetuated with no legal consequences whatsoever[50].

During this initial phase, once the negotiations have been finalised, good faith is also specified negatively as the obligation not to frustrate the reason and end of the treaty. This is deduced from article 18 a) of both Vienna Conventions in 1969 and 1986. However, this does not mean that the principle of good faith entails the requirement to be bound by the treaty in question as the state remains free to bind itself or not.

As in the negotiation phase, the difficulty of determining the breach of good faith persists during the adoption and authentication phase. This must be carried out objectively, that is to say, through the analysis of the conduct of the party in question. If we add to this the identical value of the unilateral interpretations of this conduct made by the States affected, we are once more faced with the imperfection of this principle and a third party is needed in order to decide whether or not there has been a breach. But, it must not be forgotten that this appraisal is made through the concept of good faith the interpreting party has.

In the *final phase* of the declaration of consent to be bound by the treaty, and before it comes into force, as understood from article 18 b) of the Vienna Conventions of 1969 and 1986, the same obligation not to frustrate the reason and end of the treaty persists. But, unlike the initial phase, where it is difficult to appreciate the presence or non-existence of good faith from the analysis of the conduct of the State, in this final phase, during the stage which goes from the consent to be bound and the entry in force of the treaty, "the principle of good faith can be taken into account because there is an objective criterion to enable

---

[49] Except in the following cases: acceptance of the jurisdiction of a judicial or international arbitration body, either in general or exclusively for the dispute at issue; that this measure be imposed by a treaty drawn up between the two parts; or in the case of a dispute foreseen by article 37 of United Nations Charter.

[50] Except those originated by the attitude that the other part might adopt (or the parts as the case may be) due to the reciprocity of the obligations, or as a consequence of measures involving self-control authorised by International Law (measures involving non-violent reprisals, for example). Likewise, the cases laid down in article 33 and those that follow in the United Nations Charter.

Concerning the peaceful settlement of disputes within the scope of the United Nations, cf. BADIA MARTIN, A *El arreglo pacífico de controversias en la Organización de las Naciones Unidas*. Also from the Spanish standpoint cf. ANDRES SAENZ DE SANTA MARIA, M. P., *El arbitraje internacional en la práctica convencional española (1794-1978)*, Servicio de Publicaciones de la Universidad de Oviedo, Oviedo, 1982; Asociación Española de Profesores de Derecho Internacional y Relaciones Internacionales, *El arbitraje internacional*, Zaragoza, 1989.

its appreciation, which is the text of the agreement made between the parts"[51]. According to this opinion, the existence of a text would allow the evaluation of whether or not the attitude of the State conforms with the principle of good faith. However, and despite the advantages provided by the fact that there is a text, it should not be forgotten that differing interpretations can arise when there are apparently clear texts.

Finally, it should be pointed out that the cases of culpability, corruption and coercion as regards the representative of the State and dealt with in articles 49, 50 and 51 respectively of the Vienna Conventions on the Law of Treaties also directly affect the declaration of consent and are examples of the absence of good faith, as well as coercion of the State by threatening or using the force stipulated in article 52 of both conventions.

Once the treaty comes into force, we enter the environment of article 26 of the Vienna Conventions of 1969 and 1986, that is to say, the *execution* of the treaty in good faith.[52]

As REUTER points out "the obligation of good faith is fundamental to any conduct which can be judged under international law and in the execution of all its obligations"[53]. In the Law on Treaties, the Vienna Conventions of 1969 and 1986 apply this in relation to the conduct of the parts or the future parts on conclusion, interpretation, etc. of the treaties. In the opinion of the I.L.C., the principle of good faith forms part of the regulation *pacta sunt servanda* "and means, generally speaking, that the obligation entailed by the conventional commitment must not be eluded by a purely literal application of the clauses"[54]. In ZOLLER's opinion "essentially good faith plays the role of main regulator in relation to the principle *pacta*. It also provides some other things..."[55] which materialise in the prevalence of the spirit over the letter of the text and prevents the principle *pacta sunt servanda* from degenerating into an "intellectual or material fraud" and good faith constitutes the "dominant aspect of all conventional treaties"[56]. In any event, both the principle *pacta sunt servanda* and the principle of good faith demand that the treaty *be applied* by the signatories.

It is in this phase of application of the treaty and its execution that questions regarding *interpretation* may arise. As we have repeatedly stated, the fundamental principle, the consequence of the sovereignty of States, is the identical value of the interpretation initially made by all States. Thus when a problem arises, none of the interpretations issued is entitled to prevail over the others. This principle is also

---

[51] ZOLLER, E, *La bonne foi en ..., op. cit.,* p. 78.

[52] This article states that:

> "All treaties in force oblige the parts and must be complied with in good faith".

[53] REUTER, P., *Introduction au ..., op.cit.,* p. 124.

[54] I.L.C. *Yearbook*, 1966, vol. II, pages 229 et seq.

[55] *La bonne foi en ..., op. cit.,* p. 82. The words in italics are in the original.

[56] *Ibid.*, p. 81.

based on the legal equality of the States[57]. However, the difficulty of determining the content of this "good faith" in the light of which the interpretation is to be evaluated continues to persist.

Despite the fact that good faith is a difficult notion to specify, it is possible to conclude that it obliges the contracting parts and the Judge or arbitrator requested "to interpret the treaty in a reasonable way while respecting the rule of law and the will of the authors"[58]. Thus, as regards treaties, interpreting good faith would mean that in the interpretation "of a clause not only the text should be taken into account, but also its reason and the aim of the treaty, that is to say, its spirit"[59].That is to say, the general rule for interpretation. In other words, according to the work of the I.L.C. and international case law, good faith "demands" the continued fidelity to the intention of the parts, and not causing it to fail due to a literal interpretation, nor reducing the reason and the aim of the treaty to nothing"[60].

In conclusion, once the obligatory character of acting in good faith has been determined, its weaknesses do, however, persist. We are faced with a structural or fundamental principle of a conventional or customary nature, which is difficult to specify and, therefore, there is scant possibility of proving that it has been breached[61]. As REUTER stresses, at the same time it is a question of an obligation which "is fundamental for all conduct which may be judged under international law and for the execution of all obligations"[62], which govern the process by which

---

57 See BASTID, S., *Les traités dans la vie internationale. Conclusion et effets*, Economica, Paris, 1985, p. 127. ZOLLER stresses this same aspect when she states that the International Society is a society dominated by the principle of relativism, that is to say, … a society in which the interpreters of the legal regulations are often those they will be applied to. In fact, it is in the environment of the interpretation that the reference to good faith acquires its full sense" (Commentary to article 2, paragraph 2 of the United Nations Charter in the work of COT, J-P. and PELLET, A., *La Charte des Nations Unies,* Economica, Paris, 1985, p. 98) See also CARREAU, D., *op. cit.*, p. 141.

58 CARREAU, D., *op. cit.,* p. 141.

59 CAHIER, P., "Cours général…" *op. cit.*, p. 87.

60 REUTER, P., *Introduction au ..., op. cit.*, p. 124. An example of the contrary attitude is the trade embargo ordered on May 1, 1985 by the United States against Nicaragua, and declared contrary to the objective and the aim of the Bilateral Friendship, Commerce and Navigation Treaty by the ICJ (Cf. *Reports 1986,* p. 140).

61 This occurs despite the efforts to define good faith from the reports of the ILC and international case law as a principle "which demands fidelity to the intention of the parts, without causing it to fail due to literal interpretation, nor reducing the objective and the end of the treaty to nothing" (*Introduction au droit des traités, PUF, Paris, 1985, p. 124).*

62 *Ibid.* also GONZALEZ CAMPOS, J.D., SANCHEZ RODRIGUEZ, L.I., ANDRES SAENZ DE SANTA MARIA, M. P., *op. cit.*, p. 254.

international conventional, customary and institutional norms are formed and is also present in unilateral declarations[63].

In order to minimise this difficulty in specifying the principle of good faith and permitting it to be appreciated in a specific case regarding a treaty, the Vienna Conventions of 1969 and 1986 on the Law of Treaties codified a number of criteria which make up the general rules for interpretation of the treaty. They can also be used to evaluate whether the interpretation of the specific case was made in good faith or not. However, their use does not eliminate the problem arising from two or more different interpretations of the parts to the treaty as a hypothetical interpretation made in bad faith cannot be described as such until a third party intervenes, and such an event, as has been stated above, is exceptional. Moreover, the part which hypothetically invokes an interpretation which is not in accordance with good faith would logically not accept submittal to a third party and the discrepancy would then persist and the treaty would not apply to the specific case.

Later we will dedicate time to the study of the rules of interpretation codified by the Vienna Conventions of 1969 and 1986.

3 Types and methods of interpretation: A classification based on international practice

In the preceding pages we have explained the range of views of the process of interpretation of international norms, characterised by the decisive influence of state sovereignty. This fact also explains how, owing to the non-existence of compulsory international jurisdiction as regards interpretation, it continues to be the States which, in the first instance, interpret the norms in the course of their application. Based on agreement or disagreement, the result concurs or diverges from the norm in question. Should discrepancy exist, if the norm foresees this and if the parts agree, it will be possible for a third party to intervene and the result will be an international legal or arbitrary interpretation. Otherwise the dispute will persist indefinitely. This fact shows the voluntary imperfection of the obligation regarding the peaceful settlement of disputes as the States which make up the international community have constructed it in this way.

Given the progressive institutionalisation of the International Community, it is also possible to have an interpretation given by International Organisations. In

---

[63] As regards the expression "conduct possible to judge" used by REUTER, what is the content of this? Does it perhaps mean that there is conduct which is not governed by good faith (conduct which it is not possible to judge)? If this is so, a defence would be being made of a restrictive criterion of the principle of good faith protected by the discretion of the State, insofar as it would be the State which would first appreciate whether or not the conduct in question is possible to judge or not. Thus, we would be faced with another question of interpretation previous to the norm in question.

such an event, the interpretation will generally focus on the constituent treaty of the Organisation, on the norms drawn up by it or the treaties made by it[64].

Combining this variety of factors, based on the analysis of international practice and doctrine, it is possible to draw up a classification of the different *types of interpretation* based on the following criteria: the interpreter, the content of the interpretation and the legal scope of this interpretation.

From the *interpreter's* point of view, the interpretation may stem from the States, the International Organisations and international jurisdictions (bearing in mind the interpretation of the international norms which might be made by the internal organisms of the state).

Regarding *content*, the interpretation may be general or abstract and this may be in respect to a conventional norm or a customary one.

Finally, in relation to the *judicial scope*, the interpretation may be: authentic, unilateral, collective, executive or institutional, jurisdictional (which might be obligatory or consultative). The final criterion is the extent of the interpreter's freedom.

The interpretation made by the author or authors of the act in question is *authentic*. In the latter case the two interpretations have an accumulative character[65]. In REUTER's opinion, the difficulty of the authentic interpretation lies in the fact that, from the time it is issued by the authors of the act, "the interpretation can hardly be distinguished from a modification; and so its legality, the possibility of it being retroactive is called into question"[66].

On occasions, the authentic interpretation has the appearance of being an anticipation and pre-litigation. This is the case for all the instruments of this type of interpretation (protocols, interpretative agreements, interpretative statements, exchange of notes, common statements, etc.) which are aimed at excluding an interpretation that the text of the treaty could authorise and these are carried out in order to prevent a different application of the treaty[67].

---

64 Although other situations are possible as, for example, the interpretation made by the General Assembly and by the Security Council of the United Nations of the South African mandate over Southwest Africa.

65 Thus, in the *Ambatielos Case,* the ICJ pointed out that an interpretative declaration arising from all the contracting parts must be deemed to be an "integral part of the treaty even if this has not been expressly stated" (ICJ *Reports 1952,*p. 44).

As regards this type of interpretation it should be remembered that, when the ICPJ was consulted for an opinion on the *Jaworzina Case*, it stated that "the right to authentically interpret a legal rule corresponded only to whoever had the power to modify or suppress it" (*Series A/B*, No. 18, p. 17).

For a general view of the authentic interpretation of treaties, see the work of VOICU, I., *De l'intrerprétation...*, quoted above.

66 REUTER, P., *L'introduction au ..., op. cit.,* p. 124.

67 See VOICU, I, *op. cit.,* p. 3.

It must also be added that the interpretation of its own decisions made by an international judicial or arbitration organism is also authentic.

This may also be *quasi-authentic*, in which case the interpretation is implicitly deduced from the uniform application of an instrument by the parts. As in the previous case, the conduct of all the parts as regards the act in question must be analysed[68].

Unilateral interpretation is understood to be the interpretation carried out by a single subject, generally done through diplomatic channels as each problem arises. It is not imposed on anyone but it does fix the legal position of the emitter[69]. Thus, this interpretation is important as it will bind the author as regards the others involved and this will be from the perspective of the principle of good faith and the rules of "estoppel"[70].

But the unilateral interpretation has other aspects to be taken into account. On the one hand, the unilateral interpretation of one of the parts to a treaty "may be explicit or tacitly accepted, by all the other contracting parts and so be transformed into an authentic interpretation of the treaty"[71]. On the other hand, this system may be altered insofar as this unilateral interpretation may be expressly or tacitly accepted only by some of the contracting parts. It thus becomes a *bilateral* or *multilateral interpretation* "able to cause certain effects *inter partes"*, and gives rise to situations similar to those involving the reservations to the treaties, to its modifications or the amendments *inter se*[72]. Finally, the unilateral interpretation can also be carried out within the internal environment of the state through its governmental or jurisdictional organisms. In this case, this interpretation can come into conflict with the unilateral interpretation made of the treaty by the other contracting party, owing to the identical legal value of both these interpretations and which is the direct corollary of the sovereign equality of the States[73]. Doctrine stresses that a contradiction then arises between the

68 For VOICU, the authentic interpretation breaks down into two: "the express authentic interpretation and the authentic interpretation in practice" (*op. cit.,* p. 2).

69 As SIMON points out, this is the most frequent interpretation in current International Law: that which a State gives of its rights and obligations just as they arise from an agreement it is part to or a custom by which it is acknowledged to be linked" (SIMON, D, *op. cit.,* p. 19) See also CONFORTI, B., *Diritto Internazionale,* Editoriale Scientifica, Napoli 1987, pages 102-105.

70 In the words of the ICJ: "If the interpretation of legal instruments provided by the parts themselves is not conclusive enough to determine the sense, it does, however, have great value as proof when this interpretation contains the acknowledgement by one of the parts of its obligations by virtue of an instrument" (ICJ, *Reports 1950*, pages 135 et seq.).

71 SIMON, D., *op. cit.,* pages 22 et seq.

72 In SIMON's opinion this type of interpretation "introduces the germ of incoherence into the interpretation of the treaties, and the differences in the interpretations affect the uniformity of application of the treaty by the signatory States (both the text and the note in *op. cit.*, p. 23).

73 *Ibid.*

antagonistic pretensions of the parties. Moreover, the case might arise where the interpretation carried out by the internal organism is not in line with International Law. In order to solve this contradiction, the parts need to appeal to some judicial or arbitration procedure for settling disputes, and so the unilateral interpretation of each one of these will be substituted by the interpretation given by the judicial or arbitration organism[74]. For this reason, some authors state that "the truly authentic character of the unilateral interpretation might be doubted, as it is issued by one of the parts, it cannot be considered as authorised by 'the one who has the power to modify' the rule and may not be in opposition to the other States"[75]. However, this interpretation is of great practical importance as "it contains the acknowledgement by one of the parts of its obligations" by virtue of the legal instrument in question[76].

Collective interpretation is that which comes about by the agreement of all the States who are parties to the treaty either at the time the treaty is adopted, or later, or by agreement among some of the States who are parties to the treaty, and this gives rise to a system similar to that of the successive treaties on the same matter. This type of interpretation, for example, appears in article 31 of the Vienna Conventions on the Law of Treaties of 1969 and 1986 where "parties" is used in plural.

Executive or *institutional* interpretation is that which is dictated by the organs of International Organisations in the exercise of their competencies[77], and generally its objective is the constituent treaty of the Organisation, or a norm issued or a treaty made by this Organisation. As in the interpretation made by the States, the executive interpretation may be express (for example, through an interpretative statement or decision)[78], or it may be deduced implicitly from the practice followed by the Organisation for the application of the constituent treaty.

Unlike the state interpretation, in this case the power to interpret of the body of the International Organisation in question must be attributed to it by the constituent

---

74 Cf. SUR, S., *op. cit.,* p. 95. Also SIMON, D., *op. cit.*, pages 21 et seq.

75 QUOC, DINH, N., DAILLIER, P., and PELLET, A. *Droit ..., op. cit.,* p. 247.

76 *Ibid.,* p. 248. These authors add that, through silence or the expression of agreement regarding the interpretation of the other parts, these "can accept the interpretation put forward", in which case the unilateral interpretation "becomes a collective interpretation and acquires an unarguably authentic character" (*ibid.*).

77 One variant of these three situations is that of the ICJ case which, as it is an organ of the UNO only acts at the request of the General Assembly, the Security Council, the States and other specialised bodies and organisms of the United Nations once authorisation is given by the General Assembly. The interpretation that the ICJ can make of the Charter or the institutional norms of the United Nations through advisory opinions must also be remembered. See SCHERMERS, H.G., "International Organizations and the Law of Treaties", *G.Y.I.L.*, 1999, vol. 42, pp. 56-65.

78 An example of express declarative interpretation made by the General Assembly is Resolution 2625 (XXV) which contains the Declaration on Principles of International Law concerning Friendly Relations and Co-operation among States *in accordance* with the Charter of the United Nations (the italics are mine).

treaty itself or implicitly be a necessary consequence of these competencies and powers, although in practice constituent treaties of International Organisations with an interpretation clause are scarce[79].

The interpretation carried out by International Organisations can on occasions have a creative effect as can the jurisdictional interpretation which we will examine later. One example of this, in the framework of the United Nations, is the interpretation made by the Security Council in relation to the requirement for the unanimity of all permanent Members in order to adopt decisions on all matters other than procedural. This was softened by the body interpreting the abstention of the permanent members as a sign of non-opposition to the decision of the Council in question[80].

On the other hand, it should be stressed that, as regards the Security Council, recent interpretations of Chapter VII are giving rise to doubt and preoccupation. The underlying problem, as we shall see further on, is the political interpretation (or the interpretation with political aims) of a legal norm, but its effects are imposed on the totality of the International Community as a consequence of articles 25 and 103 of the Charter. At theoretical level, the General Assembly could exercise control of the Security Council by requesting advisory opinions from the ICJ. This option has never been used until now by the General Assembly and this fact demonstrates the pre-eminence of the political interests of the Member States over the legal, despite the fact that, in principle, situations such as the one described concerning Libya can occur with other States.

There is also another kind of interpretation made by International Organisations: this is the case of interpretation of treaties between States on the occasion of the exercise of competencies by organs of these Organisations. For example, when the constituent treaty of the International Organisation establishes the primacy of its

---

79 Thus, for example, article 37.1 of the constituent treaty of the International Labour Organisation (ILO), article XIV.2 of the constituent treaty of the Unesco, article 27 of the Charter of the Organisation for African Unity (OAU), or articles 220 and 234 of the Treaty of Rome of 1957 regarding the European Community.

As regards the UNO, it has been stressed that "in the practice of the United Nations, in accordance with the criterion proposed by the San Francisco Conference, it has been admitted that this interpretation is binding if it is 'generally acceptable' by the member states. Differences regarding the meaning of this criterion persist:. Does the appeal to '*consensus*' respond to this demand?" (Quoc Dinh, N., Daillier, P. and Pellet, A., *Droit..., op. cit.*, p. 251).

80 Article 27.3 of the Charter states: "The decisions of the Security Council regarding all other questions will be taken by the affirmative vote of *nine* members, including the affirmative vote of all the permanent members; but for decisions taken by virtue of Chapter VI and paragraph 3 of article 52, the part involved in the controversy shall abstain from voting". As regards this matter, see Salmon, J., "Le fait..." *op. cit.*, pages 359 et seq.

In addition, "the effect of consent to the text of such decisions cannot be interpreted as a simple reminder or specifying of the conventional commitment adopted in the Charter. On the contrary, it may be interpreted as adhesion to the value of the rule or the series of rules declared by the decision and considered in themselves" (Dupuy, P.M., "Le juge et la règle générale", *RGDIP*, 1989/3, p. 573).

norms as regards other international agreement between States, as is the case of article 103 of the United Nations Charter[81]. As regards this point, it has been stressed that even in the event of silence regarding the foundational treaty, rather wide implicit competence of the International Organisation in question would have to be admitted. In this respect, the practice of the political organs of the UNO can be cited[82]. However, in the *Lockerbie Case*, criticism can be made of the fact that two members of the Security Council, the United States and Great Britain, which were also involved as Parties in the case before the ICJ and encouraged the adoption of Ruling 748 (1992) while the case was being heard. They, thus, modified the legal relationships between the parties involved.

Finally, there is the possibility that problems of interpretation might arise in the case of treaties made between States and International Organisations. This case shares with the controversies over interpretation between States the dependence on the consequences arising from state sovereignty and the existence of customary regulation regarding the matter which have been codified in the Vienna Convention of March 21, 1986 in this respect.

Jurisdictional interpretation is that which is carried out by a judicial body. As has been explained before, due to the structure of the International Community, where no obligatory international jurisdiction exists, the possibility of this kind of interpretation depends on the previous agreement of the Parties in the dispute on interpretation either by the necessity of state to consent in order to be bound by the conventional or institutional norm which foresees such mechanisms for solving the problems of interpretation of its norms, or by the previous acknowledgement of the jurisdiction of the international organism in question[83]. Despite the advantages of

---

[81] See GONZALEZ CAMPOS, J.D., SANCHEZ RODRIGUEZ, L. I. and ANDRES SAENZ DE SANTA MARIA, M. P. *Curso ..., op. cit.,* p. 265.

Article 103 of the United Nations Charter states that:

"In the event of conflict between the obligations contracted by the Members of the United Nations by virtue of this Charter and their obligations contracted by virtue of any other international convention, the obligations imposed by this Charter will prevail".

[82] See QUOC DINH, N., DAILLIER, P and PELLET, A, *Droit ..., op. cit.,* p. 250.

[83] This is the case of article 36.2 of the Statute of the International Court of Justice, which states that:

"2. The States which are parties to this Statute may at any time declare that they *ipso facto* acknowledge the jurisdiction of the Court for all judicial controversies which involve:

the interpretation of a treaty, with no need for a special agreement as regards any other State which accepts the same obligation".

As regards the judicial interpretation, see DE VISSCHER; C., *Problèmes d'interprétation judiciaire en droit international public,* LGDJ, Paris, 1963; JENNINGS, R., "The Internal Judicial Practice of the International Court of Justice", *BYIL*, 1988, pages 31-47; BERMAN, F., "Treaty 'interpretation' in a judicial context ", *The Yale Journal of International Law*, 29 (2004) 2, pp. 315-322; TETLEY, W., "Interpretation and construction of The Hague", *The Journal of International Maritime Law*, 10 (2004), 1, pp. 30-70.

this type of interpretation, three things ought to be borne in mind: firstly, in these cases, as we have already pointed out, the authentic interpretation of the parts will be replaced by the jurisdictional interpretation imposed on the parts. Secondly, it may happen that the parts must again appeal to this judicial or arbitration organ so that it might interpret the judgement[84]. It can also occur that third parties may be affected by the judgement[85].

Both the judicial and the arbitral interpretation are also characterised by the *obligatory* nature of the decision dictated by the international judicial or arbitral organ. This obligatory nature, however, is not present in the interpretation which the ICJ might make through *advisory opinions*.

One example of compulsory jurisdictional interpretation, at regional European level, is that of the European Communities Court of Justice (ECCJ). Its object, according to article 220 of the EEC Treaty is to ensure "that in the interpretation and application of this Treaty the law is observed". Its jurisdiction is binding and this Court also ensures uniform interpretation of European Community Law through its jurisdiction to give preliminary rulings. Where any such question is raised in a case pending before a court or tribunal of a Member State against whose decisions there is no judicial remedy under national law, "that court or tribunal shall bring the matter before the Court of Justice (article 234). The ECCJ thus ensures the uniform interpretation of Community Law both from the perspec-

---

[84] This is laid down in article 60 of the Statute of the ICJ which states that:

> "The decision will be definitive and with no right of appeal. In the event of disagreement regarding the meaning or the scope of the decision, the Court will interpret it at the request of any of the parts".

By way of example, in ICJ practice mention should be made of the cases concerning Request for Interpretation of the Judgement of 20 November 1950 in the *Asylum* case (ICJ *Reports 1950*, pages 395-404), and to the *Application for Revision and Interpretation of the Judgement of 24 February 1982 in the case concerning the Continental Shelf (Tunisia/Libyan Aral Jamahiriya (Tunisia v. Libyan Arab. Jamahiriya)* (ICJ *Reports 1985*, pages 192-232). A similar provision is article 79 of the Rules of the European Court of Human Rights, which states that:

> "1. A party may request the interpretation of a judgement within a period of one year following the delivery of that judgement.

[85] Thus, article 63 of the Statute of the ICJ, which refers to conventional norms, states that:

> "1. When it is a question of the interpretation of a convention where other States are parties apart from the parties in litigation, the Secretary will immediately notify all the States concerned.
>
> 2. Every state notified will have the right to intervene in the case; but if it exercises this right, the interpretation contained in the decision will be equally binding on it".

Article 62.1 of the same Statute covers the hypothesis as regards the interpretation of customary norms:

> "1. If a State considers it has a judicial interest which might be affected by the decision of the litigation, it may request the Court to allow it to intervene".

tive of the domestic jurisdictions of the Member States and from that of the judicial activity itself.

Concerning this kind of interpretation, there is discussion on whether it has a declarative or a creative character. Practice gives examples of both depending on the degree of liberty held by the interpreter. The innovative aspect is frequent in cases where the organism intervenes as a consequence of its compulsory jurisdiction and is less frequent when its jurisdiction is voluntary. The practice of the ECCJ is significant in this respect.

Some think that even in such hypotheses of creation the liberty of the organ is not unlimited when it interprets because it is limited by the existing legal materials[86]. Thus, the competence of the judge is "semi-discretionary, dominated by the objective of his mission to interpret, to attribute to the provisions of the treaty a meaning in accordance with the intention of the contracting parties as regards the object of its convention"[87]. However this must be stated more precisely insofar as it is the judge who appreciates and values the materials with which he works and it is from these materials, with the freedom and security conferred on him by the fact that the parts have accepted his jurisdiction, that he arrives at conclusions and builds up his decision applicable to the specific case.

One final aspect concerning jurisdictional interpretation is the *interpretation of the decision* issued by the international judicial or arbitral organ, an interpretation which will be authentic if it is made by the same organ which dictated the decision whose interpretation was requested[88].

As concerns the interpretation of judgements, case law built up on international judicial and arbitral decisions is specified in the following principles:

---

[86] See LAUTERPACHT, H., "La théorie des differands non justiciables en droit international" *R. des C.,* vol. 34 (1930-IV), pages 548 et seq.

The limitations derived from the legal materials also appear in the interpretation carried out within the framework of the internal Law of the State, whether this be of a judicial, administrative or constitutional nature. In these cases, the liberty of interpretation depends very closely on the statute that these organisms have and the role this statute attributes to them.

[87] SIMON, D., *op. cit.*, pages 143 et seq. As P.M. DUPUY points out "On extracting the quintessence from the different state conducts at legal level, opting for the legal content of declarations, attitudes and behaviour of the those affected by the law, and putting them into perspective with key concepts on which praetorian reasoning is constructed, the judge is led to extract *strong ideas* from which he draws logical conclusions more so in international law than in other fields. The level of generality which is the product of a normative synthesis at time confers a content which is quite far from what the States would have spontaneously conferred on these regulations" ("Le juge et ..." *op. cit.,* pages 570 et seq. The words in italics appear so in the original).

[88] One recent example with regard to arbitral awards is the Decision of October 21, 1994 of the Arbitral Tribunal in the case concerning the *Delimitation of the Frontier Line between Boundary post 62 and Mount Fitz Roy* (Argentina/Chile), submitted to the same Court which dictated the judgement of October 13, 1995 by Chile (*R.I.A.A.*, vol. XXII, pages 3-152 and *R.I.A.A.*, vol XXII, pages 153-207).

- The issue must be susceptible to being decided on by interpretation, which is a legal operation tending to determine the precise meaning of a norm but which cannot modify it[89]. As concerns the judgements, the interpretation is "a purely auxiliary process which can serve to explain, but not to modify what the Court has already decided with binding force and which has already been judged. Interpretation poses the question of knowing what the Court has decided with binding force in its decision and not what the Court should decide now in the light of new facts or arguments. A request for interpretation, therefore, must be based on the determination of the meaning and the scope of the decision, it cannot serve as a means to "revise" or "annul" the decision"[90].
- For the request for the interpretation of a judgement to go ahead, there must be disagreement among the parts[91].
- It suffices that both parts have manifested their differences regarding the meaning and the scope of the judgement, without the need for this divergence to be expressed in a specific manner[92].

---

[89] The ICJ states the same criterion regarding treaties, for example, in the following cases: on the *Interpretation of Peace Treaties with Bulgaria, Hungary and Romania* (cf. ICJ, *Reports 1950*, p. 229), on the *Rights of the Nationals of the United States of America in Morocco* cf. ICJ, *Reports 1952*, p. 196); and on *South West Africa phase two* (cf. ICJ, *Reports 1966*, p. 48) Also the arbitral award of October 21, 1994, already quoted. In its judgement of October 13, 1995, this same Court followed the precedents of the aforementioned ICJ and stated that "by virtue of the request «in substitution of interpretation» posed by Chile, it may interpret its judgement, but not modify it" (*op. cit.*, p. 55).

[90] The *case of the delimitation of the continental shelf between Great Britain and France* (*RIAA*, vol. XVIII, p. 366). These criteria have been repeated by the Tribunal which dictated the judgement of October 21, 1994 in its Decision on the interpretation of the previous Decision of October 13, 1995. The ICJ also in the case concerning the *Application for Revision and Interpretation of the Judgement of 24 February 1982 in the case concerning the Continental Shelf (Tunisia/Libyan Arab Jamahiriya) (Tunisia v. Libyan Arab Jamahiriya)* (cf. ICJ, *Reports 1985*, p. 223).

[91] Thus, the Decision of the Tribunal of October 13, 1995, already quoted (*op. cit.*, p. 53). The Tribunal concludes the non-existence of controversy as Chile acknowledges that there is no divergence between the parts regarding the interpretation of the previous judgement of October 21, 1994.

Concerning the ICJ, the same criterion exists, for example, in the case of the request for the interpretation of the Judgement of November 20, 1950 in the *Asylum* case (cf. ICJ, *Reports 1950*, p. 403).

[92] Thus, in the Arbitral Decision of October 13, 1995, already quoted (*op. cit.*, p. 54). Likewise the ICJ, for example, in the case concerning the *Application for Revision and Interpretation of the Judgement of 24 February 1982 in the case concerning the Continental Shelf (Tunisia/Libyan Arab Jamahiriya) (Tunisia v. Libyan Arab Jamahiriya)* (cf. ICJ, *Reports 1985*, p. 218).

- The interpretation shall be requested in relation to a specific paragraph or to a phrase of the judgement and not to the complete judgement[93].
- In no event can the interpretation exceed the limits of the judgement fixed beforehand by the conclusions of the parts. This criterion is inherent to the competence of international jurisdiction, which is limited by the attributions that the parts confer on it in the case in question. Consequently, its powers are also limited buy the maximum pretensions of the parts involved in the case. To surpass either of these would imply an *ultra vires* decision and the decision would be flawed due to excess of power[94].
- The interpretation of judgements has a particular characteristic insofar as it "not only implies the precision of the text of the points to be decided on, but also the determination of the scope, the meaning and the finality of the decision, in accordance with the considerations of this decision"[95].

Despite the existence of general regulations for the interpretation of treaties, those relating to interpretation of judgements are stricter due to the nature of the norm to be interpreted: a judicial or arbitration decision, whose interpretation does not allow the use of rules from the field of treaties such as, for example, the preparatory work or the subsequent conduct of the Parties. These can be useful for determining the common will of the Parties. So, in relation to the Award of 1902, "the Court – of Arbitration – considers that the three documents constituting the award are sufficient"[96]. Thus, in the *case concerning the delimitation of the frontier line between boundary post 62 and Mount Fitz Roy*, the Tribunal used the criterion of the text and began from the interpretative principle according to which the text must be interpreted in the sense that produces effects in accordance with international law and not contrary to it. It states that, in the case of international judgements whose legal validity is not under discussion and which have the value of

93 Thus, in the Decision of October 13, 1995, the Tribunal also mentions the "divergence of opinions between the parts on defined points" (case *concerning the delimitation of the frontier …, op. cit.*, p. 403).

94 Thus, in the Arbitral Decision of October 21, 1994 in the case concerning the *Application for Revision and ..., op. cit.*, p. 50. The ICJ also, for example, in the *Request for Interpretation of the Judgement of 20 November 1950 in the Asylum Case* (cf. ICJ, *Reports 1950*, p. 403), QUEL LOPEZ, F.J., *La interpretación, revisión y nulidad de las sentencias arbitrales internacionales*, Servicio Editorial de la Universidad del Pais Vasco, Bilbao, 2000.

95 The Inter-American Court of Human Rights, *The case of Velázquez Rodríguez, Interpretation of the judgement for compensatory indemnity, judgement of August 17, 1990 (article 67 American Convention on Human Rights), Series C*, No. 9, paragraph 26). This quotation is taken from the Decision of October 21, 1994 which we are analysing.

96 *Ibid.* The opinion of this Tribunal is based on the criterion of Queen Elizabeth II who was the arbitrator who, on December 9, 1996 dictated the decision which determined the siting of the frontierline between the two boundary posts 16 and 17 (cf. *RIAA*, vol. XVI, pages 111 et seq.).

having been judged, these "must be interpreted in such a way that they do not lead the fact that the Judge or Arbitrator have pronounced their decisions in breach of the lawful norms of the law of peoples"[97].

The last decision regarding the types of interpretation takes *the degree of freedom in the interpretation* as its reference, and this freedom depends on the general characters of the legal system in question "its greater or lesser centralisation, the hierarchy of its norms, the regulation of its competence"[98]. At international level and with the characteristics already described, when the States decide to appeal to a judicial or arbitral organ in order to submit a problem of interpretation to it, they limit their own competence in the matter in order to attribute it to the aforementioned organ in the terms considered appropriate. Likewise, when it is a question of a treaty which obliges the submittal of the problems of interpretation to a specific organ, the States themselves voluntarily accept the limitation of state competence in this respect. Finally the greater or lesser freedom for the interpretation may also depend on the type of norm to be interpreted and, if it has been written down it may also depend on how it has been drafted.

As regards the second aspect we alluded to at the beginning of this section, *the methods*, discussion arises when determining whether there are methods for the task of interpretation or not. Against a method is the argument that every interpretation can lead to several different results. Secondly, that the methods considered as positive contradict each other, for example, the grammatical method and the useful effect method. Finally, they lack judicial value because they are simply procedures of logical order or opportunity.

Those defending the existence of interpretation methods point out that these methods are inherent to every legal system. Secondly, that the interpreter could not proceed with total freedom and arbitrarily as his will would replace the will of the author of the act and the interpretation would disappear as a specific judicial activity to become confused with a task involving the creation of Law. Finally, they add that in positive International Law, it is clear that case law refers to rules, principles and methods of interpretation which it uses constantly. Therefore, they conclude that there are different *methods of interpretation* depending on the interpretative rules employed by the interpreter[99]:

---

97 The decision of October 21, 1994, *op. cit.*, p. 50. And adds, "Thus, in compliance with its legal function, a Court called on to interpret a legal norm must not only take care that its decision is supported and in keeping with international law, but must also discard anything which might produce results contrary to international law" (*ibid.*).

98 SUR, S., *op. cit.*, p. 97.

99 Concerning this point, in general, see SALMON, J., "Le fait dans l'application …", *op. cit.*, pages 353 et seq.; PASTOR RIDRUEJO, J.A., *Curso de Derecho Internacional Público y Organizaciones Internacionales*, 9th ed., Tecnos, Madrid, 2003, pages 1937 et seq., REMIRO BROTONS, A. *Derecho Internacional Público…*, *op. cit.*, pages 306 et seq.; SIMON, D., *op. cit.*, pages 98 et seq.; SUR, S. *op. cit.*, pages 252 et seq., DIEZ DE VELASCO, M., *Instituciones de Derecho Internacional Público,* 14th ed., Tecnos, Madrid, 2003, pages 183-187, CONFORTI, B., *op. cit.,* pages 97-105.

- *Grammatical, textual or objective method:* this is based on the text of the treaty "as the authentic expression of the will of the parts, stressing the primacy of the text for the interpretation"[100].
- *The teleological or functional method* focuses on the object and the aim of the treaty[101].
- *The logical-systematic method* not only takes into account the norm to be interpreted, but also all the other related norms[102].
- *The subjective method* focuses on the intention of the parts.
- *The historical-evolutionary method* takes into account the historical moment when the treaty was made and the meaning the terms had at that time"[103], as well as practice following the treaty.

As REMIRO points out, the appeal to "one or other depends on the conception of the objective of the interpretation held by the interpreter. The *objectivists* incline towards the *grammatical* or *textual* and *logical-systematic method*; the *subjectivists* prefer the teleological, sociological and *comparative* methods"[104]. That is why some authors hold that the means and methods we have analysed "are general guidelines rather than strict rules", and the interpreter should apply them with flexibility and use combinations of them[105].

A third group of authors distinguish between *means* and *rules* of interpretation "even though the distinction made is discussible"[106].

---

[100] PASTOR RIDRUEJO, J.A., *Curso ..., op. cit.*, p. 137. Cf. CONFORTI, B., *op. cit.,* pages 98 et seq. However, as BROWNLIE points out, "the textual approach in practice often leaves the decision maker with a choice of possible meanings and in exercising that choice it is impossible to keep considerations of policy out of account" (*Principles ..., op. cit.,* p. 632).

[101] "Independently of the intention of the parts, the convention insofar as it is a construction has a specific object or purpose, and the work of the Court, i.e. the ICJ, is to ascertain and establish this object or purpose and then interpret the treaty so that it becomes effective" (FITZMAURICE, G., "The Law and Procedure ..." *op. cit.,* p. 208). This process is equivalent in practice to a type of judicial legislation to the extent that the Court would fill in the gaps, correct errors and even amend the text so that obscurities or ambiguities would disappear.

[102] Cf. DIEZ DE VELASCO, M., *Instituciones ..., op. cit.,* p. 183.

[103] *Ibid.*

[104] REMIRO BROTONS, A., *Derecho Internacional Público..., op. cit.*, p. 308 (The words in italics appear so in the original). Cf. FAVRE, A., "L'interprétation objectiviste des traités internationaux", *Annuaire Suisse de Droit International,* 1960, pages 75-99.

[105] QUOC DINH, N., DAILLIER, P. and PELLET, A., *Droit..., op. cit.*, p. 256.

[106] *Ibid.*, p. 252. The *means* are "the basic or formal elements relevant to the interpretation of the text" (such as the text, the context, posterior practice, the circumstances in which the treaty was made, the preparatory work, the time when it is interpreted, the relevant rules of International Law). They also include "the instruments at the disposal of the interpreter who must use them". The *rules* are "the principles which guide the use of these means" (*ibid*).

The underlying problem is the freedom or the obligation of the interpreter "the bound or discretionary nature of his competence. The affirmation of the legal existence and the precision of a set of methods limits his power, its negation underlines his freedom"[107]. In other words, the existence of methods of interpretation limits the freedom of the interpreter while the absence of methods facilitates the interpretation. It is undeniable that the interpreters (States, International Organisations, international judicial and arbitration organisms) avail themselves of a number of rules for interpreting international norms.

The difficulties involved in interpreting arise from the type of norm as only in the field of the Law on Treaties has the codifying task of the International Law Commission (ILC) led to the affirmation of the existence of a number of rules which will be analysed later. The problems arise above all in relation to customary norms where the conduct of the States must be interpreted and the presence or not of the *opinio juris* determined. Similar problems are involved regarding institutional norms (the acts of International Organisations) and unilateral declarations, where the determining element is the conduct of the state and the intention of the parts.

---

[107] SUR, S., *op. cit.,* p. 254. Notwithstanding the specific bibliography on the interpretation of international treaties which we shall analyse later, see REUTER, P., *Introduction au Droit des Traités*, PUF, Paris, 1985.

CHAPTER II:

The Text, the Authentic Expression of the Will of the Parties, Constitutes the Subject of the Discrepancy: The Conventional Rules

1 Language, the instrument of sovereignty

Unlike the rules of custom, written rules provide the interpreter with the advantage that the task of interpretation has been supplied with a point of reference which has been pre-established by the parts: the text. This text reflects the *consensus* of the parties concerning the content of the rule and constitutes the authentic written expression of their wills.

From the perspective of this work, the presence of a written text occurs both in the conventional and the institutional rules (occasionally this is also true of unilateral declarations). Moreover, as far as treaties are concerned, the task of the interpreter is made easier by the existence of a number of rules of interpretation which arose from custom and have been codified by the ILC, with regard to the Law of Treaties between States (Vienna Convention of May 23, 1969) and to the Law of Treaties between States and International Organisations (Vienna Convention of March 21, 1986)[1] in three articles dealing with: a general rule of interpretation (article 31), complementary means of interpretation (article 32), and the interpretation of treaties authenticated in two or more languages (article 33). Therefore, these interpretative rules currently have a double nature (conventional or customary), and it should be stressed that the ICJ applies them independently of whether the parts involved in the controversy are also parties to the Vienna Convention of 1969[2].

Consequently, the method for the interpretation of conventional norms is attracted by the text of the treaty (which constitutes the authentic expression of the consensus of the signatory states and which reflects their common intention. Therefore, it is an intrinsic element and has an objective character). It is also

---

1 Cf. BROWNLIE, I., *Basic Documents in International* Law, 4th. Ed., Clarendon Press, Oxford, 1995, pages 388-425. For example, see the text of the latter in *RGDIP*, 1986/2, pages 502-540.

2 Concerning this matter, the ICJ has stated that they are rules which in many aspects "can be considered as a codification of existing customary international law on the point" (the case regarding the *Arbitral Award of 31 July, 1989*, ICJ, *Reports 1991*, p. 70).

attracted by the object and purpose of the treaty" (described by the doctrine as "the *ratio legis* of the conventional provision")[3]. These will be analysed carefully in following section of this book.

As we have stated, whereas in the norms of custom what is interpreted is the conduct of the State as an expression of its sovereign will (an interpretation which takes in the choice of action and conduct, the classification of these and the extraction of the rule of custom involved), in the specific case of the conventional norms, the interpretation begins with a detailed examination of the text to be interpreted as this text constitutes the expression of the will and the intention of the parts[4].

Unlike conventional norms in the case of institutional norms, (this work will focus on the resolutions of the General Assembly of the United Nations), we generally lack previous rules of interpretation which can guide the interpreter in his task, although the ICJ applies similar criteria to those of the Vienna Conventions, as we will see below.

In any case, even if it is true that the existence of a written text can facilitate the task of the interpreter, sometimes the international treaty does not provide such an advantage. The analysis of state practice reveals that, on many occasions, international treaties have no more value than simple recommendations, due to the way in which their obligations have been drafted. In such cases, the treaty is binding as a norm from the formal point of view, but its content must be limited to simple guidelines unless the Parties have laid down precise and detailed rules which involve specific attitudes[5]. On the other hand, certain resolutions of International Organisations, which from a formal point of view have no other value than that of a recommendation, sometimes have a precise content reminding us of a norm and entail obligations from the material point of view.

Both circumstances have been described as revealing the nomadic nature of the notion of agreement which moves from one plane to another, and which has lead to complications in the examination of these phenomena, which are frequent in international financial, development and environmental law[6].

---

3 Cf. GONZALEZ CAMPOS, J.D., SANCHEZ RODRIGUEZ, L.I. and ANDRES SAENZ DE SANTA MARIA, M.P., *op.cit.,* p. 262.

4 Before the Vienna Convention of 1969, FITZMAURICE held that to clarify its meaning "is, *ex hypothesi,* to give effect to that will and intention. If the text is not clear, recourse must be had to extraneous sources of interpretation; but the object is still the same – namely – that the text has a certain meaning, on the basis of which the parties have certain rights and obligations, and, therefore, that this is what they must have intended in concluding the treaty" (FITZMAURICE, G., "The Law and Procedure of the ICJ 1951-1954: treaty interpretation and other treaty points" *British Yearbook of International Law*, 1957, p. 207. Currently, the interpretation process must be carried out in accordance with the rules of the aforementioned Convention.

5 In this respect, see, for example, note (14) of this Chapter.

6 DUPUY, R.J., "Communaté internationale et disparités de developpement" *R. des C.,* vol. 165 (1979-IV)., p. 185. Cf. also WEIL, P., "Vers una normativité relative en Droit International", *RGDIP*, 1982/1, pages 5-47.

In our opinion, as regards the institutional norms, this is the reason why the decision on whether or not a specific norm is obligatory cannot be taken *a priori*, by it an obligatory nature depending on the norm in question, and which leads a sector of international doctrine to immediately exclude that the institutional norms might have obligatory legal effects when there is no express stipulation to this effect in the treaty constituting the Organisation[7]. On the other hand, the analysis of the content of the norm (which reflects the intentions of the parts) as well as the attitude of the parts concerning its adoption, would be clearer in order to give the precise legal force of the institutional norm in question, and in order to carry out its interpretation[8]. The IIL expressed a similar opinion in the resolution adopted in the session held in Cairo in 1987. Conclusion number 10 of this resolution keeps the drafting and the context in which the resolution was adopted by the International Organisation as criteria by which to determine the intention of the state[9]. As far as the written norms are concerned, two distinct problems arise, one referring to the institutional norms and the other to the conventional ones. In the former the problem is the interpretation of the conduct of the state and the text of the institutional norm in order to determine its nature or its legal effects. In treaties, the problem is the interpretation *strictu sensu* by recourse to the codified rules in the Vienna Conventions of 1969 and 1986.

---

7 Thus, for example, MACGIBBON, Y., "Means for the identification of International Law General Assembly Resolutions: Custom, Practice and Mistaken Identity", in the collection edited by BIN CHENG, *International Law: Teaching and Practice*, Stevens, London, 1982, pages 10-26. For this author, the Resolutions of the General Assembly are only recommendations even for the States which have voted for them: "given the powers of the General Assembly, that is all they can be" (p. 13).

8 In this respect, the ICJ was requested to give an advisory opinion on the *Legal consequences for States of the continued presence of South Africa in Namibia (South West Africa) notwithstanding Security Council Resolution 276 (1970)*, and stated the following:

> "The language of a resolution of the Security Council should be carefully analysed before a conclusion can be made as to its binding effect. In view of the nature of the powers under Article 25, the question whether they have been in fact exercised is to be determined in each case, having regard to the terms of the resolution to be interpreted, the discussion leading to it, the provisions of the Charter invoked and, in general, all circumstances that might assist in determining the legal consequences of the resolution of the Security Council" (ICJ, *Reports 1971*, p. 53).

As regards this matter, it should be pointed out that in recent practice, the Security Council has usually expressly stated which Chapter or provision of the Charter led to their adopting the resolution in question.

Concerning these problems see, for example, CASTAÑEDA, J., "Valeur juridique des résolutions des Nations Unies" *R. des C.*, vol. 129 (1970-71), pages 205-232; MOSLER, H., "Remarques sur la superposition du droit des Organisations internationales au droit des gens interétatique" in the collection *Estudios de Derecho Internacional, Homenaje al Profesor Miaja de la Muela,* Tecnos, Madrid, 1979, vol. I, pages 429-442; MCWHINNEY, E, *Les Nations Unies et la Formation du Droit,* Pedone/Unesco, Paris, 1986.

9 See Institute of International Law, *Yearbook of the Institute of International Law,* 1987, vol. 6-II, p. 281.

We insist that in order to find an answer to the first problem, a priori conclusions which immediately exclude the obligatory nature of the international norms cannot be taken into account. As was stated above, in order to solve this question with especial regard to the norms of International Organisations with constituent treaties which fail to state anything with regard to its value or judicial force (in the words of VIRALLY)[10], both the content and the language of the norm in question will be of use, as will the attitude of the States regarding that norm and the drafting process within the International Organisation. As R.J. DUPUY points out, "we must return to the long forgotten distinction between formal and material criteria, bearing in mind the tremendous flexibility of international law concerning the forms, an agreement made between states may involve much diversity"[11].

As regards the second, the interpretation *strictu sensu* of the conventional norm, the use of the interpretative rules codified in the Vienna Conventions of 1969 and 1986 must allow the interpreter to resolve the discrepancy.

The question of the *language* used in drafting the written norms (both conventional and institutional) and the unilateral declarations is closely linked to the previous two issues. As FOCSANEANU points out "every legal rule is of necessity expressed in a language which thus becomes an essential element. The interpretation and application of the rule demand a critical examination of its linguistic expression. This examination must deal with the lexical, morphological, syntactic and modern logical aspects"[12].

In this regard, as we have stated at the beginning of this work, the text expresses the will of the parties and, occasionally, it is necessary to have recourse to vague terms or terms that leave the parties a wide margin for discretion when drafting the text of the norm. This is the tribute paid by the parties in order to achieve a norm which is an instrument for formalising cooperation. This is a consequence of the sovereignty of the state and the principle of the autonomy of the will of the parties which becomes manifest during the process for drafting the norms.

---

[10] See VIRALLY, M., "Résolution et accord international", in the collection *Essays in International Law in Honour of Judge Manfred Lachs,* M. Nijhoff, The Hague, 1984, pages 299 et seq.

[11] DUPUY, R.J., "Droit déclaratoire et Droit programmatoire: de la coutume sauvage à la soft law" in the collection *L'élaboration du droit international public*, ed. Pedone, Paris, 1975, p. 140. See also VIRALLY, M., "La distinction entre textes internationaux de portée juridique et textes internationaux dépourvus de portée juridique", *Yearbook of the Institute of International Law,* vol. 60-I, 1985, pages 166-257.

[12] FOCSANEANU, L., "Les langues comme moyen d'expression du droit international", *A.F.D.I.*, 1970, pages 257 et seq. On this issue cf. REUTER, P., "Quelques réflexions sur le vocabulaire du droit international", in the collection *Mélanges en l'honneur M. le Doyen Trotabas,* Pedone, Paris, 1970, pages 423-445. See also our work "Lenguaje y Derecho Internacional", in the collection *Homenaje al Profesor D. Juan Manuel Castro Rial y Canos,* F. MARIÑO, ed. Trotta, Madrid, 2002, pages 299-318.

The states sometimes choose to formulate the obligations they are to be bound by using vague expressions or using the conditional tense "designating objectives rather than immediate obligations, programmes rather than certainties"[13]. This fact is common both to the conventional norms and the institutional ones. In the latter cases, recourse is made to the execution of Resolutions, Recommendations and Declarations. At other times, a series of obligations are listed with no indication of how they are to be developed nor are specific details gone into (this also occurs in the conventional way)[14].

Thus, from the perspective of the language used in the drafting of the *conventional* obligations, a threefold distinction can be made:

- conventional norms with specific obligations;
- conventional norms with general non-specific obligations;
- conventional norms with discretionary development of obligations[15].

For example, within the *first group* are the conventions regarding the fight against pollution of the seas by oil, which stipulate a system concerning responsibility and compensation falling upon the ship-owner and clearly drafted[16]. Also the

---

[13] DUPUY, P.M., Le Droit interrnational de l'environnement et la souveraineté des Etats. Bilan et perspectives", in the collective work *L'Avenir du Droit International de l'Environnement*, Colloque Workshop, La Haye, 1985, p. 34. See also SALMON, J., "Le fait dans l'application du droit international", *R. des C.*, t. 175 (1982-II), pages 257-414 and BOYLE, A.F., "Some Reflections on the Relationship of Treaties and Soft Law", *I.C.L.Q.*, 1999, vol. 48, nº 4, pp. 901-913.

[14] For example, article 27 of the Unesco Convention for the Protection of the World Cultural and Natural Heritage, which states:

"1. The States Parties to this Convention shall endeavour by all appropriate means, and in particular by educational and information programs, to strengthen appreciation and respect by their peoples of the cultural and natural heritage defined in Articles 1 and 2 of the Convention.

2. They shall undertake to keep the public broadly informed of the dangers threatening this heritage and of the activities carried in pursuance of this Convention" (*International Legal Materials*, 1972, p. 1358).

[15] The difficulties arising from the language used in order to state the obligation mainly appear in the obligations regarding behaviour and prevention (see on this matter, the examples quoted in the notes (14), (16) and (17) of this Chapter.

[16] Thus, article III.1 of the Convention on Civil Liability for Oil Pollution Damage of November 29, 1969, states:

"1. Except as provided in paragraphs 2 and 3 of this article, *the owner of a ship* at the time of an incident, or where the incident consists of a series of occurrences at the time of the first occurrence, *shall be liable for any pollution damage* caused by oil which has escaped or been discharged from the ship as a result of the incident" (The italics are ours).

See also the Convention of December 18, 1971 on the establishment of an International Fund for Compensation for Oil Pollution Damage.

Convention of March 29, 1972 on International Liability for Damage Caused by Space Objects[17].

In the *second group* the obligations described by VIRALLY as "good will obligations" which are characterised as leaving "a considerable margin for subjective appreciation (discretionary) which is beyond the control of a third party"[18]. These are obligations whose complete execution depends to a great extent on the good will of the subject contracting these obligations and such execution is assessed through a subjective and discretionary appreciation to the extent that "it depends exclusively on the opinion that the person owing the obligation has of the behaviour he must adopt in order to conform to this obligation, or on the circumstances which shape the current obligation", and a third party viewing the matter from the exterior cannot determine whether this appreciation conforms to the commitment acquired unless he replaces the opinion of the person bound by the obligation by his own opinion "which is clearly inadmissible". That is why "within this discretionary margin of appreciation, the person bound by the obligation remains perfectly free from the legal point of view. His will is subject to no limitations or restrictions due to the commitment he has accepted"[19].

However, this does not mean that the state which has taken on an obligation of this type does not have unlimited discretionary margin of appreciation. For these types of treaties, as in all types, the state is obliged by its manifestation of consent regarding the treaty, but drafting conditions, the required nature of the conduct to the extent that this is expressed in terms which are wide enough to dilute or reduce the obligatory content of the provision in question. These difficulties affect the other states which are parties as well as a hypothetical third party called in to interpret the norm or to determine whether the conduct of the state is in keeping with what is prescribed in the norm. We can find a good example of these types of obligations in the sector of International Law concerning the environmental protection, when conventional obligations regarding information, consultations, cooperation, negotiation and others are not specified nor developed by the conventional norm involved[20].

---

[17] Its article II, for example states:

> "A launching State shall be absolute liable to pay compensation for damage caused by its space object on the surface of the earth or to aircrafts in flight".

[18] VIRALLY, M., "The distinction between....", *op.cit.*, page 219, Cf. WEIL, P., *op.cit.*, page 44.

[19] *Ibid.*, page 334.

[20] As an example, we can quote article 1 of the Protocol for the Protection of the Mediterranean Sea Against Pollution from Land-Based Sources of May 17, 1980, which states:

> "The Contracting Parties to this Protocol (hereinafter referred to as 'the parties') *shall take all appropriate measures to prevent, abate, combat and control pollution* of the Mediterranean Sea Area caused by discharges from rivers, coastal establishments or outfalls, or emanating from any other land-based sources within their territories" (*International Legal Materials*, 1980, pages 869 et seq. The italics are ours).

Along the same lines, see the Geneva Convention on Long-Range Transboundary Air Pollution of November 13, 1979.

In this regard, an external observer such as a judicial or international arbitration institution, taking all the circumstances of a specific matter into account, can determine "whether the conduct observed by the person bound by the obligation conforms to what reasonably might be expected of him, or whether his conduct shows bad faith or the total lack of the will to comply with his commitments"[21]. It should be stressed that the hypothetical intervention of this third party can only take place if the dissenting parties agree to this or if it is imposed by the international treaty which gives rise to the controversy. Unless a third party intervenes, in practice, the discretionary nature of the matter is difficult to restrict, especially when the aforementioned weaknesses of the principle of good faith are taken into account, and the attitude of the parties must be assessed in the light of this good faith.

The last category of norms includes conventional norms containing obligations which are developed at the discretion of each party. This is the case of commitments with a specific, defined objective assessable externally by a third party "but whose practice depends on a subjective appreciation which the contracting party has stipulated he will develop more or less at his own discretion, or whose execution is subject to an appreciation of this type. In this case it is still impossible to appreciate from the exterior if the conduct has been respected or breached: it would be necessary to penetrate the conscience of the parties. As in the previous category of norms, here breach of obligation can only appear in the hypothesis of bad faith or a manifest bad will"[22], thus, the same problems regarding discretion, good faith and the hypothetical intervention of a third party already mentioned with respect to the conventional norms of the previous group (that is to say, those which contain obligations concerning good will).

This overview shows the essential role of interpretation in International Law as well as the serious difficulties that arise unless a third party intervenes in order to resolve the dispute. This must be done through the determination of the existing rights and obligations in a specific situation, as well as through the precision of the legal content of the conventional or institutional norm in question. This is a consequence of the weight of the sovereignty of the state in the structure of the International Community of the beginning of the twentioneth century.

---

21 *Ibid.* page 335. As regards this issue, see. also SKUBISZEWSKI, K., "L'élaboration des grandes conventions multilatérales et des instruments non conventionnels à fonction ou à vocation normative", *Yearbook of the Institute of International Law,* vol. 61-I, Paris, 1985, pages. 29-249 and 305-358; and vol. 61-II, Paris, 1986, pages 257-276, and the Resolution of the Institute of International Law adopted in 1987 at its session held in Cairo quoted above (Institute of International Law, *Yearbook...., op.cit.*, pages 279 et seq.).

22 *Ibid.,* pages 222 et seq. Within this group should be included the conventional obligations expressed by statements such as "shall cooperate", "shall take appropriate measures", "if possible", etc. Through these expressions the state assuming the obligation can determine what is demanded of it at a particular time at its own discretion. Despite this, these cases also involve legal obligations imposed by a conventional norm. On many occasions the texts containing obligations expressed in this manner can only establish a framework of action for the future. See, for example, the way certain obligations are expressed in the Convention on Wetlands of International Importance especially as Waterfowl Habitat made on February 2, 1971.

2 The judicial limiting of a process which is heavily dependent on the autonomy of the will of the State: The interpretative norms of the Vienna Conventions of 1969 and 1986

The situation described in the preceding pages shows the dependence of the process of interpretation on state sovereignty. In written Law, sovereignty becomes manifest through language. In other words, through the choice of the terms which suit the will that the State wishes to materialise through the text.

In an effort to limit the State's discretion when it carries out this task, the I.L.C. has codified a series of rules that must be employed in the interpretative process as regards the conventional norms. It is in the light of such rules that the divergent interpretations of the Parties must be analysed[23]. These rules are contained in articles 31 to 33 of the Vienna Conventions of 1969 and 1986 including a general rule for interpretation (Article 31), supplementary means (Article 32), and principles relating to the interpretation of treaties authenticated in two or more languages (Article 33)[24]. Finally, the entire interpretative process is based on the structural principle of good faith.

The codification made in this matter by the I.L.C. constitutes an attempt to restrict a process which is very dependent on the autonomy of the will of the States, which is characterised by the use of specific legal methods but limited to conventional norms. These rules are first imposed on the States, which must use them to make their unilateral interpretation, and also on the third party involved in the dispute. To a certain extent, they act as guides and condition the interpretation. Once the intervention of the third party takes place as a consequence of the acceptance by the parties or imposition by the treaty, the obligatory jurisdiction provides him with greater freedom to appreciate and evaluate the interpretative rules in the specific case, and he knows that his interpretation will be imposed on the parties.

---

[23] A sector of doctrine describes the work of the ILC as searching technically and with some empiricism for the general points of agreement between the states involved, in agreement with its mission for the progressive codification and development of International Law (SUR, S., *op.cit.* page 71). Previous to the two Vienna Conventions, see BERLIA, G., "Contribution à l'interprétation des traités", *R. de C.*, vol. 114 (1965-I), pages 283-333; BERNHARDT, R., *Die Auslegung völkerrechtlicher Verträge insbesondere in der neuen Rechtsprechung internationaler Gerichte*, C. Heymanns Verlag, Köln-Berlin, 1963.

[24] Among ourselves, REMIRO holds that these rules are *declarations* "although their presentation, ordering and hierarchy include aspects involving progressive development". They are also *guidelines* "to the extent that the parties to a treaty can adapt their interpretation as they see suitable". Finally, they can be *applied generally* to all treaties without prejudice to the development of particular rules as, for example, what is stipulated in article 5 of the Vienna Convention of 1986 concerning the Law on Treaties between States and International Organisations or between International Organisations (cf. REMIRO BROTONS, A., *Derecho Internacional, op. cit.*, page 309).

As we have said, the I.L.C. structures the interpretative process on the principle of good faith. Thus, as the weakness of this principle has already been explained, we should again stress the consequences this lack of specification of good faith entails for the interpretative process.

In any case, it should not be forgotten that the rules contained in both Vienna Conventions will only be applied in the event of interpretative disputes involving States or International Organisations where a third party intervenes. In such cases, they are to be applied by the third party in his interpretative work but they depend on the willingness of the Parties in dispute to submit the controversy to him (except if there is a previous obligation binding them to do so). Apart from these cases, and although these rules also oblige the Parties when they make their unilateral interpretations, knowing whether these have actually used them cannot be objectively controlled. So, they cannot just destroy the divergent interpretations of the Parties.

Finally, the usefulness and modus operandi of these rules for deciding specific cases depend on their application. And this is only effective when a third party intervenes as, unless he does, recourse to interpretative criteria cannot serve to destroy divergent interpretations which have the same value and which are both based on good faith, unless otherwise proved, which is exceedingly difficult.

In the doctrinal field, the characteristics of the interpretation of conventional norms have been underlined. Firstly, it is an *intellectual* operation aimed at understanding the treaty, specifying its meaning and determining its scope. This operation is of a declarative nature, to the extent that it states what it is and not what it should be, nor does it revise the norms nor fill in the gaps[25].

Secondly, it is also a *complex* operation involving many factors which, unless they converge, will give rise to choices regarding *meaning*, which no objective norm can prevent sharing[26].

Finally the ILC has stated that it is a *combined* operation to the extent that it demands the combination of several interpretative elements (those laid down in articles 31 to 33 of the two Vienna Conventions on the Law on Treaties)[27]. It is at this point that the integrated system rather than the autonomous operation of the elements can be appreciated.

We now move on to study the interpretative norms codified by the ILC.

The *general rule of interpretation* of article 31 is draft as follows:

> "1. A treaty shall be interpreted in good faith in accordance with the ordinary meaning to be given to the terms of the treaty in their context and in the light of its object and purpose.
>
> 2. The context for the purpose of the interpretation of a treaty, shall comprise, in addition to the text, including its preamble and annexes:

---

[25] See YASSEEN, M.K., "L'interprétation des traités d'après la Convention de Vienne sur le droit des traits", *R. des C.,* vol. 151 (1976-III), page 9.

[26] See SALMON, J., "Le fait dans l'application ….", *op. cit.*, page 357.

[27] See I.L.C., *Yearbook of the International Law Commission,* vol. 1996-II, page 103.

a) any agreement relating to the treaty which was made between all the parties in connexion with the conclusion of the treaty;

b) any instrument which was made by one or more parties in connexion with the conclusion of the treaty and accepted by the other parties as an instrument related to the treaty.

3. There shall be taken into account, together with the context:

a) any subsequent agreement between the parties regarding the interpretation of the treaty or the application of its provisions;

b) any subsequent practice in the application of the treaty which establishes the agreement of the parties regarding its interpretation;

c) any relevant rules of international law applicable in the relations between the parties.

4. A special meaning shall be given to a term if it is established that the parties so intended"[28].

By conferring this structure on article 31, the ILC wished to underline three things: firstly, the *unitary nature* of the interpretation process (thus the title "General rule of Interpretation"). Secondly, the *absence of* hierarchy among the elements which make up the interpretation (the normal meaning of the terms, context objective and purpose). Finally, the *three different principles*: interpretation in good faith, which is deduced from the norm "*pacta sunt servanda*", the presumption that the parties had the intentions which can be deduced from the normal meaning of the terms used[29] and, finally, the principle that the normal meaning of

[28] This has led REMIRO to state that, following the proposals of the ILC, the Convention chose the objectivist conception and joined the teleological interpretation to it. A secondary role has been conferred on the essential elements of the subjectivist conception (See REMIRO BROTONS, A., *Derecho Internacional ..., op. cit.*, page 309. In this regard, see CARRILLO SALCEDO, J.A., *Curso de Derecho Internacional Público*, Tecnos, Madrid, 1991, pages 163 et seq. Concerning the objectivist conception, see FAVRE, A., *op. cit.*, pages 75-98.

[29] This principle already appears in the earliest jurisprudence of the ICJ before the 1969 Vienna Convention on the Law of Treaties. Thus, in its advisory opinion on the *Conditions of Admission of a State to Membership in the United Nations* it states:

> "The Court considers it necessary to say that the first duty of a tribunal which is called upon to interpret and apply the provisions of a treaty, is to endeavour to give effect to them in their natural express the purpose of the provisions in their context and in accordance with their natural and ordinary meaning in the context in which they occur. If the relevant words in their natural and ordinary meaning make sense in their context, that is an end of the matter" (ICJ, *Reports 1950*, page 8).

And quoting the IPCJ in the *case of the Polish Postal Service in Danzig* (*Series B*, number II, page 39) it adds:

> "It is a cardinal principle of interpretation that words must be interpreted in the sense which they would normally have in their context, unless such interpretation would lead to something unreasonable or absurd" (*ibid.*).

the terms must not be determined abstractly but in their context and by reference to the objective and the purpose of the treaty[30].

As far as the doctrine is concerned, this interpretative parameter appears in two principles: *the principle of integration*, the meaning must emerge from the context of the treaty as a whole in the light of its objective and its purposes, and, the *principle of contemporary practice,* as the language of the treaty must be interpreted in the light of the norms of international law in force at the time the treaty was concluded and in the light of the contemporary meaning these terms have[31]. In this regard, in the case of the *Aegean Sea Continental Shelf*, the ICJ pointed out that the interpretation of the notion of "territorial status" must be made while taking into account its evolution, parallel to the evolution of the international system, which means that it always has the meaning given by the norms in force. Thus, the interpretation is made in accordance with the norms of International Law at the time the case is judged[32].

Pursuant to paragraph 1 of article 31, the task of interpreting begins from the presumption that the text constitutes the authentic manifestation of the intention of the parties. So, the starting point for interpretation, as the I.C.J. has so often pointed out consists of determining the meaning of the text and not in investigating *ab initio* the intention of the parties[33]. But the sense of the terms contained in the treaty is susceptible to three meanings: the ordinary, the vulgar or non-legal and the special.

With regard to these three situations, the general rule of interpretation chooses the first: the ordinary meaning to be given to the terms of the treaty and Article 31.4 takes the hypothesis of a special meaning into consideration. The interpreter shall apply the relevant interpretative criterion. It is also the interpreter who shall choose between the different meanings of the word in question, and, thus, safeguard against the error of confusing the ordinary meaning with the sense more frequently found in the vulgar language. In any case, such confusion is difficult to

---

In its first case, the advisory opinion on the *Competence of the General Assembly for the Admission of a State to the United Nations*, the I.C.J. also uses it (cf. I.C.J., *Reports 1948,* pages 61-63).

30 See ILC, *Yearbook ..., op. cit.,* page 242.

31 Cf. BROWNLIE, I., *Principles of ..., op. cit.,* page 629. See also MACLACHIAN, C., "The principle of systematic integration and Article 31(3)(C) of the Vienna Convention", *The international and comparative law quarterly* (*I.C.L.Q.*), 54 (2005), 2, pp. 279-320.

32 In this case, the Court interpreted that the notion in question ("*territorial status*") had been used with an evolutionary criteria and this intention had been brought into effect (see ICJ, *Reports 1978*, page 32). In the cases of the *Rights of Nationals of the United States of America in Morocco* and *Western Sahara*, however, the Court interpreted in accordance with the law in force at the time of the execution of the act (see, respectively, ICJ, *Reports 1952,* page 189 and *Reports 1975,* page 38).

33 This criteria is taken by the ILC from the work of the Institute of International Law (see *Yearbook of the Institute of International Law,* 1952, vol. 44, book 1, pages 190 et seq.) and from the jurisprudence of the ICJ. See a recent example in the case concerning the *territorial dispute* (CIJ, *Reports 1994*, page 22).

come across in practice as the ordinary meaning of a term in a legal, conventional and specialised context will usually be a technical and specialised meaning[34].

Therefore, the text constitutes the objective: it is the authentic expression of the common will of the parties, as was emphasised by the TPJI in the *case of the Polish war vessels in the port of Danzig*[35], and the specific ordinary sense of the term in question must be discerned through an examination of this term in context in the light of the purpose and objective of the treaty, in accordance with the general rule of interpretation of article 31.

Consequently, the primacy of the text which undermines any argumentation which might hold that the intention of the state was different from that which is reflected in the text[36]. The ICJ is very direct in this matter:

> "The two Ministers signed a text recording commitments accepted by their Governments, some of which were to be given immediate application. Having signed such a text, the Foreign Minister of Bahrain is not in a position subsequently to say that he intended to subscribe only to a 'statement recording a political understanding' and not to an international agreement"[37].

The reference to the text as the starting point for the interpretative process has again been stated by the ICJ in the case of the *Territorial Dispute* between Libyan

---

[34] In this regard, cf. for example, YASSEEN, M.K., *op. cit.*, pages, 25 et seq.; REMIRO BROTONS, A., *Derecho Internacional, op. cit., pages 310 et seq;* CARREAU, D., *Droit International Public*, 3rd edition, A. Pedone, Paris, 1991, page 141.

In the case of the *Territorial Dispute*, the I.C.J., stated:

> "42. According to Article 3 of the 1955 Treaty, the parties 'recognize that the frontiers.... are those that result' from certain international instruments. The word 'recognize' used in the Treaty indicates that a legal obligation is undertaken. To recognize a frontier is essentially to 'accept' that frontier, that is, to draw legal consequences from its existence, to respect it and to renounce the right to contest it in the future" (ICJ, *Reports 1994*, page 229).

[35] In which, in opposition to one of the allegations based on the intention of the states which were parties to the Treaty of Versailles, it stated that:

> "The Court is not prepared to adopt the view that the text of the Treaty of Versailles can be enlarged by reading into it stipulations which are said to result from the proclaimed intentions of the authors of the Treaty, but for which no provision is made in the text itself" (CPJI, *Serie A/B n° 43*, page 144).

[36] This occurs in the *case of the Maritime Delimitation and Territorial Questions between Qatar and Bahrain*, in which Qatar holds that when it subscribed to the combined communiqué it was subscribing "to a statement recording a political understating, but not to sign a legally binding agreement". The ICJ rejects this:

> "nor could any such intention, even if shown to exist, prevail over the actual terms of the instrument in question"" (ICJ *Reports* 1994, page 122).

[37] *Ibid.* An argument which is supported by the context in which the joined communiqué took place: "within the framework of the good offices of.... King Fahd Ben Abdul Aziz" of Saudi Arabia (*ibid.*, page 119).

Arab Jamahiriya and Chad: if the text is clear and as it reflects the intentions of its authors, the treaty is applied as it stands[38]. However, the Court makes further progress when it combines the criteria of the text with the other parameters of the general rule. Thus, the appeal to the purpose and the objective of the treaty confirms the interpretation allowed before[39], and this interpretation is reinforced through an examination of the context of the Treaty[40]. As can be seen, the aforementioned case constitutes a clear example of the application of the criteria of the general rule by the ICJ, and also of how it is used autonomously and not in an integrated manner.

Another example of this type is the case concerning the *Maritime Delimitation in the Area Between Greenland and Jan Mayen* in which the Court interprets article 2 of the Bilateral Agreement of December 8, 1965. In Article 1, Denmark and Norway adopted the criteria of "the common boundary" of the respective continental shelves determined by the average line whose points are equidistant from the points nearest to the base lines from where the width of the territorial seas of each of the Parties is measured. Article 2 goes on to point out that "in order that the principle set forth in Article 1 may be properly applied, the boundary shall consist of straight lines" which are defined in the Agreement itself and is located between the Skagerrak and a part of the North Sea, between the continental parts of both States. The discrepancy arises because Norway considers that this criteria is applicable to all the limitations of the continental shelf between both states, with no geographic restriction to the region of Greenland

---

[38] According to the ICJ:

> "Interpretation must above all be based upon the text of the treaty".

And it repeats the case law of the PCIJ when it ruled *on the acquisition of Polish Nationality*, and adds:

> "Having before it a clause which leaves little to be desired in the nature of clearness, it is bound to apply this clause as it stands, without considering whether other provisions might with advantage have been added to or substituted for it" (all this appears in ICJ, *Reports 1994*, pages 22 and 25).

[39] The purpose and the objective of the treaty,

> "Reading the 1955 Treaty in the light of its object and purpose one observes that it is a treaty of friendship and good neighbourliness concluded, according to its Preamble, 'in a spirit of mutual understanding and on the basis of complete equality, independence and liberty'" (*ibid.* page 25);

and adds that,

> "the object and purpose of the Treaty thus recalled confirm the interpretation of the Treaty given above,..." (*ibid.*, page 26).

[40] "The conclusions which the Court has reached are reinforced by an examination of the context of the Treaty, and, in particular, of the Convention of Good Neighbourliness between France and Libya, concluded by the parties at the same time as the Treaty" (*ibid*).

and Jan Mayen while Denmark considers that this restriction is deduced from article 2 of the Agreement.

The Court interprets by appealing firstly to the text of the agreement where the word "boundary" (in French, "lignes de délimitation") used in singular, "must refer to the one boundary defined in Article 2. If the intention had been otherwise, Article 2 would have been so worded as to make it clear that it is providing for only a part of the total boundary contemplated by the Preamble and Article 1"[41]. It then combines the rule of the text with other interpretative parameters: its context, its purpose and its objective, as well as its practice by using the general rule of interpretation properly[42].

Finally, the examination of the text together with the circumstances in which it was drafted, "within the framework of the good offices" of the King of Saudi Arabia, enabled the ICJ to conclude that the joint communiqué signed by the Foreign Secretaries of Bahrain, Qatar and Saudi Arabia constitutes an international agreement insofar as it reaffirms the previous obligations and lists the commitments the parties have consented to, thus it creates "rights and obligations in international law for the Parties"[43].

As we have explained in the preceding pages, the doctrine of the ordinary meaning implies a presumption as it is possible to establish a different meaning from the normal one. The burden of proof would fall on the part invoking this meaning.

We have pointed out in this regard that it may occur that the term in question has a *special meaning*. This is the hypothesis taken into account in paragraph 4 of article 31. Although the ILC believes that this is "quite exceptional", in such a case, as the ICJ states in the case of the *Legal Status of Eastern Greenland"*, the burden of proof will also correspond to the party invoking this meaning[44].

---

[41] Thus,

> "Considered in the light of Article 2 of the Agreement, the principle laid down in Article 1 is valid only as regards the area mentioned in Article 2" (ICJ, *Reports 1993*, page 50).

[42] It states that "The 1965 Agreement has in any event to be read in its context, in the light of its object and purpose" (*ibid.*) These criteria will be examined in their relevant section of this work.

[43] The case concerning *Maritime Delimitation and Territorial Questions between Qatar and Bahrain* (ICJ, *Reports 1994*, pages 119 and 121 respectively).

[44] I.LC., *Yearbook ..., op.cit.*, page 244. As regards the PCIJ in the case cited, it stated that:

> "The geographical meaning of the word 'Greenland', i.e. the name which is habitually used in maps to denominate the whole island, must be regarded as the ordinary meaning of the word. If it is alleged by one of the Parties that some unusual or exceptional meaning is to be attributed to it, it lies on that Party to establish its contention" (PCIJ, *Series A/B,* Number 53, page 49).

Along the same lines, cf. the advisory opinion of the ICJ in the *Western Sahara* case (ICJ, *Reports 1975,* pages 38 et seq.).

In the cases where a special meaning is invoked the tension exists between the freedom to interpret which the party invoking the meaning has and the limits to this freedom due to the fact that it is subject to the judicial determining factors of article 31.4. On condition that a third party intervenes as, otherwise, the dispute between two opposing interpretations would persist.

When a special meaning is invoked and as there are no limits to the search for the intentions of the parties, in order that the special meaning will prevail, the party concerned can introduce a number of complementary interpretative factors such as: the preparatory work or the circumstances the treaty was made in as there are the facts which can help to find the intention.

In those cases where a third party intervenes in the capacity of interpreter, and the parties are free to interpret, this freedom is not restricted and conditioned by the interpreter's competence to interpret (because this has been accepted by the parts or because it has been imposed by the treaty they are parties to) and this will enable him to discard the interpretative factors he considers to be inadequate, adopt those which are most adequate and impose his interpretation on the parties.

In fact, the use made of a number of proofs by the parties in the exercise of their freedom, will oblige the interpreter, while carrying out his task of determining the meanings of the terms the parties wish to be determined, to weigh up a series of interpretative factors including complementary factors such as the historical ones, which are generally extrinsic to the text and the context of the treaty. Only when the meaning cannot be established after the application of this combination of factors, will the interpreter apply the ordinary meaning in a determined context[45].

Paragraph 2 of article 31 specifies the content of the *context* of the treaty, including a number of intrinsic factors such as the text of the treaty itself, including the preamble and the annexes, as well as the context[46]. Both the preamble and the annexes, as well as the context will have to be weighed up while taking into account the intention of the parties. This would be done in the light of the provisions of the treaty[47].

---

45 See REMIRO BROTONS, A., *Derecho Internacional..., op.cit.,* page 311. Also, CARREAU, D., *Droit..., op. cit.,* page 141.

46 Before the codification carried out by the ILC, the PCIJ stated that the parameter of the "context" is limited insofar as its use cannot lead to "absurd or unreasonable results" (reply to an inquiry on the case of the *Polish Postal Service in Danzig,* PCIJ, *Series B,* Number 11, page 39.

47 The preamble is an integral part of the treaty and often states its purpose and objective. Sometimes it entails essential rules which determine the position of the treaty within the framework of international regulations (as in the final paragraph of the preamble of the Vienna Convention of 1969 on the Law on Treaties when it states that the rules of customary International Law will continue to govern the issues not regulated in the Convention. Cf. YASSEEN, M.K., *op. cit.*, page 35).

For the purposes of interpretation, the context also takes in factors which are extrinsic to the treaty: any agreement made by the parties regarding the treaty[48], as well as any instrument drawn up by one or more of the parties in this respect and accepted by the other parties as an instrument relative to the treaty, but it excludes unilateral documents except if these have been agreed to by one or more of the parties when the treaty is made and the parties had accepted the relation with the treaty[49]. In addition, the interpretative declarations and later unilateral practice of the parties are factors which are efficacious insofar as they can be pitted against their authors[50].

Within this framework of the interpretative process, the fact that the treaty has definitions, terminology, expressions used, etc., can be very useful for the interpreter as his objective is to "define a technical term, give a term a particular meaning, restrict the scope of an expression. They mould the language employed so that it might better reflect the intention of the parties"[51].

As regards the context, paragraph 3 of article 31 includes three types of extrinsic elements. On the one hand, all posterior agreements between the parties to the Treaty concerning its interpretation or its application and, in accordance with the ILC and the case law of the ICJ, forms part of the treaty if is previous or contem-

---

48 One example is the case concerning the *Territorial Dispute*. The context is that of the Good Neighbourliness Convention between France and Libya of 1955. The ICJ states that:

> "53. The conclusions which the Court has reached are reinforced by an examination of the context of the Treaty, and, in particular, of the Convention of Good Neighbourliness between France and Libya, concluded between the parties at the same time as the Treaty" (ICJ, *Reports 1994*, page 26).

49 Cf. ILC, *Yearbook...*, *op. cit.*, page 243. One example of this type can be found in the case concerning the *Territorial Dispute*, in which Libya holds that it from the use of the plural "frontiers" in article 3 of the treaty of 1955 it is deduced that the parts intended the delimitation of some of its frontiers and not the totality of the frontier. In the opinion of the Court,

> "...the use of the plural is,..., to be explained by the fact that there were differences of legal status between the various territories bordering on Libya, for whose international relations France was at the time responsible, and their respective frontiers had been delimited by different agreements. Tunisia was a protectorate at the time, Algeria was a *groupe de départements* and French West Africa and French Equatorial Africa were both *groupes de territories d'outre-mer*. In this context, the use of the plural is clearly appropriate, and does not have the significance attributed to it by Libya" (ICJ, *Reports 1994*, page 23. The italics are ours).

50 As regards the interpretative declarations, in the *Ambatielos case* the ICJ stated that "the provisions of the Declaration are in the nature of an interpretation clause, and, as such, should be regarded as an integral part of the Treaty". (Preliminary Exception, ICJ, *Reports 1952*, page 44).

51 YASSEEN, M.K., *op. cit.*, page 35. These formula make the treaty more specific and thus contribute to the security of the conventional relations and help to prevent probable conflicts of interpretation (cf. *ibid.*).

porary with its signing, and constitutes an authentic interpretation of the parties should it be posterior[52]. In addition, the posterior practice of the parties regarding the application of the treaty by which the agreement of the parties on its interpretation is evidenced[53] requires the analysis of the conduct during practice in order to conclude whether this interprets the agreement in question or modify it[54]. This criteria is used by the ICJ (in combination with the text, the context and the purpose or end of the treaty) in the case of the *Maritime Delimitation in the Area between Greenland and Jan Mayen*. In this later practice, the Court includes three documents, a press communiqué published by the Norwegian Foreign Ministry, the Agreement made on June 15, 1979 between Denmark and Norway regarding the delimitation of the continental shelf in the region situated between the Faroe Islands and the Norwegian economic zone as well as the delimitation between the fishing grounds throughout the Faroe Islands and the Norwegian economic zone (in which there is no mention of the existence of the agreement nor its meaning of the 1965 Agreement)[55] and the official communiqué of the 1979 Agreement to the Norwegian Parliament by the Government of this State. From its examination, the ICJ interprets that the 1965 agreement is applied exclusively to the region, in relation to which the agreement itself specifies a line of delimitation defined by coordinates and by a map, that is to say, the Skagerrak and a part of the North Sea[56].

The final extrinsic factor which forms part of the context of a treaty comes from all the norms of International Law applicable to the relationships between the

---

[52] Cf. ILC, *Yearbook ...*, *op. cit.*, page 243. Regarding the ICJ, see its statement on the *Ambatielos Case* (ICJ, *Reports 1952*, page 44).

[53] This practice constitutes an objective proof of the agreement of the parties as regards the meaning of the treaty (cf. ILC, *op. cit.*, page 243). In this respect, the following statement of the ICJ can be quoted concerning the *Corfu Cannel case*:

> "The subsequent attitude of the Parties shows that it was not their intention, by entering into the Special Agreement, to preclude the Court from fixing the amount of the compensation" (ICJ, *Reports 1949*, page 25).

Cf. Concerning this issue, the works of COT, J.P. quoted in preceding pages of this work, as well as the case law of the PCIJ in the Cases of *the Competence of the ILO with regard to the Regulation of Agricultural Work* (CPJI, *Series B* No. 2, pages 39 et seq.), *the Interpretation of Paragraph 2 of Article 3 of the Treaty of Lausanne* (CPJI, *Series B* No. 2, page 24) and *the Brazilian Loans* (CPJI, *Series A*, No. 21, page 119).

[54] Concerning these questions, see DISTEFANO, G., "La practique subséquente des États parties a un traité" (*A.F.D.I.*, 1994 pages 41-71). Also our work, "El Régimen Jurídico del Aeropuerto de Fuenterrabía: análisis del Acta hispano-francesa de 11 de julio de 1957" (*R.E.D.I.*, 1987, pages 121-141).

[55] This leads the Court to state that "….if the intention of the 1965 Agreement had been to commit the Parties to the median line in all ensuing shelf delimitations, it would have been referred to in the 1979 Agreement" (ICJ, *Reports 1993*, page 51).

[56] See *ibid.*

parties. Concerning this last factor, the ILC suppressed the reference to the temporary factor from its draft articles due both to the criticism from the States an the fact that "the relevance of the norms of international law for the interpretation of the treaties in a specific case depended on the intention of the parties, and it would be difficult to draft a norm which would take in the temporary factor completely"[57].

However, in several cases, the question of interpreting terms which have evolved together with international regulations arose. Thus, in the case of the *Aegean Sea Continental Shelf* in relation to the notion of "territorial status" and in connection with the Greek reservation which excluded the disputes concerning the territorial status of Greece from the jurisdiction of the Court. This State considered that its reservation affected the disputes on the determination of rights and the delimitation of the continental shelf. In the opinion of the Court,

> "the term 'territorial status' in the treaty practice of the time did not have the very specific meaning attributed to it by the Greek Government. As the nature of the word 'status' itself indicates, it was a generic term which in the practice of the time was understood as embracing the integrity and frontiers, as well as the legal regime, of the territory in question"[58].

Thus,

> "once it is established that the expression 'territorial status of Greece' was used in Greece's instrument of accession as a generic term denoting any matters comprised within the concept of territorial status under general international law, the presumption necessarily arises that its meaning was intended to follow the evolution of the law in force at any given time, … for it hardly seems conceivable that in such a convention terms like 'domestic jurisdiction' and 'territorial status' were intended to have a fixed content regardless of the subsequent evolution of international law"[59].

On the contrary, in other cases, the Court carries out its interpretative task by recourse to the International Law in force at the time the treaty was signed. Thus, for

---

57 ILC, *Yearbook ...*, *op. cit*, page 244.

58 ICJ, *Reports 1978*, page 31, paragraph 75. The italics are from the original. See, along the same lines, the advisory opinion of the ICJ regarding the *Western Sahara case* in relation to the non-self-governing territories (ICJ, *Reports 1975*, pages 29b et seq.).

59 *Ibid.*, p. 32, paragraph 77. And it adds that these terms,

> "must be interpreted in accordance with the rules of international law as they today, and not as they existed in 1939", which implies "to take account the evolution which has occurred in the rules of international law concerning a coastal State's rights of exploration and exploitation over the continental shelf" (*ibid.*, pages 33 et seq., paragraph 80).

example, in the Case of the *Rights of Nationals of the United States in Morocco*, where the ICJ stated,

> "Accordingly, in construing the provisions of article 20 – and, in particular the expression 'shall have any dispute with each other' – it is necessary to take into account the meaning of the word 'dispute' at the times when the two treaties were concluded. For this purpose it is possible to look at the way in which the word 'dispute' or its French counterpart was used in the different treaties concluded by Morocco: e.g., with France in 1631 and 1682, with Great Britain in 1721, 1750, 1751, 1760 and 1801. It is clear that in these instances the word was used to cover both civil and criminal disputes.

It is also necessary to take into account that, at the times of these two treaties, the clear-cut distinction between civil and criminal matters has not yet been developed in Morocco"[60].

But the general rule of interpretation of article 31.1 also points out that, in order to interpret treaties, besides analysing their terms in the context of the treaty, their *object and purpose* must be taken into account. Thus, the Vienna Convention incorporates the *teleological interpretation* to the rules of interpretation[61].

We find an example of recourse to this interpretation in the case of the *Maritime Delimitation in the Area between Greenland and Jan Mayen*. As we have stated above, in the first place, the Court appeals to the text of the agreement which shows the intention of the parties. It goes on to add that the agreement must be read in context, in the light of its purpose and end. In this case, the context is given by the Geneva Convention of 1958 regarding the continental shelf and by the domestic legislation of Denmark and Norway regarding the continental shelf which include the definition of this space contained in the Geneva Convention (and which takes into account as criteria the depth of 200 metres and the extent to which it may be exploited). Consequently, when the Agreement was signed on

---

60 ICJ, *Reports 1952*, page 189. CARRILLO SALCEDO specifies that if the text had extraordinary relevance in traditional International Law due to its coherence within a voluntary conception of law, the International Law Commission of the United Nations and the Vienna Conventions of 1969 and 1986 give clear preference to the objectivist criteria, and join it with the teleological or finalist dimension…" ("Course …," *op. cit.*, page 164).

61 In REMIROS's opinion "purpose and end constitute a criterion of interpretation in which the first factor, the purpose, involves realism and moderation, and the second, the end, involves idealism and progress. One is the fuel and the other is the smoke". (*Derecho Internacional …, op. cit.*, page 313). In YASSEEN's opinion, when it mentions these, the Vienna Convention "wished to state a criterion formed by the reasonable sense of these two terms. Thus, this criterion may be what the parties wished to achieve within the limits of the norm they have drafted" (*op. cit.*, page 57). For CARREAU, the method of teleological interpretation has an analogy "with the central criterion of admissibility of the reservations (…). The treaty must be interpreted depending on its ends", and he describe this as a "dynamic" and "activist" technique of interpretation. (*Droit …, op. cit.*, page 142).

December 8, 1965, neither Denmark nor Norway took into account the area between Greenland and Jan Mayen (located far from their respective coastlines) "as the subject of a potential future delimitation", thus, the Court considers,

> "the object and purpose of the 1965 Agreement was to provide simply for the question of the delimitation in the Skagerrak and part of the North Sea, where the whole sea-bed (with the exception of the 'Norwegian Trough') consists of continental shelf at a depth of less than 200 metres, and that there is nothing to suggest that the Parties had in mind the possibility that a shelf boundary between Greenland and Jan Mayen might one day be required, or intended that their Agreement should apply to such a boundary"[62].

Article 32 of both Vienna Conventions refer to the *means for supplementary interpretation*. It text reads,

> "Recourse may be had to supplementary means of interpretation, including the preparatory work of the treaty and the circumstances of its conclusion, in order to confirm the meaning resulting from the application of article 31, or to determine the meaning when the interpretation according to article 31:
>
> a) leaves the meaning ambiguous or obscure; or
>
> b) leads to a result which is manifestly absurd or unreasonable".

The ILC specifies that the word "supplementary" used by article 32 denotes that "the existence of independent or autonomous means of interpretation are not admitted, but only those means which enable an interpretation which is in keeping with the principles" stated in article 31[63]. It is a question of a complement of the general rule based on the current meaning of the terms and stated already in the jurisprudence of the PCIJ when, for example, in the Case of the *Treatment of Polish Nationals in Dantzig*, it states,

> "This text not being absolutely clear, it may be useful, in order to ascertain its precise meaning, to recall here somewhat in detail the various drafts which existed prior to the adoption of the text now in force"[64].

---

[62] ICJ, *Reports 1993*, pages 50 et seq.

[63] ILC, *Yearbook...*, *op. cit.*, page 245. In the opinion of the ad hoc Judge TORRES BERNARDEZ it is clear that the submittal of two different articles of the general rule of interpretation and of the complementary means "does not at all mean that there are two interpretative processes. The interpretative process is a single one and, the interpreter is free at any moment to turn his attention to the supplementary means of interpretation concerned without waiting for completion of the application of the general rule of Article 31" (case concerning the *Land, Island and Maritime Frontier Dispute*, I.C.J., *Reports 1992*, p. 720).

[64] PCIJ, *Series A/B,* Number. 44, page 33.

The ICJ takes this up again in its jurisprudence, for example in the *advisory opinion* regarding the *Competence of the General Assembly for the Admission of a State to the United Nations*, it states:

> "The Court considers it necessary to say that the first duty of a tribunal which is called upon to interpret and apply the provisions of a treaty, is to endeavour to give effect to them in their natural and ordinary meaning in the context in which they occur. If the relevant words in their natural and ordinary meaning make sense in their context that is the end of the matter. If, on the other hand, the words in their natural and ordinary meaning are ambiguous or lead to an unreasonable result, then, and then only, must the Court, by resort to other methods of interpretation, seek to ascertain what the parties really did mean when they used these words"[65].

Therefore, the supplementary means of interpretation are the preparatory work and the circumstances of the signing. As regards the former, these are the documents which are contained in the diplomatic correspondence, in the official minutes and the annexes to conferences and institutions where the negotiations took place, and this refers both to bilateral and multilateral treaties. As regards the latter, the parties which are bound by these but who have not participated in the drafting process also have the right to obtain this work[66], and they cannot allege their inadmissibility as they have been able to examine them before accepting the treaty[67].

In YASSEEN's opinion, the preparatory work does not cast much light on the matter due to the attempt of the parties to use vague, ambiguous formulas when they draft the treaty. This enables them to have a wider leeway. On the other hand, the more difficult questions are usually solved by the parties through negotiations which do not appear in the preliminary work. Thus, he points out that the recourse to preliminary work must be addressed with care, bearing in mind that this recourse is only allowed for reasons of interpretation[68].

---

65 ICJ, *Reports 1950*, page 8. That is to say, recourse to complementary methods is only possible when the use of the interpretative criteria of the general rule does not enable the problem to be solved.

66 According to CARREAU, "the projects which have led to the adoption of the text, the oral or written interventions of the participants regarding the acceptance or the rejection of amendments etc. are part of the preparatory work" (*Droit…*, *op. cit.*, page 144).

67 Cf. BROWNLIE, I., *Principles of …*, *op. cit.*, page 630.

68 See YASSEEN, M.K., *op.cit.*, page 86. BROWNLIE shows the same caution when he states that the preparatory work constitutes an "aid which must be used with discretion from the time that its use may deviate from the approximation to the text and, in particular, in the case of multilateral agreements, the documents of the procedures of the conference, treaty projects and the rest van be confusing or not very convincing" (*Principles of…*, *op. cit.*, page 630).

From an analysis of international jurisprudence, it can be deduced that the recourse to complementary means of interpretation by the international institutions of justice or arbitration takes place in the terms laid down by the two Vienna Conventions, that is to say, as a substitute for the general rule. Thus, hen the ICJ has recourse to the complementary means, it does so either to confirm the result reached through the application of the criteria of the general rule or in order to reinforce this result[69].

As regards the *circumstances in which the treaty has been concluded*, these refer to the social, historical and temporary context in which the treaty was concluded and the events which led the parties to conclude the treaty form part of these. It is in the light of these that the interpreter must decide between maintaining or confirming the *statu quo* or bring about a change demanded by the new social and historical context. Together with the historical temporary circumstances are the individual conditions of the parties, the individual conditions of the parties; the ideological, political economic and other conditions which could normally exercise influence on the attitude of the states in the different environments of international relations, *inter alia*, belonging to an ideological group, a military alliance or a determined judicial system and the fact that the state is an exporter or importer, industrialised or in the process of development[70].

As the "ad hoc" judge TORRES BERNARDEZ said from the point of view of the rules of interpretation of treaties, there is no ordinary meaning either in absolute or in abstract terms unless this is restricted by good faith in the context and in the light of the purpose and the reason for the treaty, and the interpretative factors listed in article 3 must also be borne in mind (subsequent practice and all the pertinent rules of international law) as well as the complementary means of interpretation. The elucidation of the "ordinary meaning" of the terms used in the treaty to be interpreted "requires, therefore, that due account be taken of those various interpretative principles and elements, and not only of words or expression used in the interpreted provision taken in isolation"[71].

Finally, article 33 in both Conventions takes into account the interpretation of *treaties authenticated in two or more languages*:

> "1. When a treaty has been authenticated in two or more languages, the text is equally authoritative in each language, unless the treaty provides or the parties agree that, in case of divergence, a particular text shall prevail.

---

[69] One example of this is the case of the *Land, Insular and Maritime Frontier Dispute* in which the Chamber of the ICJ states that the examination of the circumstances "constitute no more than a supplementary means of interpretation, used only where the meaning of the text is ambiguous or obscure, or the interpretation would lead to a manifestly absurd or unreasonable (see article 32 of the Vienna Convention on the Law of Treaties" (ICJ, *Reports 1992*, page 584). See also page 138, note (35) of this work.

[70] YASSEEN, M.K., *op. cit.*, page 90.

[71] The case of the *Land, Island and Maritime Frontier Dispute* (ICJ, *Reports 1992*, page 719).

2. A version of the treaty in a language other than one of those in which the text was authenticated shall be considered an authentic text only if the treaty so provides or the parties so agree.
3. The terms of the treaty are presumed to have the same meaning in each authentic text.
4. Except where a particular text prevails in accordance with paragraph 1, when a comparison of the authentic text discloses a difference of meaning which the application of articles 31 and 32 does not remove, the meaning which bests reconciles the texts, having regard to the object and purpose of the treaty, shall be adopted".

As doctrine advises undoubtedly each language has its own characteristics so that, in the event of a multi-lingual treaty, the negotiators will find it difficult establish a perfect concordance between the terms of the languages and this will give rise to problems of interpretation. The ILC was aware of the problem and highlighted this in its codification work when it pointed out that the plurality of authentic texts of a treaty always constitute an important factor as regards interpretation, as all the texts reliably state the stipulations of the agreement between the parties. However, despite the existence of several authenticated texts in Law there is only one treaty – a number of stipulations accepted by the parties and a common objective as regards these stipulations – even when two authentic texts seem to disagree. In practice, the existence of authentic texts in two or more languages sometimes complicates the interpretation of the treaty and at other times facilitates this. There are few multi-lingual treaties of more than one or two articles which do not contain any discrepancy between the texts[72].

Following the guidelines laid down by, the Vienna Conventions of 1969 and 1986 start from the unity of the treaty and the equality of the two authentic texts. Therefore, although the treaty is drafted in several languages, it continues to be a single treaty "and this unity is safeguarded by the combination of the principle that that all authentic texts are valid as it is presumed that in each of the texts of the treaty he intention was to give the same meanings to the terms. This presumption demands that everything possible be done in order to find a common meaning to the texts rather than prefer one to the other"[73]. Consequently, given the equality of the authenticated texts, what the interpreter must do in these cases is to make use

[72] ILC, *Yearbook ......*, *op. cit.*, page 246. An adds that the different mechanics of the languages, the lack of a complete "consensus ad idem", or the lack of sufficient time to coordinate the texts can lead to minor or even important discrepancies in the meaning of the texts. In such cases, the plurality of texts can constitute another important reason for ambiguity or lack of clarity in the terms of the treaty. Moreover, when the meaning of the terms is ambiguous or unclear in one language, but in others it is clear and convincing as regards the intention of the parties, the multi-lingual character of the treaty facilitates the interpretation of the text with the doubtful meaning (cf. *ibid.*, pages 246 et seq.).

[73] *Ibid.*, page 247.

of the general rule of interpretation of article 31 in order to reconcile the texts, and he may not just opt for one rather than the other nor may he forget about the normal methods of interpretation which include basing his decisions on the reason and purpose of the treaty, the preparatory work, the circumstances in which the treaty was signed, the subsequent practice, etc.

For this same reason, the interpreter cannot "*a priori*" opt for a restrictive interpretation as there is no general norm which establishes a presumption in favour of the restrictive interpretation in the event that there may be ambiguity in the multilingual texts[74].

The interpreter should solve the dispute by trying to reconcile the texts by recourse to the general norm of interpretation in order to determine the meaning of the term in question[75].

With regard to this matter, recent practice in the ICJ reveals three cases in which the interpretation of the Court was made on the basis of the translation of the treaty to a language other than the one it was authenticated in. Thus, in 1992, in the case of the *Land, Insular and Maritime Frontier*, where the interpretation of the ICJ was based on the translation of the original texts authenticated in Spanish[76]. Likewise, in the case of the maritime delimitation of the region situated between Greenland and Jan Mayen, where curiously the authentic text of the of December 8, 1965 had been established in Danish and Norwegian and the Court interpreted it based on an English translation "which has not been contested by the parties"[77]. In the case of the *Maritime Delimitation and the Territorial Questions between Qatar and Bahrain*, however, the joint communiqué or Minutes which the ICJ considers to be an international agreement was drafted in Arabic but "the English translations supplied by the Parties differ on certain points"[78].

As regards the cases of discrepancy, the two Vienna Conventions opted for the reconciliation of the texts which disagree and chose "the meaning which best reconciles the texts, having regard to the object and purpose of the treaty" as stated in article 33.4.

To conclude, unlike other norms contained in international regulations, the interpretation of conventional international norms, gives the international or internal interpreter the advantage that there are interpretative rules from the 1969 and 1986 Vienna Conventions. Their use must provide the interpreter with the solution to the possible problems that might arise in this area. However, it should be stressed that the solution to a dispute over interpretation by using the rules of the Vienna Conventions depends on the previous agreement of the parties to submit it to a

---

74 Cf. ILC (*Yearbook…*, *op. cit.*, page 247).

75 One example of this is the case of the *Elettronica Sicula S.p.A. (ELSI)*, in which the Chamber of the ICJ decided on the interpretation most in accordance with the purpose of the Treaty of Friendship, Commerce and Navigation signed by Italy and the United States on 1948 (See ICJ, *Reports 1989*, page 68).

76 Cf. ICJ, *Reports 1992*, pages 351 et seq.

77 ICJ, *Reports 1993*, page 48.

78 ICJ, *Reports 1994*, page 119.

third party (unless the treaty itself imposes this). Obviously the application of these rules is imposed on the states. In their capacity as interpreters of the treaties they sign, they are obliged to use these rules in order to carry out a unilateral interpretation. What happens is that this unilateral interpretation, which is valid for this state, remains just that. It is not imposed on the other party in disagreement which, in turn, carries out its own unilateral interpretation. We then find that these interpretations which are, in principle valid (except in cases of bad faith) and concurrent, but divergent as the discrepancy persists. What is the use of this, then? In practice, quite reduced, which shows the dependence of the process of interpretation with regard to state sovereignty.

Can the principle of good faith modulate or confine state sovereignty? In principle, unless there is evidence to the contrary and this is difficult to find, it may be supposed that the divergent interpretations are made in good faith. Fundamentally, the problem arises from the incapacity of the judicial process of interpretation (or the limitations found) in contrast with the political interest of the states in the controversy in question. These interests condition the unilateral interpretation of the parties. In other words, the judicial interpretation is conditioned and predetermined by the political interests of the states in the case being dealt with, which means that the interpretations respond to these interests. As these political interests diverge, so does the interpretation. Thus, the judicial process of interpretation is weak when a third party does not intervene. Moreover, this shows the importance of the interpretation of international norms insofar as they reflect the predominantly state structure of the International Community. In fact, in spite of the changes occurring in recent years, the pacific settlement of disputes, among which are those of continual interpretation, as in the international legal order arising after the Second World War which continues to be an order based and dependent on the will of the state. An obligation exists, as well as the political and legal means to make it effective, but its practical application, achieving its purpose still depend on the will of the state and the state in its sovereign capacity still continues to be the only judge of its interests, which in practice means a resistance to submit questions whose resolution might not coincide with the interests of the state to a third party. The primacy of politics delays or prevents the intervention of the legal process as a way to solve the dispute.

Obviously, the interpretative rules of the 1969 and 1986 Vienna Conventions are also imposed on the third party which knows the dispute, but in this case this third party has the advantage of the liberty given to him by the fact that his jurisdiction is accepted by the Parties and his decision is binding. Since his jurisdiction is accepted, this third party evaluates and weighs up the interpretative rules applicable to the specific case but he is not limited by the arguments of the Parties, nor by the interpretation given by them of the norms invoked. This shows the usefulness of the I.C.J. as well as the other international judicial or arbitration institutions in disputes concerning interpretation.

But, with respect to the I.C.J. one could ask how the Court uses the general rule codified by the I.L.C. That is to say whether the Court applies it as the I.L.C. conceived it or if, on the contrary, it is applied otherwise. As we have seen, the I.L.C.

conceived interpretation as a combined operation, as a unitary process, in which there is no hierarchy among the different elements or criteria of the general rule of Article 31 of the 1969 Vienna Convention on the Law of Treaties[79], so interpretation should be done through the simultaneous combination of all of these giving no primacy to any of the elements which make up the general rule[80]. Independently of the study of the interpretative criteria used by the I.C.J. to be examined later, it is possible to anticipate that at different times the Court uses elements of the general rule to confirm or to reinforce the interpretation reached after the sole analysis of the text of the treaty[81]. Thus, in a sense, the way the Court proceeds continues as before the codification made by the Vienna Convention of 1969 on the Law of Treaties, because it generally uses the interpretative criteria one after the other and not as a whole. An example of this kind is given by the case concerning the *Land, Island and Maritime Frontier Dispute* in which the Chamber of the Court based on the general rule of article 31, according to which "a treaty shall be interpreted 'in accordance with the ordinary meaning to be given to the terms'"[82], when this part of the general rule is completed with the context, the purpose and the reason for the treaty. Moreover, the Chamber of the ICJ bases its reasoning fundamentally on the text of the treaty in order to state that, as there is no specific mention of delimitation of the maritime spaces, it cannot be interpreted that the parties have given the Chamber the task of delimiting these[83].

---

79 In the words of Sir H. WALDOCK "a simultaneous combination of these means in a single operation" (ILC, *Yearbook of the International Law Commission*, 1996, page 200).

80 As regards this cf. TORRES BERNARDEZ, S., in his individual opinion on the case of the *Land, Insular and Maritime Dispute* (ICJ, *Reports 1992*, page 719).

81 For example, the purpose and the reason for the treaty in the case of the *Territorial Dispute* (Libya/Chad). Cf. ICJ, *Reports 1994*, page 26).

82 ICJ, *Reports 1992*, page 583. The ICJ appeals to the context in order to show that "the object of the verb 'determine' is not the maritime spaces themselves but the legal situation of these spaces. No indication of a common intention to obtain a delimitation by the Chamber can therefore be derived from this text as it stands" (*ibid.*). In addition, in order to confirm the conclusion (cf. *ibid.*). See, in the same line, the individual opinion of the ad hoc Judge TORRES BERNARDEZ on the same case (*ibid.,* page 722).

83 The Chamber appeals to comparative practice: "In considering the ordinary meaning to be given to the terms of the treaty, it is appropriate to compare them with the terms generally or commonly used in order to convey the idea that a delimitation is intended. Whenever in the past a special agreement has entrusted the Court with a task related to delimitation, it has spelled out very clearly what was asked of the Court: the formulation of principles or rules enabling the parties to agree on delimitation, the precise application of these principles or rules (see *North Sea Continental Shelf* cases, *Continental Shelf (Tunisia/Libyan Arab Jamahiriya)* and *Continental Shelf (Libyan Arab Jamahiriya/Malta)* cases), or the actual task of drawing the delimitation line (*Delimitation of the Maritime Boundary in the Gulf of Maine Area* case). Likewise, in the Anglo-French Arbitration of 1977, the Tribunal was specifically entrusted by the terms of the Special Agreement with the drawing of the line" (*ibid.*, p. 586). See the advisory opinion of judge "ad hoc" TORRES BERNARDEZ (specially, pp. 716-730).

CHAPTER III:

The Institutionalisation of the International Community Gives a New Dimension to Law Making: The Institutional Norms

1 The need for an open mind or the teaching of practice: The resolutions of the United Nations General Assembly

As we have seen in the preceding pages, the analysis of the value or legal force of institutional norms cannot be carried out, as a sector of international doctrine does[1], by basing this on a priori considerations which exclude the institutional norms, which are generally speaking the resolutions of the United Nations General Assembly, as able to have such effects. In our opinion, the answer to this question depends on the analysis of the constitutive treaty of the International Organisation and on a number of factors as, for example, the content of the norm, its language, the procedure for its approval, how it was adopted, and consequently, the attitude of the States towards the institutional norm in question.

Our study is not a trivial one. On the contrary, it acquires more and more importance as a consequence of the process of institutionalisation of the International Community. This process focuses on how international norms are formed and, in our case, this centres specifically on the appearance of a new type of norm, the institutional one as distinct from international treaties and custom[2]. Logically, once the institutional norm has been constructed, the problem of interpretation arises[3].

---

1 Cf. MACGIBBON, I., "Means for the Identification ....", *op. cit.*, pages 10-26. See also ROUCUNAS, E., "Engagements parallèles et contradictoire", *R. des C.*, VI, 206 (1987-VI), pages 9-288; SEPULVEDA, C., "Methods and Procedures for the Creation of Legal Norms in the International System of States: an Inquiry into the Progressive Development of International Law in the present Era", *German Y.I.L.*, 1990, Vol. 33, pages 444 et seq.

2 In this regard, see MCWHINNEY, E., *Les Nations Unies et la formation du droit*, Pedone/Unesco, Paris, 1986; 1986; ECONOMIDES, C., "Les actes institutionnels internationaux et les sources du Droit international", *AFDI*, 1988, pages 131-145.

3 When R. BERNHARDT published his work on the interpretation of treaties in 1963, he considered that this problem was in the initial stage of its development which made it difficult to understand (see *Auslegung...*, *op. cit.*, page 2).

We will, therefore, address the legal force of institutional norms and subsequently move on to focus on the problem of their interpretation *stricto sensu*. However, we will restrict our study only to resolutions of the United Nations General Assembly as this is the most significant example of the type of Organisation (global or universal) and the way in which its institutional norms are dealt with in the Charter (there is not a single express reference to the legal force of General Assembly resolutions). Moreover, almost all the states which make up the International Community are represented in the Assembly and there the main problems affecting this Community are discussed. Therefore, it is the example par excellence of the problem dealt with in this section.

As we have said, the context of the first question concerns the process of progressive institutionalisation of the International Community as a consequence of the appearance of International Organisations. This process, that has changed the tendency to decentralisation and the lack of institutionalisation which was a characteristic of International Law before the Second World War, has a strong effect on the formation of international norms and one of its signs is the influence of those Organisations on making International Law more positive. In this regard, the pre-eminent position of State in the formation of international norms has been influenced by the phenomenon of the International Organisations. This has had a twofold effect. On one hand, traditional proceedings for drafting of International Law by the States – fundamentally treaties and custom- had been modified due to the action of International Organisations in the process of formation of international treaties and custom.

Thus, in the framework of the United Nations resolutions of the General Assembly these had important repercussions as regards the formation of customary norms: either by declaring an international custom, by giving final shape to customary norms in process of formation, or by constituting the starting point of an international custom.

Therefore, interaction among the norms was brought about.

In the second place, for some time, the Law arising from the action of International Organisations, that is to say, the institutional norms have been added to the traditional results of the aforementioned process (treaties and customs). In other words, the shaping of the individual consent and the consensus of the States institutionalised within the framework of the International Organisations acquire a new field of action with a normative manifestation which is different from treaty and custom. This manifestation is the institutional norm.

This is why, as CARRILLO SALCEDO correctly emphasises, today it is not possible to analyse the drafting of International Law unless we take into account the influence the International Organisations in have had on making international legal norms more positive[4].

As we have stated, the question whether the legal value or force of the institutional norms arises especially with reference to those norms of International

---

4 See CARRILLO SALCEDO, J.A., *Curso*..., *op. cit.*, page 123.

Organisations whose constitutive treaty makes no mention of this or considers it to be merely recommendable.

When the constitutive treaty clearly specifies the legal value of the acts of the organisation, the reply is contained in the constitutive treaty itself. This is the case of the European Community where article 249 of the constitutive treaty clearly specifies that the general Regulations, Directives and Decisions are binding with regard to the member states[5].

The same occurs in the framework of the UN as regards some decisions of the General Assembly. Thus, those decisions regarding the approval of the general budget of the Organisation and those concerning the specialized agencies (article 17), the choice of non-permanent members of the Security Council, the election of members of the Economic and Social Committee of the Trusteeship Council, the admission of new members to the United Nations, the suspension of the rights and privileges of the Members, the expulsion of Members (article 18), the decisions regarding the establishment of subsidiary institutions (article 22), those concerning the Trusteeship System and those which affect the Trusteeship Council (articles 85 and 87), etc.

However, the constitutive treaties of International Organisations which address or specify the legal force or value of the norms created by the Organisation constitute the exception, while the general rule is silence or the description of such acts as "recommendations", "decisions", etc. Thus, we have chosen the Resolutions of the General Assembly of the United Nations as our subject of study. Some doctrinal sectors maintain that these are mere recommendations as, otherwise, the Charter would have expressly stated this as does article 25 regarding the Resolutions of the Security Council. However, in our opinion, the answer is not so simple as Sir F. VALLAT states, to say that the Assembly only has powers to discuss and recommend "would be a gross simplification"[6].

For example, as a sector of doctrine recalls, more than twenty-five of the hundred and eleven articles in the Charter and four articles of the Statute of the International Court of Justice, at least to a certain extent, confer powers of decision on the General Assembly, established as a power other than simply recommendation. Although it is true that many of these powers require the previous recommendation of some institution (normally the Security Council) in order to exercise them, and much of the material referred to by these powers of decision have less significance when compared with questions of peace keeping and security, such powers

---

5 A reinforced binding character due to the principles of primacy, immediate and uniform application enshrined in the case law of the ECCJ. About these questions see BLOKKER, N., "Decisions of International Organizations: the Case of the European Union", *N.Y.I.L.*, 1999, vol. XXX, pp. 45-74. Related to the Organization of African Unity see MALUWA, T., "International Law-Making in the Organization of African Unity: An Overview", *Rev. Afr. D.I. & Comp.*, 2000, vol. 12, nº 2, pp. 201-225.

6 VALLAT, F.A., "The competence of the United Nations General Assembly", *R des C.*, vol. 97 (1959-II), pages 225 et seq. See also ROUCOUNAS, E., *op. cit.*, pages 174-193.

should represent a clear measures of control over the performance of the Organisation as a whole.

Basically, the underlying problem involves the judicial effects of the institutional norms drawn up by the General Assembly. The plan to solve this through the simple analysis of the Charter does not adapt to the nature of the International Community at the present time, one of whose structures is characterised precisely by the existence of common interests and this occasionally leads to the fact that states that do not manifest their consent to the formation of a norm are bound by this norm as a result of the general consensus on the norm. In fact, in the social structure of common interests we see a derogation of the absolute nature that the sovereignty of the state had as regards the structure of juxtaposition, so, third party states can be affected by the consent to be bound made by a considerable number of states. One example of this derogation of state sovereignty, a consequence of the social structure of common interests, is clearly seen in the multilateral treaties and the International Conferences which deal with questions of common interest for the International Community as a whole[7].

In this context, the determination of the obligatory nature of the legal norm must be done based on the linking of this norm to the legal system which provides it with its force and which, in the event, can lay down sanctions in order to ensure respect for its norms. In our case, this system is the international one and in it, the formation of the international norms takes place through a process involving the individual consent of the state and the general consensus of the states, and it is the interaction between both stages which gives rise to the international norm in question. Therefore, the individual consent of the state and the general consensus within an International Organisation gives rise to an institutional norm. The existence of both elements which demonstrate the attitude of the state as regards the institutional norm in question is a determining factor, and not the term conferred by the Charter ("recommendation" or "decision").

Thus, the obligatory nature of the norm cannot depend on the degree of discretion or the power of appreciation which this grants to its receptor, but the attitude the receptor adopts. That the norm grants its receptor a wide degree of discretion or appreciation does not mean that it is not obligatory, thus it is not correct to talk of the existence of norms which are more or less obligatory[8]. If this involves a norm, the norm is binding. It is another matter if, due to the extent of the discretion or the power of appreciation granted by the norm, in practice it is difficult to determine whether or not the receptor has complied with the obligation contained therein. Therefore, the problems arise at the time of application.

---

[7] Which leads REUTER to state that "when the consent or the institutions arise from a sufficiently representative set of states mainly interested in one question, the consent or institution can sometime generate effects for third party states" (Principes de Droit....", *op. cit.*, pages 448 et seq.).

[8] See JACQUE, J.P., "Acte et norme en Droit International Public", *R. des C.*, vol. 227 (1991-II), page 388.

Moreover, it should be stressed that there is a contrast as regards the legal force of the resolutions of the General Assembly and the practice of this institution of the United Nations which, from its creation, has adopted over six thousand resolutions. In accordance with this doctrinal sector, if the Resolutions of the General Assembly lack legal force or the obligatory legal effects can it be accepted that the General Assembly has carried out this regulatory task while it is aware of the effects of its Resolutions? The analysis of this practice demonstrates the opposite.

However, in the field of doctrine the controversy exists on the validity and the legal effects of these resolutions[9]. Although as P.M. DUPUY points out, in fact, the debate is restricted to a limited number of these[10].

The above considerations show the mistakes involved in avoiding the problem as from pre-determined positions such as those which exclude the General Assembly from adopting resolutions with binding legal effects for its Members (apart from those laid down expressly in the Charter), and it would be better to make a detailed analysis of each resolution in the light of the factors listed at the beginning of this section. As SLOAN points out, given the difficulty or perhaps the impossibility of "making generalisations which cover all the resolutions, one has to consider all the circumstances involving a determined resolution before making an evaluation"[11].

Finally, the problem must be addressed from another more satisfactory perspective, in our opinion. This would start from the study of the process of formation of international norms and this process cannot be correctly known starting from preconceived positions such as those described above or those referred to in article 38 of the Statute of the ICJ considering that these contain the formal sources of International Law[12].

As we have mentioned above, the process for the formation of international norms in the International Community, and, therefore, the rights and obligations contained in them, is founded on two fundamental elements: the individual consent of the state and the consensus of a plurality of States.

In the International Community at the beginning of the XXI century, the State no longer acted in isolation, but within a dimension of association, and this fact had repercussions in the process for the formation of norms. In this context, the aforementioned process of formation necessarily transcends the individual basis of consent in order to constitute the expression of the social group as a whole, or particular groups of States[13].

---

9 See SLOAN, B., "General Assembly Resolutions Revisited (forty years later)" *BYIL*, 1987, page 42; Cf. QUOC DINH, N., DAILLER, P., and PELLET, A., *op. cit.*, pages 356-372.

10 DUPUY, P.M., *Droit International Public*, *op. cit.*, page 277.

11 SLOAN, B., *op. cit.*, page 42.

12 For example, BARBERIS, J, and SHAW, M.N., *International Law*, 3rd edition., Grotius, Cambridge, 1991.

13 See GONZALEZ CAMPOS, J.D., SANCHEZ RODRIGUEZ, L.I. and ANDRES SAENZ DE SANTA MARIA, M. P., *op. cit.*, page 90.

Among these elements, the first one, the individual consent of the state constitutes the necessary, initial moment for the process of formation of norms. The norm does not arise from this consent. The final moment, and thus the moment that the norm arises, takes place when the general consensus of the States is reached. Or, in other words, when there is a plurality of individual consent to being obliged by the same norm. Thus, the plurality of individual consent is transformed into a consensus of the States.

This way of addressing the process of the formation of international norms was used by the ICJ in the cases of the *North Sea Continental Shelf* and the *Fisheries Jurisdiction* in which it stated that in the process of the formation of the Law at international level, the crystallising of the norm (its birth) takes place when there is general assent (consensus) of the States[14].

In addition, this conception is put into effect in a particular way within the institutional dimension of the International Community of our days as a result of the evolution of the Community itself and it is characterised by the relational aspect, the sovereignty, having moved towards the institutional factor, and new channels for the production of consensus have been created. This is what happens within the International Organisations and the Conferences so that in these environments the crystallisation of consensus, the birth of the norm, is facilitated by the new dimension which State sovereignty has at the present time.

In short, there is a single process of formation with two elements (individual consent and the general consensus of states) which respectively constitute the initial and final phases of the process of formation.

In our opinion, from this perspective the legal effects of the institutional norm can be addressed in general, and the norms of the General Assembly of the United Nations in particular. The analysis of the conduct of the member states, manifested in the way the document is adopted, provides a satisfactory response to the first question which was posed at the start of this section. Together with this conduct, the examination of other factors will facilitate the interpretation of the will of the state regarding the document of the Organisation and will make it possible for its legal effects to be determined. The ICJ has also made statements along the same lines. For example, its advisory opinion regarding the Case of the *Legal Consequences for States of the Continued Presence of South Africa in Namibia (South-West Africa) notwithstanding Security Council Resolution 276 (1970)*, in which it stated that,

> "For it would not be correct to assume that, because the General Assembly is in principle vested with recommendatory powers, it is debarred from adopting, in specific cases within the framework of its

[14] See ICJ, *Reports 1974*, page 23. With regard to the second matter see ICJ, *Reports 1969*, page 38. The non-existence of this consensus means that the ten mile rule has not acquired "the authority of a general rule of international law" but, at any rate, it could not be used against Norway "inasmuch as she has always opposed any attempts to apply this to the Norwegian coast" (*Fisheries case*, ICJ, *Reports 1951*, page 131).

> competence, resolution which make determinations or have operative design"[15].

In addition, in its advisory opinion concerning *Certain Expenses of the United Nations*, in which it was stated that,

> "the functions and powers conferred by the Charter on the General Assembly are not confined to discussion, consideration, the initiation of studies and the making of recommendations; they are not merely hortatory. Article 18 deals with '*decisions*' of the General Assembly 'on important questions'. These 'decisions' do indeed include certain recommendations, but others have dispositive force and effect"[16].

If United Nations practice is examined, it can be seen that the General Assembly adopts different types of documents: Resolutions, Recommendations, Declarations and Decisions[17]. The following deals with the examination of this practice.

As regards the first, it is possible to classify them in four large blocks:

- Declarative Resolutions on customary norms.
- Resolutions which crystallise the customary norms *in statu nascendi.*
- Resolutions de *lege ferenda* which constitute the starting point for a custom;
- Resolutions interpreting the Charter[18].

The Declarative Resolutions of customary norms generally appear under the title of "Declaration", and its subject is the affirmation of an existing rule of law and it also constitutes a means for determining or interpreting international law, a proof of international custom or the statement of general principles of law[19].
Despite the fact that the status of the resolutions called "Declarations" do not differ from other resolutions, this particular type of resolution can serve to stress the importance of the norms announced. As the IIL points out in its Cairo Resolution, the appeal to declarations is usually convenient for dealing globally with a matter or to announce principles intended to influence the progressive development of international law[20]. As an example, Resolution 2625 (XXV) of the General Assembly on October 24, 1970 can be included. It contains the *Declaration on*

---

15 ICJ, *Reports 1971*, page 50.

16 ICJ, *Reports 1962*, page 163. The part in italics is from the original.

17 It can also draw up and adopt conventions which are annexed to the resolution in question.

18 The Institute of International Law (IIL) takes in the different types of documents under the form of Recommendations (Resolution of the Cairo meeting, September 13-21, 1987, *Yearbook of the I.I.L.*, Vol. 62-II, 1987, Pedone, Paris, pages 273-289).

19 Cf. *ibid.*, Conclusion 4.

20 Cf. *ibid.*, Conclusion 12.

Principles of International Law concerning Friendly Relations and Cooperation among States in Accordance with the Charter of the United Nations. With regard to this, in the case of *Military and Paramilitary Activities in and against Nicaragua*, the ICJ stated that it is not a repetition or a specification of the commitment assumed by the States in the Charter,

> "The effect of consent to the text of such resolutions cannot be understood as merely that of a 'reiteration or elucidation' of the treaty commitment undertaken in the Charter. On the contrary, if may be understood as an acceptance of the validity of the rule or set of rules declared by the resolution by themselves"[21].

At doctrinal level, different characteristics have been given for these types of Resolutions. Some have pointed out that declarative Resolutions are not only declarations of an existing text. On the contrary, this type of Resolution serves to define, formulate, re-formulate, clarify, specify and authenticate a text, as well as to corroborate the rule contained in it[22]. Thus, "if all, or nearly all, of the members of the United Nations say that this is the law, as in the case of interpretative resolutions, it would require strong evidence of conflicting practice to maintain the contrary"[23].

Others have highlighted the fact that declarative resolutions are a source of rules of international law similar to the consensus in the conferences for the codification and progressive development of international law[24], and they have also stated that as regards general international law, these have the same value as declarative conventions. That is to say, that if they can contribute to precision in the sense of practice (the material element of custom) on the one hand, and on the other the unanimous adoption or adoption by a large majority could be a proof of the *opinio iuris* (the spiritual element of international custom)[25]. A third opinion defends the view that the resolutions which crystallise customary norms do not create law but constitute an authorised proof of its existence[26].

---

[21] ICJ, *Reports 1986*, paragraph 188. Along the same lines, the ICJ mentions the resolution of the Sixth Inter-American Conference held on February 18, 1928, which condemned aggression and Resolution 78 of the General Assembly of American States (OAS), adopted on April 21, 1972 regarding the principles of non-intervention and the self-determination of peoples.

[22] See SLOAN, B., *op. cit.*, page 69.

[23] *Ibid.*

[24] See JIMENEZ DE ARECHAGA, E., "General Course in Public International Law", *HR*, (1978-I), vol. 159, page 31.

[25] An example of this is the statement from the ICJ in the case concerning *Military and Paramilitary Activities in and against Nicaragua* (cf. ICJ, *Reports 1986*, page 100). In this regard, see PASTOR RIDRUEJO, J.A., *Curso de ..., op.cit.*, page 175.

[26] CASTAÑEDA, J., "Valeur juridique des résolutions des Nations Unies", *HR*, (1970-I), vol. 129, page 171.

Thus, the origin of what has been said above regarding the interest and the current importance of this question can be seen. Moreover, the wealth produced by its analysis based on the practice of the General Assembly contrasts with the lack of doctrinal presentations which are restricted to discarding the fact that the institutional norms can have obligatory legal effects. The study of the practice and the appeal to the methods of analysis we have chosen prove precisely the contrary: the repercussion which these Resolutions of the General Assembly have in the formation of International Law and their effect on the sectors of these regulations referred to in their content.

The second group of Resolutions of the General Assembly are the Resolutions called resolutions *"crystallising"* the customary norms which are in the process of being formed and which contribute to the consolidation of the customary norm.

This is the case of Resolution 1962 (XVIII) which contains the *Declaration of Legal Principles governing the Activities of States in the Exploration and Use of Outer Space* adopted unanimously by the General Assembly of the United Nations on December 13, 1963. The Declaration which is the subject of this Resolution contains the legal principles which at that time reflected the International Law accepted by the members of the United Nations, and crystallised the general consensus which had been manifested in previous years as regards the general regime concerning freedom of activity in outer space. Later, these principles were codified by the *Treaty on the Principles Governing the Activities of States in the Exploration and Use of Outer Space, Including the Moon and Other Celestial Bodies*[27].

Another example which should be quoted is the Resolution belonging to the second group, Resolution 2749 (XXV) of December 17, 1970, which contains the *Declaration of Principles Governing the Sea-Bed and the Ocean Floor, and the Subsoil Thereof, Beyond the Limits of National Jurisdiction*, which proclaims that the resources are the "common heritage of mankind". In accordance with the analytical viewpoint which we have adopted above, the general consensus of the States which was manifest on voting on this Declaration accepting the legal status of common heritage of mankind which it contains as regards the seabed, has the consequence that all the States have the right to share the resources of the seabed in the area located beyond national jurisdiction.

Later, the principles contained in Resolution 2749 (XXV) were codified in 1982 by the Convention of the United Nations on the Law of the Sea which again reveals the transcendence or the effects which the Resolutions of the General Assembly have apart from what is said of these in the Charter. This fact also gives a good example of the few gaps in the doctrinal positions which maintain that the Resolutions of the General Assembly only have the effect of recommendations. As in the previous case, the Resolutions of this second group also belie this.

---

[27] Approved by the General Assembly on December 19, 1966, it was signed in London, Moscow and Washington on January 27, 1967. It has been in force since October 10, 1967.

Thus, the in Part XI of the 1982 Convention defines the legal regime of the Area of the seabed and ocean floor and subsoil thereof and includes and develops the principles of Resolution 2749 (XXV) and sets up an International Organisation (the International Seabed Authority) responsible for organising and controlling activities in the Area in accordance with the Convention.

The analysis of the practice also reveals that the crystallising of custom is intimately linked to the temporary factor in the formation process. The 1982 Convention on the Law of the Sea is a good example of this. This Convention, which came into force on November 16, 1994[28], codifies the Law of the Sea which was spread out among four Conventions. Some of the norms were already in force at customary level. However, others, such as those concerning the Area were in progressive development in 1982. Can the same be said now that they have come into force? What effects does the regime on the Area have for the States which have not ratified the Convention? In our opinion, the passage of time favours the consolidation of the legal regime for the Area and its effect could be specified in the fact that third party states are bound by it.

These questions acquire special relevance given the conclusion made on July 29, 1994 of the Agreement on the application of Part XI of the Convention of the United Nations on the Law of the Sea of December 10, 1982, which has been adopted by Resolution 48/263 of the General Assembly of July 28, 1994[29]. In addition, this agreement, whose article 2 presents it as for application and interpretation, in practice constitutes an amendment to Part XI of the 1982 Convention insofar as it declares that several articles of the aforementioned Convention cannot be applied. These articles refer to the Enterprise, decision taking by the Assembly and the Council, the Conference for Revising the 1982 Convention, the transfer of technology, policy regarding production and the financial clauses of contracts[30]. Therefore, it constitutes a good example of the way in which the States amend treaties under the appearance of their interpretation and application.

The last group of Resolutions is made up of those which have a constitutive or generating effect, also called de *lege ferenda*. These are Resolutions which through their adoption can be the basis for the practice of the States. They are thus transformed into customary International Law and constitute landmark norms in a process for the creation ad drafting of International Law by stages, and their legal value depends on the acceptance they receive in the practise of the States[31].

---

[28] See updated information on the state of this Convention in the work published by BURHENNE, W.E., *Beiträge zur Umweltbestaltung, Internationales Umweltrecht –Multilaterale Verträge*, vol. V, E. Schmidt, Berlin, pages 982:92/1 et seq.

[29] See the text in *RGDIP*, 1994/3, pages 837-857.

[30] Also the Resolution of the General Assembly in point 4, it "*Affirms* that the Agreement shall be interpreted and applied with Part XI –of the 1982 Convention- as a sole and same instrument" (*ibid.,* page 857).

[31] Cf. CARRILLO SALCEDO, J. A., *Curso…*, *op. cit.*, page 131. The italics are from the original. See also SLOAN, B., *op. cit.*, page 70.

The 1987 Cairo Resolution of the Institute of International Law includes the following categories in these types of Resolutions:

- Resolutions which contribute to the creation of an international custom;
- Resolutions which contribute to the emergence of general principles of law;
- Resolutions which restrict the field of negotiations regarding a multilateral treaty which is of general interest, especially those which provide rules to be included in a future treaty;
- Resolutions which establish policy determining the substance of a future customary or conventional law[32].

This part also includes Resolution 1514 (XV) of the General Assembly of December 14, 1960 as an example. This contains the *Declaration on the Granting of Independence to Colonial Countries and Peoples* and was classified by the ICJ in its advisory opinion on the *Namibia* Case as "a further important stage in the development of customary law"[33].

These types of Resolutions also constitute a "species of General Assembly resolutions based on established practice outside the express provisions of Chapter IV of the Charter"[34].

From the above examination, it can be concluded that there is a strong effect of consent and consensus as regards both the process of institutionalisation of the International Community and in the drafting of international law within the United Nations. In addition, it proves that it is right to address the problem of the legal effects of the Resolutions of the General Assembly based on the observed behaviour of the states when the Resolutions are adopted.

Another group is made up of the *interpretative* Resolutions of the Charter. In SLOAN's opinion, "the Charter is binding on its members as a treaty and its principles are binding on all States as general international law. Authentic interpretations would have obligatory force equal to the Charter itself and authoritative interpretations would carry almost the same weight "[35].

By virtue of article 10 of the Charter, the General Assembly can discuss and make recommendations on any matters within the framework of the Charter and its competence regarding the interpretation of the Charter is very wide. This interpretation can be explicit (as declarative resolutions) or implicit (as a decision or recommendation invoking provisions within the Charter), but in both cases they have the same legal effects as regards the member states[36].

---

32 IIL, *Yearbook of the Institute of International Law*, 1987, vol. 62-II, page 279.

33 ICJ, *Reports 1971*, page 31. Cf. Also the advisory opinion of the ICJ on the *Western Sahara* Case (*Reports 1975*, especially page 32). This Resolution was repeated and developed in subsequent Resolutions, 1541 (XV), 1980 (XVII) and 2625 (XXV).

34 SLOAN, B., *op. cit*, page 140. Chapter IV of the Charter is the one concerning the General Assembly.

35 *Ibid.* page 57.

36 See *ibid.*, page 57 et seq.

As regards the Resolutions which we have just analysed, through the *Decisions* "by virtue of powers expressly or impliedly authorised by the Charter, inherent in its nature or acquired through practice, the General Assembly may take decisions having binding force or operative effect"[37].

Finally, as concerns the *Recommendations*, in the opinion of Sir F. VALLAT, "to say that recommandations of the General Assembly are not as a rule binding on States, does not mean that they are of no legal effect whatever. Resolutions may be strong evidence of the proper interpretation of the Charter or of generally accepted principles of international law"[38]. As far as SLOAN is concerned, even the recommendations which have this characteristic *strictu sensu* involve obligations as regard cooperation, good faith and assistance, obligations applicable as regards all the recommendations validly adopted "without special regard to the size of the vote. The hortatory effect of recommendations will be strengthened by unanimity or near unanimity. Recommendations will also have value as precedents and may gain binding force through acceptance or estoppel"[39].

From the studies carried out, it can be deduced that the resolutions of the General Assembly have legal effects within the internal order of the organisation. Secondly, the resolutions are part of the customary process and have contributed to its acceleration[40]. Finally, that the determination of the legal effects of a resolution of the General Assembly depends more on the analysis of the will of the state manifested in its relation with the international norm, rather than its denomination[41].

The drafting of the Law in the General Assembly is the result of the new dimension where the manifestation of the individual consent of the state and the general consensus of the state takes place i.e. the institutional dimension. Before the institutionalisation process of the International Community, consent and consensus occur at a level which is merely relational. The institutionalisation of the International Community has led to the creation of new forums where consent and consensus are manifested, and the result is a new kind of norm: the institutional one.

The General Assembly is almost a universal forum in which takes place the presence of almost all the States which make up the International Community and it facilitates the operability of the process for drafting the institutional norm. Within the Assembly, the states manifest their attitude as regards the resolution at the same time and collectively through adopting the resolution. This resolution may

---

[37] *Ibid.* Page 139. This is the case of articles 2.5, 17 and 18 of the Charter.

[38] VALLAT, F.A., *op. cit.*, page 231.

[39] SLOAN, B., *op. cit.*, page 140. He adds that "at least in some circumstances the obligation does go further and is a duty not only to *consider* in good faith but to *act* in good faith as well. Such duty arises out of the obligations of co-operation implicit in organizational theory and expressly stated in Articles 1(3), 2(5) and 56 of the Charter of the UN" (*ibid.*, page 125).

[40] Cf. JAQUE, J.P., *op. cit.*, page 397.

[41] Cf. in this regard CARRILLO SALCEDO, J.A., *Curso ...*, *op. cit.*, pages 132 et seq.

contain a norm of International Law which already exists or is emerging, or which might be the basis and starting point for the progressive development of International Law[42].

Thus we are always dealing with a norm[43]. Consequently, it always has legal effects.

2 The examination of the attitude of the State is the determining factor: Criteria

The previous study of the legal effects of the institutional norms in general and the Resolutions of the General Assembly in particular is over, and we now address the other question in this chapter: the interpretation of the institutional norms; an interpretation which can refer both to the state conduct in order to determine the legal effects which give rise to the institutional norm, and the text of the Resolution itself.

As far as the first aspect is concerned, we again insist that the determining factor is the will of the state manifested within the International Organisation as regards the institutional norm in question. Whether this individual consent of the state exists or not is what will determine whether the norm has crystallised or not through the general consensus of the States which participate in the International Organisation[44].

In order to determine the will of the state, and therefore, the legal effects of the resolution, we can appeal to the following techniques or criteria: the drafting, the terms used, the content or the subject of the institutional norm, the procedure or way it is adopted, the context in which the resolution is drawn up and adopted, the intention of the states and the subsequent practice of the states[45].

Concerning the *content* or *subject* of the resolution, according to P.M. DUPUY the debate is restricted to a reduced number of resolutions (including the Declarations adopted on the occasion of important international conferences convoked by the UNO) and their regulatory character has been clearly established[46]. This is the case of Resolutions 2625 (XXV) and 3314 (XXIX).

---

42 See JIMÉNEZ DE ARECHAGA, E., *op. cit.*, page 34.

43 See VIRALLY, M., "Résolution et Accord International", in the collective work *Essays in International Law in Honour of Judge Manfred Lachs*, Nijhoff, The Hague, 1984. Especially page 299.

44 As regards this question from the perspective of protection of Human Rights, See CARRILLO SALCEDO, J.A., "Algunas Reflexiones sobre el valor jurídico de la Declaración Universal de Derechos Humanos". In the collection, *Hacia un nuevo orden internacional y europeo. Homenaje al Profesor M. Díez de Velasco*, Tecnos, Madrid, 1993. Especially pages 173-175.

45 The ICJ refers to these criteria in the case of the *Legal Consequences for States of the Continued Presence of South Africa in Namibia (South-West Africa) notwithstanding Security Council Resolution 276 (1970)* (See ICJ, *Reports 1971*, page 50).

46 See DUPUY, P.M. *Droit...*, *op.cit.*, page 279.

The 1972 Declaration of Stockholm and 1992 Declaration of Rio de Janeiro are good examples of the usefulness of the appeal to the criteria we are putting forward. It should be remembered that the legal effects of the former were put in doubt by the doctrine immediately after its adoption. The fact that this was by consensus was significant taking into account the obligations codified by the Declaration which had already been affirmed by international case law[47]. But the same questions arise as concerns the 1992 Declaration of Rio with regard to those aspects which mean innovation in comparison with the pre-existing regime. There is no doubt that the passage of time and the practice of the States will contribute to consolidating these obligations and to reinforcing the legal effects of the Declaration.

The analysis of the content involves three types of questions. The first, the legal or political nature of the resolution[48]. In the second place, the analysis of the terms in order to know whether it declares or recommends[49]. Finally, the nature of the question dealt with by the resolution (if this is new or has already been regulated by the International Community) which would allow us to establish whether it is a resolution which declares or crystallises an already existing norm or in the process of formation or whether it is the starting point for a new norm.

The *procedure* or *form of adoption* of the resolution enables us to know the attitude of the member states as regards the norm. In this respect some authors endeavour to disassociate the act of adoption of the resolution (procedural aspect) from the content. Thus, the procedural act of adoption would have no consequences as regards the text contained in the resolution[50]. In our opinion, this disassociation is not possible as the adoption of the Resolution is made by reference to its content. The attitude of the state at the time of the adoption of the Resolution is

---

[47] For example, Principle 21 which contains the obligation on prevention.

[48] In CARRILLO SALCEDO'S opinion, as a result of its political nature, the General Assembly adopts many resolutions which are clearly political in content "most of the time by majority, which naturally has little legal significance as concerns the process for the drafting of the general legal norms" (*Curso ...*, *op. cit.*, page 130).

[49] At doctrinal level some authors choose to put institutional norms at the same level as conventional norms for the purposes of interpretation, and propose that the analysis of the content be done by analogy in accordance with the rules of the 1969 and 1986 Vienna Conventions. SLOAN, B. (*op. cit.*, page 129) adds that "when the resolution contains a binding decision expressly authorised by the Charter or if this constitutes an agreement, it would seem reasonable to apply the treaty rule on *travaux* préparatoires" (preparatory works). VIRALLY maintains that the acceptance of the adoption of a resolution also constitutes acceptance of the terms of the resolution "so it is necessary to formulate reservations in order to disassociate, in the event of consensus" ("Résolution et ....", *op. cit.*, page 304).

[50] The adoption of a resolution would only express "an informal agreement regarding the text among all the states which, through their representatives, have contributed to this adoption", whether by majority, unanimously or by consensus (VIRALLY, M., "Résolution et ...", *op. cit.*, page 301).

determined by its content, by the text, therefore the conduct observed at the time of the adoption is also the conduct manifested with regard to the text of the resolution[51]. From the time that consent to be bound by the resolution and the consensus ad idem are manifested within the General Assembly, the legal effects arise[52].

On adoption by *voting*, this expresses the agreement of the states which *vote in favour*. The favourable votes must include both the states whose support might be necessary for the effective application of the resolution and the states of all the economic and legal systems[53]. That is to say, it must be a *representative vote* of the majority in question so that those proposing the resolution or those who invoke it for regulatory objectives may endeavour to make it "the expression of a collective *opinio iuris*, which is creative or simply demonstrates a regulatory intention attributable to the international community as a whole[54].

The majority is essential. In fact, it is not the same for the resolution to be the subject of a general agreement and ample consensus among the states belonging to the main legal systems (which grants greater relevance and legal authority) which, on the contrary, finds opposition from a sufficiently representative minority (which will prevent the resolution from having legal effects)[55].

---

[51] Thus VIRALLY himself is inclined to recognise that the adoption of the resolution confers on the regulatory provisions of the text a legal authority which is above its formal classification, and he states that the resolution is of a *mixed nature*: "formally it is a unilateral act of the committee of the conference which produced it. Due to the conditions of its adoption, it expresses the content of the inter-governmental agreement and is thus of a conventional colouring" ("Résolution et ….", *op. cit.*, pages 301 et seq).

[52] Following this line of thought, the resolution of the IIL at its Cairo meeting in 1987, in its conclusion number 13, states: "A law declaring resolution, adopted without negative vote or abstention, creates a presumption that the resolution contains a correct statement of law. That presumption is subject to rebuttal". And Conclusion number 14 adds: "In situations where a rule of customary law is emerging from State practice or where there is still doubt whether a rule, though already applied by an international organ or by some States, is a rule of law, a resolution adopted without negative vote or abstention may consolidate a custom or remove doubts that might have existed" (*op. cit.*, 283-285).

[53] SLOAN, B., *op. cit.*, page 131.

[54] DUPUY, P.M., *Droit* ……, *op. cit.*, pages 279 et seq.

[55] See in this regard CARRILLO SALCEDO, J.A., *Curso* ..., *op. cit.*, page 130. Other criteria apart from the representative nature is, according to P.M. DUPUY, the establishment of a control mechanism which is more or less institutionalised for the monitoring of the resolution by the member states. This control could consist of a periodical examination of the conditions of application laid down in the resolution by an institution of the Organisation (*Droit* ..., *op. cit.*, page 280)

The criteria of the representative nature appears backed by the IIL in its Cairo Resolution, "The authority of a resolution is enhanced when it is adopted by a representative majority that includes the main legal systems" (*op. cit.*, page 285).

In any case, it is evident that the state which votes in favour of the Resolution adheres to the validity of the norm or set of norms declared by the Resolution[56].

Obviously the states which vote against are free from the legal effects of the Resolution voted by a majority. This is initially true, but it should be added that this refusal may be affected by the general consensus as regards the resolution in question on condition that the criteria examined as concerns the manner of adoption of the institutional norm are respected.

As regards those who *abstain*, the doctrinal opinions diverge among those who sustain that these states do not oppose but disassociate from the agreement[57] and those who consider that the abstention is the same as acquiescence[58]. As was the case in the criteria examined above, the reply in the cases of negative votes and abstentions is determined by the number of negative votes or abstentions as if these are substantial or qualitatively significant the effect of stating law or creating rules by the resolution would be weakened[59].

If the resolution is adopted by *consensus*, this shows the unanimity of the agreement of the states concerning the content of the norm, and the authority of the resolution is thus reinforced[60]. JACQUE states that if the vote on a resolution implies that there is already agreement on the content of the resolution among the members of the majority, this agreement is even more evident when the resolution is adopted by consensus. The same happens when reservations are formulated regarding the resolution by some States. This indicates that they grant a certain value to the commitment contained in the resolution as they feel the need to be more specific[61]. These reservations do not produce legal effects when it is a matter of resolutions which state existing law[62].

---

56 As stated by the ICJ in the case of *Military and Paramilitary Activities in and against Nicaragua* (ICJ, *Reports 1986*, para. 188).

57 Cf. VIRALLY, M., "Résolution.......", *op. cit.*, page 301.

58 SLOAN, B., *op. cit.*, page 131.

59 See IIL, *op. cit.*, page 285.

60 In accordance with Conclusion number 16 of the Resolution of the IIL of 1987, at the Cairo session, "the authority of a resolution is enhanced when it is adopted by consensus".
The Declaration of Stockholm in 1972 constitutes an example of a Resolution adopted by consensus.
It should be added that when the resolution is voted unanimously, it force seems, in principle, greater than when it is adopted by consensus.

61 See JACQUE, J.P., *op. cit.*, page 398. This author describes this agreement as "an informal legal agreement among states", which must be deduced from the examination of the circumstances involved in the adoption of the resolution (*ibid*).

62 As concerns the reservations, the Cairo Resolution of the IIL in its Conclusion number 17, states that "Where a resolution may be subjected to reservations either in the explanations of votes or in other statements, the effect of such reservations is to qualify or limit the extent of approval by the reserving State. Depending on its contents a reservation may mean less than rejection of the rule. It may be merely an expression of doubt. If a resolution expresses existing law, a State cannot exclude itself from the binding force of that law by making a reservation" (*op. cit.*, page 285).

From the viewpoint of the interpretation, the resolution adopted by consensus or by a unanimous vote will have a particular interpretation as proof of an *opinio iuris* in the customary process: it may testify to a political agreement. But it will be necessary to make a wider examination of the context in order to affirm that we are in the presence of a legal agreement and not a political one[63].

In the cases of adoption of the resolution by consensus, the absence of protests can mean an acceptance of the resolution where each state commits itself given that the objection of a single state would be sufficient for the resolution not to be adopted. In other words, the acceptance of the consensus means that each member state participates individually in the adoption of the resolution, which leads VIRALLY to state that this is why the member states of the institution which pronounces by consensus "cannot disassociate from the agreement made in his manner except as regards particular points and through active conduct, by formulating reservations before or after the adoption of the resolution"[64].

But it should not be forgotten that the great Resolutions are adopted through negotiation procedures which are similar to the great general treaties. This means that the resolutions are prepared in restricted groups and are then submitted to the plenary institution. Generally, they are discussed and voted on article by article and, more and more frequently, the states explain their vote in order to specify their positions more. This process of drafting the resolution shows the existence of an exchange of points of view and a meeting of wills within the assembly which is very similar to what takes place on the drafting of multilateral treaties[65]. PASTOR RIDRUEJO hit the nail on the head when he stressed the characteristic of consensus: "the proposal of the resolution made by the President of the Organisation has been drafted through consultations, negotiations and transactions among the delegations concerned, that is to say, it is the subject of a compromise, so, when the President submits it to the institution, he already knows that it will not give rise to objections". These objections are understood to be those which are sufficiently substantial to prevent the adoption of the resolution given that practice shows that the state delegations can express minor objections (which adopt the form of reservations) but do not involve the intention to prevent the formation of the resolution[66].

---

63 See JACQUE, J.P., *op. cit.*, page 398.

64 See VIRALLY, M., "Résolution ...", *op. cit.*, page 303.

65 Which leads P.M. DUPUY to state that in such cases, whether it is wished or not, "it is a matter of the expression of a meeting of wills, although rather diluted... which is facilitated by the organic framework of the intervention, whose nature is conventionally deaf and difficult to respond to" (*op. cit.*, page 281).

66 PASTOR RIDRUEJO, J.A., *Curso ...*, *op. cit.*, page 710. Also CARRILLO SALCEDO who, after he had stressed the negotiation process of the resolution among the states which make up the political groups which constitute the General Assembly, he states that "when this negotiation becomes fruitful and makes the adoption of a resolution possible by consensus or by general agreement, the resolution in question is in fact a concerted judicial act of a non-conventional nature, that is to say, an agreement between states expressed at a judicial act as distinct from an international agreement, with undeniable legal value as a new procedure for drafting legal norms in contemporary International Law..." (*Curso...*, *op. cit.*, page 134).

A third criteria is the *intention* of the states, which can be known through the language employed in the drafting of the resolution; if it is clearly imperative, recommendatory, using the conditional tense, leaving a wide discretionary margin to the states, etc.[67].

The importance of the drafting as regards the Resolutions of the General Assembly has also been stressed by international case law. Thus, the ICJ in the case of *Military and Paramilitary Activities in and against Nicaragua* it states that,

> "... just as the wording of certain General Assembly declarations adopted by States demonstrates their recognition of the principle of the prohibition of force as a definitely matter of customary international law, some of the wording in those declarations operates similarly in respect of the right of self-defence (both collective and individual)"[68].

In addition, as we have stated above, the mode of adopting the resolution, by voting (unanimously or by majority) or by consensus, also constitutes an indication of the intention of the states as regards the resolution.

There are no discrepancies concerning the competence of the General Assembly to interpret the Charter through *interpretative resolutions*. We have referred to its extent as a result of the empowerment contained in article 10 to discuss and make recommendations on any matter within the framework of the Charter. As regards the effect of the attitude of the states, it is considered that this interpretation is generally accepted when there is a unanimous or almost unanimous vote of the aforementioned resolution[69]. Thus, it has been said that "every interpretation holds within it the seeds of development. This is true whether it purports to be strictly textual or is frankly teleological. Interpretations may explain, clarify, elaborate, develop or supplement the Charter, or they may slip into modification or informal amendment. The line between interpretation and modification, like the line between codification and development, is a thin one and the distinction is often difficult, if not impossible, to make. Development often takes place under the guise of interpretation and the test of general acceptability remains the best guide in either case"[70].

---

[67] The IIL in Conclusion number 10 of the Cairo Resolution of 1987 highlights as criteria for appreciating the intention of states both the drafting and the context of a resolution as these help to determine the scope of the norm, and adds that the presence of "references to international law or equivalent phrases, or the deliberate omission, are relevant but not in themselves" (IIL, *op. cit.*, page 281). See also AMERASINGHE, C.F., "Interpretation of texts in Open International Organizations", *BYIL*, 1994, pages 175-209.

[68] ICJ, *Reports 1986*, para. 193.

[69] Cf. SLOAN, B., *op. cit.*, page 59. This presumption could only be destroyed if the rejection of the resolution were to be proved by subsequent practice (*ibid.*).

[70] *Ibid.*, page 60.

The last criteria is *subsequent practice*, which places the resolutions of the General Assembly of the United Nations in relationship with custom[71] (with the three manifestations which we have explained in the previous section). Practice, in this case, takes in both the resolution itself and the votes of the states which reflect their positions with regard to the resolution[72].

Subsequent practice of the states as regards the resolution in question also allows us to confirm the attitude of these states concerning the legal value of the resolution and the interpretation of the Charter. It should not be forgotten that the Charter is a living text and thus the subsequent practice enables us to know the contemporary interpretation of the Charter made by current members. From this perspective, the changes occurring in the International Community since the Charter was drafted are evident. The balance consigned to the Charter after the Second World War has been extensively altered, first, due to the universalising of the Community itself as a result of decolonisation and, more recently, due to the disappearance of the soviet block and the subsequent break up of the USSR. The Charter is the same but the context in which it is applied has changed profoundly. Some of the provisions (for example, Chapter VII) recover vitality and the Organisation is confronted with new challenges. Within the framework of this Chapter, the provisions of the Charter concerning the prohibition of the use of force and the protection of human rights receive new applications, and questions arise such as the control of the legality of the acts of the Security Council. The principle of non-intervention is also affected by the new international context.

Considering the profundity of the changes which have occurred, the analysis of the subsequent practice of the States concerning the resolutions of the General Assembly acquire a new dimension. Thus, it is also useful to consider "the frequency and density of the repetition of certain principles through voluntary repetitive resolutions", both in the course of the sessions of the General Assembly and other plenary meetings of universal international organisations such as the IWO, the WHO or the FAO[73].

Although it is true that the United Nations Charter points out that the General Assembly can only adopt "decisions" and "recommendations", this does not prevent this institution from adopting other kinds of decisions ("declarations"), nor that the

---

71 See CARRILLO SALCEDO, J.A., *Curso* …., *op. cit.*, page 130.

72 According to SLOAN the "resolutions -or at least the votes of States on resolutions- are a part of state practice", and constitute "a material source of customary law and must be taken into account in considering the current state of the law" (*op. cit.*, page 74). And he adds, the "resolutions are evidence" (*ibid.*, page 85).

73 DUPUY, P.M., *Droit* …., *op. cit.*, 283. SLOAN adds other factors such as the time and the circumstances, "the international climate in which the resolution was adopted must influence its weight" (*op. cit.*, page 128). These changes give rise to another problem which is the replacement of the commitments and the text of the past by new individual and collective consent. Cf. also AMERASINGHE, C.F., "Interpretation of texts….", *op. cit.*, pages 198-200.

declarations and recommendations have obligatory legal effects. All the resolutions, independently of their names, have legal effects. The scope of these resolutions and their precision will have to be determined case by case by recourse to the criteria examined. How can this conclusion be reconciled with the absence of provisions in the Charter expressly capacitating the General Assembly to create law with binding legal effects? As it is true that the sovereignty of the state only has the limitations accepted by the states themselves – except for the limitation deriving from imperative norms – and that the will of the state reflected in the Charter does not state anything with regard to creation of law by the general Assembly, it is no less true that, in the General Assembly, the process for the formation of the institutional norms takes place through the channels and procedures laid down in the Charter. These procedures, in which the states have an active participation, channel the opinions of the majority and provide them with a regulation expression (which is the institutional norm)[74].The individual consent of each state and the *consensus ad idem* of the generality of the states are manifest, are crystallised through the procedures laid down in the Charter. At the meetings of the General Assembly, consent and consensus produce the institutional norm. But this is not the only thing. The institutional norm created in this way also expresses the *opinio iuris* of the states in the General Assembly. This is one of the more relevant aspects resulting from the institutionalisation of the International Community. Unlike the past, at the present time, it is not a reduced group of states (the Great Powers) which express the will of the International Community. On the contrary, practically all this community represented in the General Assembly – independently of the degree of power and economic development – which participates in the drafting of this norm of international law which is the institutional norm.

The phenomenon which we have just described has also been specified as PASTOR RIDRUEJO points out by a displacement of the centre of gravity of the material element of the custom, the practice, towards the spiritual element or *opinio iuris*, as a result of the demands made by the universalising, democratisation and socialisation of international law. Today the important thing is not always the practice or the material element of the custom, but the *opinio iuris* or legal conviction. And this *opinio iuris generalis* "is also adequately manifested through the resolutions of the General Assembly of the United Nations"[75].

The state consensus, in which the resolution is crystallised, is arrived at after a long process with several stages, at which the individual consent of the state regarding the resolution is manifested (this consent is specified in the negotiations, deliberations, transactions and consultations regarding the text), and this consent is manifested or exteriorised later in the form of adoption of the norm.

---

74 See DUPUY, P. M., *Droit ...*, *op. cit.*, page 290.

75 PASTOR RIDRUEJO, J. A., *Curso ...*, *op. cit.*, page 177. One of the results of current situation after the changes which have occurred is the new protagonism of the Great Powers and the role they play in the General Assembly. This has led to the fact that international law declarations or texts are not being adopted as frequently as between 1960 and 1990.

In our opinion, the classical manifestation of the ICJ in its advisory opinion on the *Legal Consequences for States of the Continued Presence of South Africa in Namibia (South-West Africa) notwithstanding Security Council Resolution 276 (1970)* in the sense that, "an international instrument has to be interpreted and applied within the framework of the entire legal system prevailing in at the time of the interpretation"[76], backs up the position we have adopted as regards the legal force of the resolutions of the General Assembly. At the present time, the relevance of the General Assembly is considerably greater than when the Charter was drafted. The ideological context has also been modified and facilitates the conclusion of norms which express the general consensus of the member states. Finally, the process for the drafting of the resolution is also different from the process at the time the Charter was drawn up. In short, International Society has changed radically. All these changes affect the legal force of the resolutions of the General Assembly and their study cannot be addressed using the schemes of 1945. When the resolution is adopted, it has already passed through the filter of negotiation, it has been the subject of transactions, deliberations and consultations. The final text faithfully reflects the will of the state.

Therefore, the determining factor is not the denomination the institutional norm receives but the attitude of the states with regard to it. This attitude may appear as the manifestation of the *opinio iuris* concerning the norm (or the set of norms) in question, and may be considered as from then independently of the other provisions, especially those of an institutional nature, to which it is submitted at the conventional level of the Charter[77].

Finally, the resolutions of the General Assembly have legal effects, they are norms of International Law[78]. Whether or not they have obligatory legal force as regards the specific persons involved is something that must be analysed case by case based on the criteria examined above.

An additional reflection should be added: the role played by the Resolutions of the General Assembly of the United Nations in the contemporary International Community. As we have stated above, practically all the states which make up this world or universal community participate in the General Assembly and make pro-

---

[76] ICJ, *Reports1971*, page 31.

[77] Cf. ICJ, *Military and Paramilitary Activities in and against Nicaragua, Reports 1986*, para. 188.

[78] According to VIRALLY, the resolutions of the International Organisations "are the expression of a political agreement made between states which have participated in its adoption. Insofar as they share specific commitments for the states, these commitments must be considered as politically binding the states which have accepted them", and they do not have a value inferior to those the states assume in other actions apart from the institutions of the international organisations or at conferences convened to adopt an agreement" ("Résolution ....", *op. cit.*, pages 305 et seq.). However as P. M. DUPUY points out., "the nature and the intensity of the relations maintained between the two regulation orders, the political order and the legal order" remain to be known. (*Droit ...*, *op. cit.*, page 281).

nouncements on questions and problems which are classical or new. Thus, analysis of the Charter, once more than sixty years have elapsed since it came into force, with schemes which lead to literal interpretations of the Charter in relation to the resolutions of the General Assembly, does not allow the role which this institution and its norms play in the International Community at the beginning of the XXI century to be addressed satisfactorily.

Following this line of thought, it should be remembered that questions not laid down in the Charter or only listed in it have been dealt with and developed later based on resolutions adopted by the General Assembly. This is the case, for example, of the sectors of the international legal system concerning the international protection of the environment and human rights, whose first norms were the resolutions of the General Assembly[79].

The same evolutionary nature of the international legal system positively affects the relevance of the resolutions of the General Assembly as concerns the new problems confronting the International Community and which are the subject of attention by this legal system require responses in accord with this evolution and one of the characteristics of this evolution is the fundamental role played by the International Organisations in general and the UNO in particular, as well as the institutional norms they draw up. Consequently, the process for forming the international norms cannot be addressed exclusively from the classical perspective, reduced to conventional and customary norms, but the evolution which we have described must also include the growing relevance of the institutional norms within this system. Otherwise, both the study of the process of formation of international norms and the phenomenon of the International Organisations will be incomplete as it ignores a reality which is more and more established as a consequence of the progressive institutionalisation of the International Community. This institutionalisation is characterised by the negotiation, discussion, deliberation, transaction and flexibility at the time the decisions are taken or the norms are drafted.

Finally, we agree with SEPULVEDA when he states that a "*corpus* is being produced and this cannot be undervalued any longer. It is becoming policy, principles, norms, procedures, attitudes which satisfy the needs of the International Community rather than individual interests or the aspirations of a state, independently of how powerful a state or group of states might be. The process has just begun and is irreversible"[80].

---

[79] For example, the 1972 Declaration of Stockholm, the Universal Declaration of Human Rights of December 10, 1948, the Declaration on Protection Against Torture or Cruel, Inhuman or Degrating Treatment or Punishment of December 9, 1975, etc. As regards the Human Rights sector cf. KISS, A. Ch., "Le rôle de la Déclaration universelle des droits de l'homme dans le développement du droit international", *Bulletin des Droits de l'Homme*, éd spéciale, Nations Unies, New York, 1988, pages 51-56. The same can be said as regards the principle of self-determination of peoples.

[80] SEPULVEDA, C., "Methods ....", *op. cit.*, page 466. The italics are from the original.

CHAPTER IV:

Conduct, the Expression of the Will of the State, Constitutes the Subject of the Discrepancy: The Customary Norms

1 The conduct of the State and its appreciation are tributaries of sovereignty

In the preceding pages we have mentioned the disputes which arise even when the will of the States is written down and expressed in the text of the norm (whether this is conventional or institutional), due to the possibility of unilateral interpretations of their provisions, which are all valid but divergent. It is understandable that discrepancy or disagreement can be manifested more easily when it concerns the existence or content of a non written norm.

In written Law, language is the instrument of sovereignty. States use it to shape their will choosing the terms and composition which better reflects their wills and interests. The written materialization of that will is no other than the result of the exercise of the sovereign liberty International Law recognises the State to have.

The effects of sovereignty, or its consequences, are also manifested subsequently when, on the occasion of the application of the norm the problems of interpretation arise. In order to modulate the discretion of the State, International Law has enshrined the principle of good faith as a fundamental norm which governs or should govern international relations. Later, and with the same aim, the sector of International Law concerning the Law on Treaties contains a series of interpretative rules that enable the Parties in a dispute concerning interpretation to resolve it. Nevertheless, as we have said before, the settlement of disputes, in general, and those of interpretation, in particular, depends on specific means in order to achieve those objectives, and is limited to offering the States a series of resources (political and legal) subordinated to the previous will of the Parties concerned. Consequently, unless there is an agreement or the imposition of a specific means for settlement by a treaty, the obligation to resolve the dispute by pacific means will continue to affect the Parties in order to prevent the dispute from degenerating into a situation prohibited by International Law, but this will not achieve its resolution.

The principle of good faith as well as the interpretative rules of the 1969 and 1986 Vienna Conventions are norms which are also tributaries of the sovereignty of the State. They exist. They rule the application of International Law and States must observe them, but the conception the concerned Parties have of their application to specific cases is not necessarily the same. The contrary is in fact true. The discrepant Parties argue the validity of their respective arguments, which lead to confrontation as they are contrary, and both parties base their arguments on the principle of good faith as well as on the interpretative rules of the Vienna Conventions. As we have mentioned before, they are all unilateral interpretations, valid but divergent. Unless a third arty intervenes, the dispute will persist. In turn, from the perspective of this third party, who is also limited in his task of interpretation by the rules mentioned above.

The panorama we have once more briefly described can be applied to the interpretation of the customary norms. In this regard, the same difficulties and conditioning factors arise. But, due to their customary nature, these become more acute. In effect, if the discrepancy is possible with regard to the written norm – a written text showing the previous agreement concerning the content retained by this text-that possibility is greater when it concerns a customary norm because here the language is supplied by the conduct of the State. As regards these types of norms, the dispute is determined by the invocation of the customary norm with respect to the specific case and this can be a matter of the existence of the norm or of its content and interpretation. But with one particularity: in this case there are no rules in order to guide the interpreter in the resolution of the problem oriented to limiting or marking out the discretion of the State, which is the first interpreter in this field. Even when a third party, on the occasion of a previous case, had specified the content of the customary norm different interpretations of the explanation given by this third party can be given.

Thus, we are moving on thin ice due to the lack of a written text as well as of interpretative rules. But it is also a field in which the role of that third interpreter acquires a greater projection because it is this third party who will determine not only the interpretation but also the existence or not of the norm, its content, as well as the reasonable nature of its application to the specific case.

To carry out this task, the judicial interpreter has been endowed with a number of elements or criteria through case law: practice, which must be generalised, constant and uniform, the temporary element, and the *opinio iuris* whose application to the specific case will allow him to determine the existence of the norm and the resolution of the discrepancy. In practice, States usually resort to those same elements in order to support the invocation of a customary norm or of its content[1]. However, unlike written law, the leeway given to the international judge or arbitrator is greater. First, because he is the only one who can determine the existence of the customary norm. Secondly, because he specifies its content and these con-

---

1 For SUR, custom "appears as the result of an accumulation of successive connected interpretations" (*op. cit.*, p. 189).

siderations are repeated in subsequent case law[2]. Finally, it is the ICJ itself which evaluates the elements of international custom, adapting them in the course of time, specifying them, reducing them to essentials and giving priority or a greater incidence to one of those elements depending on the appraisal of the Court. There are immediate effects upon the Parties concerned in the case in question because the decision of that third party is obligatory.

Thus, International case law becomes a way of systematising Law and has immediate effect initially upon the Parties concerned and is then projected upon the International Community as it is repeated, developed and specified by the same body which pronounced the decision[3].

These characteristics of the interpretation of customary norms guide doctrine to state that in this task the third party (international judge or arbitrator) has in a certain way a sort of "creative, quasi-legislative role and this must be understood as such"[4] or as having "a type of regulatory power"[5].

Such assertions show the important relevance of the judicial or arbitral interpreter's function in this process, and that, both, as regards the hypothesis of proceedings in contentious cases as well as in advisory proceedings. As we have said, case law decisions do not only have effects as regards the specific case so it is not difficult to understand the importance of the interpretations of the ICJ, especially in an International Community as we have today in which there is no body to which States must by obligation turn to in order to resolve problems of interpretation due to decentralized and non hierarchical structure of this Community. This fact, as we have stated in preceding pages, leads to the existence of concurrent interpretations of the Parties involved in a specific problem of interpretation. Interpretations that are opposed, unilateral, but have the same validity independently of the fact that any one of these can be an interpretation that could be imposed on third States.

Thus, the interpretations of the ICJ which are located initially at the same level as those made by the Parties concerned are highly important, and are eventually

---

2 Which leads H. TORRIONE to state that, as regards customary law, the interpretation occurs when the norm is produced "no customary law comes about unless a previous process of interpretation has taken place" (*L'influence des conventions de codification sur la coutume en droit international public*, eds. Universitaires, Fribourg, 1989, p. 224). See also GUGGENHEIM, P., *Traité de droit international public*, 2nd ed., vol. I, Geneva, 1967, pages 93 et seq. and KAMMERHOFER, J., "Uncertainty in the formal sources of international law: customary international law and some of its problems", *European Journal of International Law*, 15 (2004) 3, pp. 523-553.

3 See in this regard the case of the *Maritime Delimitation in the Area Between Greenland and Jan Mayen* (ICJ, *Reports 1993*, p. 62, para. 5 in fine) the value given by Article 38 of the Statute of the I.C.J. as a subsidiary means for the determination of rules of law must not be forgotten.

4 HAGGENMACHER, R., "La doctrine du droit coutumier dans la pratique de la Cour internationale", *RGDIP*, 1986/1, page 114.

5 DUPUY, P.M., *Droit ...*, *op. cit.*, page 229.

imposed as a result of the acceptance of their jurisdiction in each specific case and may have effects on the rest of the International Community to the extent that they fix the position of the Court as regards the question addressed. Thus, it has been stated that the decisions of the ICJ are endowed with considerable real authority, and fill a vacuum[6].

In the *process of interpretation of custom*, three phases can be distinguished:

- The *determination of its existence* which implies an operation for the selection of facts, attitudes and conduct of the Parties in question by the interpreter. Thus, the Parties themselves invoke a practice to support their respective thesis, which is generally combined with other kinds of considerations, based on the principles within which they wish to frame it. At first, unilateral acts (of domestic or International Law such as acts of International Organizations, advisory opinions of the I.C.J., etc.) whose recognition or opposability can condition custom, play an important role[7].
- The *classification* of such attitudes and conduct as customary practice. This fact makes it possible to establish the scope of the customary norm and to determine whether it is imposed on the State in question or not[8].

The *determination of the content of the norm* and the extraction of the rights and obligations applicable to the case in question[9].

The interpretative task of the Judge as regards the customary norms is not limited to an analysis of the facts as such. In this sense it is said that these facts would by themselves enable the judge to provide the solution to the problem. Consequently, the judge must "analyse, classify, evaluate or minimise such facts, as the Parties do, based on a thesis whose choice depends to a great extent

---

6 TORRIONE, H., *op. cit.*, p. 228. He adds that I.C.J. case law, "in a general way, is a manifestation of the existence inside the International Community of a coordinated interpretation of customary law imposed upon particular interpretations" (cf. *ibid.*). On the other hand, the value which Article 38 of the I.C.J. Statute gives to judicial decisions as a means for the determination of rules of law must be taken into account.

7 See TORRIONE, H., *op. cit.*, p. 215. On this question, as regards the importance of precedents in the formation of a customary norm, see Roben, V., "Le précédent dans le jurisprudence de la Cour internationale", *German Yearbook of International Law*, 1989, vol. 32, pages 382-407.

8 Thus, the interpretation is not only an act of knowledge, but, once all the judicially possible solutions have been considered, includes an act of will: the choice of promoting one of these (cf. TORRIONE, H., *op. cit.*, page 221).

9 Thus, in the case of the *Maritime Delimitation in the Area Between Greenland and Jan Mayen*, the I.C.J. states that the "statement of an 'equitable solution' as the aim of any delimitation process reflects the requirements of customary law as regards the delimitation both of continental shelf and of exclusive economic zones" (I.C.J., *Reports 1993*, p. 59). In the case concerning *Land, Island and Maritime Frontier Dispute*, the ICJ stated that, when proof exists, acquiescence and recognition can be used as factors for the interpretation of the customary applicable law (cf. ICJ, *Reports 1992*, page 401).

on his appraisal[10]. For this task, the ICJ also has recourse to international case law. Thus, in the case of the *Maritime Delimitation of the Area Between Greenland and Jan Mayen*, it states that the judicial decisions based on the customary law applied to the delimitation of the continental shelf between coasts situated opposite each other have considered the middle line to be a provisional line which can be adjusted or displaced in order to reach an equitable result, and adds that the special circumstances appear as circumstances which can modify the result produced by an automatic application of the principle of equidistance[11].

As we have state before, in order to carry out this task, the interpreter has created a number elements or criteria in the light of which he will determine the existence and content of the customary norm as regards the specific case. These criteria are quoted in Article 38 of the Statute of the I.C.J. when it speaks of international custom as "evidence of a general practice accepted as law" and it is from here that the Court extracts and develops them, specifying their content and adapting them to the case it is called to pronounce on.

With regard to those elements or criteria, and without prejudice to the analysis we will make in the next Section of this Chapter, doctrine has focused especially on the *opinio juris* or legal conviction that action is being taken in accordance with law to the extent that the determination of this element in the specific case depends on the exclusive evaluation of the judge. It has been said that the *opinio juris* depends on the interpreter while the other elements of custom would be "simple standards or criteria of evaluation, formal frameworks through which the interpreter would appreciate the material that is submitted to him"[12]. Thus an attempt is made to show the dependence that the *opinio iuris* has with regard to the international judge because it is the judge who appreciates whether that legal conviction of its obligatory nature is or is not present in the norm invoked by the Parties. All depends on him, so the weight of the element of practice which has been built up by precedents and subsequent conduct is displaced towards that of *opinio iuris*. This is why it is stated that more attention will be paid to the interpreter and to the conditions determining his perception of the phenomenon than "the elements alleged to build customary law[13]. Along the same lines P. M. DUPUY holds that the theory of the two elements on which the ICJ bases interna-

---

[10] HAGGENMACHER, R., *op. cit.*, p. 118. On the interpretation of customary norms by the internal judge see with regard to France, TREBOUL, G. "Le droit international non ecrit devant le juge administrative. Quelques reflexions", *RGDIP*, 1991/2, p. 321-370.

[11] See ICJ, *Reports 1993*, p. 60.

[12] HAGGENMACHER, R., *op. cit.*, p. 117. See also MENDELSON, M.H., "The Formation of Customary International Law", *R.C.A.D.I.*, 1998, vol. 272, pp. 155-410 and YEE, S., "The News that Opinio Juris 'Is not a Necessary Element of Customary (International) Law' Is Greatly Exaggerated", *G.Y.I.L.*, 2000, vol. 43, pp. 227-238.

[13] HAGGENMACHER, R., *op. cit.*, p. 117. And in the opinion of P.M. DUPUY, as the basis of the validity of the norm invoked "lies less in the conviction of the States than in that of the judges" ("Le juge et ...", *op. cit.*, p. 586).

tional custom is insufficient to explain the bases of the validity of the rule, and only serves to present "as a formalised procedure what is, in fact, a more or less spontaneous social process"[14].

Is the leeway of the international judge (or arbitrator) really so broad? In this regard, some hold that the conviction of the international judge concerning the existence of the customary norm "must be preceded by a similar conviction from the States themselves – that is to say, the *opinio iuris*- and be based upon it"[15]. However, who carries out this evaluation? Undoubtedly the third party who has knowledge of the dispute. Along the same lines there is the reflection provoked by the reading of article 38.1.b) of the Statute of the ICJ when it refers to international custom as proof of a practice "generally accepted as law". It is true that the existence or not of that general acceptance will be established starting from the analysis of the conduct of the State. But, who determines that the conduct of the State in the specific case is due to its conviction of its obligatory nature? Only the third party to whom the dispute is submitted can decide this. And this third party, which criteria will he use? Which criteria does the I.C.J. use? As we will see later, neither the frequency nor the regular character of the acts (whether these be action or lack of action) are sufficient. It is necessary for the *opinio iuris* to be present but the perception of its presence or not in the rule invoked in the specific case corresponds to the judge, and this shows the extensive liberty the judge has at the time he evaluates the elements which make up the customary norm as he construes this[16]. Finally we must refer to the cases of *interaction* between custom and treaty because interpretation has a relevant place in this field too. Thus, in treaties of codification as regards the need to determine what the treaty involves concerning progressive development and what it has of codified customary law.

It has been said that that task is a problem of interpretation of the concepts of progressive development as well as of codified customary law, whose resolution

---

[14] And he adds that "When it wa hindered by the drafting of article 38 of the Statute, the Court tried to emancipate itself in this way" (DUPUY, P.M., "Le juge et ...", *op. cit.*, p. 586).

[15] TORRIONE H., *op. cit.*, p. 233. Cf. FERRARI BRAVO, L., "Méthodes de recherche de la coutume internationale dans la pratique des Etats", *R. des C.*, vol 192 (1985-III), pages 233-330. Especially pages 246 et seq.

[16] This fact is stressed by Judge M. SOERENSEN in his dissenting opinion concerning the case of the *North Sea Continental Shelf* when he states,

> "The *possibility has thus been reserved* – by the Court– *of recognizing* the rapid emergence of a new rule of customary law based on the recent practice of States. This is particularly important in view of the extremely dynamic process of evolution in which the international community is engaged at the present stage of history" (ICJ, *Reports 1969*, p. 243). The italics are ours.

will require the consideration of the date when the provisions of the treaty can be applied[17].

Secondly, interaction between custom and treaty is also present in relationship to subsequent law because, due to the same value of both norms, custom can interpret, modify or revoke a treaty. This leads us to the interpretation of the treaty by the subsequent practice of the Parties. In this case the behaviour or the conduct of the Parties is sometimes held as a way to evaluate the intention of the Parties, helping the interpreter to specify the sense of the text. But the conduct of the Parties can appear to create a new rule of law. In this case, this conduct must be taken into account in the same way as the other obligations that link the Parties. As Cot states, "in one case subsequent practice, *a guide showing the will of the Parties*, is a means of interpretation. In the other, *the source of a new obligation*, it gives rise to a legal norm"[18].

The ICJ has again pronounced on the relationship between conventional and customary norms (from the perspective of their application and interpretation) in recent cases such as those of the *Military and Paramilitary Activities in and Against Nicaragua* and of the *Maritime Delimitation in the Area Between Greenland and Jan Mayen*[19]. As is already known, in the first case, as a result of the reservations of the United States of America which prevented the Court from applying international treaties to the dispute, it was obliged to pronounce on the existence of conventional and customary rules with identical content. In this case, it was a matter of the rules regarding the prohibition of the threat and use of force, non-intervention in the internal affairs of a State, and individual or collective self-defence. The ICJ and the 1974 Final Act of Helsinki on cooperation and security in Europe, which analysed the conduct of the U.S.A. as well as that of Nicaragua with regard to these principles in order to conclude the existence of an *opinio iuris* of both States with regard to the aforementioned obligations[20].

---

17 Vid Sur, S., *op. cit.*, p. 192. One example of interaction examined recently by the ICJ is the case of the *Maritime Delimitation in the Area between Greenland and Jan Mayen* where, in relationship with the delimitation of the continental shelf, the Court states that the fact that the 1958 Geneva Convention, ratified by Denmark and Norway, should be applied to the present case, "does not mean that Article 6 thereof can be interpreted and applied either without reference to customary law on the subject, or wholly independently of the fact that a fishery zone boundary is also in question in these waters" (I.C.J., *Reports 1993*, p. 58).

18 Cot, J.P. "La conduite subséquente des parties à un traité", *RGDIP*, 1966, vol. 70 p. 638 (vid also p. 663). The italics are in the original. On the other hand this is a retroactive interpretation which the treaty again takes up from the beginning "nothing prevents it from developing problems little by little regulated by the treaty" (Sur, *op. cit.*, pages 192 et seq.) For an example of practice subsequent to the treaty see Cot, J.P., "L'interprétation de l'accord franco-américain…", *op. cit.*, pages 370 et seq.

19 See ICJ, *Reports 1986* and *Reports* 1993, respectively.

20 See ICJ, *Reports 1986*, pages 99, 100 and 107. In the case of the *Maritime Delimitation in the Area Between Greenland and Jan Mayen* the I.C.J used the arbitral award of the case on the *Gulf of Maine* and stated that "the equidistance/special circumstances rule of the 1958 Convention is, in the light of this 1977 Decision, to be regarded as expressing a general norm based on equitable principles"(I.C.J., *Reports 1993*, p. 58).

In the second, the Court, among other questions, addressed the matter of the delimitation of fishing zones between States with coasts located opposite each other and stated that the achievement of an equitable solution is a requirement derived from customary International Law. In order to achieve this, conventional law requires the examination of all "special circumstances"[21] while "customary law based upon equitable principles on the other hand requires the investigation of 'relevant circumstances'", and this concept can be described as "a fact necessary to be taken into account in the delimitation process"[22]. Although these are different categories due to their origin and denomination, both share the fact that their use must enable the achievement of an equitable result (in one case, the delimitation of spaces belonging to States with coasts opposite each other; in the other, the delimitation of fishing zones between States in the same situation).

The I.C.J. reached the conclusion that it was right to resort to the median line, drawn provisionally, as first step in the operation of delimitation, and then addressed whether in the case submitted to its competence there were special circumstances justifying the adjustment or the displacement of that median line (which is the criterion regarding adapting the median line to the special circumstances)[23]. The Court will reach a positive conclusion when it appreciates the following special circumstances: the disparity of coastal lengths in the relevant area, the access to resources and the presence of ice in that zone[24].

As regards a separate existence of conventional and customary norms relating to the same matter, the I.C.J., in the case concerning *Military and Paramilitary Activities in and Against Nicaragua*, states that the fact that such obligations are codified or incorporated into multilateral conventions does not mean that they cease to exist and to be applied as principles of customary law, even with regard to States that are Parties to such conventions. Thus,

> "Principles such as those of the non-use of force, non-intervention, respect for the independence and territorial integrity of States, and the freedom of navigation, continue to be binding as part of customary

---

[21] A criterion retained by the 1958 Geneva Convention on Territorial Sea and Contiguous Zone and on Continental Shelf regarding the delimitation of these spaces when it is a question of States whose coasts are located opposite each other.

[22] This is deduced from general International Law as developed trough the case law of the Court and arbitral case law, and through the work of the Third United Nations Conference on the Law of the Sea", which also uses the concept of "relevant circumstances" (I.C.J., *Reports 1993*, p. 62).

[23] See *ibid*., p. 64.

[24] See *ibid*., pages 67, 70 et seq. and 72, respectively. Nevertheless, the Court will reject others: the population, socio-economic factors and the cultural factor (*ibid*., pages 73 et seq.).

> law, despite the operation of provisions of conventional law in which they have been incorporated "[25].

Therefore, one norm does not supplant the other[26]. However, in addition, two identical norms in conventional International Law and in customary International Law "are also distinguishable by reference to the methods of interpretation and application"[27]. In conclusion, according to the ICJ "it is clear that customary international law continues to exist and to apply, separately from international treaty law, even when the two categories of law have an identical content"[28].

Concerning this question the I.I.L., in its resolution approved on 1995 in Lisbon, has adopted a criterion which departs from international case law. Its Conclusion No. 12 says that even when an a priori hierarchy between treaty an custom as sources of International Law does not exist, "however, as a matter of the application of international law in cases of dispute, relevant norms deriving from a treaty binding upon the parties to the dispute will prevail over norms deriving from customary law, save where the norm deriving from a treaty contravenes a rule of jus cogens, or has been subsequently modified by a latter norm of customary law"[29]. This position of the I.I.L. is not irrelevant. Firstly, it is surprising that it asserts this primacy because the I.C.J. in the case concerning *Military and Paramilitary Activi-*

---

[25] ICJ, *Reports 1984*, pages 424 et seq., para. 73. The ICJ repeats this assertion in its Judgement on the merits of the case, on 27 june1986 (I.C.J., *Reports 1986*, p. 93, para. 174) In this last it adds,

> "even if a treaty norm and a customary norm relevant to the present dispute were to have exactly the same content, this would not be a reason for the Court to take the view that the operation of the treaty process must necessarily deprive the customary norm of its separate applicability" (*ibid.*, p. 94, paragraph 175).

[26] The ICJ adds, "It rather demonstrates that in the field in question, the importance of which for the present dispute need hardly be stressed, customary international law continues to exist alongside treaty law. The areas governed by the two sources of law thus do not overlap exactly, and the rules do not have the same content" (I.C.J., *Reports 1986*, p. 94, para. 176).

[27] As "A State may accept a rule contained in a treaty not simply because it favours the application of the rule itself, but also because the treaty establishes what that State regards as desirable institutions or mechanisms to ensure implementation of the rule. Thus, if that rule parallels a rule of customary international law, two rules of the same content are subject to separate treatment as regards the organs competent to verify their implementation, depending on whether they are customary rules or treaty rules" (*ibid.*, pp. 95 et seq. paragraph 178).

[28] I*bid.*, p. 96, para. 179. Cf. GONZALEZ CAMPOS; J.D., SANCHEZ RODRIGUEZ, L.I., ANDRES SAENZ DE SANTA MARIA, M. P., *Curso …*, *op. cit.*, pages 123-125. See also RODRIGUEZ CARRION, A., *Lecciones de Derecho Internacional Público*, 5th ed., Tecnos, Madrid, p. 231 et seq. The same criterion is adopted by the I.I.L. in conclusion number 11 of its Lisbon resolution (see I.I.L., *Yearbook of the Institute of International Law*, 1995, vol. 66-I, Pedone, Paris, 1995, pages 247-248.

[29] IIL, *Yearbook…*, *op. cit.*, p. 248.

ties in and against Nicaragua[30] stated the opposite criterion. In addition, the exception based on the primacy of the *jus cogens* over the Law of Treaties as stated in Article 53 of the 1969 Vienna Convention on the Law of Treaties states, a treaty is void if, at the time of its conclusion, it conflicts with a peremptory norm of general international law, so that it can not pose problems of hierarchy. It simply does not exist nor produce any legal effect. And in the case of a new norm of general International Law, article 64 of the same Convention states that "if a new peremptory norm of general international law emerges, any existing treaty which is in conflict with that norm becomes void and terminates". Finally, to accept that conclusion of the I.I.L. would lead in practice to important legal consequences when interpreting basic sectors of International Law such as those conventionally taken into account in the Charter of the United Nations but later developed and specified by resolutions of the General Assembly. One of the consequences would be that the I.C.J. would be limited in its jurisdictional function if it had to necessarily give primacy to the Charter, despite the hypothesis present in Article 103 of the Charter, disregarding the customary development of its most fundamental obligations.

2 The interpreter limits the discretion of the State. The conception of the interpreter prevails as regards the discrepancy: The dependence of the State

In the preceding pages we have shown interpreter's task in relationship with customary norms. Here, we will analyse I.C.J. case law.

The starting point of the interpretative process of the Court itself is usually taken to be the referral to article 38.1, b) of its Statute, according to which the Court,

> "whose function is to decide in accordance with international law such disputes as are submitted to it shall apply:
>
> b) international custom, as evidence of a general practice accepted as law;"[31].

Nevertheless, it should be remembered that it is the Court that appreciates, values and gives content to each one of these elements.

As we have stated before, the general theory of international custom is a construction built up by the I.C.J. starting from Article 38.1.b) of its Statute and based on its case law. Effectively, through the different cases submitted to it in this regard, the Court has specified the conditions the element of practice must have, the consequences derived from passivity and abstention, the characteristics of the temporary element, the necessity of a legal conviction or an *opinio iuris*, who has the burden of proof and, finally, the elements required for the existence of a gen-

[30] Cf. ICJ, *Reports 1986*, pages 95 et seq.

[31] Cf. CAHIER, Ph., "Cours général ...", *op. cit.*, pages 223-247.

eral, regional or local custom (besides the hypothesis concerning interaction between custom and treaty already studied).

With regard to *practice*, this is constituted by acts carried out by State bodies responsible for international relations, by bodies of International Organizations as well as by the domestic law of States with international relevance (legislative measures, judicial decisions, etc.). In any of these situations, we find precedents which acquire value at the time they are generalised[32] independently of the fact that some of them could constitute elements which demonstrate the official position of the State regarding the point in question.

This is why States, in their mutual relationships, have a vigilant attitude as regards the conduct of other States. Especially, in cases concerning them where they expressly manifest their refusal to admit certain conduct in order to prevent the legal relevance of the precedent. Analysis of practice also shows that, on occasions, the States satisfy some expectations of other States but make the reservation that such acceptance is that it is limited to the specific case and this precedent regarding its conduct does not serve for future cases. Or they also admit, on occasions, the expectations of others but manifest that such conduct must be interpreted *ex gratia* and not because they feel themselves legally bound. Taking these considerations into account only clear precedents "acquire value to determine the existence of a custom as expression of the consent of the State"[33].

As concerns the relationship with *the element of practice*, the I.C.J. addressed this in one of its first cases concerning the *Asylum Case*, and stressed two points: first, that the conduct in question can be active or passive, as we will see later, and must be "in accordance with a constant and uniform usage practised by the States in question" and then, that this usage "is the expression of a right appertaining to the State" which invokes it[34]. This is the State with the burden of proof[35].

---

[32] Vid RODRIGUEZ CARRION, A., *Lecciones de ..., op. cit.*, pages 224 et seq. Cf. FERRARI BRAVO, L., *op. cit.*, page 246 and BROWNLIE, I., "Some problems in the evaluation of the practice of status as an element of custom", in *Studi di diritto internazionale in onnore di Gaetano Arangio Ruiz*, 2004, vol. I, pp. 313-318.

[33] GONZALEZ CAMPOS, J.D., SANCHEZ RODRIGUEZ, L., and ANDRES SAENZ DE SANTA MARIA, M. P., *Curso ..., op. cit*, p. 111. The words in italics corresponds to the original. Cf. also, JIMENEZ DE ARECHAGA, E., "The work and the jurisprudence of the International Court of Justice", *B.Y.I.L.*, 1987, pages 1-38.

[34] It adds that "This follows from article 38 of the Statute of the Court, which refers to international custom 'as evidence of a general practice accepted as law'" (ICJ, *Reports 1950*, pages 275 et seq.).

[35] In the *Asylum Case* referred to, the ICJ states,

> "The Party which relies on a custom of this kind must prove that this custom is established in such a manner that it has become binding on the other Party. The Colombian Government must prove that the rule invoked by it is in accordance with a constant and uniform usage practised by the States in question, and that this usage is the expression of a right appertaining to the State granting asylum and a duty incumbent on the territorial State" (*ibid.*).

In the *Fisheries Case*, the I.C.J. adds that evidence shall be "convincing" (I.C.J., *Reports 1951*, p. 138).

Later, in the case concerning the *Continental Shelf (Libyan Arab Jamahiriya)*, the I.C.J. will state that this practice shall be effective[36].

Secondly, the practice is not usable against the State which has repeatedly opposed it. This conclusion derives from I.C.J. jurisprudence in the *Asylum Case* and in the *Fisheries Case*. In the first case, the Court said that even in the case that the right of asylum existed only between certain States of Latin America,

> "it could not be invoked against Peru which, far from having by its attitude adhered to it, has, on the contrary, repudiated it by refraining from ratifying the Montevideo Conventions of 1933 and 1939, which were the first to include a rule concerning the qualification of the offence in matters of diplomatic asylum"[37].

In the *Fisheries Case* and with regard to the British argument of the ten mile rule as a rule of International Law on the closing of bays, the Court said that even if this were so (and it was not the case), such a rule "would appear to be inapplicable as against Norway inasmuch as she has always opposed any attempt to apply it to the Norwegian coast"[38].

Thirdly, practice must be *constant* and *uniform*. Both characteristics appear since the sentence of the I.C.J. concerning the *Asylum Case* in 1950, and mean that practice shall be consistent and repeated on successive occasions without contradictory conduct. In such cases, the Court emphasizes the lack of consistence that hinders the possibility of speaking about a regional custom concerning the right of diplomat asylum,

> "The facts brought to the knowledge of the Court disclose so much uncertainty and contradiction, so much fluctuation and discrepancy in the exercise of diplomatic asylum and in the official views expressed on various occasions, there has been so much inconsistency in the rapid succession of conventions on asylum, ratified by some States and rejected by others, and the practice has been so much influenced by considerations of political expediency in the various cases, that it is not possible to discern in all this any constant and uniform usage, accepted as law, with regard to the alleged rule of unilateral and definitive qualification of the offence"[39].

---

[36] "The material of customary international law is to be looked for primarily in the actual practice and *opinio iuris* of States" (ICJ, *Reports 1985*, pages 29 et seq., para. 27).

[37] ICJ, *Reports 1950*, pages 277 et seq.

[38] ICJ, *Reports 1951*, page 131.

[39] ICJ, *Reports 1950*, page 278. In the *Fisheries Case* the I.C.J. states,

> "although the ten-mile rule has been adopted by certain States both in their national law and in their treaties and conventions, and although certain arbitral decisions have applied it as between these States, other States have adopted a different limit. Consequently, the ten-mile rule has not acquired the authority of a general rule of international law" (I.C.J., *Reports 1951*, p. 131).

This criterion is repeated in subsequent cases. Thus, in the case of the *Temple of Preah Vihear*, where the Court stated that,

> "when a country has evinced as clearly as Thailand did in 1950, and indeed by its consistent attitude over many years, an intention to submit itself to the compulsory jurisdiction of what constituted at the time the principal international tribunal, the Court could not accept the plea that this intention had been defeated and nullified by some defect not involving any flaw in the consent given, ..."[40].

In addition, the conduct which gives rise to this practice can be *active* (as we have just seen), or *passive*. An example of this, which had negative effects for the passive State is the judgement in the case concerning the *Temple of Preah Vihear* as a result of the passivity of Thailand in relation to the frontier maps drawn up by the mixed Franco-Thai Commission which placed the temple in Cambodian territory. The Court said,

> "Even if there were any doubt as to Siam's acceptance of the map in 1908, and hence of the frontier indicated thereon, the Court would consider, in the light of the subsequent course of events, that Thailand is now precluded by her conduct from asserting that she did not accept it. She has, for fifty years, enjoyed such benefits as the treaty of 1904 conferred on her, ... France, and through her Cambodia, relied on the Thailand's acceptance of the map ... It is not now open to Thailand, while continuing to claim and enjoy the benefits of the settlement, to deny that she was ever a consenting party to it"[41].

---

[40] ICJ, *Reports 1961*, p. 34. In the case of the *Arbitral Award Made by the King of Spain on 23 December 1906*, the Court states that Nicaragua,

> "by express declaration and by conduct, recognized the Award as valid and it is no longer open to Nicaragua to go back upon that recognition and to challenge the validity of the Award" (I.C.J., *Reports 1960*, p. 213).

Also in the case of the *North Sea Continental Shelf*, concerning the equidistance principle of Article 6 of the 1958 Geneva Convention, where it states that the cases cited "are inconclusive, and insufficient to bear the weight sought to be put upon them as evidence of such a settled practice, ..." (I.C.J., *Reports 1969*, p. 45).

[41] ICJ, *Reports 1962*, page 32. And adds,

> "as a whole, Thailand's subsequent conduct confirms and bears out her original acceptance, and that Thailand's acts on the ground do not suffice to negative this. Both Parties, by their conduct, recognized the line and thereby in effect agreed to regard it as being the frontier " (*ibid.*, p. 33).

In the *Fisheries Case*, it is the United Kingdom of Great Britain which suffers the consequences of its prolonged abstention when it did not react when Norway pronounced the Decree of 1869 which contained the criterion of the delimitation of ten miles in order to close off bays. When Great Britain alleged it did not know of this system of delimitation, the ICJ responded that,

Also in the case of the *Legal Consequences for States of the Continued Presence of South Africa in Namibia (South West Africa) notwithstanding Security Council Resolution 276 (1970)*, in which South Africa questioned the legality of Resolution 284 (1970) of the Security Council as it had been adopted despite the abstention of two of its permanent members, contradicting what is laid down in article 27.3 of the Charter when it states that the "decisions of the Security Council on all other matters shall be made by an affirmative vote of nine members, including the concurring votes of the permanent members;". The I.C.J. answered that,

> "by abstaining, a member does not signify its objection to the approval of what is being proposed; in order to prevent the adoption of a resolution requiring unanimity of the permanent members, a permanent member has only to cast a negative vote. This procedure followed by the Security Council, which has continued unchanged after the amendment in 1965 of Article 27 of the Charter, has been generally accepted by Members of the United Nations and evidences a general practice of that Organization"[42].

The case law of the I.C.J. repeats these characteristics of practice (general, constant and uniform) until 1969, the year of the case concerning the *North Sea Continental Shelf*, which constitutes a point of inflexion in the opinion of the Court as regards the two elements of custom: the general character of practice and the temporary element.

Until that case, the Court did not reduce its requirements concerning both elements. On the contrary, in its judgement in the North Sea Continental Shelf, the I.C.J. tones down the criterion of the *generality of practice*, stating that,

> "it might be that, even without the passage of any considerable period of time, a very widespread and representative participation in the convention might suffice of itself, provided it included that of States whose interests were specially affected"[43].

> "As a coastal State on the North Sea, greatly interested in the fisheries in this area, as a maritime Power traditionally concerned with the law of the sea and concerned particularly to defend the freedom of the seas, the United Kingdom could not have been ignorant of the decree of 1869 which had at once provoked a request for explanations by the French Government. Nor, knowing of it, could it have been under any misapprehension as to the significance of its terms, which clearly described it as constituting the application of a system" (I.C.J., *Reports 1951*, p. 139).

Cf. also the quoted case of the *Arbitral Award Made by the King of Spain on 23 December 1906* involving Nicaragua and Honduras (I.C.J., *Reports 1960*, p. 214), where passivity acts against Nicaragua.

42 ICJ, *Reports 1971*, p. 22, para. 22.

43 ICJ, *Reports 1969*, p. 42. Cf JIMENEZ DE ARECHAGA, E., The work and ...", *op. cit.*, pages 31 et seq. and VISMARA, F., "La prova di una pratica generale acettata come diritto nella prassi della Corte internazionale di giustizia", *Comunità Internazionale*, 2000, vol. LV, nº 3, pp. 439-463.

This evolution finds its most recent expression in the case concerning the *Military and Paramilitary Activities in and Against Nicaragua*, when the Court clearly states that it is not to be expected that in the practice of States the application of the rules in question should have been perfect:

> "The Court does not consider that, for a rule to be established as customary, the corresponding practice must be in absolutely rigorous conformity with the rule. In order to deduce the existence of customary rules, the Court deems it sufficient that the conduct of States should, in general, be consistent with such rules, and that instances of State conduct inconsistent with a given rule should generally have been treated as breaches of that rule, not as indications of the recognition of a new rule. If a State acts in a way prima facie incompatible with a recognized rule, but defends its conduct by appealing to exceptions or justifications contained within the rule itself then whether or not State's conduct is in fact justifiable on the basis, the significance of that attitude is to confirm rather than to weaken the rule"[44].

As regards the *temporary element*, as we have stated, the change in the interpretation of the I.C.J. is also found in its judgement concerning the *North Sea Continental Shelf*. Here, the Court states that a considerable period of time is not required for a custom to be built up but it must be the practice of the States specially affected[45]. Until then, the cases addressed by the Court involved practice over along period of time. Thus, in the case of the *Right of Passage over Indian Territory*, the practice involved more than 125 years; in the case of the *Temple of Preah Vihear*, 50 years; in the *Fisheries Case*, more than 60 years.

Consequently, the temporary element must be relativised at the time the customary norm is interpreted[46]. The change of criterion or its adaptation is justified by

---

[44] ICJ *Reports* 1986, p. 98, para. 186. Cf. DUPUY, P.M., Le juge et …", *op. cit.*, p. 573.

[45] The ICJ states,

> "Although the passage of only a short period of time is not necessarily, or of itself, a bar to the formation of a new rule of customary international law on the basis of what was originally a purely conventional rule, an indispensable requirement would be that within the period in question, short though it might be, State practice, including that of States whose interests are specially affected, should have been both extensive and virtually uniform in the sense of the provision invoked;- and should moreover have ocurred in such a way as to show a general recognition that a rule of law or legal obligation is involved" (I.C.J., *Reports 1969*, p. 43).

[46] This relativisation is backed up by the rapidity in the transmission of information in the contemporary International Community and expressed in specific terms, as CAHIER shows, in the fact that the conduct of the different States is known almost immediately by the rest of the International community. On the other hand, the increased number of international conferences and meetings of the bodies of International Organizations provides States with the opportunity to make public its statements on any question, this was not possible in the last Century nor at the beginning of the XXth Century (cf. "Cours …", *op. cit.*, p. 226).

the I.C.J. due to the necessity of taking into account the action of factors that are characteristic of the socio-historical structure of the international order. So, in the *Fisheries Case* where the I.C.J. takes geographical factors into consideration in order to evaluate the interests of the States in question), the economic interests "peculiar to a region, the reality and importance of which are clearly evidenced by a long usage (United Kingdom v. Norway)[47], the existence of social necessity[48], etc. Finally, the I.C.J. resorts to the element of the *opinio iuris* in its case law concerning the interpretation of customary norms[49]. Thus, in the case of the *North Sea Continental Shelf*, the ICJ states that,

> "Not only must the acts concerned amount to a settled practice, but they must also be such, or be carried out in a such a way, as to be evidence of a belief that this practice is rendered obligatory by the existence of a rule of law requiring it. The need for such a belief, i.e., the existence of a subjective element, is implicit in the very notion of the *opinio iuris sive necessitatis*. The States concerned must therefore feel that they are conforming to what amounts to a legal obligation. The frequency, or even habitual character of the acts is not in itself enough"[50].

The necessity of the presence of such legal obligation is repeated subsequently in the case of the *Continental Shelf (Libyan Arab Jamahiriya/Malta*[51], and in the case of the *Military and Paramilitary Activities in and against Nicaragua*[52].

---

[47] ICJ, *Reports 1951*, p. 133.

[48] Cf. in this regard, the case of the *Fisheries Jurisdiction (United Kingdom v. Iceland),* (ICJ, *Reports 1974*, pages 191 et seq.).

[49] This was present in the case law of the PCJI, as in the *Lotus case*, when it states that,

> "Only if such abstention were based on their being conscious of having a duty to abstain would it be possible to speak of an international custom" (P.C.I.J. *Series A*, No. 10, 1927, p. 28).

[50] This is the conviction which differentiates these acts from "many international acts, e.g., in the field of ceremonial and protocol, which are performed almost invariably, but which are motivated only by considerations of courtesy, convenience or tradition, and not by any sense of a legal duty"(both quotations are from the I.C.J., *Reports 1969*, p. 44). The italics corresponds to the original.

[51] Thus,

> "the material of customary international law is to be looked for primarily in the actual practice and *opinio juris* of States, even though multilateral conventions may have an important role to play in recording and defining rules deriving from custom, or indeed in developing them" (I.C.J., *Reports 1985*, p. 29, paragraph 27. The part in italics corresponds to the original).

[52] In which the ICJ states that,

> "The Court must satisfy itself that the existence of the rule in the *opinio juris* of States is confirmed by practice (I.C.J., *Reports* 1986, p. 98, paragraph 184. The italics correspond to the original).

This latter case also has the additional interest derived from the fact that it concerns the interpretation by the I.C.J. through non conventional acts of the customary norm concerning the illegality of the use or threat of force (due to the reservations of the United States of America as regards the jurisdiction of the Court). In that case, the search for the *opinio iuris* is carried out by the Court through the analysis of the resolutions of the United Nations as well as of the declaration on principles governing the mutual relations of States participating in the Conference on Security and Cooperation in Europe (Helsinki, 1 August 1975). Its conclusions confirm the attitude we have taken in the preceding pages when stating that it is not reasonable to reject in aprioristically the legal character of institutional norms[53].

In order to determine the existence of an *opinio iuris* concerning the binding value of the duty of States to refrain from use or threat of force, the ICJ first analyses the attitude of the Parties in the dispute with regard to United Nations General Assembly resolutions. The Court acts in such a way to specify if it is possible to deduce from that attitude "with the necessary care" the existence of such legal conviction. According to the Court,

> "This *opinio iuris* may, though with all due caution, be deduced from *inter alia*, the attitude of the Parties and the attitude of States towards certain General Assembly resolutions, and particularly resolution 2625 (XXV) entitled 'Declaration on Principles of International Law concerning Friendly Relations and Co-operation among States in accordance with the Charter of the United Nations'. The effect of consent to the text of such resolutions cannot be understood as merely that of a 'reiteration or elucidation' of the treaty commitment undertaken in the Charter. On the contrary, it may be understood as an acceptance of the validity of the rule or set of rules declared by the resolution by themselves"[54].

And adds,

> "It would therefore seem apparent that the attitude referred to expresses an *opinio iuris* respecting such rule (or set of rules), to be thenceforth treated separately from the provisions, especially those of an institutional kind, to which it is subject on the treaty-law plane of the Charter"[55].

---

[53] The existence of the *opinio iuris* of the States as specified by the I.C.J. in the case concerning the *Delimitation of the Maritime Boundary in the Gulf of Maine Area* "can be tested by induction based on the analysis of a sufficiently extensive and convincing practice, and not by deduction from preconceived ideas". (I.C.J., *Reports 1984*, p. 229). The same can be stated with regard to the legal effects of the resolutions of the United Nations General Assembly.

[54] ICJ, *Reports 1986*, pages 99 et seq.

[55] *Ibid.*

The same conclusion derives from the 1975 Helsinki Declaration, in which the States participating repeat the same prohibition. In opinion of the I.C.J.,

> "Acceptance of a text in these terms confirms the existence of an *opinio iuris* of the participating States prohibiting the use of force in international relations"[56].

According to doctrine, the *opinio iuris* referred to by the Court means that what is really important is to prove that such States have consented, accept the practice as custom, and this is done through practice. Therefore, the *opinio iuris* is the proof that they have consented, and that the practice has become a norm[57].

In the opinion of P.M. DUPUY, the recent case law of the ICJ also illustrates another procedure, different from article 38 of its Statute, through which the international judge can identify the general rule, and in which the practice is not only relativised but can be said to be made subsidiary as regards the principle which illustrates it[58]. This author bases his statement on the case of the *Border Dispute between Mali and Burkina Fasso* in which the Court based the "general principle" of *uti possidetis* not on the practice of the State but on the political phenomenon of decolonisation, of which it is a logical consequence. Also, in the case concerning *Military and Paramilitary Activities in and against Nicaragua* where, in the opinion of P.M. DUPUY, "practice is neither relativised, nor derived from the logic of the principle it demonstrate, nor excluded. It is simply absent and the authority of the rules involved seems be *derived* from the ethical principles justifying them. The judge does not extract the rule from the assent of States"[59]. With this conduct the Court acts outside Article 38 of its Statute[60], which leads P. M. DUPUY to state that these attitudes of the Court with regard to the general rule respond to a notable evolution of the international legal system, and the case law examined by him

---

[56] *Ibid.* p. 100. The ICJ follows the same reasoning with regard to the relation with other obligations affected by this matter, such as the principle of non-intervention,

> "It is easy to find numerous expressions of an *opinio iuris* on the existence of this principle in customary international law" (*ibid.*, p. 106); and cites General Assembly Resolutions 2625 (XXV) and 2131 (XX), this latter relating to the Declaration on the Inadmissibility of Intervention in the Domestic Affairs of States and the Protection of their Independence and Sovereignty. It finally uses its own jurisprudence stated in the *Corfu Channel* case (cf. *ibid.*, p. 107).

[57] GONZALEZ CAMPOS, J.D., SANCHEZ RODRIGUEZ, L.I. and ANDRES SAENZ DE SANTA MARIA, M.P., *Curso* ..., *op. cit.*, p. 117. Cf. also THIRLWAY, H., "The Law and Procedure of the International Court of Justice", 1989, *op. cit.*, pp. 143-157.

[58] DUPUY, P.M., *Droit* ..., *op. cit.*, p. 576. The italics are in the original.

[59] *Ibid.* p. 579. The italics are in the original.

[60] To the extent that "on being released at different levels from reference to international practice, in order to affirm the legal validity of certain general rules, the Court has undoubtedly overlooked the statutory conditions under which it is allowed to apply international law" (*Droit*..., *op. cit.*, p. 580).

reaffirms that there are general principles within the system endowed with manifest autonomy as regards custom[61].

Definitively, from the analysis we have made the substantial liberty the international judge has to give more or less importance to one or other of the elements we have analysed in order to specify the existence of a custom can be deduced.

Independently of the elements which are part of the general theory of custom built up by the I.C.J. and which we have seen through the preceding examples, its statements about the existence of *regional*[62] and *local*[63] customs should also be taken into account.

In relationship with this last point, it adds,

> "This practice having continued over a period extending beyond a century and a quarter unaffected by the change of regime in respect of the intervening territory which ocurred when India became independent, the Court is, in view of all circumstances of the case, satisfied that that practice was accepted as law by the Parties and has given rise to a right and a correlative obligation"[64].

The importance of the I.C.J.'s interpretative task regarding customary norms can be appreciated by its effects upon certain sectors of international order. This is the case, firstly, of the *formation of customary international norms*, through the construction of a general theory of custom based on three elements: practice with its characteristics (general, constant and uniform)[65], the temporary factor[66]and the

---

[61] *Ibid.*, pages 580 et seq.

[62] Cf. The *Asylum Case* (ICJ, *Reports 1950*, pages 275 et seq.).

[63] On the occasion of the case of the *Right of Passage over Indian Territory*, in which the practice had extended over 125 years,

> "It is difficult to see why the number of States between which a local custom may be established on the basis of a long practice must necesarily be larger than two. The Court sees no reason why long continued practice between two States accepted by them as regulating their relations should not form the basis of mutual rights and obligations between the two States" (I.C.J., *Reports 1960*, p. 39).

[64] *Ibid.*, p. 40.

[65] In the following cases: the *Asylum Case* (*Reports 1950*, pages 275 et seq.), the *Fisheries* (*Reports 1951*, pages 136 et seq.), of the *Right of Passage over Indian Territory* (*Reports 1960*, pages 39 et seq., the *Arbitral Award Made by the King of Spain on 23 December 1906* (*Reports 1960*, p. 213), the *Temple of Preah Vihear* (*Reports 1961*, p. 34), the *Legal Consequences for States of the Continued Presence of South Africa in Namibia South West Africa) notwithstanding Security Council Resolution 276 (1970)* (*Reports 1971*, p. 53). The Court accepts nuances of these characteristics in the following cases: the *North Sea Continental Shelf* (*Reports 1969*, p. 42), the *Continental Shelf (Libyan Arab Jamahiriya/Malta)* (*Reports 1985*, pages 29 et seq., para. 27), and the *Military and Paramilitary Activities in and against Nicaragua* (*Reports 1986*, pages 98 et seq. paragraphs 185 and 186).

opinio iuris[67]. Its decisions on the interaction between treaty and custom come into this area with the affirmation of the separate existence of both norms even when they have the same content[68] In addition, the recognition of the existence of regional[69] and local[70] customs.

Secondly, with regard to *institutional norms*, the I.C.J. has specified the character of abstention in the adoption of United Nations Security Council Resolutions[71], and has recognised the legal effects deriving from the acceptance of institutional norms[72].

Thirdly, it has affirmed the principle of estoppel and the consequences deriving from this[73].

Fourth, in the sector of the international system concerning the Law of the Sea, the Court has pronounced on the system of straight baselines as a method of delimitation as regards bays due to the presence of geographical characteristics[74] and the absence of an obligation to have recourse to the principle of equidistance and special principles, from a customary point of view, as regards the delimitation of continental shelves.

Finally, the interpretation of the I.C.J. has also addressed the following sectors of International law: the concept of "terra nullius", the principle of "uti possidetis", the legality of the threat or use of nuclear weapons, the immunity from

---

66 Those constituted over a long period of time: (cases: the *Fisheries* (*Reports 1951*, p. 131) the *Right of Passage over Indian Territory Reports* 1960, p. 40), and the *Temple of Preah Vihear (Reports 1961*, p. 34), becomes progressively relativised by the Court (cases concerning the *North Sea Continental Shelf* (*Reports 1969*, p. 43), the *Continental Shelf (Libyan Arab Jamahiriya/Malta*), (*Reports 1985*, pages 29-30, paragraph 27), and the *Military and Paramilitary Activities in and against Nicaragua* (*Reports 1986*, p. 98, paragraph 186).

67 In the Cases: the *North Sea Continental Shelf* (*Reports 1969*, pages 28 and 44), the *Continental Shelf (Libyan Arab Jamahiriya/Malta)* (*Reports 1985*, pp. 29-30, paragraph 27), and the *Military and Paramilitary Activities in and against Nicaragua* (*Reports 1986*, p. 100, paragraph 188). Already, in the jurisprudence of the P.C.I.J. in the *Lotus Case* (*Series A*, No. 9, pages 18-21).

68 The case of the *Military and Paramilitary Activities in and against Nicaragua* (*Reports 1986*, page 94, para. 175).

69 The *Asylum Case* (*Reports 1950*, pages 276-278).

70 The case of the *Right of Passage over Indian territory* (*Reports 1960*, pages 39-43).

71 The case of the *Legal Consequences for States of the Continued Presence of South Africa in Namibia South West Africa) notwithstanding Security Council Resolution 276 (1970)*, (*Reports 1971*, p. 53).

72 In the case of the *Military and Paramilitary Activities in and against Nicaragua* (*Reports 1986*, pages 99 et seq.). See Chapter X of this work.

73 In the following cases: the Fisheries (*Reports 1951*, pages 131-138) the *Arbitral Award Made by the King of Spain on December 23, 1906* (*Reports 1960*, pages 213 et seq.), and the *Temple of Preah Vihear* (*Reports 1961*, pages 32-34).

74 The *Fisheries Case* (*Reports 1951*, page 139).

criminal jurisdiction in other States and the inviolability of an incumbent Minister for Foreign Affairs, the concept of occupied territory and international obligations resulting for the occupying Power, as well as the question related to the legal consequences of the commission of an internationally wrongful act[75].

In all these cases the *interpretative parameters* used by the Court had been: the practice of the States (with the characteristics we have already seen), the requirement of a certain length of time (quantitatively minimized in the cases submitted to the Court since 1969), and the existence of a legal conviction of States regarding the obligatory character of such conduct (the *opinio iuris*). In all these cases, it is the Court which freely makes its own assessment of the different elements giving more weight to some of them then to the others, specifying its content, while modulating, its application to the specific case.

The analysis of case law also shows the evolution undergone by the I.C.J. in its conception of the different situations of dependence of States once they accept the jurisdiction of the Court. That is to say, they are at the mercy of the appreciations the Court will make and they are aware that it will always be able to justify the construction it chooses.

[75] See Chapter IX of this work.

Chapter V:

Does the Declaration Express the Will of the State or Is It the Interpreter Who Builds It? The Unilateral Declarations

1 Another sign of the dependence of the State with regard to the interpreter: The determination of the effects of the declaration

Until now we have analysed the problem of interpretation with regard to the three types of norms existing in the international order: conventional, institutional and customary. While in the first the interpreter has a text reflecting the will of the Parties and also certain rules applicable in the matter, with regard to institutional and customary norms the question acquires other features. As we have seen, interpretation of institutional norms requires the carrying out of a double analysis to determine which has been the will of the State. This analysis includes the text of the norm (the drafting and the terms employed) as well the conduct of the State with regard to the norm at the time of its adoption. Unlike the preceding case, here the interpreter has no interpretative rules imposed by International Law. But, according to the I.C.J., it can be said that the adoption of a General Assembly resolution on a question of the Charter is not a merely reiteration or clarification of treaty commitments undertaken in the Charter. We have already specified the existence of some criteria aiding the interpreter in his task of interpretation of the attitude of the State with regard to the institutional norm. Consequently, we will not insist on it. While the two preceding situations have in common the existence of a text (although the interpretation of institutional norms also requires the examination of the conduct or attitude of the State with regard to the resolution in question), in the case of customary norms, the will of the State is manifested through practice, that is, its conduct, the acts carried out by it that reveals this will. The non-existence of interpretative rules on the matter gives the interpreter substantial liberty because it is he, who is not limited by any kind of rule and appreciates the arguments of the Parties and their conduct in order to give an opinion of the conduct analysed. The sole, but slight conditioning is the definition of customary rule contained in Article 38.1.b) of the Statute of the I.C.J. which, in a certain way, is the framework in which the international judge must analyse the customary norm because it contains the characteristics that conduct must have in order to be considered as a norm. Nevertheless, we have already seen how the Court can go beyond this conditioning through its own interpretation of the content of each one of the elements cited in Article 38.1.b). The example of the *opinio iuris* is relevant because it is the Court that appreciates its existence and determines its content.

With regard to customary norms the I.C.J. acts as a creator of law rather than as an interpreter, and the most relevant example is its construction concerning the general theory of international custom.

Something similar occurs with regard to the unilateral declarations, as we will see. Here, interpretation has two factors in common with institutional norms: the text of the declaration and the conduct of the States which makes the declaration. From its analysis, the Court deduces the intention of the author of the declaration in the specific case and whether it wishes or not to assume a legal obligation. In addition, in common with customary norms there is the fact of a construction of the Court which starts from the declaration that manifests the will of its author, in opinion of the Court.

But, what is surprising about this construction of unilateral declarations built up by the I.C.J. is that the intention deduced by the Court from the declaration does not coincide with the appreciation of the same declaration that its author and the States directly concerned have. Otherwise, they would not have had resort to the Court.

As we will have the possibility of verifying, under the theory of the unilateral declarations the I.C.J. again shows its creative aspect: before its judgement in the *Nuclear Tests* case, this manner of creating international rights and obligations did not appear in its case law or in the books of Public International Law. On the other hand, it reflects the dependence of State with regard to the Court because it is the Court which reserves the interpretation of the intention of the States and provides it with content. This content cannot coincide with the appreciation the author has of his own declaration but, nevertheless, it will produce legal effects.

2 The criteria retained by the interpreter in order to affirm the binding character of the declaration

As is known, the possibility of the existence of legal obligations, whose origin would lie in the consent of a sole State appears, for the first time, in the *Nuclear Tests* case, in which it is stated that "it is well recognized that declarations made by way of unilateral acts, concerning legal or factual situations, may have the effect of creating legal obligations. Declarations of this kind may be, and often are, very specific"[1]. In this case, this involves stopping French nuclear testing in the atmosphere. As this matter is sufficiently well known due to the fact that it is a

[1] ICJ, *Reports 1974*, p. 267. See CASTILLO, L. De, "Comentarios sobre el derecho internacional de los actos jurídicos unilaterales", in *Estudios de derecho internacional en homenaje al profesor Ernesto Rey Caro*, Zlata Drnas de Clément ed., 2002, vol. I, pp. 23-57.

classic example of unilateral declaration, therefore, we will only highlight the elements we consider more relevant for our study.

From the analysis of the declarations made by the President of the French Republic and by the French Ministers of Defence and of Foreign Affairs the Court reached the conclusion that the French intention in making those declarations was not to carry out more nuclear tests in the atmosphere. Nevertheless, this is a conclusion neither Australia nor New Zealand reached using the same declarations as the Court in its interpretation. As neither of these States would have requested the Court that it should adjudge and declare that the carrying out of nuclear weapon tests in the atmosphere is not consistent with International law, and order the French Republic to cease carrying out these tests. Even, the *Attorney-General* of Australia, on 26 September 1974, in reply to a question asked in the Australian Senate said that the French statements about proceeding to carry out underground tests in the future "falls far short of a commitment or undertaking that there will be no more atmospheric tests conducted by the French Government at its Pacific Tests Centre" and that, "in legal terms, Australia has obtained nothing from the French Government which protects it against any further atmospheric tests should the French Government subsequently decide to hold them"[2].

In consequence, it can be said that the requests made by Australia and New Zealand show their perception of the inexistence of a French obligation as a consequence of its own declarations. The intervention just quoted manifests this.

But neither does France appear to have that perception. Thus, the French Government and the Minister of Defence, in two declarations made on 7 February and on 2 May 1973, assert the legality of the tests and that neither the cancellation nor the modification of the programme was envisaged. Later, in 1974, the statements concerning the cessation of nuclear tests in the atmosphere as well as the intention to proceed to underground testing took place.

It is known that the French Republic has failed to appear before the Court, as this would be to its detriment. So the Court, after stating that, in view of the non-appearance of the Respondent, "it is especially incumbent upon the Court to satisfy itself that it is in possession of all the available facts", and stated that it was necessary to consider the French statements subsequent to 1973 – not made before the Court but made in public – in order to discern "whether they embody any modification of intention as to France's future conduct"[3] The ICJ is even more explicit and claims expressively and with absolute clarity its autonomy to determine the meaning and scope which the author wanted a unilateral declaration to have[4]. In this way, the

---

2 ICJ, *Reports 1974*, p. 262.

3 *Ibid.*, p. 264.

4 Thus,

> "The Court must however form its own view of the meaning and scope intended by the author of a unilateral declaration which may create a legal obligation, …" (*ibid.*, p. 269, paragraph 50).

The ICJ repeats this argument in the case of the *Frontier Dispute* (ICJ, *Reports 1986*, p. 573, paragraph 39).

Court became the interpreter of the French unilateral declaration and the results are known. But is this not an act of creation rather than interpretation?

Additionally, this case is a good example not only of the consequences derived from the acceptance of the jurisdiction of the Court but, also, of the non appearance before it. This latter aspect, in the *Nuclear Tests* case, also involves an interpretation of the French declarations by the Court; which could not be coincident with the will or the intention of that State. In any case, it is also possible, that the appearance of France before the Court would not have changed the thesis of the Court.

In opinion of the I.C.J., from the declarations made by the French authorities during 1974, the intention of France not to proceed in the future to nuclear tests in the atmosphere can be deduced. Unlike Australia and New Zealand, the I.C.J. gives legal effects to the French declarations starting from the presumption that France makes such declarations with the intention of producing legal obligations[5]. The relevancy is that the Court puts itself in the place of France and sustains that this State considers itself obliged by the terms of its declarations. Upon this basis – or upon this interpretation of the French intention – it builds its theory of unilateral declarations stating that,

> "When it is the intention of the State making the declaration that it should become bound according to its terms, that intention confers on the declaration the character of a legal undertaking, the State being thenceforth legally required to follow a course of conduct consistent with the declaration. An undertaking of this kind, if given publicly, and with an intent to be bound, even though not made within the context of international negotiations, is binding. In these circumstances, nothing in the nature of a *quid pro quo* nor any subsequent acceptance of the declaration, nor even any reply or reaction from other States, is required for the declaration to take effect, since such a requirement would be inconsistent with the strictly unilateral nature of the juridical act by which the pronouncement by the State was made"[6].

The Court bases the grounds of the obligatory nature of these kinds of declarations on the principle of good faith as it is "one of the basic principles governing the creation and performance of legal obligations, whatever their source, …"[7]. As occurs in treaty law with the rule *pacta sunt servanda*, which is based on the prin-

---

[5] Because "these statements were not made *in vacuo*.", but in relation to a specific legal or *de facto* situation (*Reports 1974*, p. 269). The italics correspond to the original.

[6] The case of the *Nuclear Tests* (ICJ, *Reports 1974*, p. 267).

[7] ICJ, *Reports 1974*, p. 268. and adds,

> "Trust and confidence are inherent to international cooperation, in particular in an age when this cooperation in many fields is becoming increasingly essential" (*ibid.*).

ciple of good faith, in the case of unilateral declarations, the Court states that "so also is the binding character of an international obligation assumed by unilateral declarations. Thus interested States may take cognisance of unilateral declarations and place confidence in them, and are entitled to require that the obligation thus created be respected"[8].

We thus verify that, as far as the States are concerned, this principle, which has been described with its lack of sharpness, and which does not prevent the persistence of the controversy deriving from valid, but divergent, unilateral interpretations when the States are not obliged to submit the interpretation to a third party, and in the hands of the Court it receives specific content. The Court grants feasibility to the principle of good faith and makes it applicable. The result is the obligatory nature of the international undertaking assumed by the unilateral declaration.

Nevertheless, the problem of interpretation does not disappear. For example, in the field of international treaties. The statement of the I.C.J. as regards the *Nuclear Tests* case to the effect that States concerned may take unilateral declarations into account and place their trust in them, and they are entitled to require that the obligation thus created be respected, and is transferable to that field: the States concerned may take what has been agreed to in the Treaty into account and trust in it and they are entitled to require that the obligation thus created be respected. Nevertheless, in practice, problems can arise. We have seen that, with regard to treaties, divergent interpretations of the States participating can arise regarding the same text. Respect for the obligation so created is interpreted in a different manner by the Parties and, while the discrepancy persists, that obligation is not applied.

If this happens with regard to a written text which reflects the will of its authors, as can be imagined the problems become greater when the object of interpretation is a unilateral declaration. Especially when, as the I.C.J. has stated, it is the author of that act alone who becomes bound. It is the author who finds his sovereignty limited. In consequence, a defence of a restrictive interpretation of such limitation will always be made. The beneficiary, on the contrary, will always invoke the interpretation most favourable to him (which, in turn, will be restricted to the debtor). Thus, with regard to Treaties, if the problems of interpretation occur, much more with regard to unilateral declarations in relationship where the author of the declaration as well as its beneficiary will interpret differently the elements which, in the opinion of the I.C.J., are present in each unilateral declaration. And this, because its effects are also undergone in a different manner (one as beneficiary; the other or others as debtor or debtors of the obligation).

Another consequence deriving from the principle of good faith is the *irreversible character of the declaration* which, according to one sector of doctrine, is a delicate matter. According to this opinion, although there are no legal acts or "perpetual" norms, the transformation of international legal acts is protected by certain guarantees. Therefore, as regards the unilateral acts, the power of repen-

---

[8] *Ibid.*

tance must be admitted, but the exercise of this must not be left to the free choice of the States. That is to say, the discretional right of States to be released from the obligations resulting from its own undertakings cannot be recognised, as this would imply ignoring the rights extracted by the other States as regards these undertakings and will gravely attack judicial security[9].

In the *Nuclear Tests* case, the I.C.J. stresses this when it states that the obligation undertaken by the French Government cannot be interpreted "as having been made in implicit reliance on an arbitrary power of reconsideration" as it assumed an obligation whose precise nature and limits must be understood in accordance with the terms in which they were publicly expressed[10].

In this interpretative process, another rule involved in the appreciation of the unilateral declaration is that concerning the authors: these must be subjects with capacity to bind the State, and it is not necessary that such declarations be addressed to a State in particular or be accepted by a State. In the *Nuclear Tests* case the declarations held by the I.C.J. were made by the President of the French Republic as well as by the Ministers of Defence and Foreign Affairs[11].

In the Case of the *Legal Status of Eastern Greenland*, its predecessor the PCJI retained the declaration made by the Norwegian Minister of Foreign Affairs[12]. In the Case of the *Minquiers and Ecrehous*, the I.C.J. considers the letter of the French Navy Minister in which it was stated that the Iles Des Minquiers were in the possession of Great Britain as "evidence of the official French view at that time"[13].

---

[9] Cf. QUOC DINH, N., DAILLIER, P., and PELLET, A, *Droit ...*, *op.cit.*, p. 354. And add that it must be admitted that a State cannot be released from its obligations arising from unilateral acts except by recourse to the usual procedures for the pacific settlement of controversies. In the end, the problem of the obligation to negotiate in good faith would arise. (cf. *ibid.*).

[10] See ICJ, *Reports 1974*, pages 269 et seq.

[11] In the words of the Court,

> "There can be no doubt, in view of his function, that his public communications or statements, oral or written, as Head of State, are in international relations acts of the French State. His statements, and those of members of the French Government acting under his authority, up to the last statement made by the Minister of Defence (of 11 October 1974), constitute a whole. Thus, in whatever form these statements were expressed, they must be held constitute an engagement of the State, having regard to their intention and to the circumstances in which they were made (*ibid.*, p. 269).

[12] The Court states,

> "The Court considers it beyond all dispute that a reply of this nature given by the Minister of Foreign Affairs on behalf of his Government in response to a request by the diplomatic representative of a foreign Power, in regard to a question falling within his province, is binding upon the Country to which the Minister belongs" (P.C.I.J., *Series A/B*, No. 53, p. 71).

[13] ICJ, *Reports 1953*, p. 71. In his individual opinion, Judge BASDEVANT considered that the letter in question was issued by a Minister "without authority to make decisions pertaining to questions of territorial sovereignty" (*ibid.*, p. 80).

Nevertheless, the Chamber of the I.C.J. that judged the case of the *Border Dispute* did not gave binding legal effects to the declaration of the head of State of Mali made on 11 April 1975 during an interview with France Presse in the course of which he stated that his Government would comply with the decision of the Mediation Commission set up by the Organization of African Unity because, in the opinion of the Court, that decision did not express the intention of Mali to be bound by the works of the Commission. Concerning this question there were also some nuances confirming the decision of the I.C.J. We will analyse these later in relationship with the element of the "intention" that, according to the construction of the Court, must be present in unilateral declarations.

The third element employed by the I.C.J. to specify the legal effects the unilateral declarations is that these take place with regard to a *de facto* or *de lege situation*. This appreciation of the Court is made on the basis of a presumption. So, in the *Nuclear Tests* case, where the Court says that it is "entitled to presume, at the outset, that these statements were not made *in vacuo*" but in relation to the tests which constitute the very subject of the case, although France did not come forward in the case[14].

The fourth criterion employed by the I.C.J. in order to conclude that unilateral declarations produce legal effects is *the intention of the Parties to be legally bound*; which, in its opinion, implies the interpretation of the act in question taking into account that if that act were limitative of the future freedom of action of the Parties it should be interpreted in a restrictive way[15].

In order to determine the intention of the author of the declaration, the Court employs two criteria: the factual circumstances in which the act occurred[16]. And its content, because "it is from the actual substance of these statements, and from the circumstances attending their making, that the legal implications of the unilateral act must be deduced"[17]. By combining these in the case of the nuclear Tests, the I.C.J. concludes that, through the declarations in this regard made in 1974 by the President of the French Republic as well as by the Minister for Foreign Affairs, the French Government made public its intention to effectively terminate the nuclear tests in the atmosphere.

---

14 *Ibid.*

15 Thus the ICJ states,

> "…, not all unilateral acts do not imply obligations; but a State may choose to take up a certain position in relation to a particular matter with the intention of being bound, the intention is to be ascertained through interpretation of the act. When States make statements by which their freedom of action is to be limited, a restrictive interpretation is called for" (I.C.J., *Reports 1974*, p. 267).

Cf. regarding this judgement THIRLWAY, H., "The Law and Procedure of the International Court of Justice", *B.Y.I.L.*, 1989, pages 8-17.

16 See the case of the *Border Dispute* (ICJ, *Reports 1986*, p. 574).

17 Case of the *Nuclear Tests* (ICJ, *Reports 1974*, p. 269).

Consequently, what is important in the opinion of the Court is the intention to assume legal obligations or the adoption of a certain statement on a specific matter. Nevertheless, it should not be forgotten that it is the Court itself that concludes the existence of legal obligations derived from the statements made by the French authorities. Neither France nor Australia, nor New Zealand arrived at such a conclusion. The I.C.J. affirms the existence of legal obligations with regard to France through the interpretation it made of the French intention and it derives from the declarations quoted.

Thus, the Court considers that in announcing that the 1974 series of atmospheric tests would be the last, the French Government conveyed to the world at large – including New Zealand and Australia – its intention to "effectively" terminate these tests and,

> "was bound to assume that other States might take note of these statements and rely on their being effective. The validity of these statements and their legal consequences must be considered within the general framework of the security of international intercourse, and the confidence and trust which are so essential in the relations among States"[18].

As we have said before, the I.C.J. employs two criteria in order to appreciate the intention of the author of the declaration: its real content and the circumstances in which it is made. Combining both criteria with the clarity, in its opinion, of the French declaration, the Court – in the *Nuclear Tests* case – concludes that such declarations constitute an undertaking with legal effect[19] and is irreversible in the sense that it does not imply an "arbitrary power of reconsideration"[20].

One immediate consequence of the construction made by the ICJ on the basis of the declarations made by France is that it is led to consider that the objective pursued by the plaintiffs had been achieved and the claim no longer had any objective[21]. This reasoning enables the Court not to reply to the first request made by

---

[18] *Ibid.* However, none of the States affected by this matter perceived it in the same way.

[19] "The objects of these statements are clear and they were addressed to the international community as a whole, and the Court holds that they constitute an undertaking possessing legal effect. The Court considers that the President of the Republic, in deciding upon the effective cessation of atmospheric tests, gave an undertaking to the international community to which his words were addressed (*ibid.*, pages 269 et seq.).

[20] On the other hand,

> "The Court finds further that the French Government has undertaken an obligation the precise nature and limits of which must be understood in accordance with the actual terms in which they have been publicly expressed" (*ibid.*).

[21] Thus, it states,

> "Therefore, the Court is in a situation in which the objective of the plaintiff had effectively been reached insofar as the Court verified that France adopted the undertaking not to proceed with the nuclear tests in the atmosphere in the South Pacific".

Australia and New Zealand, that it should adjudge and declare that the carrying out of atmospheric nuclear tests in the South Pacific was not consistent with International Law. Concerning this question the Court seems to suffer from a certain anxiety as it declares,

> "The Applicant has clearly indicated what would satisfy its claim, and the Respondent has independently taken action; the question for the Court is thus one of interpretation of the conduct of each of the Parties. The conclusion at which the Court has arrived as a result of such interpretation does not mean that it is itself effecting a compromise of the claim; the Court is merely ascertaining the object of the claim and the effect of the Respondent's action, and this it is obliged to do. Any suggestion that the dispute would not be capable of being terminated by statements made on behalf of France would run counter to the unequivocally expressed views of the Applicant both before the Court and elsewhere[22].

As regards the second objective of the action, that the Court should order the French Republic to stop these tests), this is indirectly achieved through the answer of the Court[23].

Nevertheless, the I.C.J. justifies its non-pronouncement on the specific requests of Australia and New Zealand. Its reasoning shows the broad margin of appreciation the Court has once a controversy is submitted to it, the Court itself interprets the claim and the scope of its own judicial function[24].

As it is aware of this, it tries to justify it. In the *Nuclear Tests* case, it states that it is the Court's duty to isolate the real issue in the case and to identify the object of the claim and adds that the Court is entitled to interpret the submissions of the Parties and that it has never been contested because this is one of the attributes of its judicial functions[25]. Along the same lines and in the same case it states that it is the Court that must ascertain the true objective and purpose of the claim and in doing so it cannot confine itself to the ordinary meaning of the words used; it must take into account the application as a whole, the arguments of the plaintiff before the Court, the diplomatic exchanges brought to its attention as well as the public statements made on behalf of the Government making the claim[26].

---

22 *Ibid.* Consequently, there is no longer a controversy which requires the decision of the Court.

23 "The Applicant has repeatedly sought from the Respondent an assurance that the tests would cease, and the Respondent has, on its own initiative, made a series of statements to the effect that they will cease. Thus the Court concludes that, the dispute having disappeared, the claim advanced by Australia no longer has any object. It follows that any further finding would have no *raison d'être*. (*ibid.*, p. 271).

24 A similar pronouncement is made, as we shall see, in the case of the *Border Dispute*.

25 See *Reports 1974*, p. 262. And in support of its thesis it cites case law both of the PCIJ and its own (see *Ibid.*, pages 262 et seq.).

26 See *ibid.*, p. 263.

This reasoning will provoke serious criticism from the Court from the part of several judges who, in their separate opinions, will remind the Court that it is entitled to interpret the submissions of the Parties but it is not authorized to introduce inadequate submissions[27]. However, the critical tone becomes more acute when these judges state that in their opinion the Court does not interpret the text, the requests of Australia and New Zealand, but has altered or mutilated it to conclude what the Applicant had called "the main prayer in the Application", that is, the request for a declaration of the illegality of nuclear atmospheric tests in the South Pacific Ocean. In their opinion, "a radical alteration or mutilation of an applicant's submission under the guise of interpretation has serious consequences because it constitutes a frustration of a party's legitimate expectations that the case which it has put before the Court will be examined and decided on"[28].

In conclusion, the construction, rather than the interpretation, made by the I.C.J. in the *Nuclear Tests* case allows the Court to elude a pronouncement on the conformity or not of the atmospheric nuclear tests with International Law[29], a pronouncement which would have been highly interesting and was what the applicants had asked for.

The aspect we consider more important in the construction of unilateral declarations made by the I.C.J. is that which concerns the *intention* of the author of the declaration. In the case already analysed as in other subsequent ones, the common denominator is that it is the Court itself which, on occasion of the dispute submitted to it, substitutes the author of the declaration because it is the Court itself which specifies the intention of the author of the declaration. This way of acting takes shape, in practice, in the substitution of the real will of the State through the interpretation of the declaration of the State made by the judicial body. The I.C.J.

---

[27] "If, however, the Court lacks the power to reformulate inadequate submissions, *a fortiori* it cannot reformulate submissions as clear and specific as those in this case" (*ibid.*, p. 316). It is the joint dissident opinion of judges ONYEAMA, DILLARD, JIMENEZ DE ARECHAGA and WALDOCK.

[28] *Ibid.*, p. 317. And adds,

> "In this instance the serious consequences have an irrevocable character because the Applicant is now prevented from resubmitting its Application and seising the Court again by reason of France's denunciation of the instruments on which it is sought to base the Court's jurisdiction in the present dispute (*ibid.*).

[29] Regrettably, the Court makes no pronouncement,

> "It may be argued that although France may have undertaken such an obligation, by a unilateral declaration, not to carry out atmospheric nuclear tests in the South Pacific Ocean, a judgement of the Court on this subject might still be of value because, if the judgement upheld the Applicant's contentions, it would reinforce the position of the Applicant by affirming the obligation of the Respondent. However, the Court having found that the Respondent has assumed an obligation as to conduct, concerning the effective cessation of nuclear tests, no further judicial action is required" (*ibid.*, p. 271).

had already stated this in the *Nuclear Tests* case and repeated it later in the *Frontier Dispute* case,

> "Thus it all depends on the intention of the State in question, and the Court emphasized that it is for the Court to 'form its own view of the meaning and scope intended by the author of a unilateral declaration which may create a legal obligation'"[30].

The problem is that an external observer has no resources to risk giving the answer of the Court in the specific case. So, in the case concerning *Military and Paramilitary Activities in and against Nicaragua*, the I.C.J. concludes that the communication made on July 12, 1979 by the Junta of the Government of National Reconstruction of Nicaragua and transmitted to the General Secretary of the Organization of American States is not a unilateral declaration of Nicaragua from which any legal undertaking can be inferred.

In that communication, the Government of Nicaragua enumerated a list of the objectives of the Nicaraguan Junta and stated, in particular, its intention of installing a new régime through a peaceful, orderly transition and of respecting human rights under the supervision of the Inter-American Commission on Human Rights[31]. However, the ICJ,

> "is unable to find anything in these documents, whether the resolution or the communication accompanied by the 'Plan to secure peace', from which it can be inferred that any legal undertaking was intended to exist"[32].

In the *Frontier Dispute* case, Burkina Faso invoked the existence of a unilateral declaration of the head of State of Mali, on 11 April 1975 during an interview with the France Press agency, during which he stated that,

> "Mali extends over 1,240,000 square kilometres, and we cannot justify fighting for a scrap of territory 150 kilometres long. Even if the Organization of African Unity Commission decides objectively that the frontier line passes through Bamako, *my Government will comply with the decision*"[33].

---

30 ICJ, *Reports 1986*, p. 573. The ICJ repeats what was stated in the case of the *Nuclear Tests*.

31 Cf. ICJ. *Reports 1986*, p. 131.

32 *Ibid.*, p. 132.

33 ICJ, *Reports 1986*, p. 571. The italics are ours. The Commission mentioned is a Mediation Commission set up on 26 December 1974 following an armed conflict between the two countries which broke out on 14 December 1974. One of its tasks was to seek a solution to the frontier dispute on the basis of existing legal documents. That Mediation Commission set up a Military Sub-Commission and a Legal Sub-Commission. The latter Commission comprises an outline solution (cf. *ibid.*).

For Burkina Faso, this declaration made the report of the Legal Sub-Commission endorsed by the summit meeting of Heads of State or Government held at Lome on 17 and 18 June 1975 binding, because Mali had proclaimed itself, on 11 April 1975, already bound by the report which might have been made by the Mediation Commission (on which this Sub-Commission depends). Mali challenges this interpretation and remarks that the Mediation Commission had no power of decision and that the statement of its President made on 11 April 1975, "was merely 'a witticism of the kind regularly uttered at press conferences', which implied 'no more than that Mali is anxious to consider the Commission's recommendations with goodwill and in good faith'"[34].

Once this declaration has been placed in its context, the conclusion of the Court seems to be correct. Effectively, both States recognize that the O.A.U. Mediation Commission was not a jurisdictional body and lacked the power to take legally binding decisions. Furthermore, it never completed its work, it took no steps formally to take note of the reports of its sub-commissions and it did not submit any definitive overall solution for consideration by the Parties. Moreover, through a final communiqué, on the occasion of the meeting held on 17 and 18 June 1975 at Lome by the Mediation Commission, both States agreed to the establishment of a neutral technical committee to determine the location of some villages, to reconnoitre the frontier and to make proposals for the setting up of the Commission. However, this neutral technical committee could not fulfil its mission. In addition, these occurrences are posterior to Mali's declaration, from which Burkina Faso concludes the existence of legal effects and which demonstrate the persistence of the dispute. Consequently, the I.C.J. concludes that if the Parties had had the intention to accept the binding character of the conclusions the Mediation Commission wanted, the normal method would have been an international agreement. After this, the Court specifies the differences between this case and that of the *Nuclear Tests* as, in the latter, France argued that the tests were lawful so that it could not accept the terms of a negotiated solution with each of the applicants without jeopardizing its contention that its conduct was lawful.

But the Court repeated its case law on the matter, and stated that it is for it to "form its own view of the meaning and scope intended by the author of a unilateral declaration which may create a legal obligation"[35], which means that it might be possible that the opinion of the Court regarding that intention could be imposed on the author of the declaration even when he stated that its intention was different.

The difference of criterion between the *Nuclear Tests* case and that of the *Frontier Dispute* is justified by the I.C.J. because the circumstances of the latter are

> "radically different. Here, there was nothing to hinder the Parties from manifesting an intention to accept the binding character of the conclusions of the Organisation of African Unity Mediation Commission by the normal method: a formal agreement on the basis of reciprocity.

34 *Ibid.*, p. 573.

35 *Ibid.*

> Since no agreement of this kind was concluded between the Parties, the Chamber finds that there are no grounds to interpret the declaration made by Mali's head of State on 11 April 1975 as a unilateral act with legal implications in regard to the present case"[36].

As can be verified, the reasoning of the Court is different from that employed in the *Nuclear Tests* case (where the unilateral declaration is also made in the course of a press conference). There, the Court considers that, in the declarations made by the French Republic, the intention to stop such tests is present. In the *Frontier Dispute* case, nevertheless, the I.C.J. states that, if that had been the will of the Parties there was nothing to hinder them from manifesting an intention to accept the binding character of the conclusions of the Mediation Commission by the normal method of a formal agreement, "on the basis of reciprocity"[37]. Once more it is the I.C.J. which substitutes the will of the State but, in this case, its criterion and that of the author of the declaration of the State coincide.

Which, then, is the criterion followed by the Court to confer legal effects on some unilateral declarations and to refuse it as regards others or, in its own words, to form its own view of the meaning and scope intended by the author of the unilateral declaration? Why is it necessary to have a formal agreement in certain cases and not in others? Can this disparity as regards criterion by the fact that the in latter case judgement was made by a Chamber of the Court, and it was possible to have different interpretations within the Court?

The last element used by the I.C.J. in relationship with unilateral declarations concerns its *form*, which, in its opinion, is irrelevant. Already in 1961, in the *Temple of Preah Vihear* case, the I.C.J. stated that in contrast to private Law, International Law places its emphasis on the intentions of the parties so that, when law prescribes no particular form, "parties are free to choose what form they please provided their intention clearly results from it"[38].

In the *Nuclear Tests* case el Court went deeper into this matter and stated that this is not a domain in which international law imposes any special or strict requirements. Whether the statement or declaration is made orally or in writing makes no essential difference, because such statements "made in particular circumstances may create commitments in international law, which does not require that they should be couched in written form. Thus the question of form is not decisive"[39]. What is truly relevant is to know whether the language employed in any given declaration does reveal the clear intention of its author[40].

---

36 *Ibid.*, p. 574.

37 *Ibid.*

38 ICJ, *Reports 1961*, p. 31.

39 ICJ, *Reports 1974*, pages 267 et seq.

40 See the case of the *Temple of Preah Vihear* (ICJ, *Reports 1961*, p. 32). Consequently, it can be deduced that in the case of verbal declarations, such an intention would have to be deduced from the terms employed in the declaration.

In the *doctrinal field* some sectors, specially in France, include a number of acts with negotiable content within unilateral legal acts, for example, promise, renunciation and recognition[41]. This conception is inspired in the theory of the legal affairs characteristic of Domestic Law, and projects those categories onto the international legal order. Starting from those points of view, each one of such unilateral acts (promise, renunciation, recognition) is analysed in the international legal order in order to show their finality and effects[42]. However, as other authors point out if the unilateral legal act, no matter how it has been manifested, (promise, renunciation, recognition) involves an obligatory common foundation, good faith and the commencement of an obligation is based on the consent of the State, which must be appreciated in each specific case in order to establish the intention to be bound in a specific situation, the individualised examination of the manifestations of consent in accordance with their finality, are irrelevant[43]. That is to say, the determining factor is the individual manifestation of the consent to be bound independently of the form this might adopt or be exteriorised.

In conclusion, it is a third party apart from the States concerned in the declaration who appreciates the constitutive elements of a unilateral legal act (generally, an international judicial or arbitral body). And this only occurs if the dispute is submitted to it. It is that body which interprets the will of the State, its intention expressed in the unilateral declaration. From the analysis of international arbitral and judicial practice it can be seen that on the occasion of such interpretation the body in question generally carries out a task of law making which constitutes a restriction to the sovereignty of the author of the declaration. Effectively, when the international arbitral or judicial body appreciates the presence of the constitutive

---

41 For example, CARREAU, D., *Droit ..., op. cit.*, pages 205-223. Especially pages 205-208; QUOC DINH, N., DAILLIER, P., PELLET, *Droit ..., op. cit.*, pages 350-356; DUPUY, P.M., *Droit ..., op. cit.,*, pages 242-245; RUZIE, D., *Droit International Public*, 9th ed., Dalloz, Paris, 1993, pages 48-49. In Spanish doctrine see RODRIGUEZ CARRION, A., *Lecciones de Derecho Internacional Público*, 5th ed., Tecnos, 2002, p. 171.

42 GONZALEZ CAMPOS, J.D., SANCHEZ RODRIGUEZ, L.I., ANDRES SAENZ DE SANTA MARIA, M. P., *Curso ..., op. cit.*, p. 74. Cf. in general: SUY, E., *Les actes juridiques unilatéraux en Droit international public*, L.G.D.J., Paris, 1962;VENTURINI, G., "La portée et les effets juridiques des attitudes et des actes unilatéraux des Etats", *R des C.* , vol. 112 (1964-II), pages 369-466; MIAJA DE LA MUELA, A., "Los actos unilaterales en las relaciones internacionales", *R.E.D.I.*, vol. 20, 1967, pages 429-464; JACQUE, J.-P., *Eléments pour une théorie de l'acte juridique en droit international public* , Paris, L.G.D.J., 1972. More recently, cf. SICAULT, J., "Du caractère obligatoire des engagements unilatéraux en Droit international public", *R.G.D.I.P.* , 1979, pages 633-688; SKUBISCEWSKI, K., "Les actes unilatéraux des Etats", in the collection edited by BEDJAOUI, M., *Droit International. Bilan et perspectives*, vol. I,Paris, 1991, pages 231-250.

43 *Ibid.*, p. 75. Along the same lines we have: GUTIERREZ ESPADA, C., *Derecho Internacional Público 1: Introducción y Fuentes*, 4th ed., PPU, Barcelona, 1993, p. 387; PASTOR RIDRUEJO, J.A., *Curso de Derecho Internacional Público y Organizaciones Internacionales*, 9th ed., Tecnos, Madrid, 2003, p. 169.

elements of a unilateral declaration, the immediate consequence is the limitation of the sovereignty of the author of the declaration insofar as it is obliged by its content. What is important in this process is the *law making character* of the interpreter's task. It is the interpreter who determines the existence or not of the intention of the State to become bound, it is the interpreter who recognizes the legally binding effects of the declaration made[44], who concludes the capacity of the author of the declaration to bind[45], who extracts obligatory effects from the circumstances and content of the declaration[46].

3 The declarations of acceptance of the obligatory jurisdiction of the ICJ

Article 36.2 of the Statute of the I.C.J. provides that States parties to the Statute, "may at any time declare that they recognize as compulsory *ipso facto* and without special agreement, in relation to any other State accepting the same obligation, the jurisdiction of the Court in all legal disputes", as concerns the interpretation of a treaty, any question of International Law, the existence of any fact which, if established, would constitute a breach of an international obligation, as well as the nature or extent of the reparation to be made for the breach of an international obligation[47].

The system of compulsory jurisdiction in this form is summed up as a variety of bilateral relationships between those declaring[48], and its characteristics are mutuality (the parties must be declaring States) and reciprocity (the parties must have recognised the compulsory jurisdiction with the same scope).

---

44 Sometimes the interpreter recognises these (case of the *Nuclear Tests*, the case of the *Legal Status of Eastern Greenland*), and sometimes he negotiates them (case of the *Border Dispute*).

45 Positive in the case of the *Nuclear Tests* (the President of the French Republic and the French Minister of Foreign Affairs), in the case concerning the *Legal Status of Eastern Greenland* (the Norwegian Minister of Foreign Affairs) and in the case of *Minquiers and Ecrehos* (the French Navy Minister). Negatively in the *Frontier Dispute* case (the Mali head of State).

46 Positive in the case of the *Nuclear Tests*, negative in the case of the *Frontier Dispute*. Both cases have in common the fact that the declarations were made at press conferences.

47 According to the constant case law of the ICJ "a determination of the existence of the 'same obligation' requires the presence of two parties to a case, and a defined issue between them, which conditions can only be satisfies when proceedings have been instituted" (the case of *Military and Paramilitary Activities in and against Nicaragua* , I.C.J., *Reports 1984*, p. 420).

48 Cf. TORRES BERNARDEZ, S., "La reciprocidad en el 'sistema de jurisdicción obligatoria' establecido en el Artículo 36. Párrafo 2 del Estatuto de la Corte Internacional de Justicia", *Cursos de Derecho Internacional de Vitoria-Gasteiz 1988*, Servicio Editorial de la Universidad del País Vasco, Bilbao, 1989, p. 365.

In opinion of the I.C.J. declarations of acceptance of the compulsory jurisdiction of the Court are

> "facultative, unilateral engagements, that States are absolutely free to make or not to make. On making the declaration a State is equally free either to do so unconditionally and without limit of time for its duration, or to qualify it with conditions or reservations. In particular, it may limit its effect to disputes arising after a certain date; or it may specify how long the declaration itself shall remain in force, or what notice (if any) will be required to terminate it"[49].

However, the unilateral character of declarations does not signify that the State making the declaration is free to amend the scope and the contents of its solemn commitments as it pleases. This is not so because such declarations, "though they are unilateral acts, establish a series of bilateral engagements with other States accepting the same obligation of compulsory jurisdiction, in which and the conditions, reservations and time-limit clauses are taken into consideration"[50]. One example of this, in relation to the withdrawal of the declaration of acceptance of the compulsory jurisdiction of the Court, is its statement in the case concerning *Military and Paramilitary Activities in and against Nicaragua*, when the United States withdrew its declaration of acceptance, the Court specifies that this withdrawal will produce its effects six months later (which was the period stipulated by this State in its declaration of acceptance of the obligatory jurisdiction of the ICJ drawn up in 1946). As the Court states, the principal question concerning the notification made by the United States in 1984 is to specify whether the United States was free to disregard the six month's notice clause which, freely and by its own choice, it had appended to its 1946 Declaration. When this clause was established, the United States,

> "entered into an obligation which is binding upon it vis-à-vis other States parties to the Optional-Clause system. Although the United States retained the right to modify the contents of the 1946 Declaration or to terminate it, a power which is inherent in any unilateral act of a State, it has, nevertheless assumed an inescapable obligation towards other States accepting the Optional-Clause, by stating formally and solemnly that any such change should take effect only after six months have elapsed as from the date of notice"[51].

---

[49] ICJ, *Reports 1984*, p. 418.

[50] See *ibid.*

[51] ICJ, *Reports 1984*, p. 419. See of a general nature, BARBERIS, J., "Los actos jurídicos unilaterales como fuente del Derecho Internacional Público", in the collective work *Hacia un nuevo orden internacional y europeo. Homenaje al Profesor M. Díez de Velasco* , Tecnos, Madrid, 1993, pp. 101-116.

The principle of good faith examined previously in other parts of this work, also plays an essential role in the declarations of acceptance of the compulsory jurisdiction of the *Military and Paramilitary Activities in and against Nicaragua* when it was stated that in the establishment of this network of engagements, which constitutes the Optional Clause system,

> "the principle of good faith plays an important role; the Court has emphasized the need in international relations for respect for good faith and confidence in particularly unambiguous terms, …"[52].

That is why the States concerned may "take cognisance of unilateral declarations and place confidence in them, and are entitled to require that the obligation thus created be respected"[53]. Consequently, the principle of good faith also applies when withdrawing the declaration of acceptance[54]. According to the Court, the principle of good faith appears in the application by analogy of the treatment laid down by Treaty Law which prescribes "a reasonable period for the withdrawal form or termination of the treaties that contain no provision regarding the duration of their validity", and, as regards the matter in hand, it concludes that the lapse of time from April 6 to April 9, 1984 does not constitute a "reasonable time"[55]. As the ICJ states, the notice clause is an integral part of the declaration of acceptance of its jurisdiction and is an important part of the declaration. Therefore notification made outside this reasonable period cannot abolish the obligation of the State to be submitted to the obligatory jurisdiction of the Court as regards the State which has accepted the same obligation[56].

Concerning these types of declarations, the only formality required is for it to be deposited before the Secretary General of the United Nations in accordance with paragraph 4 of article 36 of the Statutes of the Court[57], and the Court adds that "the precise form and language in which they do this is left to them, and there is no suggestion that any particular form is required, or that any declarations not in such form will be invalid"[58].

---

[52] Referring later to the *Case of the Nuclear Tests* (ICJ, *Reports 1984*, p. 418. the italics are ours).

[53] ICJ, *Reports 1984*, p. 418.

[54] As stated by the ICJ in the Case of *Military and Paramilitary Activities in and against Nicaragua* already mentioned.

[55] *Ibid.,* p. 420. In addition, does this pretension of the USA to modify its declaration of acceptance of the jurisdiction of the ICJ of 1946 in order to hinder the claim of April 9, 1984, not constitute an example of bad faith which remains impaired by the application of the principle of good faith by the Court?. This seems to be the case.

[56] Cf. *ibid.* p. 421.

[57] See *ibid.*, p. 412.

[58] The *Temple pf Preah Vihear* (ICJ, *Reports 1961*, p. 32. Although custom and tradition have normally led the countries which accept the obligatory jurisdiction of the Court to use a certain type of drafting for reasons of comfort, but the use of such formula is not imperative (cf. *ibid.*).

In this regard, in the Case of the *Temple of Preah Vihear*, the ICJ stated that the only pertinent question was to know whether the drafting used clearly reveals the intention "in the terms of paragraph 2 of Article 36 of the Statute, 'to recognize as compulsory *ipso facto* and without special agreement, in relation to any other State accepting the same obligation, the jurisdiction of the Court in all legal disputes' concerning the categories of questions enumerate in that paragraph"[59].

In order to determine this intention, in the case cited above, the ICJ has recourse to "its normal canons of interpretation, the first of which, according to the established jurisprudence of the Court, is that words are to be interpreted according to their natural and ordinary meaning in the context in which they occur"[60]. Therefore, it transfers the rules of interpretation of the Law on Treaties to the declaration of acceptance of its jurisdiction.

This did not occur in the Case of the *Anglo-Iranian Company* (previous to the codification carried out by the CDI as regards treaties) in which, faced with the British argument that a legal text, the Iranian declaration of acceptance of the compulsory jurisdiction of the Court, must be interpreted in such a way that a reason and meaning could be attributed to their words, the ICJ was much more cautious as it stated that such proceedings were justified when what is to be interpreted is the text of a treaty. However,

> "The text of the Iranian Declaration is not a treaty text resulting from the negotiations between two or more States. It is the result of unilateral drafting by the Government of Iran, which appears to have shown a particular degree of caution when drafting of the text of the Declaration… This caution is explained by the special reasons which led the Government of Iran to draft the Declaration in a very restrictive manner"[61].

As can be appreciated, unlike classical unilateral declarations, where the obligations arise for the State declaring by reason of the declaration alone, which in turn generates rights for third parties, the declarations of acceptance of the obligatory jurisdiction of the ICJ are contained in a conventional framework governed by the principles or conditions of reciprocity ad mutuality, by virtue of which, the declaration of the compulsory jurisdiction of the Court (mutuality) is not sufficient, and this declaration must recognise the compulsory jurisdiction for the specific dispute

---

[59] *Ibid.*

[60] *Ibid.* Which leads to the conclusion that these types of declarations cannot have another sense or meaning than that of the acceptance of its jurisdiction (cf. *ibid.*).

[61] ICJ, *Reports 1952*, p. 105. In its declaration of acceptance of the compulsory jurisdiction of the ICJ, Iran excluded controversies concerning the application of all the treaties accepted by it before the ratification of the declaration of acceptance of this jurisdiction, "this intention has found an adequate expression in the text of the Declaration as interpreted above by the Court" (*ibid.*, p. 106).

(principle of reciprocity). The result is that the Court is confined within the limits of the declarations of the States in question.

It should be added that the principle of reciprocity refers to the extension and the substance of the obligations, including the reservations these might contain, and not to the formal conditions regarding the creation, duration or denouncement. Therefore, reciprocity cannot be invoked by a State in order not to respect the terms of its own declaration, no matter what its field of application, its limits or its conditions might be[62]. On the contrary, the principle or condition of reciprocity intervenes at this time in order to determine whether, in the light of the interpretation and the comparison that the Court has made of the content of the two declarations, it can be concluded that the controversy is restricted to these narrower limits which represent the area for which the applicant and the respondent have accepted "the same obligation" with regard to the exercise of the compulsory jurisdiction by the Court"[63].

This principle is also present with regard to the reservations made on a State accepting the jurisdiction and can be re-conducted to two categories: "reservations" (by virtue of which, the declaration of acceptance of the compulsory jurisdiction of the ICJ is limited to the controversies which arise after the declaration comes into force), and the "reservations *ratione temporis*" (which are drafted with regard to facts or situations which are posterior to the declaration of acceptance coming into force and constitute a limitation to the field of application of the principle of reciprocity of article 36.2 of the Statute)[64]. The interpretation in these cases is based on the distinction made by the ICJ in its case law between "facts and situations that have guide to a dispute" and the "dispute in itself"[65].

In conclusion, according to the Court, the content of the principle or condition of reciprocity comes from the fact that both the applicant and the respondent have accepted the "same obligation" with regard to the reason for the proceedings defined in the claim, which is a rule contained in article 36.2 of its Statute. It also serves as a criterion in such jurisdiction in order to determine the condition of those declaring from both States, that is to say, in order to check whether the "principle of mutuality", which is equally required by the system is being complied with[66].

As we have been able to verify, the interpretation of the declarations of acceptance of the jurisdiction of the ICJ is carried out by the ICJ with the same criteria already examined with regard to unilateral declarations *strictu sensu*, and the text

---

[62] Cf. ICJ, *Reports 1984*, p. 419.

[63] Torres Bernardez, S., "La 'reciprocidad' ….", *op. cit.*, p. 388.

[64] As the ICJ pointed out in the Case of the *Interhandel*, reciprocity allows the State which has accepted the wider jurisdiction of the Court to avail itself of the reservations to this acceptance drawn up by the other party and not expressed in its acceptance, it is "here" that the effect of reciprocity ends" (ICJ, *Reports 1959*, p. 23).

[65] In this regard, see Torres Bernardez, S., "La 'reciprocidad'….", *op. cit.*, pages 408 et seq.

[66] Cf. *ibid.*, p. 388.

is the starting point in order to determine the intention of the parties. The interpretation of this text is carried out by the ICJ by recourse to the general rule of interpretation, in consonance with the conception the Court itself has of the system of the optional clause in the sense of the establishment of a network of undertakings as a result of the conventional framework it is contained within[67].

[67] Cf. the case of the *Military and Paramilitary Activities in and against Nicaragua* (ICJ, *Reports 1984*, p. 418).

Part Two:

Analysis of International Practice: The Interpretative Canons Employed by International Case Law

CHAPTER VI:

The International Court of Justice (I.C.J.)

1 Introduction

The competence of the I.C.J. in matters of interpretation is drawn up in Article 36 of its Statute in the following terms:

> "1.The jurisdiction of the Court comprises all cases which the parties refer to it and all matters especially provided for in the Charter of the United Nations or in treaties and conventions in force.
>
> 2. The states parties to this Statute may at any time declare that they recognise as compulsory *ipso facto* and without any special agreement, as regards any other state accepting the same obligation, the jurisdiction of the Court in all legal disputes concerning:
>
> a) the interpretation of a treaty;
>
> b) any question of international law".

Article 36 is completed with article 38 which states that, in such disputes as are submitted to it, the Court shall apply international conventions and international custom. In matters of interpretation this is specified by the necessity to apply the 1969 and 1986 Vienna Conventions on the Law of Treaties, both of which contain the interpretative rules we have seen.

Consequently, five situations are envisaged. The first, when States involved in a dispute on interpretation decide voluntarily or as a consequence of having recognised the jurisdiction of the Court to be compulsory, to submit it to this Court[1]. Secondly, as a body of the United Nations, the I.C.J. is competent to interpret the Charter through advisory opinions[2]. The third situation is when States agree by treaty that

---

1 In relation to other norms, paragraph b) of Article 36 is applicable because it involves all legal disputes concerning "any question of international law".

2 In its advisory opinion concerning the *Western Sahara* the Court recalls its status as a body of the United Nations and that its acts (advisory opinions and judgements) constitute a way for the I.C.J. to participate in U.N. action (cf. *Reports 1975*, p. 21). As regards this matter see ROSENNE, S.,, *The Law and Practice of the International Court*, M. Nijhoff, Dordrecht, 1985.

any dispute concerning its interpretation will be submitted to the I.C.J.[3] Fourthly, interpretation derived from the application of general or particular conventions to the specific case was included in Article 38.1 a) of the Statute of the I.C.J.

The last situation is that of the interpretation of the judgements of the Court included in Article 60 of its Statute:

> "In the event of dispute as to the meaning or scope of the judgement, the Court shall construe it upon the request of any party".

Finally, the I.C.J. can also intervene in matters of interpretation on the occasion of the issue of advisory opinions "on any legal question"[4].

The analysis we have made of the case law of the I.C.J. from its origin until today reveals, firstly, that for the Court as well as for the I.L.C. interpretation is a *legal question*. The Court had already made it clear in 1948, in its advisory opinion on the *Conditions of Admission of a State to Membership in the United Nations (Article 4 of the Charter)* stating that:

> "To determine the meaning of a treaty provision – to determine, as in this case, the character (exhaustive or otherwise) of the conditions for admission stated therein – is a problem of interpretation and consequently a legal question"[5].

Later, in 1975, it again stated its opinion on the occasion of the interpretation of the expression "legal question" in Article 65.1 of its Statute (already referred to) and present also in Article 96 of the U.N. Charter[6]. On this occasion, the Court says that:

---

[3] Thus, the Convention against Torture and Other Cruel, Inhuman or Degrading Treatment or Punishment, of December 10, 1984 (art. 30).

In this case as well as in that of a dispute of interpretation between two or more States, Articles 62 and 63 of the Statute of the Court shall be applied. Article 62 states:

> "1. Should a state consider that it has an interest of a legal nature which may be affected by the decision in the case, it may submit a request to the Court to be permitted to intervene.
>
> 2. It shall be for the Court to decide upon this request".

Article 63 states:

> "1. Whenever the construction of a convention to which states, other than those concerned in the case, are parties is in question, the Registrar shall notify all such states forthwith.
>
> 2. Each state so notified has the right to intervene in the proceedings; but if it uses this right, the construction given by the judgement will be equally binding upon it".

[4] Article 65.1. Chapter IV of the Court's Statute has to do with this question.

[5] I.C.J., *Reports 1948*, p. 61.

[6] Article 96 says:

> "1. The General Assembly or the Security Council may request the International Court of Justice to give an advisory opinion on any legal question.
>
> 2. Other bodies of the United Nations and specialised agencies, which may at any time be so authorised by the General Assembly, may also request advisory opinions from the Court on legal questions arising within the scope of their activities".

"although these pronouncements were made in somewhat different contexts, they indicate that the references to any legal question in the above mentioned provisions of the Charter and Statute are not to be interpreted restrictively"[7].

As concerns the argument that advisory opinions of the I.C.J. have to do with legal questions only when it pronounces directly upon the rights and obligations of the States, the Court considers that to accept this would be the same as to admit a restrictive interpretation of its advisory jurisdiction. It affirms this in the following terms:

"Thus, to assert that an advisory opinion deals with a legal question within the meaning of the Statute only when it pronounces directly upon the rights and obligations of the States or parties concerned, or upon the conditions which, if fulfilled, would result in the coming into existence, modification or termination of such a right or obligation, would be to take too restrictive a view of the scope of the Court's advisory jurisdiction"[8].

From the point of view of the *interpretative canons*, from 1948 to 2006 – the period we have chosen for the present work – the I.C.J. uses the following:

– the natural and ordinary meaning[9];

---

7 I.C.J., advisory opinion concerning the *Western Sahara, Reports 1975*, p. 20, paragraph 18.

8 *Ibid*., p. 20, paragraph 19.

9 In the following cases: Advisory Opinion concerning the *Conditions of Admission of a State to Membership in the United Nations (Article 4 of Charter)* (I.C.J., *Reports 1948*, p. 63), Advisory Opinion concerning the *Competence of the General Assembly for the Admission of a State to the United Nations* (I.C.J., *Reports 1950*, p. 8), Advisory Opinion concerning the *Interpretation of Peace Treaties with Bulgaria, Hungary and Rumania* (I.C.J., *Reports 1950*, p. 227), *Asylum case* (I.C.J., *Reports 1950*, p. 279), *Anglo-Iranian Oil Company* (I.C.J., *Reports 1952*, p. 104), *Rights of Nationals of the United States of America in Morocco* (I.C.J., *Reports 1952*, p. 195), the *Ambatielos case* (I.C.J., *Reports 1952*, p. 41), Advisory Opinion concerning the *Admissibility of Hearings of Petitioners by the Committee on South West Africa* (I.C.J., *Reports 1956*, p. 28), *Right of Passage over Indian territory* (I.C.J., *Reports 1957*, p. 142), *Aerial incident of 27 July 1955* (I.C.J., *Reports 1959*, p. 142), Advisory Opinion concerning the *Constitution of the Maritime Safety Committee of the Intergovernmental Maritime Consultative Organization* (I.C.J., *Reports 1960*, p. 158-161), *Temple of Préah Vihear* (I.C.J., *Reports 1961*, p. 32), *South West Africa* (I.C.J., *Reports 1962*, p. 336), *Aegean Sea Continental Shelf* (I.C.J., *Reports 1978*, p. 22, paragraph 52), *Arbitration Award of 31 July 1989* (I.C.J., *Reports 1991*, p. 69 et seq., paragraph 48); *Land, Island and Maritime Frontier Dispute (El Salvador/Honduras)* I.C.J., *Reports 1992*, p. 586); *Maritime Delimitation in the Area between Greenland and Jan Mayen* (I.C.J., *Reports 1993*, p. 50); *Territorial Dispute (Libyan Arab Jamahiriya/Chad* (I.C.J., *Reports 1994*, p. 22); *Maritime Delimitation and Territorial Questions involving Qatar and Bahrain* (I.C.J., *Reports 1994*, p. 121 and *Reports 1995*, pages 17-19); Advisory Opinion concerning *Legality of the Use by a State of Nuclear Weapons in Armed Conflict,*(I.C.J., *Reports 1996, pages 75-76, paragraphs 19-21); Kasikili/Sedudu Island (Bot-*

- the context[10];
- the object and purpose of the treaty[11];
- the intention of the Parties[12];

---

swana/Namibia) (I.C.J., *Reports 1999); Legality of Use of Force (Serbia and Montenegro v. Belgium)* (I.C.J., *Reports 2004,* para.101); *Sovereignty over Pulau Ligitan and Pulau Sipadan (Indonesia/Malaysia),* (I.C.J., *Reports 2002*).

[10] In the following cases: *Aerial Incident of 27 July 1955* (I.C.J., *Reports 1959*, p. 142), Advisory Opinion concerning *the Constitution of the Maritime Safety Committee of the Intergovernmental Maritime Consultative Organization* (I.C.J., *Reports 1960*, p. 158), Advisory Opinion concerning *Certain Expenses of the United Nations (Article 17, paragraph 2, of the Charter)* (I.C.J., *Reports 1962*, p. 162), advisory opinion on the *Legal Consequences for States of the Continued Presence of South Africa in Namibia (South West Africa) notwithstanding Security Council Resolution 276 (1970)* (I.C.J., *Reports 1971*, p. 31), *Western Sahara* (I.C.J., *Reports 1975*, p. 40, paragraph 85), *Aegean Sea Continental Shelf* (I.C.J., *Reports 1978*, p. 43, paragraph 105), *Arbitration Award of 31 July 1989* (I.C.J., *Reports 1991*, p. 69, paragraph 48); *Maritime Delimitation in the Area between Greenland and Jan Mayen* (I.C.J., *Reports 1993*, p. 50); *Territorial Dispute (Libyan Arab Jamahiriya/Chad)* (I.C.J., *Reports 1994*, p. 25); *Maritime Delimitation and Territorial Questions involving Qatar and Bahrain* (I.C.J., *Reports 1994*, p. 119 and *Reports 1995*, p. 17); Advisory Opinion concerning *the Legality of the Use by a State of Nuclear Weapons in Armed Conflict,* (I.C.J., *Reports 1996*, pages 75-76, paragraphs 19-21); *LaGrand case (Germany v. United States of America)* (I.C.J., *Reports 2001*, para. 102); *Sovereignty over Pulau Ligitan and Pulau Sipadan (Indonesia/Malaysia),* (I.C.J., *Reports 2002*).

[11] In the following cases: Advisory Opinion concerning *Reservations to the Convention on Genocide* (I.C.J., *Reports 1951*, p. 24), *Rights of Nationals of the United States of America in Morocco* (I.C.J., *Reports 1952*, p. 196), *Constitution of the Maritime Safety Committee of the Intergovernmental Maritime Consultative Organisation* (I.C.J., *Reports 1960*, p. 170), Advisory Opinion concerning *Certain Expenses of the United Nations (Article 17, paragraph 2, of the Charter)* (I.C.J., *Reports 1962*, p. 158 et seq.), *South West Africa* (I.C.J., *Reports 1962*, p. 343), *South West Africa (Second Phase)* (I.C.J., *Reports 1966*, p. 48, paragraph 91), Advisory Opinion concerning the *Western Sahara* (I.C.J., *Reports 1975*, p. 40, paragraph 84); *Maritime Delimitation in the Area between Greenland and Jan Mayen* (I.C.J., *Reports 1993*, p. 50); *Territorial Dispute (Libyan Arab Jamahiriya/Chad)* (I.C.J., *Reports 1994*, p. 25 and *Reports 1995*, p. 17); *Oil Platforms* (I.C.J., *Reports 1996*, p. 813); Advisory Opinion concerning *Legality of the Use by a State of Nuclear Weapons in Armed Conflict* (I.C.J., *Reports 1996*, pages 75-76 paragraphs 19-21); *Avena and other Mexican Nationals* (I.C.J., *Reports 2004*, p. 26, para. 40; p. 38, para 84); *Legality of Use of Force (Serbia and Montenegro v. Belgium)* (I.C.J., *Reports 2004*, para.102); *LaGrand case (Germany v. United States of America)* (I.C.J., *Reports 2001*, para.102); *Sovereignty over Pulau Ligitan and Pulau Sipadan (Indonesia/Malaysia),* (I.C.J., *Reports 2002*).

[12] In the following cases: Advisory Opinion concerning *Reservations to the Convention on Genocide* (I.C.J., *Reports 1951*, p. 23), *Ambatielos* (I.C.J., *Reports 1952*, p. 45), *Rights of Nationals of the United States of America in Morocco* (I.C.J., *Reports 1952*, p. 198), Advisory Opinion about the *Admissibility of hearings of Petitioners by the Committee on South West Africa* (I.C.J., *Reports 1956*, p. 28), *Sovereignty over Certain Frontier Land* (I.C.J., *Reports 1959*, p. 221 et seq. and p. 225), *Right of Passage over Indian Territory* (I.C.J., *Reports 1960*, p. 38), advisory opinion on the *Legal Consequences for States of the Continued*

- the principle of effectiveness[13];
- the preparatory work[14];
- the subsequent practice[15];
- the spirit of the treaty[16];
- equity[17];
- treaties authenticated in two or more languages[18];

Presence of South Africa in Namibia (South West Africa) notwithstanding Security Council Resolution 276 (1970) (I.C.J., *Reports 1971*, p. 31), *Elettronica Sicula S.p.A. (ELSI)*, (I.C.J., *Reports 1989*, p. 42, paragraph 50); *Maritime Delimitation in the Area between Greenland and Jan Mayen* (I.C.J., *Reports 1993*, p. 50); *Territorial Dispute (Libyan Arab Jamahiriya/Chad* (I.C.J., *Reports 1994*, p. 22 and *Reports 1995*, p. 17).

13 In the following cases: *Corfu Channel* (I.C.J., *Reports 1949*, p. 24), Advisory Opinion concerning the *Interpretation of Peace Treaties with Bulgaria, Hungary and Rumania* (I.C.J., *Reports 1950*, p. 229); *South West Africa (Second Phase)* (I.C.J., *Reports 1966*, p. 48); *Legal Consequences for States of the Continued Presence of South Africa in Namibia (South West Afrcia) notwithstanding Security Council Resolution 276 (1970)* (I.C.J., *Reports 1971*, p. 35); *Aegean Sea Continental Shelf*(I.C.J., *Reports 1978*, p. 22); *Territorial Dispute (Libyan Arab Jamahiriya/ Chad* (I.C.J., *Reports 1994*, p. 25).

14 In the following cases: Advisory Opinion concerning the *Conditions of Admission of a State to Membership in the United Nations (Article 4 of Charter)* (I.C.J., *Reports 1948*, p. 63); advisory opinion on *the Competence of the General Assembly regarding Admission to the United Nations* (I.C.J., *Reports 1950*, p. 8), *South West Africa* (I.C.J., *Reports 1962*, p. 344); *Aegean Sea Continental Shelf* (I.C.J., *Reports 1978*, p. 32, paragraph 77); *Border and Cross-Border Armed Action (Nicaragua v. Honduras), Jurisdiction and Admissibility)* (I.C.J., *Reports 1988*, p. 85); *Territorial Dispute (Libyan Arab Jamahiriya/Chad* (I.C.J., *Reports 1994*, p. 27 and *Reports 1995*, pages 17 and 21); *Kasikili/Sedudu Island (Botswana/Namibia)* (I.C.J., *Reports 1999); Avena and other Mexican Nationals* (I.C.J., *Reports 2004*, p. 26, para. 40; pp. 38-39, para. 87 and 88); *Legality of Use of Force (Serbia and Montenegro v. Belgium)* (I.C.J., *Reports 2004*, para.103-113); *Sovereignty over Pulau Ligitan and Pulau Sipadan (Indonesia/Malaysia),* (I.C.J., *Reports 2002).*

15 In the following cases: Advisory Opinion concerning the *Constitution of the Maritime Safety Committee of the Intergovernmental Maritime Consultative Organization* (I.C.J., *Reports 1960,* p. 167); *Land, Island and Maritime Frontier* Dispute (I.C.J., *Reports 1992*, p. 586) *Maritime Delimitation in the Area between Greenland and Jan Mayen* (I.C.J., *Reports 1993*, p. 51); *Oil Platforms* (I.C.J., *Reports 1996*, p. 815); Advisory Opinion concerning the *Legality of the Use by a State of Nuclear Weapons in Armed Conflict*,(I.C.J., *Reports 1996*, p. 75, paragraph 19); *Kasikili/Sedudu Island* (Botswana/Namibia) *(*I.C.J., *Reports 1999).*

16 In the case concerning *Haya de la Torre* (I.C.J., *Reports 1951*, p. 81).

17 In the following cases: *South West Africa (Second Phase)* (I.C.J., *Reports 1966*, p. 48, paragraph 90), and the *Territorial Dispute* (I.C.J., *Reports 1986*, p. 567 et seq., paragraph 28).

18 In the following cases: Advisory Opinions concerning the *Conditions of Admission of a State to Membership in the United Nations* (Article 4 of Charter) (I.C.J., *Reports 1948*, p. 61), and the *Applicability of Article VI, Section 22, of the Convention on the Privileges and Immunities of the United Nations* (I.C.J., *Reports 1989*, p. 194). Also in the cases concerning *Maritime Delimitation in the Area between Greenland and Jan Mayen*

– Inter-temporal law[19].

Now we move on to analyse the case law of the I.C.J. concerning these criteria. Two periods can be distinguished as regards this matter: the periods before and after the codification made by the 1969 Vienna Convention on the Law of Treaties in this regard. As a result of this analysis we will be able to conclude whether the I.C.J. uses the general rule of interpretation as it was conceived by the I.L.C. or whether it is applied otherwise.

2 General canons employed

2.1 The natural and ordinary meaning of the terms

As the Court has repeated recently, the text is the starting point of the interpretative process: "interpretation must be based, above all, upon the text of the treaty" and if it is clear due to the fact that it reflects the intention of its authors it is applied as it stands[20].

This general rule of interpretation, which, in the words of the Court before codification in this matter, is one of "its normal canons of interpretation"[21], is asserted by the I.C.J. since its firsts judgements and continue the line laid down by its predecessor, the P.C.I.J. Already in 1950, for example, it stated that the first duty of a court which is called upon to interpret the provisions of a treaty is to

---

(I.C.J., *Reports 1993*, p. 48); and *Maritime Delimitation and Territorial Questions between Qatar and Bahrain* (I.C.J., *Reports 1994*, p. 119). In this last case the treaty is drafted in Arabic but the dispute arose from the English translation given to the I.C.J. by the Parties. More recently, in the following cases: LaGrand (Germany v. United States of America) (I.C.J., *Reports 2001*, para. 99); *Avena and other Mexican Nationals* (I.C.J., *Reports 2004*, p. 26, para. 40); *Kasikili/Sedudu Island (Botswana/Namibia)* (I.C.J., *Reports 1999*); *Sovereignty over Pulau Ligitan and Pulau Sipadan (Indonesia/Malaysia)* (I.C.J., *Reports 2002*).

19 In the following cases: *Rights of Nationals of the United States of America in Morocco* (I.C.J., *Reports 1952*, p. 189), *Western Sahara* (I.C.J., *Reports 1975*, p. 38 et seq., paragraphs 79 and 80), and *Aegean Sea Continental Shelf* (I.C.J., *Reports 1978*, p. 31 et seq., paragraphs 74 to 77).

20 Case concerning the *Territorial Dispute (Lybian Arab Jamahiriya/Chad* (I.C.J., *Reports 1994*, p. 22). And "if the intention had been otherwise, Article 2 would have been so worded as to make it clear that it is providing for only a part of the total boundary contemplated by the Preamble and Article 1" (case concerning *Maritime Delimitation in the area between Greenland and Jan Mayen,* I.C.J., *Reports 1993*, p. 50).

21 The complete quotation is as follows:

> "the Court must apply its normal canons of interpretation, the first of which, according to the established jurisprudence of the Court, is that words are to be interpreted according to their natural and ordinary meaning in the context in which they occur" (I.C.J., Case concerning the *Temple of Preah Vihear, Reports 1961*, p. 32).

More recently, in 1992, the Court repeats its expression "normal canons of interpretation" in order to refer, later, to the "basic rule of Article 31 of the Vienna Convention on the Law of Treaties, ..." (*Land, Island and Maritime Frontier Dispute,* I.C.J., *Reports 1992*, p. 582 et seq.).

endeavour to give effect to them "in their natural and ordinary meaning in the context in which they occur"[22]. While interpreting in such a way, if the relevant words make sense in their context, that is the end of the matter.

From the analysis of the I.C.J. case law we have made, it has been shown that the rule of the "natural and ordinary meaning" of the terms was completed, before the 1969 Vienna Convention on the Law of Treaties, with the following guidelines. *First*, only if the words "in their natural and ordinary meaning are ambiguous or lead to an unreasonable result, then, and then only, must the Court, by resort to other methods of interpretation, seek to ascertain what the parties really meant when they used these words"[23].

Secondly, the rule of the "natural and ordinary meaning" is not an absolute one. This was stated by the I.C.J. in the case concerning *South West Africa (Preliminary Exceptions)*:

> "where such a method of interpretation results in a meaning incompatible with the spirit, purpose and context of the clause or instrument in which the words are contained, no reliance can be validly placed on it"[24].

Third, the choice of this method (as described by the I.C.J.) does not mean that the Court gives priority to grammatical or literal interpretation and that this method always prevails[25]. This would only be possible if the grammatical arguments were "compelling and decisive"[26].

---

[22] I.C.J., advisory opinion on the *Competence of the General Assembly for the Admission of a State to the United Nations* (*Reports 1950*, p. 8). This general rule of interpretation is also used in the case concerning the *Arbitration Award of 31 July 1989* (I.C.J., *Reports 1991*, p. 69, paragraph 48). Cf. FITZMAURICE, G., "The Law and Procedure …", *op. cit.*, pages 203 et seq.

[23] I.C.J., advisory opinion on the *Competence of the General Assembly for the Admission of a State to the United Nations*, (*Reports 1950*, p. 8. In supporting this criterion, what the Court does is to follow the jurisprudence of the P.C.I.J. in the case concerning the *Polish Postal Service in Danzig* when it stated that:

> "it is a cardinal principle of interpretation that words must be interpreted in the sense which they would normally have in their context, unless such interpretation would lead to something unreasonable or absurd" (P.C.I.J., *Series B, No. II*, p. 39).

[24] I.C.J., *Reports 1962*, p. 336. After the 1969 Vienna Convention, the I.C.J. repeats this quotation and confirms the criterion contained in it. So, in the case concerning the *Arbitration Award of 31 July 1989* (I.C.J., *Reports 1991*, p. 69 et seq., paragraph 48).

[25] In fact, the Court:

> "cannot base itself on a purely grammatical interpretation of the text. It must seek the interpretation which is in harmony with a natural and reasonable way of reading the text, …" (case concerning the *Anglo-Iranian Oil Company*, *Reports 1952*, p. 104). See also the preceding footnote.

[26] Thus, in the *Aegean Sea Continental Shelf Case*, the I.C.J. points out that

> "Consequently, only if the grammatical arguments were compelling and decisive would the Court be convinced that such is the effect which ought to be given to the words. … But those arguments do not appear to the Court to be so compelling as has been suggested" (*Reports 1978*, p. 22, paragraph 52).

Fourth, when it is possible to interpret the treaty giving to the words their natural and ordinary meaning, the Court considers that it may not interpret them by giving them a different meaning[27].

The *last* specification of the principle of the "natural and ordinary meaning" resulting from the jurisprudence of the Court before the codification made by the 1969 Vienna Convention is, that it is not permissible to resort to preparatory works when the text of the treaty is clear[28].

In its more recent jurisprudence, the I.C.J. affirms that the method as well the principles "are reflected in Articles 31 and 32 of the Vienna Convention on the Law of Treaties, which may in many respects be considered as a codification of existing customary international law on the point"[29], and that "in accordance with

---

27 So, in the advisory opinion concerning the *Competence of the General Assembly for the Admission of a State to the United Nations*:

> "When the Court can give effect to a provision of a treaty by giving to the words used in it their natural and ordinary meaning, it may not interpret the words by seeking to give them some other meaning. In the present case the Court finds no difficulty in ascertaining the natural and ordinary meaning of the words in question and no difficulty in giving effect to them" (I.C.J., *Reports 1950*, p. 8).

Its quotation in the *Ambatielos* case is along the same lines when it states :

> "The Court cannot accept an interpretation which would have a result obviously contrary to the language of the Declaration and to the continuous will of both Parties ..." (I.C.J., *Reports 1952*, p. 45). Also, "it introduces a distinction in the plain language of the Declaration for which the Court sees no justification" (*ibid.*, p. 41).

28 Thus, in the advisory opinion concerning the *Conditions of Admission of a State to Membership of the United Nations (Article 4 off the Charter)*, where the Court stated:

> "The Court considers that the text is sufficiently clear; consequently, it does not feel that it should deviate from the consistent practice of the Permanent Court of International Justice, according to which there is no occasion to resort to preparatory work if the text of a convention is sufficiently clear in itself" (*Reports 1948*, p. 63).

And in the advisory opinion concerning the *Competence of the General Assembly for the Admission of a State to the United Nations*, after stating what was quoted in the preceding footnote added:

> "Some of the written statements submitted to the Court have invited it to investigate the *travaux préparatoires* of the Charter. Having regard, however, to the considerations stated above, the Court is of the opinion that it is not permissible, in this case, to resort to *travaux préparatoires*" (I.C.J., *Reports 1950*, p. 8), because the natural and ordinary meaning in this case allows it to give sense to the words.

29 I.C.J., case concerning the *Arbitration Award of 31 July 1989, Reports 1991*, p. 70, paragraph 48. Also in the case concerning *Oil Platforms*:

> "The Court recalls that, according to customary international law as expressed in Article 31 of the Vienna Convention on the Law of Treaties of 23 May 1969, a treaty must be interpreted in good faith and in accordance with the ordinary meaning to be given to its terms in their context and in the light of its object and purpose. Under Article 32, recourse may be had to supplementary means of interpretation such as the preparatory

customary international law, reflected in Article 31 of the 1969 Vienna Convention on the Law of Treaties, a treaty must be interpreted in good faith and in accordance with the ordinary meaning to be given to its terms in their context and in the light of its object and purpose. Interpretation must be based above all upon the text of the treaty. As a supplementary measure, recourse may be had to means of interpretation such as the preparatory work of the treaty and the circumstances of its conclusion"[30].

In relationship with Article 35, paragraph 2 of the Statute of the Court, that refers to "the special provisions contained in treaties in force" in the context of the question of access to the Court it states:

> "Taking the natural and ordinary meaning of the words 'special provisions', the reference must in the view of the Court be to treaties that make 'special provision' in relation to the Court, and this can hardly be anything other than provision for the settlement of disputes between the parties to the treaty by reference of the matter to the Court"[31].

It specifies, too, that in order to admit an interpretation other than that which results from the natural meaning of the terms, "a decisive reason" would be re-

---

work and the circumstances in which the treaty was concluded" (I.C.J., *Reports 1996*, p. 812). Cf. also, *Kasikili/Sedudu Island (Botswana/Namibia), Judgement,* I.C.J., *Reports 1999 (II)*, p. 1059, para. 18; *Sovereignty over Pulau Ligitan and Pulau Sipadan (Indonesia/Malaysia)*, I.C.J., *Reports 2002*, para. 37; *Oil platforms (Islamic Republic of Iran v. United States of America)*, I.C.J., *Reports 2003*, para. 40; *Legality of Use of Force (Serbia and Montenegro v.Belgium)*, I.C.J., *Reports 2004*, para. 100.

30 I.C.J., case concerning the *Territorial Dispute (Libyan Arab Jamahiriya/Chad, Reports 1994, Judgement*, pages 21-22, paragraph 41. Cf. also its Advisory Opinion concerning *Legality of the Use by a State of Nuclear Weapons in Armed Conflict*,, (I.C.J., *Reports 1996*, p. 75, paragraph 19) and its decisions in the following cases: *Oil platforms (Islamic Republic of Iran v. United States of America)*, (I.C.J., *Reports 2003*, para. 40); *Legality of Use of Force (Serbia and Montenegro v. Belgium)*, I.C.J., *Reports 2004*, para. 100.

31 Case concerning *Legality of Use of Force (Serbia and Montenegro v.Belgium)*, I.C.J., *Reports 2004*, para. 101. As for the words "treaties in force" the Court interpret them as "those which were in force on the date of the institution of proceedings in a case in which such treaties are invoked. In favour of this latter interpretation, it may be observed that the similar expression 'treaties and conventions in force' is found in Article 36, paragraph 1, of the Statute, and the Court has interpreted it in this sense (for example, *Questions of Interpretation and Application of the 1971 Montreal Convention arising from the Aerial Incident at Lockerbie, (Lybian Arab Jamahiriya v. United Kingdom), Preliminary Objections, Judgement,* I.C.J., *Reports 1998*, p. 16, para. 19). The expression 'treaty or convention into force' in Article 37 of the Statute has also been read as meaning in force at the date proceedings were instituted (*Barcelona Traction, Light and Power Company, Limited, Preliminary Objections, Judgement,* I.C.J., *Reports 1964*, p. 27)" (*ibid.*).

quired[32]. Also, that "in order to illuminate the meaning of words agreed upon in 1890, there is nothing that prevents the Court from taking into account the present-day state of scientific knowledge, as reflected in the documentary material submitted to it by the Parties (compare *Controversia sobre el recorrido de la traza del límite entre el Hito 62 y el Monte Fitz Roy (Argentina/Chile) [Dispute concerning the course of the frontier between B.P. 62 and Mount Fitz Roy (Argentina/Chile)]*, also known as the *"Laguna del desierto"* case, Arbitral Award of 21 October 1994, *International Law Reports (ILR)*, Vol. 113, p. 76, para. 157; *Revue générale de droit international public (RGDIP),* Vol. 2, 1996, p. 592, para. 157)"[33].

Finally, it should be added that this interpretative rule is on occasions combined by the Court with other interpretative criteria such as those of the context, the object and the purpose of the treaty[34].

2.2 The context

Before the codification made by the 1969 Vienna Convention, in the case law of the I.C.J. the preamble of the treaty as well as its annexes (if there are any) are part of the treaty. Thus, for example in the *Ambatielos* case, where the Court said that "the provisions of the Declaration are in the nature of an interpretation clause, and, as such, should be regarded as an integral part of the Treaty, even if this was not stated in the terms"[35]. The limitation of this rule of interpretation resides in the fact that its use shall not lead to something unreasonable or absurd[36].

---

[32] So, in the advisory opinion concerning the *Conditions of Admission of a State to Membership of the United Nations (Article 4 of Charter)*:

> "To warrant an interpretation other than that which ensues from the natural meaning of the words, a decisive reason would be required, and this has not been established" (*Reports 1948*, p. 63).

Cf. also *Kasikili/Sedudu Island (Botswana/Namibia), Judgement,* I.C.J., *Reports 1999 (II)*, p. 1059, para. 18; *Sovereignty over Pulau Ligitan and Pulau Sipadan (Indonesia/Malaysia)*, I.C.J., *Reports 2002*, para. 37; *Oil platforms (Islamic Republic of Iran v. United States of America)*, I.C.J., *Reports 2003*, para. 40; *Legality of Use of Force (Serbia and Montenegro v.Belgium)*, I.C.J., *Reports 2004*, para. 100.

[33] Case concerning *Kasikili/Sedudu Island (Botswana/Namibia), Judgement,* I.C.J., *Reports 1999 (II)*, p. 1059, para. 20.

[34] So, recently in the cases concerning *Maritime Delimitation in the Area between Greenland and Jan Mayen* (I.C.J., *Reports 1993*, p. 50) and the *Territorial Dispute (Libyan Arab Jamahiriya/Chad* (I.C.J., *Reports 1994*, p. 25 and *Reports 1995*, pages 17-19).

[35] I.C.J., *Reports 1952*, p. 44.

[36] Cf. the case concerning the *Polish Postal Service in Danzig* (P.C.I.J., *Series B*, No. 11, p. 39).

More recently: "Any other interpretation would encounter serious difficulties: it would deprive the phrase of its effect and could, moreover, well lead to an unreasonable result" (case concerning *Maritime Delimitation and Territorial Questions involving Qatar and Bahrain, Judgement, Reports 1995*, p. 19).

In that period, the use by the Court of the criterion of the context as a principle to take into account in the interpretative process has a secondary characteristic: it will be used only if doubts remain after turning to the natural and ordinary meaning of the terms[37]. Also, as a complement to the principle of the natural and ordinary meaning[38].

According to paragraphs a) and b) of Article 31.2 of the 1969 Vienna Convention, for the purpose of the interpretation of a treaty, context comprises, in addition to the text (including its preamble and annexes), any agreement relating to the treaty which has been made between all the parties in connection with the conclusion of the treaty, as well as any instrument which was made by one or more parties in connection with the conclusion of the treaty and accepted by the other parties as an instrument related to the treaty.

---

[37] Thus, in the case concerning the *Aerial Incident of July 27th, 1955 (Israel v. Bulgaria)* in which the Court said:

> "Finally, if any doubt remained, in order to interpret Article 36, paragraph 5, the Court should consider it in its context bearing in mind the general scheme of the Charter and the Statute which is the foundation of the jurisdiction of the Court regarding the consent of States. It should, as is stated in the case of the *monetary gold removed from Rome in 1943*, be careful not to run counter to a well-established principle of international law embodied in the Court's Statute, namely, that the Court can only exercise jurisdiction over a State with its consent" (*I.C.J., Reports 1954*, p. 32)" (I.C.J., *Reports 1959*, p. 142).

The I.C.J. also uses context after analysing the text of the provision in its task of interpretation. For example, in its advisory opinion concerning *Certain Expenses of the United Nations (Article 17, paragraph 2, of the Charter)*, where the analysis of Article 17 is carried out taking into account "its place in the general structure and scheme of the Charter" which constitute its context (*Reports 1962*, p. 162). Also recently in the cases concerning *Maritime Delimitation in the Area between Greenland and Jan Mayen* (I.C.J., *Reports 1993*, p. 50) and the *Territorial Dispute (Libyan Arab Jamahiriya/Chad)* (I.C.J., *Reports 1994*, p. 26).

[38] For example, in the advisory opinion concerning the *Constitution of the Maritime Safety Committee of the Inter-Governmental Maritime consultative Organisation*, in which the I.C.J. states:

> "The meaning of the word 'elected' in the article cannot be determined in isolation by recourse to its usual or common meaning and attaching that meaning to the word where it is used in the Article. The word obtains its meaning from the context in which it is used. If the context requires a meaning which connotes a wide choice, it must be construed accordingly, just as it must be given a restrictive meaning if the context in which it is used so requires" (I.C.J., *Reports 1960*, p. 158).

And in the advisory opinion on *Certain Expenses of the United Nations (Article 17, paragraph 2, of the Charter)* after analysing the text of the article interpreted, the Court passes to "its place in the general structure and scheme of the Charter" which constitutes its context (I.C.J., *Reports 1962*, p. 162).

After 1969, the study of the case law of the Court concerning the criterion of the context shows that it is used to situate the question put to the Court[39], to situate the international instrument submitted for interpretation[40], to situate the terms of the question[41] or to confirm or reinforce the conclusion arrived at by the Court[42].

---

39 So, for example, in the *Western Sahara* case, the resolution of the General Assembly in which the opinion of the I.C.J. is requested shows that the two questions contained in the request:

> "have been put to the Court in the context of proceedings in the General Assembly directed to the decolonisation of Western Sahara in conformity with resolution 1514 (XV) of 14 December 1960", in which Morocco and Mauritania claimed this territory (I.C.J., *Reports 1975*, p. 40, paragraph 85).

40 So, in the advisory opinion on the *Legal Consequences for States of the Continued Presence of South Africa in Namibia (South West Africa) notwithstanding Security Council Resolution 276 (1970)*, in which, after recalling "the primary necessity of interpreting an instrument in accordance with the intentions of the parties at the time of its conclusion", it adds:

> "Moreover, an international instrument has to be interpreted and applied within the framework of the entire legal system prevailing at the time of the interpretation" (I.C.J., *Reports 1971*, p. 31), also taking into account the important developments of the legal order in this sector.

Also, recently, in the case concerning *Maritime Delimitation and Territorial Questions involving Qatar and Bahrain* (I.C.J., *Reports 1994*, p. 119). Here, context is given by the good offices of King Fahd Ben Abdul Aziz, of Saudi Arabia.

41 So, for example, in the case concerning the *Arbitral Award of 31 July 1989* (I.C.J., *Reports 1991*, p. 69, paragraph 48), where the I.C.J. textually repeats its case law given in the advisory opinion on the *Competence of the General Assembly for the admission of a State to the United Nations* (I.C.J., *Reports 1950*, p. 8). Also in the *Aegean Sea Continental Shelf* case, where the Court says:

> "Consequently, it is in that context – …- that the meaning of the Brussels Joint communiqué of 31 May 1975 has to be appraised. When read in that context, the terms of the Communiqué do not appear to the Court to evidence any change in the position of the Turkish Government with regard to the conditions under which it was ready to agree to the submittal of the dispute to the Court" (I.C.J., *Reports 1978*, p. 43).

Cf. also *LaGrand case (Germany v. United States of America)*, C.I.J., *Reports 2001*, para. 77 and 102: "The context in which Article 41 has to be seen within the Statute is to prevent the Court from being hampered in the exercise of its functions because the respective rights of the parties to a dispute before the Court are not preserved" (para. 102).

42 As confirmation, in the *Land, Island and Maritime Frontier Dispute (El Salvador/Honduras: Nicaragua intervening)* case, in which the Court places the phrase "in the wider context, first of the Special Agreement as a whole, and then of the 1980 General Peace Treaty, to which the Special Agreement refers" (I.C.J., *Reports 1992*, p. 583).

In order to reinforce its conclusions, in the case concerning the *Territorial Dispute (Libyan Arab Jamahiriya/Chad)* (I.C.J., *Reports 1994*, p. 26).

2.3 The object and purpose of the treaty

In the case law before 1969, in the opinion of the Court, the recourse to the criterion of the object and purpose of the treaty reveals the intention of the Parties. Thus, in the advisory opinion concerning *Reservations to the Convention on Genocide*[43], in which the I.C.J. states:

> "the Convention was manifestly adopted for a purely humanitarian and civilising purpose. It is indeed difficult to imagine a convention that might have this dual character to a greater degree, since its object on the one hand is to safeguard the very existence of certain human groups and on the other to confirm and endorse the most elementary principles of morality. In such a convention the contracting States do not have any interests of their own; they merely have, one and all, a common interest, namely, the accomplishment of those high purposes which are the *raison d'être* of the convention"[44].

The I.C.J. concludes that it is not possible to make reservations regarding this Convention:

> "The *object and purpose* of the Genocide Convention imply that it was the intention of the General Assembly and of the States which adopted it that as many States as possible should participate … The *object and purpose* of the Convention thus limit both the freedom to make reservations and to object to them. It follows that it is the compatibility of a reservation with the *object and purpose* of the Convention that must furnish the criterion for the attitude of a State making the reservation on accession as well as for the appraisal by a State objecting to the reservation"[45].

Secondly, the interpretative criterion of the object and purpose of the treaty has priority when both are clearly stated in the treaty. For example, in its preamble[46].

---

[43] I.C.J., *Reports 1951*. In this advisory opinion and as regards the *origins*, the Court states:

> "The origins of the Convention show that it was the intention of the United Nations to condemn and punish genocide as 'a crime under international law' involving a denial of the right to existence of entire human groups, a denial which shocks the conscience of mankind and results in great losses to humanity, and which is contrary to moral law and to the spirit and aims of the United Nations (Resolution 96 (I) of the General Assembly, December 11th 1946)" (*ibid.*, p. 23).

[44] *Ibid.*

[45] *Ibid.*, p. 24. The italics are ours.

[46] So, in the case concerning the *Rights of Nationals of the United States of America in Morocco*:

> "The purposes and objects of this Convention were stated in its Preamble in the following words: 'the necessity to establish, on fixed and uniform bases, the exercise of the

Thus, in the case concerning the *Rights of Nationals of the United States of America in Morocco*, where the I.C.J., in relationship with treaties said that the interpretation of the provisions of the Act must take into account its purposes, "which are set forth in the Preamble …"[47].

The same happens concerning the *South West Africa* case regarding the system of mandates of the League of Nations, in which the I.C.J. states that:

> "The manifest scope and purpose of the provisions of this Article indicate that Members of the League were understood to have a legal right or interest in the observance by the Mandatory of its obligation both toward the inhabitants of the Mandated Territory, and toward the League of Nations and its Members"[48].

Third, the Court uses the object and purpose of the treaty to lay aside any interpretation of its provisions which are not in harmony with these[49].

Finally, the analysis of the object and purpose of the treaty can be made by the Court only in order to interpret the treaty and never to rectify or revise it[50].

In the jurisprudence of the I.C.J. after 1969 the recourse to the criterion of the object and purpose of the treaty takes place when the terms "by themselves do not

---

right of protection in Morocco and to settle certain questions connected therewith …'. In these circumstances, the Court can not adopt a construction by implication of the provisions of the Madrid Convention which would go beyond the scope of its declared purposes and objects. Furthermore, this contention would involve radical changes and additions to the provisions of the Convention. The Court, in its Opinion -Interpretation of Peace Treaties (Second Phase) (I.C.J., *Reports* 1950, p. 229)- stated: 'It is the duty of the Court to interpret the Treaties, not to revise them'" (I.C.J., *Reports 1952*, p. 196).

47 *Ibid.*, p. 197. See also the advisory opinion of the I.C.J. concerning *Certain Expenses of the United Nations (Article 17, paragraph 2, of the Charter)*, where the Court analyses the purposes of the United Nations in order to determine whether an expense has been incurred in order to achieve one of these.(I.C.J., *Reports 1962*, pages 162 et seq.).

48 I.C.J., *Reports 1962*, p. 343.

49 So, in the advisory opinion concerning the *Constitution of the Maritime Safety Committee of the Inter-Governmental Maritime Consultative Organisation*:

> "The Court cannot subscribe to an interpretation of 'largest ship-owning nations' in Article 28 (a) which is out of harmony with the purposes of the Convention …" (I.C.J., *Reports 1960*, p. 171).

50 In this regard, in the case concerning *South West Africa, Second Phase* the I.C.J. states:

> "91. It may be urged that the Court is entitled to engage in a process of 'filling in the gaps', in the application of a teleological principle of interpretation, according to which instruments must be given their maximum effect in order to ensure the achievement of their underlying purposes. The Court need not here enquire into the scope of a principle the exact bearing of which is highly controversial, for it is clear that it can have no application in the circumstances in which the Court would have to go beyond what can reasonably be regarded as being a process of interpretation, and would have to engage in a process of rectification or revision" (I.C.J., *Reports 1966*, p. 48).

have a very precise meaning". This is the case of the advisory opinion concerning the *Western Sahara*, in relation to the interpretation of the expression "legal ties" present in Resolution 3292 (XXIX) of the General Assembly of the United Nations. There, the I.C.J. states:

> "That expression, however, unlike '*terra nullius*' in Question I, was not a term having in itself a very precise meaning. Accordingly, in the view of the court, the meaning of the expression 'legal ties' in Question II has to be found rather in the object and purpose of General Assembly resolution 3292 (XXIX), by which it was decided to request the present advisory opinion"[51].

Also, to confirm the interpretation arrived at through the analysis of the text of the treaty[52], to clarify the meaning to be given to the terms of the treaty[53], as well as to reject a certain interpretation[54].

2.4 The subsequent practice

In the period before 1969, this criterion is used to throw light on the study of the question by the Court[55] or in order to know the intention of the Parties[56].

---

[51] I.C.J., *Reports 1975*, p. 32.

[52] For example, in the case concerning the *Territorial Dispute (Libyan Arab Jamahiriya/Chad)*:

> "The object and purpose of the Treaty thus recalled confirm the interpretation of the treaty given above, …" (I.C.J., *Reports 1994*, p. 26).

Also in the case concerning the *Maritime Delimitation in the Area between Greenland and Jan Mayen* (see I.C.J., *Reports 1993*, p. 50 seq.). In the case concerning *Sovereignty over Pulau Ligitan and Pulau Sipadan (Indonesia/Malaysya)* resort to the object and purpose of the 1891 Convention is complemented with the preamble to that Convention: "This interpretation is, in the Court's view, supported by the very scheme of the 1891 Convention" (*Reports 2002*, para. 51). Cf. also *Legality of Use of Force (Serbia and Montenegro v. Belgium)*, I.C.J., *Reports 2004*, para. 100.

[53] Case concerning *Kasikili/Sedudu Island (Botswana/Namibia), Judgement,* I.C.J., *Reports 1999 (II*, para. 43.

[54] "The Court considers that such a general formulation cannot be interpreted in isolation from the object and purpose of the Treaty in which it is inserted … It follows that the object and purpose of the Treaty of 1955 was not to regulate peaceful and friendly relations between the two States in a general sense" (case concerning *Oil Platforms, Reports 1996*, pages 813-814). Cf. also *LaGrand case (Germany v. United States of America*): "The object and purpose of the Statute is to enable the Court to fulfil the functions provided for therein, and in particular, the basic function of judicial settlement of international disputes by binding decisions in accordance with Article 59 of the Statute" (para. 102).

[55] In the advisory opinion concerning the *Constitution of the Maritime Safety Committee of the Inter-Governmental Maritime Consultative Organisation* the I.C.J. says:

After 1969, the I.C.J. uses it to confirm the interpretation made[57], and detract from the argument of one of the Parties as it is not supported by the subsequent practice of the State[58]. Also, to conclude from all of the foregoing that the subsequent practice of the parties did not result in any "agreement between the parties regarding the interpretation of the treaty or the application of its provisions", within the meaning of Article 31, paragraph 3 (a) of the 1969 Vienna Convention on the Law of Treaties, nor did it result in any "practice in the application of the treaty which establishes the agreement of the parties regarding its interpretation", within the meaning of subparagraph (b) of that same provision[59].

In the case concerning the *Land, Island and Maritime Frontier Dispute (El Salvador/Honduras: Nicaragua intervening)*, after considering the customary and conventional character of the subsequent practice in matters of interpretation, the Chamber of the Court does not take this practice into account because none of the considerations raised by Honduras can prevail "over the absence from the text of any specific reference to delimitation"[60].

It is also stated by the Court that a map cannot be consider either an "agreement relating to a treaty which was made between all the parties in connection with the conclusion of the treaty" or an "instrument which was made by a party in connection with the conclusion of the treaty and accepted by the other parties as an instrument related to that treaty", both within the meaning of Article 31, paragraphs

---

> "An examination of certain Articles of the convention and the actual practice which was followed in giving effect to them throws some light on the court's consideration of the question" (I.C.J., *Reports 1960*, p. 167).

56 Thus, in the *Corfu Channel* Case:

> "The subsequent attitude of the Parties shows that it was not their intention, by entering into the Special Agreement, to preclude the Court from fixing the amount of the compensation" (I.C.J., *Reports 1949*, p. 25).

57 Case concerning *Kasikili/Sedudu Island (Botswana/Namibia), Judgement,* I.C.J., *Reports 1999 (II)*, para. 80.

58 See the cases concerning *Maritime Delimitation in the Area between Greenland and Jan Mayen* (I.C.J., *Reports 1993*, p. 51 s.), the *Land, Island and Maritime Frontier Dispute (El Salvador/Honduras: Nicaragua intervening)* (I.C.J., *Reports 1992*, p. 586) and the *Oil Platforms* (I.C.J., *Reports 1996*, p. 815). In the latter: "The practice followed by the Parties with regard to the application of the Treaty does not lead to a different conclusion".

59 Case concerning *Kasikili/Sedudu Island (Botswana/Namibia), Judgement,* I.C.J., *Reports 1999 (II)*, para. 79.

60 Adding that, whenever in the past a special agreement has entrusted the Court with a task related to delimitation, it has spelled out "very clearly" what was asked of the Court: the formulation of principles or rules enabling the parties to agree on delimitation, the precise application of these principles and rules or the task involved in drawing the delimitation line (cf. I.C.J., *Reports 1992*, p. 586). The customary nature of Article 31, paragraph 3 of the Vienna Convention of 23 May 1969 on the Law of Treaties, is also declared by the Court in the case concerning *Sovereignty over Pulau Ligitan and Pulau Sipadan (Indonesia/ Malaysya)* (cf. *Reports 2002*, para. 37).

2 (a) and (b) of the Vienna Convention on the Law of Treaties, because it does not "fall into the category of physical expressions of the will of the State or States concerned"[61].

2.5 The preparatory work

In the case law previous to 1969, preparatory work is used when it is not possible to reach a satisfactory result in the interpretation through the preceding methods[62]. In consequence, these have a subsidiary character. Thus, and continuing with the case law of the P.I.C.J., the I.C.J. considers that it is not possible to resort to preparatory works if the text of the treaty is clear[63]. Nor is this possible if the natural meaning of the terms would be enough to enable interpretation. Finally, the I.C.J. uses preparatory works as an interpretative criterion as regards the subsequent practice of the Parties in order to reject that preparatory works would allow the conclusion that Parties had referred therein to a determined practice[64].

---

[61] Case concerning *Sovereignty over Pulau Ligitan and Pulau Sipadan (Indonesia/Malaysia)* (cf. *Reports 2002*, para. 88).

[62] So, in the advisory opinion on the *Competence of the Assembly regarding Admission to the United Nations*:

> "In the present case the Court finds no difficulty in ascertaining the natural and ordinary meaning of the words in question and no difficulty in giving effect to them. Some of the written statements submitted to the Court have invited it to investigate the *travaux préparatoires* of the Charter. Having regard, however, to the considerations stated above, the Court is of the opinion that it is no permissible, in this case, to resort to *travaux préparatoires*" (I.C.J., *Reports 1950*, p. 8).

In the *South West Africa (Preliminary Objections)* case, however, the I.C.J. uses, among other criteria, the preparatory works when it says that the article in question:

> "was embodied in the draft agreement between the Principle Allied and Associated Powers and was proposed to the Council of the League by the representative of the United Kingdom as the original mandatory on behalf of South Africa, the present Mandatory for South West Africa" (I.C.J., *Reports 1962*, p. 344).

[63] So, in the advisory opinion on the *Conditions of Admission of a State to Membership of the United Nations (Article 4 of Charter)* the I.C.J. says:

> "The Court considers that the text is sufficiently clear; consequently, it does not feel that it should deviate from the consistent practice of the Permanent Court of International Justice, according to which there is no occasion to resort to preparatory work if the text of a convention is sufficiently clear in itself" (I.C.J., *Reports 1947-1948*, p. 63).

In a similar way see the case concerning the *Territorial Dispute (Libyan Arab Jamahiriya/Chad)* (I.C.J., *Reports 1994*, p. 26).

[64] In the advisory opinion concerning *Reservations to the Convention on Genocide*:

> "The preparatory work of the Convention contains nothing to justify the statement that the contracting States implicitly had any definite practice in mind. Nor is there

After 1969, the resort by the I.C.J. to preparatory works takes place in order to reinforce the reading of the provision in question made by the Court[65], to specify the scope and the object of the treaty in question[66] or to confirm its interpretation[67]. Nevertheless, these must be used with caution[68].

> any such indication in the subsequent attitude of the contracting States: neither the reservations made by certain States nor the position adopted by other States towards those reservations permit the conclusion that assent to one or other of these practices had been given" (I.C.J., *Reports 1951*, p. 25 et seq.).

As concerns this question see QUEL LOPEZ, F.J., *Las reservas a los tratados internacionales (un examen de la práctica española)*, Servicio Editorial de la Universidad del País Vasco, Bilbao, 1991, pages 89-222.

65 Thus, in the case concerning *Border and Cross-Border Armed Actions (Nicaragua v. Honduras), Jurisdiction and Admissibility* where the I.C.J. says:

> "Further confirmation of the Court's reading of Article XXXI is to be found in the *travaux préparatoires*. In this case these must of course be resorted to only with caution, as not all the stages of the drafting of the texts at the Bogotá Conference were the subject of detailed records" (I.C.J., *Reports 1988*, p. 85).

Cf. also the cases cocnerning *Legality of Use of Force (Serbia and Montenegro v.Belgium)*, I.C.J., *Reports 2004*, para. 103, and *Kasikili/Sedudu Island (Botswana/Namibia), Judgement,* I.C.J., *Reports 1999 (II)*, para. 46.

66 So, in the case concerning *Fisheries Jurisdiction (United Kingdom v. Iceland)*, in which, after recalling its jurisprudence concerning the subsidiary character of preparatory works when the text of the treaty is sufficiently clear, it undertakes the review of the negotiations that led to the 1961 Exchange of Notes:

> "having regard to the peculiar circumstances of the present proceedings, – the failure to appear of one of the Parties- and in order fully to ascertain the scope and purpose of the 1961 Exchange of Notes, …" (I.C.J., *Reports 1973*, pages 10 and 56).

67 In the case concerning the *Territorial Dispute (Libyan Arab Jamahiriya/Chad)*: "The Court considers that it is not nercessary to refer to *travaux préparatoires* to elucidate the content of the 1955 Treaty; but, as in previous cases, it finds it possible by reference to the *travaux* to confirm its reading of the text, namely, that the treaty constitutes an agreement between the parties which, *inter alia*, defines the frontiers" (I.C.J., *Reports 1994*, p. 27). More recently, it states: "In short, it is clear that none of the sources of interpretation referred to in the relevant Articles of the Vienna Convention on the Law of Treaties, including the preparatory work, contradict the conclusions drawn from the terms of Article 41 read in their context and in the light of the object and purpose of the Statute. Thus, the Court has reached the conclusion that orders on provisional measures under Article 41 have binding effect" (*LaGrand case Germany v. United States of America, Reports 2001*, para. 101). Cf. also the case concerning *Sovereignty over Pulau Ligitan and Pulau Sipadan (Indonesia/Malaysia)* (cf. *Reports 2002*, para. 53).

68 "The *travaux préparatoires* of the Doha Minutes must be used with caution in the present case, on account of their fragmentary nature. In the absence of any document relating the progress of the negotiations, they appear to be confined to two draft texts submitted by Saudi Arabia and Oman successively and the amendments made to the latter" (case concerning *Maritime Delimitation and Territorial Questions between Qatar and Bahrain, Judgement*, I.C.J., *Reports 1995*, p. 21).

2.6 Treaties authenticated in two or more languages

Before the 1969 Vienna Convention on the Law of Treaties, we find an example of a problem of this kind in the advisory opinion concerning the conditions of *Admission of a State to the United Nations (Charter, Art. 4)* where the I.C.J. analyses the English and French texts of Article 4, paragraph 1 of the Charter, concluding that

> "the text of this paragraph, by the enumeration which it contains and the choice of its terms, clearly demonstrates the intention of its authors to establish a legal rule which, while it fixes the conditions of admission, determines also the reasons for which admission may be refused;"[69].

As we have seen, as concerns treaties authenticated in two or more languages, Article 33 of the 1969 and 1986 Vienna Conventions states that the text is equally authoritative in each language in which it has been authenticated (paragraph 1), presuming that the terms of the treaty have the same meaning in each authentic text (paragraph 3). Paragraph 4 states that when a comparison of the authentic texts reveals a difference of meaning which the application of Articles 31 and 32 of both Vienna Conventions does not remove, the meaning which best reconciles the texts, "having regard to the object and purpose of the treaty, shall be adopted".

Nevertheless, in the case concerning *Elettronica Sicula S.p.A. (ELSI)*, in the opinion of GIULIANO, the Chamber of the I.C.J. seems to prefer the meaning more in accordance with the purpose of the treaty defined in Article VII, paragraph 1, of the 1948 Friendship, Commerce and Navigation Treaty made between Italy and the United States[70].

More recently, in three cases, the Court made its interpretation starting from translations to English of a treaty authenticated in Danish and Norwegian – where

---

[69] I.C.J., *Reports 1948*, p. 62.

[70] This Article states:

> "The United States contended that 'immovable property or interests therein' is a phrase sufficiently broad to include direct ownership of property rights held trough a subsidiary that is not a United States corporation. The argument turned to a considerable extent on the difference in meaning between the English 'interests' and the Italian '*diritti reali*'. 'Interests' in English no doubt has several possible meanings. But since it is in English usage a term commonly used to denote different kinds of rights in land (for example rights such as charges, or easements, and many kinds of 'future interests'), it is possible to interpret the English and Italian versions of Article VII as meaning much the same thing; especially as the clause in question is in any event limited to immovable property. The Chamber however has some sympathy with the contention of the United States, as being more in accord with the general purpose of the FCN Treaty" (*Reports 1989*, p. 79). Cf. GIULIANO, M., et alt., *op. cit.*, p. 355.

Cf. also the advisory opinion of the I.C.J. on the *Conditions of Admission of a State to Membership in the United Nations (Article 4 of the Charter)* (*Reports 1948*), p. 62.

there was no discrepancy between the Parties –, and of an Arabic text as regards its translation to English where discrepancy did exist[71], as well as a text in Spanish translated to English by the Parties for the purposes of their dispute before the Court[72].

In another, the dispute which exists between the Parties concerns the interpretation of Article 41 of the Statute of the Court, which is worded in identical terms in the Statute of the I.C.J. and of the Permanent Court of International Justice. Nevertheless, the Court finds itself faced with two texts "which are not in total harmony"[73] as well as with the fact that neither the Statute of the Court nor the Charter of the United Nations indicates how to proceed in cases of divergence between the equally authentic versions of the Statute[74].

2.7 The intention of the Parties

This element is present in the interpretative task of the Court since its first case law. Already in 1959, in its advisory opinion concerning *Reservations to the Convention on Genocide*, the I.C.J. takes this into account when it analyses the origin and character of this Convention:

> "The origins of the Convention show that it was the *intention* of the United Nations to condemn and punish genocide as a 'crime under international law' involving a denial of the right of existence of entire human groups, a denial which shocks the conscience of mankind and results in great losses to humanity, and which is contrary to moral law and to the spirit and aims of the United Nations …
>
> The Genocide Convention was therefore *intended* by the General Assembly and by the contracting parties to be definitively universal

71 See the cases concerning *Maritime Delimitation in the Area between Greenland and Jan Mayen* (I.C.J., *Reports 1993*, p. 48); and *Maritime Delimitation and Territorial Questions between Qatar and Bahrain* (I.C.J., *Reports 1994*, p. 119).

72 It is the "Special Agreement between El Salvador and Honduras to submit to the decision of the International Court of Justice the Land, Island and Maritime Boundary Dispute existing between the two States, signed in the City of Esquipulas, Republic of Guatemala, on 24 May 1986". The Parties provided the Chamber with a joint translation into English of this special Agreement. A French translation of the agreed English translation of the Special Agreement was prepared by the Registry of the I.C.J. (cf. I.C.J., *Reports 1992*, p. 356).

73 I.C.J., *LaGrand (Germany v. United States of America), Reports 2001*, para. 101.

74 The Court concludes: "It follows from the object and purpose of the Statute, as well as from the terms of Article 41 when read in their context, that the power to indicate provisional measures entails that such measures should be binding, inasmuch as the power in question is based on the necessity, when the circumstances call for it, to safeguard, and to avoid prejudice to, the rights of the parties as determined by the final judgment of the Court. The contention that provisional measures indicated under Article 41 might not be binding would be contrary to the object and purpose of that Article" (*ibid.*, para. 102).

in scope. It was in fact approved on December 9th, 1948, by a resolution which was unanimously adopted by fifty-six States"[75].

The analysis of the intention of the Parties enables the rejection of interpretations contrary to this intention[76] and the correct interpretation[77].

After 1969 the Court states "the primary necessity of interpreting an instrument in accordance with the intentions of the parties at the time of its conclusion"[78].

In the case law of this period the element of the intention of the Parties has been detailed by the Court in several ways. On the one hand, by stating that the intention of the Parties shall be on record expressly for it to prevail over an important principle of International Law such as the principle concerning the exhaustion

---

[75] I.C.J., *Reports 1951*, p. 23. The italics are ours.

[76] So, in the *Ambatielos* case:

> "The Court cannot accept an interpretation which would have a result obviously contrary to the language of the Declaration and to the continuous will of both Parties to submit all differences to arbitration of one kind or another" (I.C.J., *Reports 1952*, p. 45).

Also in the advisory opinion concerning the *Admissibility of Hearings of Petitioners by the Committee on South West Africa*, where the I.C.J. states:

> "Accordingly, in interpreting any particular sentences in the Opinion of the Court of 11 July 1950, it is not permissible, in the absence of express words to the contrary, to attribute to them a meaning which would not be in conformity with this *paramount purpose* or with the operative part of that Opinion" (I.C.J., *Reports 1956*, p. 28). The italics are ours.

Cf. also the decisions of the I.C.J. in the cases concerning *Sovereignty over Certain Frontier Land* (I.C.J., *Reports 1959*, p. 225) and *Maritime Delimitation in the Area between Greenland and Jan Mayen* (I.C.J., *Reports 1993*, p. 50). In the last, the I.C.J. states that if the intention of the Parties were to be different, the provision of the treaty would be drafted otherwise.

[77] For example, in the case of the *Rights of Nationals of the United States of America in Morocco*:

> "In this case, there is a clear indication of the *intention of the parties* to the effect that certain matters are to be dealt with by the consular tribunals and to this extent it is possible to interpret the provisions of the Act as establishing or confirming the exercise of consular jurisdiction for these limited purposes" (I.C.J., *Reports 1952*, p. 198). The italics are ours).

Also, in the case concerning the *Right of Passage over Indian territory*, where the Court states:

> "It therefore appears that the Treaty of 1779 and the *sanads* of 1783 and 1785 were intended by the Marathas to effect in favour of the Portuguese only a grant … and not to transfer sovereignty over the villages to them" (I.C.J., *Reports 1960*, p. 38).

[78] I.C.J., advisory opinion on the *Legal Consequences for States of the Continued Presence of South Africa in Namibia (South West Africa) notwithstanding Security Council Resolution 276 (1970)*, *Reports 1971*, p. 31.

of local remedies in matters of diplomatic protection[79]. On the other hand, by giving priority to the criterion of the intention of the text when the text is invoked by a Party to justify an interpretation other than the one deriving from it[80]. At least, stating that by introducing the term (in the case, "main channel") into the draft treaty, "the contracting parties must be assumed to have intended that a precise meaning be given to it. For these reasons, the Court will therefore proceed first to determine the main channel. In so doing, it will seek to determine the ordinary meaning of the words 'main channel' by reference to the most commonly used criteria in international law and practice, to which the Parties have referred"[81].

Nevertheless, it should be remembered that the intention of the Parties is expressed in the terms of the treaty, as it is part of the element of the intention of the general rule of Article 31 of the 1969 Vienna Convention on the Law of Treaties. In other words, intention is not an autonomous interpretative criterion nor does that intention exist independently of the treaty. On the contrary, it is expressed in the text of the treaty itself[82]. In this sense, the Court "finds that the intention of the parties to clarify the 1891 delimitation and the complementary nature of demarcation operations become very clear when the text of the Agreement is examined carefully"[83].

---

[79] This question is present in the *Elettronica Sicula S.p.A. (ELSI)* case, where the I.C.J. states:

> "The Chamber has no doubt that the parties to a treaty can therein either agree that the local remedies rule shall not apply to claims based on alleged breaches of that treaty; or confirm that it shall apply. Yet the Chamber finds itself unable to accept that an important principle of customary international law should be held to have been tacitly dispensed with, in the absence of any words making clear an intention to do so" (I.C.J., *Reports 1989*, p. 42, paragraph 50).

[80] This is the situation in the case concerning *Maritime Delimitation and Territorial Questions between Qatar and Bahrain* where the I.C.J. contests the argument of Bahrain considering its intention at the time of the signature of the joint communiqué as the signature of a statement recording a political understanding and not an international agreement, saying that "nor could any such intention, even if shown to exist, prevail over the actual terms of the instrument in question" (I.C.J., *Reports 1994*, p. 122).

[81] Case concerning *Kasikili/Sedudu Island (Botswana/Namibia), Judgement,* (I.C.J., *Reports 1999 (II)*, p. 1061, para. 27. Cf. also para. 43).

[82] In the case concerning the *Land, Island, and Maritime Frontier Dispute (El Salvador/Honduras: Nicaragua intervening)* the Court sates that "it must have regard to the common intention as it is expressed in the words of the Special Agreement" (I.C.J., *Reports 1992*, p. 584). Also: "There is no doubt that the Court's jurisdiction can only be established on the basis of the will of the Parties, as evidenced by the relevant texts" (case concerning *Maritime Delimitation and Territorial Questions between Qatar and Bahrain, Judgement,* I.C.J., *Reports 1995*, p. 23).

[83] Case concerning *Sovereignty over Pulau Ligitan and Pulau Sipadan (Indonesia/Malaysia*) (cf. I.C.J., *Reports 2002*, para. 71).

2.8 The rule of practical effect

The principle of effectiveness (that is the translation of the Latin maxim *ut res magis valeat quam pereat*) is present in the jurisprudence of the I.C.J. specially before 1969 and it is used by the Court only if it does not lead to results contrary to the letter and spirit of the treaty[84]. In this sense, the I.C.J. follows its predecessor the P.C.I.J.[85].

In other words, "the Court cannot remedy a deficiency if, in order to do so, it has to exceed the bounds of normal judicial action"[86]. Consequently, in its case law subsequent to 1969, the Court rejects interpretations contrary to those deriving form the reading of the text when this text clearly manifests the intention of the Parties[87].

2.9 The spirit of the treaty

The spirit of the treaty is used to remove another interpretation in the case concerning *Haya de la Torre* (therefore, anterior to the 1969 Vienna Convention on the Law of Treaties) in which the I.C.J. analyses Article 1 of the Havana Convention which orders the delivery of persons charged with crimes of common law to the

---

[84] Cf. in this regard, the advisory opinion of the I.C.J. in the case concerning *Interpretation of Peace Treaties with Bulgaria, Hungary and Rumania, Second Phase* (*Reports 1950*, p. 229).

[85] So, in the *Corfu Channel* case where the I.C.J. quoting the P.C.I.J. says:

> "In its Order of August 19th, 1929, in the Free Zones Case, the Court said (*Series A*, No. 22, p. 13): 'in case of doubt, the clauses of a special agreement by which a dispute is referred to the Court must, if it does not involve doing violence to their terms, be construed in a manner enabling the clauses themselves to have appropriate effects'" (I.C.J., *Reports 1949*, p. 24).

And adds:

> "It would indeed be incompatible with the generally accepted rules of interpretation to admit that a provision of this sort occurring in a special agreement should be devoid of purport or effect" (*ibid.*).

Along the same lines, in the advisory opinion in the case concerning *Interpretation of Peace Treaties with Bulgaria, Hungary and Rumania, Second Phase*:

> "The principle of interpretation expressed in the maxim: *Ut res magis valeat quam pereat*, often referred to as the rule of effectiveness, cannot justify the Court in attributing to the provisions for the settlement of disputes in the Peace Treaties a meaning which, as stated above, would be contrary to their letter and spirit" (I.C.J., *Reports 1950*, p. 229). The italics correspond to the original.

The same quotation is reproduced by the I.C.J. in its judgement concerning the *South West Africa, Second Phase* case (I.C.J., *Reportsl 1966*, p. 48).

[86] I.C.J., *South West Africa, Second Phase* case (*Reports 1966*, p. 48).

[87] "Any other construction would be contrary to one of the fundamental principles of interpretation of treaties, consistently upheld by international jurisprudence, namely that of effectiveness" (the case concerning the *Territorial Dispute*, I.C.J., *Reports 1994*, p. 25).

territorial authorities but does not have any similar provision as regards crimes of a political nature and states:

> "This silence cannot be interpreted as imposing an obligation to surrender the refugee in case the asylum was granted to him contrary to the provisions of article 2 of the Convention. Such an interpretation would be *repugnant to the spirit* which animated that Convention in conformity with the Latin-American tradition in regard to asylum, a tradition in accordance with which political refugees should not be surrendered"[88].

2.10 Equity

The equity we take into account in this work is not that of Article 38, paragraph 2 of the I.C.J. Statute[89], but that other which constitutes an element of application or interpretation of International Law. Unlike the first, this latter is conceived as an alternative method which, with the previous consent of the Parties, authorizes the Court to give a decision in accordance with International Law:

> "It is always open to parties to a dispute, if they wish the Court to give a decision on a basis of *ex aequo et bono*, and are so agreed, to invoke the power which, in those circumstances, paragraph 2 of this same Article 38 confers on the court to give a decision on that basis, notwithstanding the provisions of paragraph 1. Failing that, the duty of the court is plain"[90].

As an interpretative method, in its jurisprudence, the Court defines its content more precisely:

> "It is clear that the Chamber cannot decide *ex aequo et bono* in this case. Since the Parties have not entrusted it with the task of carrying out an adjustment of their respective interests, it must also dismiss any possibility of resorting to equity *contra legem*. Nor will the Chamber apply equity *praeter legem*. On the other hand, it will have regard to equity *infra legem*, that is, this form of equity which

[88] I.C.J., *Reports 1951*, p. 81. The italics are ours.

[89] That says:

> "2. This provision shall not prejudice the power of the court to decide a case *ex aequo et bono*, if the parties agree thereto".

[90] I.C.J., *South West Africa, Second Phase* case (*Reports 1966*, p. 48). The italics correspond to the original.

> constitutes a method of interpretation of the law in force, and is one of its attributes"[91].

This kind of equity is present in the case law of the I.C.J. concerning the delimitation of land frontiers where it plays an interpretative function, focusing the content of the norm on the concrete case in accordance with the requirements of justice[92]. Sometimes equity has also played a complementary or integrated role offering the international judge or arbitrator a criterion to resolve the questions of detail not specifically contemplated by the applicable norm[93].

Another example of equity as an element of interpretation occurs when equity is part of the applicable rule of International Law. This is the case of maritime delimitations, with regard to which the Court states that the purpose "is not a matter of finding simply an equitable solution, but an equitable solution derived from the applicable law"[94]. In order to achieve this, the I.C.J. recalls that, when applying international law "a court may choose from among several possible interpretations of the law the one which appears, in the light of the circumstances of the case, to be closest to the requirements of justice"[95].

2.11 Inter-temporal law

In matter of interpretation, timeless Law is composed of two rules: one, general and, the other, its exception.

Accordingly to the general rule (or principle of contemporariness) the terms of the treaty are interpreted in conformity with their sense and scope at the time of the

---

[91] Expressed in the application of the principles and rules considered applicable by the Court in the case in question (I.C.J., *Frontier Dispute*, *Reports 1986*, p. 567 et seq., paragraph 28). The underlining corresponds to the original.

[92] Cf. JUSTE RUIZ, J., "La equidad en el Derecho Internacional Público: aspectos actuales", I.H.L.A.D.I., Santo Domingo, 1989, p. 9.

[93] Cf. *ibid.* In this case this would be a kind of equity *infra legem* allowing the judge to make the profile more specific and adjust them to the requirements of the case in question and remain within the framework of applicable Law. Nevertheless, in practice, it is sometimes very difficult to distinguish this complementary function of equity from other kinds of supplementary applications (*praeter legem*) or abolition (*contra legem*), considered as unacceptable (cf. *ibid.*).

[94] I.C.J., *Fisheries Jurisdiction*, *Reports 1974*, p. 33, paragraph 78. About this question see JUSTE RUIZ, J., "Delimitaciones marinas en Africa Occidental: el laudo Arbitral sobre la delimitación de la frontera marítima entre Guinea y Guinea-Bissau", *R.E.D.I.*, 1990/1, pages 7-41.

[95] I.C.J., case concerning the *Continental Shelf (Tunisia/Libyan Arab Jamahiriya)*, *Reports 1982*, p. 60, paragraph 71. See also JUSTE RUIZ, J., "Delimitaciones marinas en Africa Occidental ...", just quoted.

conclusion of the treaty[96]. Thus, in the case concerning the *Western Sahara* with regard to the expression “terra nullius”:

> “it therefore seems clear that the words … have to be interpreted by reference to the law in force at that period. The expression ‘*terra nullius*’ was a legal term of art employed in connection with ‘occupation’ as one of the accepted legal methods of acquiring sovereignty over territory … In the view of the Court, therefore, a determination that Western Sahara was a ‘*terra nullius*’ at the time of colonization by Spain would be possible only if it were established that at that time the territory belonged to no-one in the sense that it was open to acquisition through the legal process of ‘occupation’”[97].

The second rule is an exception to the above insofar as it is broken if the Parties have had the intention of using the terms with an evolutionary character[98]. Thus, in the case of the *Aegean Sea Continental Shelf*, in relation to the notion of “territorial status” the I.C.J. states that those terms must be interpreted

> “in accordance with the rules of international law as they exist today, and not as they existed in 1931 …”, which implies “to take account of the evolution which has occurred in the rules of international law concerning a coastal State’s rights of exploration and exploitation over the continental shelf”[99].

---

[96] This rule is applied by the I.C.J., for example, with regard to the notion of “dispute” in the treaties concluded in the XVII century between Morocco and France and in the XVIII and XIX centuries between Morocco and Great Britain (cf. the case concerning the *Rights of nationals of the United States of America in Morocco* I.C.J., *Reports 1952*, p. 189), and with regard to the concept of “terra nullius”, in the *Western Sahara* case (cf. I.C.J., *Reports 1975*, p. 38).

[97] I.C.J., *Reports 1975*, p. 38.

[98] This rule is also applied by the I.C.J., for example, with regard to the notion of “mandate”, in the *South West Africa (Preliminary Objections)* case,(cf. I.C.J., *Reports 1962*, p. 330 et seq.); with regard to the concepts of “the strenuous conditions of the modern world” and “the well-being and development” embodied in Article 22 of the Covenant of the League of Nations, in the case concerning the *Legal Consequences for States of the Continued Presence of South Africa in Namibia (South West Africa) notwithstanding Security Council Resolution 276 (1970)*, (*Reports 1971*, p. 31); and in the case of the *Aegean Sea Continental Shelf* with regard to the notion of “territorial status” (cf. I.C.J., *Reports 1978*, p. 33 et seq.).

[99] I.C.J., *Reports 1978*, p. 33 et seq.

3 Does the I.C.J. use the interpretative canons as they were conceived by the I.L.C.?

We have analysed the interpretative criteria regarding the interpretation of treaties present in the case law of the I.C.J. and studied the Law of Treaties from the socio-historical perspective before and after the 1969 Vienna Convention, and we will now move on to address the way in which the Court uses the interpretative elements in order to be able to determine whether the practice is in accordance with the construction made by the I.L.C. in the codification which concluded in the Vienna Convention.

As we have seen in Chapter II of the present work, the I.L.C. conceived interpretation as a combined operation structuring the general rule of Article 31 of the 1969 Vienna Convention starting from a series of inter-related elements with no criterion of hierarchy and based on the principle of good faith. These elements – the natural and ordinary meaning of the terms of the treaty, the context of the treaty, its object and purpose –, are said by the I.L.C., to constitute a *single rule*: the general rule of interpretation. These elements are part of this general rule of interpretation and are "closely" linked. The same occurs with the references to the context (Article 31.2), with any subsequent agreement or practice and with any relevant rule of applicable International Law in the relations between the Parties (Article 31.3). Thus, interpretation is described as a "combined operation"[100].

In conclusion, it is a question of a single rule composed of different elements and not isolated unrelated elements applicable to the specific case.

As we have recalled, the order in which the elements composing the general rule of article 31 are quoted does not correspond to criteria of hierarchy but to "considerations of logic"[101]. Nevertheless, in the interpretative process the text is the starting point. So, it is logical that the first element of the general rule be the natural and ordinary meaning to be given to the terms of the treaty in their context, taking into account its object and purpose. So, logic also requires that the elements included in the "context" be quoted immediately afterwards followed by subsequent agreements and practice as well as the relevant rules of applicable International Law concerning the relations between the Parties. This last point is included because, in the opinion of the I.L.C., from the logical point of view, these elements are extrinsic to the text. However, the three are of a compulsory nature and, have the same rank as the other elements of the general rule.

Returning once more to the case law of the I.C.J., the Court speaks of "normal rules of treaty interpretation", and describes the general rule of Article 31 as the "basic rule" and considers the text as the starting point of the interpretative

[100] Cf. I.L.C., *Yearbook ..., op. cit.*, p. 241.

[101] *Ibid.*

process[102]. In this regard, the reference to the different elements of the general rule used to make an exclusively textual interpretation more precise or to reject it is present in the cases concerning the *Arbitration Award of 31 July 1989* and the *Aegean Sea Continental Shelf* case[103].

Nevertheless, this procedure is unusual in the case law of the Court. On the contrary, the I.C.J. usually gives excessive primacy to the textual element without combining it with the other elements of the general rule. Thus, in the case concerning the *Land, Island and Maritime Frontier Dispute*, in which the Court states the necessity of a "decisive reason" in order to admit an interpretation other than that resulting from the ordinary meaning of the words and that, in considering the ordinary meaning to be given to the terms of the treaty, "it is appropriate to compare them with the terms generally or commonly used" in order to convey the idea in question (in the specific case, a delimitation)[104].

This primacy given to the text is also present in the way the Court uses the other elements of the general rule. So, resort to the context of the terms of the treaty is made in order to situate the question put to the Court[105], to situate the instrument submitted to interpretation[106], to situate the terms in question[107], and to confirm[108] or to reinforce[109] the conclusion arrived at.

The subsequent practice – which is part of the context according to Article 31.3b) – is also used in order to confirm the interpretation drawn from the text[110], but it

---

[102] So, in the case concerning the *Land, Island and Maritime Frontier Dispute* (cf. I.C.J., *Reports 1992*, p. 582 s.). Cf. also the case concerning the *Territorial Dispute (Libyan Arab Jamahiriya/Chad)* (I.C.J., *Reports 1994*, p. 22); saying that if the intention had been otherwise Article 2 would have also been worded otherwise (cf. the case concerning *Maritime Delimitation in the Area between Greenland and Jan Mayen*, I.C.J., *Reports 1993*, p. 50).

[103] In the first, the I.C.J. says that the rule of interpretation according to the natural and ordinary meaning of the words employed is not an absolute one. So, "where such a method of interpretation results in a meaning incompatible with the spirit, purpose and context of the clause or instrument in which the words are contained, no reliance can be validly placed on it" (I.C.J., *Reports 1991*, p. 69 s.). Cf. the second case in I.C.J., *Reports 1978*, p. 22.

[104] I.C.J., *Reports 1992*, p. 586.

[105] Cf. the *Western Sahara* case (*Reports 1975*, p. 40).

[106] In the cases concerning the *Consequences for States ...* (cf. I.C.J., *Reports 1971*, p. 31) and the *Maritime Delimitation and territorial Questions between Qatar and Bahrain, Jurisdiction and Admissibility* (cf. I.C.J., *Reports 1994*, p. 119).

[107] In the cases concerning the *Arbitration Award of 31 July 1989* (cf. I.C.J., *Reports 1991*, p. 69) and the *Aegean Sea continental Shelf* (cf. I.C.J., *Reports 1978*, p. 43).

[108] In the case concerning the *Land, Island, and Maritime Frontier Dispute* (cf. I.C.J., *Reports 1992*, p. 583).

[109] In the *Territorial Dispute* case (cf. I.C.J., *Reports 1994*, p. 26).

[110] In the case concerning *Maritime Delimitation in the Area between Greenland and Jan Mayen* (cf. I.C.J., *Reports 1993*, p. 51 et seq.).

cannot prevail over the absence from the text of any specific reference to the question invoked[111].

The last elements quoted in the general rule of Article 31, in accordance with the logical order used by the I.L.C., are the object and purpose of the treaty. The starting point of the I.L.C. was the assumption that the text is the authentic expression of the intention of the Parties[112].After stating in 1971 the "fundamental" necessity of interpreting a certain instrument in accordance with the intentions of the Parties at the time of its conclusion, in 1992 the I.C.J., coincided with the I.L.C. when it stated that the intention of the Parties is in the text[113]. In the meantime, it has clarified that this intention must be expressly on record[114].

With regard to this way of proceeding, it should be added that the Court should bear in mind that the intention of the Parties is not an autonomous interpretative criterion but the purpose of the legal operation which constitutes interpretation. The purpose of interpretation is to discover the intention of the Parties and in order to achieve this, it must resort to the rules codified in Articles 31 to 33 of the 1969 Vienna Convention. In other words, the intention of the Parties does not float independently of the interpretation resulting from the application of these rules. The I.C.J. seems to forget this because it uses the element of the intention as if it were an autonomous interpretative criterion.

The same occurs as regards the object and purpose of the treaty: they are used when the terms in themselves do not have a very precise sense[115]. Moreover, in order to confirm the interpretation reached solely by resort to the text of the treaty[116].

Finally, the interpretation of treaties by the I.C.J. is generally carried out without taking into account the elements in combination and individually as stated in the general rule of article 31. Consequently, the interpretative elements which compose this are used in succession not jointly (as they were conceived by the I.L.C.). From the analysis we have made of the case law of the I.C.J. after the 1969 Vienna Convention on the Law of Treaties, it is also possible to see the use of elements of the general rule of Article 31 made by the Court for the purposes of Article 32 (this is the case of the context, the object and the purpose of the treaty). Thus, they are employed in a way not conceived by the I.L.C.

---

[111] In this case, a delimitation Cf. the case concerning the *Land, Island, Maritime and Frontier Dispute* (I.C.J., *Reports 1992*, p. 586).

[112] I.L.C., *Yearbook ...*, *op. cit.*, p. 242.

[113] In the case concerning the *Land, Island and Maritime Frontier Dispute* (cf. I.C.J., *Reports 1992*, p. 584. Consequently, when intention is invoked in order to justify an interpretation different from that resulting from the text, the latter has primacy (cf. the case concerning maritime delimitation and territorial questions ..., I. C.J., *Reports 1994*, p. 122).

[114] Cf. the case concerning *Elettronica Sicula S.p.A. (ELSI)*, (I.C.J., *Reports 1989*, p. 50).

[115] Cf. I.C.J., the *Western Sahara* case, *Reports 1975*, p. 32.

[116] In the cases concerning the *Territorial Dispute (Libyan Arab Jamahiriya/Chad* (cf. I.C.J., *Reports 1994*, p. 26) and *Maritime Delimitation in the Area between Greenland and Jan Mayen* (cf. I.C.J., *Reports 1993*, p. 50 et seq.).

Unlike what happens with the elements of the general rule, it is possible to assert that the I.C.J. uses the supplementary means of interpretation correctly. So, with regard to preparatory works, these are used by the Court to clarify the scope and object of the treaty[117], to confirm the interpretation reached – even if, in its opinion, this is not necessary[118] – or to reinforce the interpretation[119]; and it states that the resort to preparatory works is not allowed if the text is clear[120].

[117] For example, in the case concerning *Fisheries Jurisdiction* (cf. I.C.J., *Reports 1973*, pages 10 and 56).

[118] Cf. the case concerning the *Territorial Dispute (Libyan Arab Jamahiriya/Chad*, (I.C.J., *Reports 1994*, p. 27).

[119] Cf. the case concerning *Border and Cross-Border Armed Actions (Nicaragua v. Honduras), Jurisdiction and Admissibility* (I.C.J., *Reports 1988*, p. 85).

[120] Cf. the case concerning the *Territorial Dispute (Libyan Arab Jamahiriya/Chad* (I.C.J., *Reports 1994*, p. 26).

CHAPTER VII:

Arbitral Tribunals

1 Introduction

The study of recent jurisprudence shows that some arbitration Tribunals, before and during interpretation, address the legal nature of the interpretative rules codified in the 1969 Vienna Convention on the Law of Treaties. They state that they are "generally accepted rules of International Law" and that case law as well as doctrine have shown that the Convention reflects the current and past state of the International Law of treaties since, as far as treaties are concerned, it codifies the customary law in force which contains the rules used to interpret treaties[1].

A detailed example of the resort to the rules of Articles 31 and 32 of the Vienna Convention is found in the Award of 14 February 1985 relating to the case concerning the *Maritime Delimitation between Guinea and Guinea-Bissau*. This case is also special as neither of the States is party to the Vienna Convention. However, the Arbitral Tribunal points out that both States recognize that Articles 31 and 32 of that Convention constitute the rules of International Law applicable to the interpretation of the 1886 Agreement. So, the Tribunal will apply them as international custom recognized between States[2].

More recently, in its award of 21 October 1994 on the case concerning a boundary dispute between Argentina and Chile concerning *the course of the frontier between B.P. 62 and Mount Fitz Roy*, the Arbitral Tribunal recalls the existence in International Law of rules which are used for the interpretation of any legal instrument, "be it a treaty, a unilateral instrument, an arbitral award, or a resolution of an international organization[3].

---

1 Thus, in the Decision of 16 May 1980 relating to the case concerning the *question whether the re-evaluation of the German Mark in 1961 and 1969 constitutes a case for application of the clause in article 2 (e) of Annex I A of the 1953 Agreement on the German External Debt made involving Belgium, France, Switzerland, the United Kingdom of Great Britain and Northern Ireland and the United States of America on the one hand and the Federal Republic of Germany on the other* (*R.I.A.A.*, vol XIX, p. 91 et seq.).

2 *Ibid.*, p. 165. On this decision and the questions of interpretation see JUSTE RUIZ, J., "Delimitaciones marinas en ...", *op. cit.*, pages 16 et seq.

3 This is the case of the rule of the natural and ordinary meaning of the terms, the rule of reference to the context and the rule of the practical effect, which "are all general rules of interpretation" (*R.I.A.A.*, vol. XXII, p. 25, para. 72. This case is also interesting because both, Argentina and Chile, agree on the existing interpretative principles applicable to the interpretation of the judgement of 1902.

As in the preceding Chapter, we will analyse the arbitral case law concerning the interpretative criteria based on whether it preceded or followed the 1969 Vienna Convention on the Law of Treaties.

2 General Criteria Employed

2.1 The natural and the ordinary meaning of the terms

The reference to the ordinary meaning of the terms as a rule of interpretation appears in the earliest case law decisions. Thus, in the case of *William E. and William Barron v. the U.S.A. (n. 633)*, in 1871, in which the arbitration body stated that:

> "The first rule of hermeneutics, legal or otherwise, is that interpretation means finding in good faith that meaning of certain words, if they are doubtful, which those who used the words must have desired to convey, according to the usage of speech (*usus loquendi*), the existing laws, common sense, and the general intent of that whole of which the doubted passage forms a part; and does not mean what ingenuity may apparently succeed in forcing into a passage"[4].

If the analysis of the language is the starting point for the process of interpretation, the rule of the ordinary meaning of the terms logically receives the same treatment[5] due to the fact that the first step in that process is the analysis of the text of the treaty[6]. Progressively, this argument of the arbitral case law will be based less on

---

[4] Decision of 16 August 1871 (COUSSIRAT-COUSTERE, V., and EISEMAN, P.M., *op. cit.*, vol. I, p. 30. In this regard, the decision of the arbitrator in the *case of the Treaty of Limits of 1858*, involving Costa Rica and Nicaragua, of 26 July 1899:

> "All concur that words are to be taken as far as possible in their first and simplest meanings – 'in their natural and obvious sense, according to the general use of the same words', 'in the usual sense, and not in any extraordinary or unused acceptation'" (*ibid.*, p. 31).

[5] So, for example, in the "arbitral opinion" of the 20th February 1953, relating the *case of the Gold of the National Bank of Albania*:

> "Selon la doctrine unanime du droit des gens, il est indiqué de prendre comme point de départ du processus d'interprétation des dispositions conventionnelles entre Etats le sens usuel des termes employés par les Etats contractants, et de ne l'abandonner que si leur signification n'est pas compatible avec l'objet et le but de ces engagements" (*R.S.A.*, vol. XII, pages 19-52).

[6] In this regard, the decision of the Italian-U.S. Conciliation Commission (Peace Treaty of February 10, 1947) in the case of *Albert Flegenheimer (No. 182)*, of 20 September 1958:

> "The starting point of the *processus* of all interpretation of an international treaty is the text on which the two Parties have agreed; it is evident that the main point of an international agreement lies in the concordant intent of such Parties and that, without this concordance, there are no rights or obligations which arise therefrom" (*R.S.A.*, vol. XIV, pages 328-390; COUSSIRAT-COUSTERE, V., and EISEMAN, P.M., *op. cit.*, vol. III, t. 1, p. 112).

doctrinal works and on resolutions of the Institute of International Law and more on the case law of the P.C.I.J.[7], as well as on that of the I.C.J.[8].

The analysis of the arbitral case law before the 1969 Vienna Convention on the Law of Treaties also shows that the burden of proof falls on the Party which invokes a particular meaning of a term[9] (here there is a parallelism with the affirmation of the same criterion in the case law of the I.C.J.)[10].

The problem caused by *ambiguous provisions* requires special consideration. Here, the general rule is that "where the agreement is susceptible to two interpretations, that interpretation is to be taken which is least onerous upon the party which must render the service or suffer the loss under the agreement"[11]. Usually, the ambiguous clause is interpreted, firstly, against the party which drafted it[12], but another decision says that "the rule that, in case of doubt, the text of a treaty is to be interpreted against the party which drafted it, can only be applied when, as in

---

7 Thus, the Italian- U.S.Conciliation Commission (Peace Treaty of February 10, 1947), in its Decision of 12 December 1959 concerning the case of *Eugenio Fubini et alt. (No. 201)*:

> "The rules on the art of interpreting international treaties require that the interpreter rely, first of all, on the text that must be applied, in giving the terms employed by the contracting States their natural meaning ...
>
> In its case law, the Permanent Court of International Justice rendered the same opinion and refused to give any consideration to the provisions that were not to be found in the text" (*R.S.A.*, vol. XIV, pages 421-434; COUSSIRAT-COUSTERE, V., and EISEMAN, P.M., *op. cit.*, vol. III, t. 1, p. 113).

8 Thus, in the Arbitral Award of 3 July 1958 concerning the *Agreement on the German External Debt (of February 27, 1953)*, in which the Arbitral Tribunal stated,

> "According to the practice of the International Court of Justice, words and phrases are to be given their normal, natural and unstrained meaning in the context in which they occur" (COUSSIRAT-COUSTERE, V., and EISEMAN, P.M., *op. cit.*, vol. III, t. 1, pages 110-111).

9 Thus, in the Decision of 3 September 1924, in the *case of the German Claims*, where the Claims Commission declared:

> "C'est donc à celui qui prétend que néanmoins, dans le cas qui nous occupe, les expressions en question ont été employées dans un sens spécial qu'incombe le fardeau d'en fournir la preuve" (*R.S.A.*, vol. I, pages 431-528; COUSSIRAT-COUSTERE, V., and EISEMAN, P.M., *op. cit.*, vol. II, p. 25). See also other aspects of these decision in relation to the expression "entreprise d'utilité publique" (*ibid.*, pages 25-33).

10 Along the same lines and more recently, see the Judgement of 21 October 1994 of the Arbitration Tribunal in the case concerning the *Dispute concerning the course of the frontier between B.P. 62 and Mount Fitz Roy (Argentina/Chile), op. cit.*, p. 103, para. 149).

11 French-Venezuelan Commission, 1902, Decision of the 31th July 1905, in the *Heirs of Jean Maninat case* (France/Venezuela), *R.I.A.A.*, vol. X, p. 78; COUSSIRAT-COUSTERE, V., and EISEMAN, P.M., *op. cit.*, vol. I, p. 41).

12 *David Goldenberg et Fils case*, Decision of the 27th September 1928 (COUSSIRAT-COUSTERE, V., and EISEMAN, P.M., *op. cit.*, vol. II, p. 36).

the case of the Treaty of Versailles, one of the parties handed the prepared text to the other party for signature"[13].

Similarly, in case of doubt and faced with the ambiguous provision, a restrictive interpretation should be made[14].

The arbitral jurisprudence after 1969 repeats that language constitutes the starting point of the interpretative task: "it is that language which is to be interpreted" in accordance with the general rule as stated in Article 31 of the 1969 Vienna Convention on the Law of the Treaties[15].

From the different meanings which the provision under interpretation could have, primacy is given to the "clear", "natural" or "ordinary" meaning. However, it does not have an exclusive effect insofar as Article 31.4 of the Convention allows the special meaning, if it is established that the Parties so intended[16]. But a word or a phrase can have one meaning in a context and another one in another context. So, as regards arbitral jurisprudence, the concept of the "ordinary meaning in its context" constitutes a most precise guide in the interpretative task[17].

The treaty shall be considered as a whole interpreting the different clauses in such a manner as to avoid depriving it any of its provisions of effectiveness in order to give it to others[18].

In the case concerning a boundary dispute between Argentina and Chile concerning *the course of the frontier between B.P. 62 and Mount Fitz Roy*, the Arbitral Tribunal analyses the criterion of the text with regard to international decisions. The

---

13 The *Case of the pensions of officials of the Saar Territory* (Germany/Governing Commission of the Saar Territory), Decision of the 4th September 1934 (*R.I.A.A.*, vol. III, p. 1564 et seq.; COUSSIRAT-COUSTERE, V., and EISEMAN, P.M., *op. cit.*, vol. II, p. 36).

14 So, for example, the Italian-U.S. Conciliation Commission in its Decision of 22 October 1953:

> "There can be no doubt (as to the scope of the treaty). But if there were any doubt, the rule should be invoked according to which the debtor party must profit from the benefit of the doubt and also that, in case of doubt, restrictive interpretation is necessary" (*R.I.A.A.*, vol. XIV, p. 167; COUSSIRAT-COUSTERE, V., and EISEMAN, P.M., *op. cit.*, vol. III, t. 1, p. 131). See the Decision of 24 June 1961 of the same Commission, in the *Mary De Pascale et al. case (no. MD/1018)* (*R.I.A.A.*, vol. XVI, p. 234; COUSSIRAT-COUSTERE, V., and EISEMAN, P.M., *op. cit.*, vol. III, t. 1, p. 132).

15 Decision of 26 January 1972 relating the case concerning *claims arising out of decisions of the Mixed Greek-German Arbitral Tribunal set up under Article 304 in Part X of the Treaty of Versailles (involving Greece and the Federal Republic of Germany)*, (*R.I.A.A.*, vol. XIX, p. 53).

16 *Ibid.*

17 *Ibid.*, p. 55. In the same sense see the case concerning *Filleting within the Gulf of St. Lawrence involving Canada and France*, (*R.I.A.A.*, vol. XIX, p. 248).

18 Decision of 26 January 1972 relating the case concerning *claims arising out of decisions of the Mixed Greek-German Arbitral Tribunal set up under Article 304 in Part X of the Treaty of Versailles (involving Greece and the Federal Republic of Germany)*, (*R.I.A.A.*, vol. XIX, p. 60).

Tribunal starts from the interpretative principle according to which the text shall be interpreted in the sense in which it produced effects in accordance with and not contrary to International Law, and later stated that the same criterion shall be applied in relation to international judgements whose legal validity is not discussed and have the value of *res judicata*[19]. In this case, judgements shall be interpreted in such a manner that they do not lead to the judge or the arbitrator giving a decision in violation of the norms of International Law. Thus, while carrying out its jurisdictional function, a tribunal called to interpret a legal norm shall not only pay attention to the fact that its decision shall be based and adjusted to International Law but, it shall also reject the fact that it could produce results contrary to this[20].

In this same case, in relation to the interpretation of the expression "water-parting", the arbitral Tribunal combines three interpretative rules: that of the ordinary meaning[21], that of practical effect[22] and the principle of contemporaneityness[23].

2.2 The context

This is a long standing interpretative criterion in arbitral case law. In 1911, in the *Walfish Bay Boundary* case involving Germany and Great Britain, it was said that, in order to resolve the dispute and to determine the interpretation of the terms in question, resort shall be made to:

> "general principles of law, which are the same as the principles of international law, and according to which it is necessary to consider, in order to determine the intention which inspires an arrangement or act, the grammatical value of the terms used, the consequences which result from understanding them in one sense or the other, and the facts or antecedent circumstances which contribute to explain them"[24].

---

19 In its words, "it must now be added that in the international legal system *res judicata* also applies to the meaning of the terms used in the propositions which make up an arbitral award and that this meaning cannot be altered by any use subsequent to the decision or by the evolution of the language, or by the acts or decisions of one of the parties to the dispute" (Decision of 21 October 1994, *R.I.A.A.*, vol. XXII, p. 39, para. 122.

20 Cf. *ibid.*, p. 25, para. 76.

21 Criterion used by the Parties and the Arbitrator in the arbitration of 1898-1902 (*ibid.*, p. 47 et seq., para. 149. Also in p. 44, para. 135).

22 *Ibid.*, p. 45, para. 137.

23 In order to determine exactly the meaning of this expression at that time (cf. *ibid.*, p. 43, para. 128). On the other hand, the Tribunal considers that the concept of "water-parting" in the Award of 1902 is protected by the *res judicata* and is not susceptible of any subsequent change through usage, evolution of the language, or acts or decisions of one of the Parties to the dispute (cf. *ibid.*, p. 43, para. 130).

24 Arbitral Award of 23 May 1911 (*R.I.A.A.*, vol. XI, pages 267-308; COUSSIRAT-COUSTERE, V., and EISEMAN, P.M., *op. cit.*, vol. I, p. 31 et seq.).

Through time, and before 1969, this criterion is used with a variety of purposes. So, for example, as a complement to the grammatical interpretation[25], in order to avoid erroneous interpretations as a consequence, for example, of the consideration of an isolated phrase[26], to know the intention of the Parties[27], to determine the

[25] So, for example, in the case concerning the *Interpretation of the Air Transport Services Agreement, of 27 March 1946* (France v. United States of America):

> "Interpretation, as a logical operation that seeks to establish with the maximum possible certainty what the common intention of the Parties was, can only succeed in determining the meaning to be attributed to a term appearing in a clause of the treaty, in the framework and as a function of the clause as a whole. In its turn, a clause should be interpreted with reference to the content of the treaty considered in its entirety; and, if the agreement comprises other instruments which complete or modify it, all these instruments should, if necessary, be taken into consideration in the interpretation of the clause" (COUSSIRAT-COUSTERE, V., and EISEMAN, P.M., *op. cit.*, vol. III-1, p. 123).

Likewise, see the case concerning the *Interpretation of the Tardieu-Jaspar Agreement* of 12 January 1930, Belgium v. France, (*R.I.A.A.*, vol. III, pages 1703-1716; COUSSIRAT-COUSTERE, V., and EISEMAN, P.M., *op. cit.*, vol. II, p. 35), and the decision of 8 March 1951, case *Società Mineraria e Metallurgica di Pertusola (n. 95)*, (*R.I.A.A.*, vol. XIII, pages 179-197; COUSSIRAT-COUSTERE, V., and EISEMAN, P.M., *op. cit.*, vol. III, t. 1, p. 116).

[26] In words of the Mixed Commission of Claims in the case *Paula Mendel et alt. versus Germany*(Germany/United States), in its decision of 13 August 1926:

> "But the language here relied on by the claimants cannot be construed as an isolated phrase. The pertinent provisions of the whole Treaty must be considered in the light of the conditions existing at the time of its conclusion, the nature and cause of the damages and injuries which had been inflicted and the allocation of responsibility therefore, in order to apply the master rule governing the construction of all treaties, that the intention of the parties must be sought out and enforced even though this should lead to an interpretation running counter to the literal terms of an isolated phrase, which read in connection with its context is susceptible of a different construction" (*R.I.A.A.*, vol. VII, pages 380-389; COUSSIRAT-COUSTERE, V., and EISEMAN, P.M., *op. cit.*, vol. II, p. 34).

[27] Thus:

> "The task of interpretation, however, is not exhausted by assigning to the words their linguistic meaning and arriving at the result by help of grammatical rules. Its aim is to get at the intention of the parties in so far as it can be said to have been expressed by the words.

To that end it is here necessary also to look at the purpose of the phrase in the sentence as a whole and in general at all the circumstances which are capable of showing the idea the parties have wanted to express by the phrase" (case concerning *Dampfschiffahrtsgesellschaft "Argo" v. The Hanseatic Maritime Agency*, Arbitral Award of 21 June 1928, in COUSSIRAT-COUSTERE, V., and EISEMAN, P.M., *op. cit.*, vol. II, p. 35).

object and scope of the treaty[28], to try to resolve the discrepancy due to the fact of the vagueness of the terms in the languages in which the treaty was drafted[29], etc.

As with the criterion of the object and purpose of the treaty, with regard to the context, the arbitral case law before 1969 also gives up doctrine as its basis substituting this by quotations of judgements of the P.C.I.J. and of the I.C.J.[30] insofar as these courts decide on questions of interpretation.

After 1969 the criterion of the context is used in the arbitral case law as a complement to the grammatical interpretation[31] or to specify clearly the terms[32]. But

---

28 So, for example, in the case concerning *Compagnie du Katanga versus Colonie du Congo Belge*:

> "The general principles of law and equity make it incumbent upon the judge for the purpose of determining the object, the scope or the range of an agreement, to investigate the common intention of the parties, bearing in mind the state of affairs at the time of the conclusion of the agreement, and considering the circumstances, the personalities of the parties and the aim pursued by each of them in contracting" (*B.Y.I.L.*, 1964, pages 184-194; COUSSIRAT-COUSTERE, V., and EISEMAN, P.M., *op. cit.*, vol. II, p. 35).

29 Cf. the case concerning *the question whether the re-evaluation of the German Mark ... , op. cit.*, pages 94 and 100.

30 So, for example, the French-Italian Conciliation Commission in its decision of 16 March 1956 concerning the *Interpretation and Application of the Provisions of Article 78, para. 7, of the Peace Treaty concerning Ethiopian territory (No. 201)*:

> "it is a cardinal principle of interpretation that words must be interpreted in the sense they would normally have in their context, unless such interpretation would lead to something unreasonable or absurd" (*R.I.A.A.*, vol. XIII, pages 636-658; COUSSIRAT-COUSTERE, V., and EISEMAN, P.M., *op. cit.*, vol. III, t. 1, p. 116 et seq.).

Cf. also the decision of the French-Italian Conciliation Commission, of 9 July 1962, concerning the case *Société des Comptoirs Dufay et Gigandet et al. (n. 284)*, in *R.I.A.A.*, vol. XVI, pages 199-219; COUSSIRAT-COUSTERE, V., and EISEMAN, P.M., *op. cit.*, vol. III, t. 1, p. 120.

31 So, the Arbitral Tribunal for the *Agreement on German External Debts (of February 27, 1953)* in its decision of 26 January 1972:

> "74. The Agreement must be considered as a whole. The different clauses must be so interpreted as to avoid depriving any one of them of practical effect in order to credit others with a literal meaning" (*I.L.R.*, vol. XLVII, pages 423-462; COUSSIRAT-COUSTERE, V., and EISEMAN, P.M., *op. cit.*, vol. III, t. 1, p. 126).

Also the cases concerning maritime delimitation ..., (*op. cit.*, p. 173) and Filleting within the Gulf of St. Lawrence, (*op. cit.*, p. 248).

32 So, for example, in the interlocutory award of the Iran-United States Claims Tribunal of 20 August 1986 concerning the case *Islamic Republic of Iran v. The United States of America*:

> "It is a general principle of treaty interpre-tation, recalled in Article 31, para. 2, of the Vienna Convention on the Law of Treaties, that the terms of a treaty must be construed in their context, which contains, *inter alia*, any agreement which was made between all the parties in connection with the conclusion of the treaty" (COUSSIRAT-COUSTERE, V., and EISEMAN, P.M., *op. cit.*, vol. III, t. 1, p. 127).

Article 31.3 c) of the 1969 Vienna Convention states that together with the context any subsequent agreement between the Parties or any subsequent practice in the application of the treaty as well as any relevant rules of International Law applicable to the relations between the Parties shall be taken into account. We find an example of the resort to this criterion in the case concerning *Filleting within the Gulf of St. Lawrence* involving Canada and France in which the Tribunal says that having been required to decide according to International Law it is in the obligation to take into account the norms contained in Article 31.3 c) of the 1969 Vienna Convention on the Law of Treaties[33].

2.3 The object and purpose of the treaty

This interpretative criterion is used less in arbitral case law than precedent. Before 1969 the resort to this means a literal interpretation can be put aside[34], as well as an extensive interpretation[35].

After 1969, it is used in different cases where the arbitral body defines more precisely that the object and purpose do not form any independent basis for interpretation, but are rather "factors to be taken into account in the determination of the 'meaning to be given to the terms of the treaty'. The terms themselves should be given primary weight in the analysis of the text"[36]. So, the presumptions obtained trough the resort to the object and purpose of the treaty are confirmed by "a general terminological analysis of the texts considered"[37].

---

[33] Cf. *ibid.*, p. 254.

[34] So, for example, the Mixed Claims Commission involving Germany and the United States of America in its decision of 13 August 1926, in the case *Paula Mendel et alt. v. Germany*:

> "Such a literal construction of the language quoted finds no support in the other provisions of the Treaty and is repugnant to the objects and purposes of the Treaty as a whole. It cannot stand alone and must fall" (*R.I.A.A.*, vol. VII, pages 380-389; COUSSIRAT-COUSTERE, V., and EISEMAN, P.M., *op. cit.*, vol. II, p. 24).

[35] Thus, the decision of April 15, 1935 concerning the *Maison Hermann Schlessiger case*, involving Germany and Rumania:

> "The result wished band the Parties of a convention can not be, however, considered as reached moreover the limits of the commitments really adopted band them to realize it; the result wished can not, in sane interpretation, serve to determine those commitments" (the original is in French. The translation was made band us; *R.S.A.*, vol. III, pages 1641-1655; COUSSIRAT-COUSTERE, V., and EISEMAN, P.M., *op. cit.*, vol. II, p. 25).

[36] Iran-United States Claims Tribunal, *United States-Iran, Case No. A 17*, Interim Judgement of 13 May 1985 (COUSSIRAT-COUSTERE, V., and EISEMAN, P.M., *op. cit.*, vol. III, t. 1, p. 109).

[37] Case concerning *Maritime Delimitation involving Guinea and Guinea-Bissau*, *op. cit.*, p. 176.

The study also reveals the usefulness of the analysis of treaty preambles in order to determine the object and purpose of the treaty in question. Thus, in the case concerning the *Beagle Channel* the Arbitral Tribunal states:

> "19. Although Preambles of treaties do not usually – nor are they intended to – contain provisions or dispositions of substance – (in short they are not operative clauses) – it is nevertheless generally accepted that they may be relevant and important as guides to the manner in which the Treaty should be interpreted, and in order, as it were, to 'situate' it in respect of its object and purpose"[38].

An example of the resort to the object and purpose of the treaty but within the framework of article 33.4 of the 1969 Vienna Convention (treaties authenticated in two or more languages) is given by the case concerning *the re-evaluation of the German Mark* in which, since the discrepancy between the three texts authenticated (in English, French and German)persisted, the arbitral Tribunal was unable to resolve it by applying Articles 31 and 32 of the quoted Convention, and stated that it would analyse the meaning by harmonizing the texts, while taking into account the object and purpose of the treaty. In its opinion, the reference to the object and purpose of the treaty means nothing else than that "any person having to interpret a multilingual international treaty has the opportunity to resolve any divergence in the texts which persist, after the principles of Articles 31 and 32 of the VCT have been applied, by opting for a final interpretation or for one or other of the texts which in its opinion most closely approaches the 'object and purpose' of the treaty"[39].

2.4 The subsequent practice

Before 1969 subsequent practice is a supplementary means of interpretation[40], "susceptible to either confirming, or contradicting, and even possibly of correcting the conclusions furnished by the interpretations based on an examination of the text and the preparatory work, for the purposes of determining the common intention of the Parties when they concluded the Agreement"[41].

---

[38] *I.L.R.*, 1978, vol. LII, p. 132; COUSSIRAT-COUSTERE, V., and EISEMAN, P.M., *op. cit.*, vol. III, t. 1, p. 109.

[39] *Op. cit.*, p. 109.

[40] So, for example, in the case concerning the *Interpretation of the Air Transport Services Agreement involving the United States of America and Italy, of 6 February 1948* (*R.I.A.A.*, vol. XVI, pages 81-102).

[41] Case concerning the *Interpretation of the Air Transport Services Agreement of 27 March 1946*, involving France and the United States of America, Judgement of 22 December 1963 (COUSSIRAT-COUSTERE, V., and EISEMAN, P.M., *op. cit.*, vol. III, t. 1. p. 155. In the same sense the Arbitral Commission *on Property, Rights and Interests in Germany*, in its decision of 26 May 1966 (*ibid.*, pages 162-163), and the Iran-United States Claims Tribunal in its Declaration of 27 December 1983 (*ibid.*, pages 166-167). See also the cases concerning *re-evaluation of the German Mark*, (*op.cit.*, p. 104) and the *maritime delimitation*, (*op. cit.*, p. 180).

However, this practice is only taken into account if it reflects the balanced position of the Parties in question. On the contrary,

> "A definite difference of opinion having thus clearly come to light, it follows, that from the moment that this occurred, the practice of the Parties in the application of the Agreement can no longer be used as a supplementary means of interpreting the agreement itself, because it would only be of import for this purpose if it brought to light the same positions or principle or, at least, positions that were not directly opposed"[42].

This practice is different from that required for the building of a customary norm. In the words of the arbitral body in the advisory opinion concerning the *interpretation of the Agreement of 6 February, 1948 concerning the air transport services*, involving Italy and the United States of America, the matter at issue is not to deduce a legal standard from the practice followed:

> "but merely to reveal the interpretation the parties gave to the provisions in dispute, which can serve as additional evidence in ascertaining the intentions of the parties and illustrate their intent as of the time the Agreement was concluded …

The position would be different if the point at issue involved concluding from practice that there had been a subsequent amendment of the Agreement, …"[43].

After 1969, the arbitral case law determines more clearly that, in addition to matters concerning the formation of customary norms as regards interpretation the resort to the subsequent practice of the Parties, this includes active and passive behaviour[44].

---

[42] *Interpretation of the Air Transport Services Agreement of 27 March 1946* (COUSSIRAT-COUSTERE, V., and EISEMAN, P.M., *op. cit.*, vol. III, t. 1, p. 157). In the case of the *Iran-United States Claims Tribunal*, this states:

> "This practice must, however, be a practice of the parties to the treaty and one which establishes the agreement of the parties regarding the interpret of that treaty" (*ibid.*, p. 167).

[43] It uses the assertion of the I.C.J. in its advisory opinion concerning the *International Status of South-West Africa*, according to which:

> "Interpretation placed upon legal instruments by the parties to them, though not conclusive as to their meaning, have considerable probative value when they contain recognition by a party of its own obligations under an instrument" (I.C.J., *Reports 1950*, pages 135)" (*R.I.A.A.*, vol. XVI, pages 81-102; *R.G.D.I.P.*, 1968, vol. LXXII, pages 461-486; COUSSIRAT-COUSTERE, V., and EISEMAN, P.M., *op. cit.*, vol. III, t. 1., p. 158 et seq.).

[44] So, for example, in the case concerning the *Beagle Channel*, in which the Arbitral Tribunal states:

In relation to the interpretation of awards, in the case of the *Dispute concerning the course of the frontier between B.P. 62 and Mount Fitz Roy (Argentina/Chile)*, the Arbitral Tribunal analyses the arguments of the parties based on their respective conduct subsequent to the 1902 Award, which constituted the object of the case. In the opinion of the Tribunal, "such conduct is not directly related to the Court's mandate, since it involves facts subsequent to the Award which the Court is required to interpret"[45]. Nevertheless, reference will be made to that conduct in the awareness that it shall prevent an analysis of the facts so invoked turning it aside from the strict fulfilment of its function[46], which is the interpretation of the arbitrator's intention manifested in the Award of 1902.

2.5 Preparatory works

The analysis of arbitral case law shows that, before 1969, resort to preparatory works takes place in cases of obscurity of the treaty to be interpreted[47], that is to say, of a subsidiary nature[48]. In some cases, due to the long duration of the nego-

"Under these circumstances the silence of Argentina permits the inference that the acts tended to confirm an interpretation of the meaning of the Treaty independent of the acts of jurisdiction themselves" (*I.L.R.*, vol. LII, p. 224, para. 169 a); COUSSIRAT-COUSTERE, V., and EISEMAN, P.M., *op. cit.*, vol. III, t. 1, p. 165).

45 The Tribunal repeats the affirmation made by the Arbitrator in 1966 in the sense that, concerning the subsequent practice of the Parties, including the conduct of individuals and local authorities, the Court cannot understand how this practice can throw light on the intention of the Arbitrator (cf. *op. cit.*, p. 50 para. 162).

46 *Ibid.*, para. 163.

47 So, for example, in the judgement of 19 September 1949, concerning the *Interpretation of article V of the Constitution of the United Nations Educational, Scientific and Cultural Organization (Unesco)*:

"With regard to the *travaux préparatoires* preceding the Unesco Constitution, to which reference has been made, the tribunal is bound to remark that in any case it would only be proper for it to take these into account if the text of the Constitution were not sufficiently clear in itself -which in fact is not the case". The arbitral Tribunal bases its argumentation on the jurisprudence of the P.C.I.J. concerning preparatory works (*A.D.*, XVI (1949), pages 331-337. Also in COUSSIRAT-COUSTERE, v. and EISEMAN, P.M., *Repertoire de la Jurisprudence Arbitrale Internationale*, vol. III, t. 1, Nijhoff, Dordrecht, 1991, pages 135-136).

48 This criterion is based by arbitral case law on P.C.I.J. case law:

"The documentary history of the negotiations, or as it is generally called the 'legislative history', is in fact rightly considered by case law and doctrine to be a proper subsidiary guide for the interpretation of treaties. This principle was initially asserted by the Permanent Court of International Justice in its Decision of February 4, 1932, regarding the *Treatment of Polish Nationals in Danzig*, in which it stated: 'This text not being absolutely clear, it may be useful, in order to ascertain its precise meaning, to recall here somewhat in detail the various drafts which existed prior to the adoption of the text now in force' (*Series A/B*, No. 44, p. 33).

tiations leading to the treaty, "involving initiatives and important acts", or because the Parties have used them in abundance in their argumentation, within this framework,

> "both Parties have largely resorted in their pleadings to subsidiary methods of interpretation, and in this framework have attributed a preponderant place to the documentary history of the negotiations; they here also, in general, expressly recognized the legitimate nature and the particular value of a study of the preparatory work"[49].

But they also generally confirm the interpretation reached[50].

In relation to the resort to preparatory works to interpret a multilateral treaty, an interesting problem appears concerning treaties in whose process of elaboration States that adhered to it later did not participate. As regards this, the arbitral case law oscillates among the following situations: it does not take them into account because in its opinion its analysis is not acceptable[51]; it does not take them into account (even if the Parties agree as concerns their content) because they have not been published[52]; or it analyses them[53]. But the analysis of the arbitral case law

---

The same principle was subsequently formulated in the most explicit manner by the Court in its Decision of March 17, 1934, regarding the *Lighthouses Case involving France and Greece*, in which it stated: 'Where the context does not suffice to show the precise sense in which the Parties to the dispute have employed these words in their Special Agreement, the Court in accordance with its practice, has to consult the documents preparatory to the Special agreement in order to satisfy itself as to the true intention of the Parties' (*Series A/B*, No. 62, p. 13)" (Judgement of 22 December 1963 concerning *Interpretation of the Air Transport Services Agreement dated March 27, 1946* involving France and the United States of America, *R.I.A.A.*, vol. XVI, pages 11-71; *R.G.D.I.P.*, 1965, pages 189-258; COUSSIRAT-COUSTERE, V. and EISEMAN. P.M., *op. cit.*, vol. III, t. 1., p. 147 et seq.).

49 *Ibid.*, COUSSIRAT-COUSTERE, V., and EISEMAN, P.M., *op. cit.*, vol. III, t. 1, p. 148.

50 So, for example, the Arbitral Tribunal in the case concerning the *Agreement on German External Debts*, in its Judgement of 16 May 1980 (*op. cit.*, p. 109).

51 So, for example, in the case concerning *the interpretation of Article V of the Unesco Constitution*:

> "In any event the Tribunal could not have taken the verbatim record of the Conference of allied Ministers in London into consideration, as certain States which signed the Constitution did not participate in that Conference" and quotes as a precedent the Judgement of the P.C.I.J. in the case concerning the *International Commission of the Oder, Series A/B*, No. 36, p. 42 (*A.D.*, 1949, vol. XVI, pages 331-337; COUSSIRAT-COUSTERE, V., and EISEMAN, P.M., *op. cit.*, vol. III, t. 1, p. 136).

52 Thus, in the case concerning *German External Debts*, Judgement of 3 July 1958, where after analysing the preparatory works of the Agreement in question, the Arbitral Tribunal states:

> "The Tribunal does not feel that in interpreting Article VII it can give any evidential value to such assertions, based as they are on no published record, even should the parties agree as to their accuracy" (*International Law Reports*, 1958-I, vol. XXV, p. 63; COUSSIRAT-COUSTERE, V., and EISEMAN, P.M., *op. cit.*, vol. III, t. 1, p. 136).

reveals that the principle not to resort to preparatory works in order to interpret multilateral treaties with regard to States that adhere to them afterwards is not of an absolute character. It depends on the power of appreciation of the judge of the circumstances of each case[54].

After 1969 the arbitral case law affirms the existence of certain limits to the resort to preparatory works: they shall be written, it is possible to resort to them later, they shall be accessible and known by all the Contracting Parties participating in the elaboration of the treaty, States adhering to it later shall be able to consult them and to take them into account[55]. This is why both the 1969 and 1986

---

53 So, for example, the *Arbitral Commission on Property, Rights and Interests in Germany* in its decision of 14 November 1959:

> "The purpose to be considered is the common and reasonable purpose of the Convention at the time of its conclusion and not the purpose which each Party desired to achieve for its part, and still less that which the States which subsequently acceded to the Convention might imagine. The Commission is of the opinion that, by recourse to the *travaux préparatoires*, it will be possible to establish with certitude what was the common purpose of the Contracting Parties ..." (COUSSIRAT-COUSTERE, V., and EISEMAN, P.M., *op. cit.*, vol. III, t. 1, p. 141).

54 So, for example, the *Arbitral Commission on Property, Rights and Interests in Germany* in its decision of 14 November 1959:

> "The principle of interpretation relied on by the complainant is thus by no means absolute. In international cases recourse has sometimes been had to the *travaux préparatoires* of multilateral treaties to which one of the States in a case was not a party and did not subsequently accede; thus the Permanent Court of International Justice, in the case of the Free Zones involving France and Switzerland, relied on the *travaux préparatoires*, including those relating to Article 435 of the Treaty of Versailles, a multilateral treaty which had not been signed by Switzerland and to which it has never acceded (...).
>
> The Commission is of opinion that the problem of recourse to the *travaux préparatoires* of a multilateral treaty, even if they were neither published nor made accessible to one of the Parties, should be left to the discretion of the judge and solved in accordance with the circumstances of the case" (*ibid.*, p. 143).

And it adds:

> it is "not by virtue of the rule of international law which prescribes that they cannot be invoked against acceding States, but by virtue of the particular circumstances of the case before it, since the consideration of these *travaux préparatoires* can induce it as well to confirm as to invalidate the interpretation given by Italy to the treaty provision in question" (*ibid.*, p. 140).

55 So, for example, the Arbitral Tribunal of the Agreement on the German External Debts in its Judgement of 16 May 1980 concerning the Y*oung Loan*:

> "34. a few words seem necessary at this point to define the concept of *travaux préparatoires*. It must first be stressed that the term must normally be restricted to material set down in writing -and thereby actually available at a later day. This means that oral statements and opinions non recorded in minutes or conference papers cab apparently be regarded as a component of *travaux préparatoires* only in exceptional

Vienna Conventions consider them to be supplementary means of interpretation, of a restrictive nature[56].

Finally, with regard to the interpretation of awards, the inexistence of ambiguities justifies not resorting to preparatory works[57].

2.6 Treaties authenticated in two or more languages

The problems concerning interpretation of treaties authenticated in two or more languages were dealt with by the International Law Commission which, based on the equal value of each text, proposed the solution retained in Article 33.4 of both 1969 and 1986 Vienna Conventions: the meaning which best reconciles the texts, having regard to the object and purpose of the treaty.

Before both Conventions the problem also appears in cases submitted to international arbitration. So, the decisions of arbitral bodies state the same value of all the treaties in question at the time of their interpretation[58]. Consequently, the in-

---

cases. They can in any event be considered only if made in an official capacity and during the negotiations themselves. (…).

A further prerequisite if material is to be considered as a component of *travaux préparatoires* is that it was actually accessible and known to all the original parties. … While a State which accedes to a multilateral treaty at a later stage is able, *before* accession, to examine all the available *travaux préparatoires, i.e.* to make itself familiar with them, before it gives its 'yes or no', …" (COUSSIRAT-COUSTERE, V., and EISEMAN, P.M., *op. cit.*, 1980, vol. III, t. 1, p. 151; *I.L.R.*, vol. LIX, pages 544-545; *R.G.D.I.P.*, 1980/4, pages 1158-1206).

56 So, the Arbitral Tribunal in the case concerning *Filleting within the Gulf of St. Lawrence* in its Judgement of 17 July 1986 stated:

"That having been said, the Tribunal is well aware that international case law – in particular the decisions of the International Court of Justice – exercises the utmost caution in resorting to the preparatory work or the documentary background of negotiations leading up to the conclusion of the treaty. It is also aware of the restrictive attitude adopted at the Vienna Conference on the Law of Treaties following a United States amendment to do away with the hierarchy set up by the International Law Commission between the different means of interpretation" (COUSSIRAT-COUSTERE, V., and EISEMAN, P.M., *op. cit*, vol. III, t. 1, p. 154).

57 So, in the *Dispute concerning the course of the frontier between B.P. 62 and Mount Fitz Roy (Argentina/Chile)*, Award of 21 October 1994:

"The interpretation of the 1902 Award contains no ambiguities which would justify application of the rule allowing recourse to the preparatory work" (*R.I.A.A.*, vol. XXII, p. 49, para. 156).

58 So, "there is no doubt that each one of them shall equally serve to interpret the Treaty" (case concerning the *Frontier in the Area of the Manica Plateau*, Portugal/United Kingdom, Decision of 30 January 1897, COUSSIRAT-COUSTERE, V., and EISEMAN, P.M., *op. cit.*, vol. I, p. 42. The translation was made by us).

terpreter shall use all them[59]. The case concerning the *Krankenversorgung der Bundesbahnbeamten versus the Austrian Republic* is a good example of this. In it, the Arbitral Tribunal affirms that in the case of a multilingual multilateral treaty where all the versions are equally valid, according to the rules of interpretation recognized in Public International Law, the interpretation which reconciles all the versions of the treaty shall be adopted. The Tribunal adds that "if a common meaning to all these versions can be found, a historic interpretation specific merely to one text should be rejected in advance, since the will of the contracting parties must be determined according to the treaty itself. International case-law establishes that, when a word receives a different meaning in two States, it must be interpreted according to the language more favourable to the obliged State"[60].

One rule applied to this type of problem is that of the "clear text": to interpret the obscure text in the light of the clear text[61]. But, as we have shown in the opening pages of the present work, clearness as well as ambiguity of a text can not be asserted *a priori*, before carrying out its interpretation.

In any case, in both situations we are faced with older rules superseded by the 1969 Vienna Convention on the Law of Treaties. According to this Convention, interpretation of treaties authenticated in two or more languages shall be carried out, in the last analysis, "having regard to the object and purpose of the

---

[59] So: "a) The Commission does not deny that the texts of the Treaty (of Peace with Italy of 1947), prepared in three languages, all have the same value as authenticated originals, and that the interpreter must reconcile them one with the other" (Italian-United States Conciliation Commission, Decision of 20 September 1958 in the case *Albert Flegenheimer (No. 182)*, *R.I.A.A.* vol. XIV, pages 328-390; COUSSIRAT-COUSTERE, V., and EISEMAN, P.M., *op. cit.*, vol. III, t. 1., p. 170).

[60] Case concerning *Krankenversorgung der Bundesbahnbeamten c. Republique d'Autriche*, Binding opinion No. 37 of the Austro-German Tribunal, of 14 November 1962 (COUSSIRAT-COUSTERE, V., and VINCENT, P.M., *op. cit.*, vol. III, t. 1, p. 171).

[61] So, for example, the Claims Commission in the case concerning the *German Claims*, in its decision of 3 September 1924:

> "The situation is so here: there is a clear text -the English text- and a text which is not clear and whose sense shall be derived by interpretation -the French text-. Both texts are equally authoritative. Both have been submitted to the signature of the Parties. In this case, it seems not to be allowed to make abstraction of the English text and to interpret the French text as the English text did not exist. On the contrary, the clear text, the English text, will provide the best middle to interpret the French text. Both texts are evidently called to express the same ideas. If there were two texts equally clears but not according between them, the preference of the text comporting less obligations to the obliged Party could be sustained. But if one of the texts is clear and not the other, the solution is to interpret the text less clear in the light of the other text and accordingly to the meaning of the terms resulting of this last text" (*R.I.A.A.*, vol. I, p. 439; COUSSIRAT-COUSTERE, V., and EISEMAN, P.M., *op. cit.*, vol. II, pages 36-37).

treaty" (Article 33.4); in fact, this was already taken into account by the arbitral case law[62].

The case concerning the *Re-evaluation of the German Mark* is a good example of the evolution of arbitral case law. Here, the arbitral Tribunal deals with the problem of a treaty authenticated in English, French and German. It begins its reasoning recalling that all texts have the same legal force so it is not possible to take past practice in which priority was given to the basic or original text. Also, because this would be contrary to the general rule of interpretation codified in Article 33.1 of the 1969 Vienna Convention on the Law of Treaties which gives the same status to the authenticated texts in the case of multilingual treaties[63]. The Tribunal will resolve the case trough the application of Article 33.4 of that Convention.

2.7 The intention of the Parties

In its Judgement of 21 October 1994, in the case of the *Dispute concerning the course of the frontier between B.P. 62 and Mount Fitz Roy (Argentina/Chile)*, the Arbitral Tribunal resorts to the intention of the Parties as well as to that of the Arbitrator who gave the Award of 1902 in order to interpret the expression "water-parting". With regard to the Arbitrator, the Tribunal states that in any of the written documents constituting the Award of 1902 – the decision of the Arbitrator and the report of the Tribunal- no proof can be found in order to assert that the intention of the Arbitrator had been that of detaching itself from the concept of "water-parting" which was given to it by the Parties and was coincidental with the ordinary meaning attributed to that term at that time[64].

---

[62] For example, in the case concerning the *Young Loan (n. 6-10)*, in which the Arbitral Tribunal of the Agreement on the German External Debts, of 27 February 1953, in its Judgement of 16 May 1980, states that:

> "The repeated reference by Article 33 (4) of the VCT to the 'object and purpose' of the treaty means in effect nothing else than that any person having to interpret a plurilingual international treaty has the opportunity of resolving any divergence in the texts which persists, after the principles of Article 31 and 32 of the VCT have been applied, by opting, for a final interpretation, fot the one or the other text which in his opinion most closely approaches the 'object and purpose' of the treaty. Application of article 33 (4) of the VCT to the case under decision means that the Arbitral Tribunal has the right -and the duty- to adopt that interpretation of the clause in dispute which most closely approaches the object and purpose of the L(ondon) D(ebt) A(greement) (of February 27, 1953)" (*I.L.R.*, 1980, vol. LIX, p. 529 et seq.; *R.G.D.I.P.*, 1980/4, pages 1158-1206; COUSSIRAT-COUSTERE, V., and EISEMAN, P.M., *op. cit.*, vol. III, t. 1., p. 175).

[63] *R.I.A.A.* vol. XIX, p. 92. On the other hand, this case is also a good example of the combination of the interpretative criteria of the arbitral Tribunal. It uses the following: the natural and ordinary meaning, the context, the object and purpose of the treaty, the subsequent practice and the preparatory works.

[64] Cf. *ibid*, p. 42, para. 127.

Concerning the intention of the Parties, the Tribunal is called to analyse this as a consequence of the discrepancy between them concerning Chile's extreme claim in the arbitration of 1898-1902. In order to determine this claim the Tribunal analyses what Chile stated at that time[65], and concluded that it was specified in the continental watershed. At this point, the Tribunal addresses the interpretation of the Chilean claim in the cases where the maps presented by Chile represented the line of the *divortium aquarum* "with some divergences from the reality on the ground or in those other cases in which the line was unknown because the areas were unexplored"[66]. In its search for that intention the Arbitral Tribunal concludes that in the interventions made by Chile before the Arbitrator of 1898-1902 this State "established an order of priority among the manifestations of its wishes (the written texts and the maps) and asserted that the natural and effective continental water-parting prevailed". In other words, "the water-parting present in nature, over its representations on maps and regardless of the accuracy thereof. The same criterion applies to the unexplored regions and to the ones which have been insufficiently explored"[67].

In the opinion of the Tribunal, that conclusion is in agreement with the principles of good faith and contemporaneity because it is based on precise texts manifesting Chile's intention in that arbitration "clearly and conclusively", as well as on geographic knowledge the Parties had in 1902[68].

---

[65] "This Court believes, therefore, that Chile's extreme claim in 1898-1902 shall must be sought in that country's presentations before that Arbitrator" as it was not possible to interpret what was decided at that time "in accordance with criteria submitted to the 1991 Court but which were not validated in the original decision, for that would be to take up matters which were not covered by the 1902 Award and which, in consequence, cannot serve as a basis for interpreting it" (*ibid.*, p. 29, para. 85).

[66] Cf. *ibid.*, p. 31, para. 91.

[67] *Ibid.*, p. 31, para. 94. The Tribunal also concludes that Chile's extreme claim in 1898-1902 concerning the frontier sector submitted to the decision of the Court, "was the natural and effective continental *divortium aquarum*, except in the case of Mount Fitz Roy" (*ibid.*, p. 36, para. 109).

[68] *Ibid.*, p. 69, paras. 95-96. Regarding this last the Tribunal states that in 1902, "there were still unexplored areas of the frontier and other areas which were insufficiently known, something which is not the case today. Chile argued that neither the inaccuracy of the maps nor the lack of knowledge of a region could serve as an excuse for not applying the invariable criterion of demarcation which, in its opinion, was the continental water-divide. It asserted that the same principles should also be applied to the unexplored regions, even when the outcome was uncertain, and that it was ready to accept the consequences. Thus, the conclusion of this Court to the effect that Chile claimed in any event the natural and effective continental water-parting has been established on the basis of the geographical knowledge of 1902, i.e., in strict conformity with the principle of contemporaneity" (*ibid.*, p. 34, para. 97).

2.8 The rule of practical effect

As we have seen, before 1969 the arbitral case law had already stated that with regard to treaties thepractical effect consisted of the fact that their interpretation shall be done in a manner that it should not be vain and illusory[69]. However, its application cannot lead to an interpretation distant of what the Parties did establish[70].

The jurisprudence posterior to 1969 emphasizes that the rule of practical effect is "embodied in uninterrupted and constant legal practice" and states that "a provision must always be interpreted in such a way as to have a certain effect"[71], repeating that its application cannot lead to an interpretation removed from what was established by the Parties[72]. It also emphasizes that it is a principle "generally accepted as one of the main principles of treaty interpretation"[73].

3 Does the arbitral jurisprudence use the interpretative canons as they were conceived by the I.L.C.?

When appraising the way in which arbitral case law applies Articles 31, 32 and 33 of the 1969 Vienna Convention on the Law of Treaties in matters of interpretation, account shall be taken of one fundamental fact characterising and differentiating it

---

[69] Permanent Court of Arbitration, Judgement of 25 June 1914, *Timor Island* (*R.I.A.A.*, vol. IX, pages 490-509; COUSSIRAT-COUSTERE, V., and EISEMAN, P.M., *op. cit.*, vol. I, p. 34). See also in the same line the decision of the Arbitral Tribunal of 22 January 1926 concerning the case *Cayuga Indians v. United States*, (*ibid.*, pages 35-36); *R.S.A.*, vol. VI, pages 175-190.

[70] Thus, for example, the decision of the Advisory Panel of 30 November 1965, in the case concerning the *Legality of a system for the selective adjustment of quotas (International Coffee Agreement)*:

> "The principle of 'effectiveness' in the interpretation of treaties, whatever its scope, cannot justify so sharp a departure from the structure established by the parties" (*I.L.R.*, 1965, vol. LXII, p. 428; COUSSIRAT-COUSTERE, V., and EISEMAN, P.M., *op. cit.*, vol. III, t. 1, p. 128).

[71] The case of the *Dispute concerning the course of the frontier between B.P. 62 and Mount Fitz Roy (Argentina/Chile)*, Decision of 21 October 1994, p. 45, para. 137. In this case the Tribunal states that the term "local water-parting'" used by the Arbitrator in 1902 in this sector, "must be interpreted so as to have an applicable meaning and outcome" (*ibid.*).

[72] In this sense see the decision of 17 July 1986 in the case concerning *Filleting within the Gulf of St. Lawrence between Canada and France* (*R.G.D.I.P.*, 1986, pages 734-735; COUSSIRAT-COUSTERE, V., and EISEMAN, P.M., *Ibid.*, p. 129) and the decision of 26 January 1972 concerning *Claims arising out of decisions of the Mixed Greek-German Arbitral Tribunal set up under Article 304 in Part X of the Treaty of Versailles (involving Greece and the Federal Republic of Germany)*, (*R.I.A.A.*, vol. XIX, p. 60).

[73] Iran-United States Claims Tribunal, interlocutory award of 20 August 1986 (COUSSIRAT-COUSTERE, V., and EISEMAN, P.M., *op. cit.*, vol. III, t. 1, p. 131).

from the I.C.J. case law: this is always done by the same organ and occasionally by some of its Chambers. Arbitral case law, on the other hand, is given by different bodies constituted by the Parties for the specific case. The fact that, due to the plurality of unrelated arbitral bodies, this could lead to less uniformity of the arbitral case law in the matter, in practice, however, the result is not so. In effect, it can be said that the case law of the arbitral bodies in matters of interpretation after the 1969 Vienna Convention on the Law of Treaties shows a correct application of the rules and criteria conceived by the I.L.C. In this sense, the general rule of Article 31 is applied as it was conceived, that is, integrally, starting from the natural and ordinary meaning of the terms (choosing the special meaning – Article 34.1 – if it was the intention of the Parties)[74], in its context and taking into account its object and purpose[75].

The context is also correctly conceived, and, as stated in Article 31.2, all the clauses of the treaty are part of it, including the preamble, as well as any agreement of the Parties related to the conclusion of the treaty[76].

Together with the context, arbitral case law also retains any subsequent agreement and practice (passive as well as active), as well as any pertinent rule of International Law applicable to the relations between the Parties (Article 31.3)[77].

The supplementary character of the resort to preparatory works tasks is also taken into account according to Article 32 of the 1969 Vienna Convention. The arbitral case law stresses its limits: they shall be written, accessible and known by all Contracting Parties, as well as by States adhering afterwards to the treaty in question. Resort to these shall also be possible after the treaty. They are conceived, in consequence, with a restrictive character[78].

---

[74] So in the Judgement of 26 January 1972 in the case concerning *Claims arising out of decisions of the Mixed Greek-German Arbitral Tribunal set up under Article 304 in Part X of the Treaty of Versailles (involving Greece and the Federal Republic of Germany)*, (*R.I.A.A.*, vol. XIX, p. 53).

[75] The object and purpose do not form any independent basis for interpretation "but rather factors to be taken into account in the determination of the 'meaning to be given to the terms of the treaty'" with special incidence in the interpretation of treaties authenticated in two or more languages (cf. the cases *Iran-United States of America, Case N. A 17*, *op. cit.*, p. 109; *Maritime Delimitation involving Guinea and Guinea-Bissau*, *op. cit.*, p. 176; and *re-evaluation of the German Mark*, *op. cit.*, p. 109).

[76] Cf. the case quoted in the preceding footnote as well as those concerning the *Agreement on the German External Debts* (*I.L.R.*, vol. XLVII, pages 423-462; COUSSIRAT-COUSTERE, V., and EISEMAN, P.M., *op. cit.*, vol. III, t. 1, p. 126); *Maritime Delimitation ...* (*op. cit.*, p. 173); *Filleting within the Gulf of St. Lawrence* (*op. cit.*, p. 248); and *Iran v. United States of America* (COUSSIRAT-COUSTERE, V., and EISEMAN, P.M., *op. cit.*, vol. III, t. 1, p. 127).

[77] Cf. the examples of the cases concerning the *Filleting within the Gulf of St. Lawrence*, *Iran v. United States of America* and the *dispute about the run of the borderline between border stone 62 and the Mount Fitz Roy (Argentine/Chile)*, we have quoted in the present Chapter.

[78] Cf., for example the case concerning the *Agreement on the German External Debts* (*op. cit.*, p. 151).

With regard to treaties authenticated in two or more languages, the criterion of article 33.4 of the Vienna Convention is applied correctly. If their interpretation is not possible through application of Articles 31 and 32, the arbitral Tribunal in question states that it shall analyse the meaning which best reconciles the texts, having regard to the object and purpose of the treaty and choosing the text more near to them[79].

In conclusion, as far as interpretation is concerned – unlike the I.C.J.- arbitral case law uses the interpretative criteria in the way they were conceived in this matter by the I.L.C.

[79] Cf. the cases concerning the *re-evaluation of the German Mark* (*op. cit.*, p. 109); and *Loan Young (n. 6-10)* (*op. cit.*, p. 529-530).

Part Three:

Rules and Criteria Employed in Relation to the Interpretation of Certain Categories of Norms and International Instruments

Chapter VIII:

Conventional Instruments or Instruments of a Statutory Nature

1 Interpretation of treaties *stricto sensu*

As this question has been fully dealt with in the preceding pages, reference can be made to the information already provided in this regard[1].

2 The Charter of the United Nations

The firsts interpretations of the Charter of the United Nations took place in a specific socio-historical context as regards problems inherent to the Organization itself when the United Nations was getting under.

One of the questions treated by the Court concerns the *legal nature* of the Charter, which is a multilateral treaty, "albeit a treaty having certain special characteristics". Consequently, it follows the principles and rules generally applicable to the interpretation of treaties. Thus, the interpretation of the Charter is essentially a legal and not a political task (as some States pretended)[2]. In this sense, the Court itself, in its Advisory Opinion concerning conditions for the *Conditions of Admission of a State to Membership in the United Nations (Article 4 of the Charter)*, recalls that as it is "the principal judicial organ of the United Nations", as regards any article of the Charter it may exercise "an interpretative function which falls within the normal exercise of its judicial powers"[3].

---

1 See Chapter II of this work.

2 So, it states:

> "It is true that most interpretations of the Charter of the United Nations will have political significance, great or small. In the nature of things it could not be otherwise. The Court, however, cannot attribute a political character to a request which invites it to undertake an essentially judicial task, namely, the interpretation of a treaty provision" (I.C.J., Advisory Opinion concerning *Certain Expenses of the United Nations, Reports 1962*, p. 155).

3 I.C.J., *Reports 1948*, p. 61.

Another aspect of the Charter interpreted by the Court in this initial period concerns *the conditions a State must fulfill with in order to be able to become a member of the United Nations*, quoted in Article 4.1 of the Charter[4]. The I.C.J. states that the text of this paragraph of Article 4, "by the enumeration which it contains and the choice of its terms, it clearly demonstrates the intention of its authors to establish a legal rule which, while it fixes the conditions of admission, determines also the reasons for which admission may be refused; ..."[5].

Article 4.1 establishes the following requisite conditions: the applicant must be a State, it must be peace-loving, it must accept the obligations of the Charter, it must be able – in the judgement of the Organization – to carry out these obligations and be willing to do so. In the opinion of the I.C.J., these conditions, must be regarded "not merely as the necessary conditions, but also as the conditions which suffice"[6].

Article 4.2 states that "the admission of any such state to membership in the United Nations will be effected by a decision of the General Assembly upon the recommendation of the Security Council". In the opinion of the I.C.J. – which has no doubts concerning the sense of this text – that procedure and no other is what is envisaged by the Charter[7], and both certifications are "indispensable" for the Organization to appraise if the State in question complies or not with the conditions of Article 4.1 of the Charter.

A third question in relation to the Charter concerns *the obligation of the Member States to bear the expenses of the Organization as apportioned by the General Assembly*, contained in Article 17 of the Charter. From the interpretation made by the I.C.J. in its Advisory Opinion concerning *Certain Expenses of the United Nations* it turns out that the term "expenses of the Organization" means "all the expenses and

---

[4] This Article says:

> "1. Membership in the United Nations is open to all other peace-loving states which accept the obligations contained in the present Charter and, in the judgement of the Organization, are able and willing to carry out these obligations".

[5] I.C.J., Advisory Opinion concerning *Conditions of Admission of a State to Membership in the United Nations (Article 4 of the Charter), Reports 1948*, p. 62.

[6] *Ibid.*, p. 62. And adds:

> "To warrant an interpretation other than that which ensues from the natural meaning of the words, a decisive reason would be required which has not been established" (*ibid.*, p. 63).

[7] I.C.J., Advisory Opinion concerning the *Competence of the General Assembly for the Admission of a State to the United Nations*:

> "In the present case the Court finds no difficulty in ascertaining the natural and ordinary meaning of the words in question and no difficulty in giving effect to them. Some of the written statements submitted to the Court have invited it to investigate the *travaux préparatoires* of the Charter. Having regard, however, to the considerations above stated, the Court is of the opinion that it is not permissible, in this case, to resort to *travaux préparatoires*" (p. 8).

not just certain types of expenses which might be referred to as 'regular expenses'". Thus, "an examination of other parts of the Charter shows the variety of expenses which must inevitably be included within the 'expenses of the Organization' just as much as the salaries of staff or the maintenance of buildings"[8].

In order to specify whether a certain expense corresponds or not to the United Nations, the I.C.J. completes its previous consideration with the analysis of the general structure and economy of the Charter, the functions of United Nations' bodies as well as the purposes of the Organization[9]. If the expense in question complies with the conditions required by the quoted analysis, it will always be an expense of the U.N.O.

In relationship to Article 17 of the Charter, the I.C.J. has also interpreted *the function of the General Assembly in order to approve the budget of the Organization*. In the opinion of the Court, the budgetary power of the General Assembly "is not absolute" so, where expenditure arises out of obligations, the General Assembly has no alternative but to honour these engagements and awards of the Administrative Tribunal of the United Nations which fall within this category (among which are the decisions of the Administrative Tribunal of the United Nations agreeing to compensation for staff)[10].

The *relationship between the U.N.O. and its staff* have been interpreted by the Court from a threefold viewpoint: the body with competence to resolve those disputes, the compulsory character of the judgements of the United Nations' Administrative Tribunal and its consequences. With regard to the first question, the Court has stated the non existence in the charter of a body with competence to resolve the disputes between the Organization and its staff. It is true that, in the Charter, there is no provision for allowing one of the principal bodies to resolve such disputes. On the other hand, Article 105 of the Charter gives to the U.N.O. immunity of jurisdiction in the territory of each of its Members. In the opinion of the Court, if the U.N.O. did not provide jurisdictional or arbitration protection for its staff members to resolve the disputes that could arise between them and the Organization, such a situation would not be compatible with the aims of the Charter to favour freedom and justice for human beings nor with U.N.O.'s aim to promote those aims[11]. The answer is founded by the Court on the theory of the implied powers of the Organization. So, the legal power to establish a tribunal competent to resolve disputes between the Organization and its staff members is essential "in order to ensure the efficient working of the Secretariat and to give effect to the paramount consideration of securing the highest standards of efficiency,

8 I.C.J., *Reports 1962*, p. 161.

9 Cf. *ibid.*, pages 161 set seq.

10 Advisory Opinion concerning the *Effects of Awards of Compensation Made by the United Nations Administrative Tribunal* (I.C.J., *Reports 1954*, p. 59). And in this regard, the attribution of the budgetary power to the General Assembly could not be considered as "implying a right to refuse the execution of an obligation derived from an award of the Administrative Tribunal" (*ibid.*).

11 Cf. *ibid.*, p. 57.

competence and integrity", and "it appears from the Charter itself that such a power is conferred by necessary implication"[12].

Which is the body with competence to create this? In the opinion of the I.C.J., Articles 7.2, 22 and 101.1 show that the General Assembly "has the power to establish a tribunal competent to render judgements binding on the United Nations" as well as to ensure justice between the Organization and its staff members[13].

Concerning the compulsory character of the judgements of that Tribunal with regard to the General Assembly, the I.C.J. states that the Administrative Tribunal of the United Nations was established as an independent and truly judicial body competent to pronounce final judgements without appeal within the limits of its functions. It also states that it was an exclusive competence of the General Assembly to specify the nature and scope of the measures through which it would exercise its power to establish a tribunal[14].

On the other hand, the compensation awards of the Administrative Tribunal of the United Nations in favour of staff members are part of the obligations which the Organization has already incurred and that the General Assembly shall assume even though they do not appear in the budgets approved by the latter, the Court repeats that the binding effect of these awards derives from their authority as *res judicata* as well as from the binding force they have for the Organization of the United Nations. Consequently, the attribution to the General Assembly of the budgetary power of the Charter could not be considered as implying the right to refuse obligations deriving from an award of the Administrative Tribunal. So, the General Assembly has no right to refuse to give effect to an award of the United Nations Administrative Tribunal in favour of a staff member of the United Nations whose contract of service has been terminated without his consent[15].

The *relations between the bodies and the consequences* on the way the Tribunal acts had also been interpreted by the Court through a two fold appraisal. Thus, the statement of the I.C.J. in the case concerning *Certain Expenses of the United Nations* can be classified as advanced as it asserts its competence to examine something which the U.N.O. has excluded. In this case, the exclusion was the French amendment rejected by the General Assembly. The I.C.J. considers that this rejection does not constitute a directive to the Court "to exclude from its consideration the question whether certain expenditures were decided on in conformity with the Charter', if the Court finds such consideration appropriate"[16]. In its opinion, it is not to be assumed that the General Assembly would thus seek to fetter or hamper the Court in the discharge of its judicial functions. On the contrary, "the Court must have full liberty to consider all relevant data available to it in forming an opinion on a question submitted to it for an advisory opinion"[17].

---

[12] *Ibid.*

[13] *Ibid.*, p. 58.

[14] Cf. *ibid.*

[15] Cf. *ibid.*, p. 62.

[16] I.C.J., *Reports 1962*, p. 157.

[17] *Ibid.*

As an example of a restrictive appraisal, its statement in the Advisory opinion concerning *Legal Consequences for States of the Continued Presence of South Africa in Namibia (South-West Africa) notwithstanding Security Council Resolution 276 (1970)* can be quoted, as an example that the Court has no powers of judicial control and appeal with regard to decisions taken by the bodies of the United Nations[18].

More recently, the I.C.J. again interpreted the Charter on the occasion of the case concerning *Questions of Interpretation and Application of the 1971 Montreal Convention arising from the Aerial Incident at Lockerbie (Libyan Arab Jamahiriya v. United States of America)*, Provisional Measures, in which the Libyan Arab Jamahiriya requested the Court for provisional measures[19]. As is known, this case arose from the request made to Libya by the United Kingdom and the United States to extradite two Libyan nationals indicted on 14 November 1991, by a Grand Jury of the United States District of Columbia for having caused a bomb to be placed aboard PAN AM flight 103 on 21 December 1988 over Lockerbie, in Scotland, which caused its destruction[20].

According to the Montreal Convention, Libya is obliged to exercise its jurisdiction for the purposes of prosecution[21] and to judge its citizens[22]. With regard to the

---

[18] It adds that, as far as this case is concerned, the request for an advisory opinion does not have to do with the validity of Resolution 2145 (XXI) of the General Assembly nor the resolutions connected with the Security Council nor whether it is in agreement with the Charter. However, "in the exercise of its judicial function and since objections have been raised, the Court will examine these when it gives the grounds before pronouncing on the judicial consequences deriving from these resolutions " (*ibid.*, p. 45).

[19] I.C.J., *Reports 1992*, pages 114-118.

[20] Libya asks the Court to adjudge and declare:

- that Libya has fully complied with all of its obligations under the Montreal Convention;
- that the United States has breached, and is continuing to breach, its legal obligations to Libya under Articles 5(2), 5(3), 7, 8(2) and 11 of the Montreal Convention; and
- that the United States is under a legal obligation immediately to cease and desist from such breaches and from the use of any and all force or threats against Libya, and from all violations of the sovereignty, territorial integrity, and the political independence of Libya.

[21] According to Article 5, paragraphs 2 and 3:

> "2. Each Contracting State shall likewise take such measures as may be necessary to establish its jurisdiction over the offences mentioned in Article 1, paragraph 1 (a), (b) and (c), and in Article 1, paragraph 2, in so far as that paragraph relates to those offences, in the case where the alleged offender is present in its territory and it does not extradite him pursuant to Article 8 to any of the States mentioned in paragraph 1 of this Article.
>
> 3. This Convention does not exclude any criminal jurisdiction exercised in accordance with national law".

[22] According to Article 7 of the same Convention:

> "The Contracting State in the territory of which the alleged offender is found shall, if it does not extradite him, be obliged, without exception whatsoever and whether or

extradition, requested by the United Kingdom and by the United States, this is taken into account in Article 8. The first paragraph of this article states that the offences shall be deemed to be included as extraditable offences" and the second paragraph specifies that "extradition shall be subject to the other conditions provided by the law of the requested State". Finally, cooperation in criminal proceedings appears in Article 11[23]. These are the provisions whose breach by the United Kingdom is invoked by Libya.

In this context, on 21 January 1992, the Security Council of the United Nations approved resolution 731 (1992) which urges Libya "immediately to provide a full and effective response to those requests so as to contribute to the elimination of international terrorism"[24].

Three days after the close of the hearings before the I.C.J., and as there was no decision of the Court, on 31 March 1992 the Security Council adopted resolution 748 (1992), in which it places the dispute under Chapter VII of the Charter, stating that:

> "the failure by the Libyan Government to demonstrate by concrete actions its renunciation of terrorism and in particular its continued failure to respond fully and effectively to the requests in resolution 731 (1992) constitute a threat to international peace and security, …"[25].

In this case, two types of problems are present: one is the interpretation and application of the Montreal Convention (especially Article 14.1)[26]. The other, the most

---

not the offence was committed in its territory, to submit the case to its competent authorities for the purpose of prosecution. Those authorities shall take their decision in the same manner as in the case of any ordinary offence of a serious nature under the law of that State".

23 This states:

"1. Contracting States shall afford one another the greatest measure of assistance in connection with criminal proceedings brought in respect of the offences. The law of the State requested shall apply in all cases.

2. The provisions of paragraph 1 of this Article shall not affect obligations under any other treaty, bilateral or multilateral, which governs or will govern, in whole or in part, mutual assistance in criminal matters".

24 I.C.J., *op. cit.*, p. 123.

25 *Ibid.* Chapter VII of the Charter was also applied by the Security Council when Kuwait was invaded by Iraq.

26 Which states:

"1. Any dispute between two or more Contracting States concerning the interpretation or application of this Convention which cannot be settled by negotiation, shall, at the request of one of them, be submitted to arbitration. If within six months of the date of the request for arbitration the Parties are unable to agree on the organization of the arbitration, any one of those Parties may refer the dispute to the International Court of Justice by request in conformity with the Statute of the Court".

important: is that it is not only the interpretation of the Montreal Convention but the interpretation of the Charter of the United Nations (especially, the institutional balance between the Security Council and the I.C.J.).

In relation to the former, it is clear that the I.C.J. could not intervene within the framework of Article 14.1 of the Montreal Convention because at that time the parties concerned were only at the negotiation stage, and the submission for arbitration at the request of one of the Parties when the dispute cannot be settled by negotiation had not been effected, nor had the dispute been submitted to the I.C.J. because the Parties were unable to agree on the organization of the arbitration. In other words, in this case the intervention of the Court takes place outside the framework of Article 14.1 of the Montreal Convention.

Nevertheless, concerning the second problem, the I.C.J. voluntarily did not take advantage of the occasion it had to interpret the Charter from the perspective of the institutional balance between the Security Council and the Court itself[27].The I.C.J., used Articles 25 and 103 of the Charter[28], and built up an interpretation giving priority to the obligations of the Charter of the United Nations and did not interpret the Montreal Convention nor did it point out provisional measures (as Libya had requested). Through this reasoning and supported by Resolution 748 (1992), the I.C.J. voluntarily avoided the dealing with the grounds for the case and failed to comply with its duties as the principal judicial organ of the United Nations. Thus, it accepted the application of Chapter VII of the Charter and gave in to the political interests of the Security Council.

This fact is especially serious due to the disproportionate framework within which the Security Council places the dispute: the aforementioned Chapter VII of the Charter, entitled "Action with respect to threats to peace, breaches of the peace, and acts of aggression". It must not be forgotten that the Security Council places the dispute within such a framework because this is how it can adopt measures impossible to adopt any other way. Consequently, the decision of the I.C.J.

---

[27] This problem is resolved in other areas such as European Community Law, but insufficiently within the framework of the Charter. Statements of the I.C.J. can be found in the following cases: *United States Diplomatic and Consular Staff in Tehran* (I.C.J., *Reports 1980*, pages 21 and 22, paragraph 40), and *Military and Paramilitary Activities in and against Nicaragua* (I.C.J., *Reports 1984*, pages 433-435, paragraphs 92 to 97), which we will study later on. See on this question, SANCHEZ RODRIGUEZ, L.I., "La invasión de Kuwait por Iraq y la acción del Consejo de Seguridad de las Naciones Unidas", *Cursos de Derecho Internacional de Vitoria-Gasteiz. 1991*, pages 15-60. Also ORAKHELASHVILI, A., "The Impact of Peremptory Norms on the Interpretation and Application of United Nations Security Council Resolutions", *E.J.I.L*, Vol. 16, Nr. 1, February 2005, pp. 59-88.

[28] Concerning, the former, the obligation of Member States to accept and carry out the decisions of the Security Council in accordance with the Charter, and, concerning the latter, the fact that, in event of a conflict between the obligations of the Members of the United Nations under the Charter and their obligations under any other international agreement, their obligations under the Charter shall prevail.

affects the institutional balance of the United Nations because, as a consequence of the attitude of the Court, primacy is given to the power of the Security Council to the detriment of the rule of law which must be ensured by the Court.[29] Effectively, the I.C.J. should have reminded the Security Council of the existence of other mechanisms in the Charter, other than those in Chapter VII, in order to ensure prompt and effective action by the United Nations for the maintenance of international peace and security such as those mechanisms in Chapter VI concerning the "Peaceful Settlement of Disputes" which are, moreover, in accordance with the purposes and principles of the United Nations quoted in Articles 1 and 2 of the Charter.

The attitude and reasoning of the I.C.J. are more surprising because they contradict its own previous jurisprudence concerning the adoption of provisional measures[30] and the institutional balance of the Charter[31]. In relation to the latter, the I.C.J. has specified that:

> "Whereas Article 12 of the Charter expressly forbids the General Assembly to make any recommendation with regard to a dispute or situation while the Security Council is exercising its functions in respect of that dispute or situation, no such restriction is placed on the functioning of the Court by any provision of either the Charter or the Statute of the Court. The reasons are clear. It is for the Court, the principal judicial organ of the United Nations, to resolve any legal questions that may be in issue between parties to the dispute; and the resolution of such legal questions by the Court may be an impor-

[29] In other words, there occurs "an overlap of attributes which leads to a conflict of competence among institutions" (ANDRÉS SÁENZ DE SANTA MARÍA, P., "De maximis non curat praetor…? …, *op. cit.*, page 333). Sea also ARANGIO RUIZ, G., "On the Security Council's 'Law-Making'", *R.D.I.*, 2000, vol. LXXXIII, nº 3, pp. 609-725.

[30] Thus, in the case concerning *Military and Paramilitary Activities in and against Nicaragua*, when the United States argued that the matter were essentially one for the Security Council since it concerned a complaint by Nicaragua involving the use of force, the I.C.J. recalled its jurisprudence in the case concerning *the United States Diplomatic and Consular Staff in Tehran*:

> "In the preamble to this second resolution the Security Council expressly took into account the Court's Order of 15 December 1979 indicating provisional measures; and it does not seem to have occurred to any member of the Council that there was or could be anything irregular in the simultaneous exercise of their respective functions by the Court and the Security Council. Nor is there in this any cause for surprise (I.C.J., *Reports 1980*, p. 21, par. 40)" (I.C.J., *Reports 1984*, p. 433, paragraph 93).

[31] Where Article 36, paragraph 3 states:

> "In making recommendations under this Article, the Security Council should also take into consideration that legal disputes should as a general rule be referred by the parties to the International Court of Justice, in accordance with the provisions of the Statute of the Court".

tant, and sometimes decisive, factor in promoting the peaceful settlement of the dispute"[32].

Moreover, the fact that Article 24 of the Charter confers on the Security Council primary responsibility for the maintenance of international peace and security does not mean that the Court could not intervene as the responsibility of the Council in the matter is not exclusive. Effectively,

> "The Charter accordingly does not confer *exclusive* responsibility upon the Security Council for the purpose. While in Article 12 there is a provision for a clear demarcation of functions between the General Assembly and the Security Council, in respect of any dispute or situation, that the former should not make any recommendation with regard to that dispute or situation unless the Security Council so requires, there is no similar provision anywhere in the Charter with respect to the Security Council and the Court. The Council has functions of a political nature assigned to it, whereas the Court exercises purely judicial functions. Both organs can therefore perform their separate but complementary functions with respect to the same events"[33].

In the case concerning *United States Diplomatic and Consular Staff in Tehran*, with the same mentality the I.C.J. examined the simultaneous exercise of their respective functions by the Security Council and by the Court itself, stating clearly that, whereas Article 12 of the Charter expressly forbids the General Assembly to make any recommendation with regard to a dispute or situation while the Security Council is exercising its functions in respect of that dispute or situation, "no such restriction is placed on the functioning of the Court by any provision of either the Charter or the Statute of the Court"[34]. In its opinion, the reasons are clear:

---

[32] I.C.J., case concerning *Military and Paramilitary Activities in and against Nicaragua, Reports 1984*, pages 433-434, paragraph 93.

[33] *Ibid.*, p. 435, paragraph 95. The words in italics correspond to the original. The I.C.J. reinforces its argument and recalls its statement in the case concerning the *Corfu Channel*, and says:

> "It must also be remembered that, as the *Corfu Channel* case (I.C.J., *Reports 1949*, p. 4) shows, the Court has never shied away from a case brought before it merely because it had political implications or because it involved serious elements of the use of force. The Court was concerned with a question of a 'demonstration of force' (*loc. cit.*, p. 31) or 'violation of a country's sovereignty' (*ibid.*); the Court, indeed, found that:
>
> 'Intervention is perhaps still less admissible in the particular form it would take here; for, from the nature of things, it would be reserved for the most powerful States, and might easily lead to perverting the administration of international justice itself (*ibid.*, p. 35)'" (case concerning *Military and Paramilitary Activities in and against Nicaragua, I.C.J., Reports 1984*, p. 435, paragraph 96). The words in italics correspond to the original.

[34] I.C.J., *Reports 1980*, p. 22.

> "It is for the Court, the principal judicial organ of the United Nations, to resolve any legal question that may be in issue between parties to a dispute; and the resolution of such legal questions by the Court may be an important, and sometimes decisive, factor in promoting the peaceful settlement of the dispute"[35].

Finally, the fact that the I.C.J. approved the use of Article 103 of the Charter by the Security Council does not take not into account the fact that in this case that provision was not applicable because there was no conflict between the obligations under the Charter and those under the Montreal Convention. Effectively, the Montreal Convention in its Article 5.2 provides that the State in whose territory the alleged offender is present and does not extradite him (extradition conceived by the Montreal Convention as "discretional"), shall establish its jurisdiction over the offences committed. In addition, Libyan law does not allow the extradition of Libyan nationals. Consequently, taking these aspects into consideration together with the fact that International Law does not oblige States to extradite, the refusal of Libya to do so was in accordance with Law. Moreover, Libya had acted in conformity with the Montreal Convention because it had established its jurisdiction from the time it was informed that two Libyan nationals had been indicted by a Grand Jury of the United States District of Columbia of having caused a bomb to be placed aboard the PAN AM flight 103 on 21 December 1988 over Lockerbie, in Scotland. It also requested the assistance of the judicial authorities of the United States in the criminal proceedings, in accordance with paragraph 1 of Article 11 of the Montreal Convention. This is why it is not possible to speak about the existence of a contradiction between the Convention and the Charter of the United Nations. What happened is quite different, as it was impossible to achieve the extradition of the two Libyan nationals by legal means, the United States, the United Kingdom and France, promoted Resolution 748 (1992) in order to achieve their goal through political means, taking advantage of the discretion the Security Council has to classify the situations it is aware of and to declare their legal grounds.

The resort to Article 103 in this case is only an instrument to reinforce the reasoning of the Security Council and the I.C.J. accepted this instead of analysing the legality of Resolution 748 (1992), even at the stage of provisional measures, because it is manifestly incompatible with the Charter that the political organ of the United Nations hindered the I.C.J. from achieving its judicial function. As BEDJAOUI says, the fact of placing the Court in a situation of subordination with regard to the political organ of the United Nations is contrary to the principle of separation or independence

---

35 *Ibid.*, adding that this is what is recognized in Article 36, paragraph 3, of the Charter when it states that:

> "In making recommendations under this Article the Security Council should also take into consideration that legal disputes should as a general rule be referred by the parties to the International Court of Justice in accordance with the provisions of the Statute of the Court".

of the judicial power[36]. In other words, the Security Council is also submitted to the Charter and to International Law[37].

A last question examined by the I.C.J. in relation to the Charter concerns the *consequences of a treaty not registered with the Secretariat of the United Nations*, as stated in Article 102 of the Charter. In the opinion of the Court, the fact of not registering the treaty in question does not affect its validity and it will continue to link the Parties. The sole consequence is that, in the absence of registration, the treaty in question cannot be invoked by the Parties before an organ of the United Nations[38].

3 The system of Mandates and the validity of the obligations inherent to it despite the disappearance of the League of Nations

As is known, the Covenant of the League of Nations created the system of Mandates with regard to colonized peoples and these required, as Article 22 states, "that the tutelage of such peoples should be entrusted to advanced nations who by reason of their resources, their experience or their geographical position can best undertake this responsibility, and who are willing to accept it, and that this tutelage should be exercised by them as Mandatories on behalf of the League"[39].Therefore, as an international legal category the system of mandates constitutes an international status recognised by all of the Members of the League of Nations which:

> "was created, in the interest of the inhabitants of the territory, and of humanity in general, as an international institution with an international object – a sacred trust of civilization. It is therefore not possible to draw any conclusion by analogy from the notions of mandate in national law or from any other legal conception of that law. The international rules regulating the Mandate constituted an interna-

[36] BEDJAOUI, M., *Nouvel ordre mondial et contrôle de légalité des actes du Conseil de Sécurité*, Bruylant, Bruxelles, 1994, p. 88. See also TORRES BERNARDEZ, S., "Some considerations on the respective roles of the Security Council and the International Court of Justice with respect to 'the prevention of aggravation of disputes' in the domain of the pacific settlement of international disputes or situations", *International Legal Issues Arising under the United Nations Decade of International Law*, Kluwer, Netherlands, 1995, pages 663-708.

[37] See TORRES BERNARDEZ, S., "Perspectivas en la contribución de las Naciones Unidas al mantenimiento de la paz y la seguridad internacionales: comentarios y observaciones sobre la Declaración de los Miembros del Consejo de Seguridad de 31 de enero de 1992", in *Hacia un nuevo orden internacional y europeo. Estudios en homenaje al Profesor Manuel Díez de Velasco*, Tecnos, Madrid, 1993, pages 751-752.

[38] See the case concerning *Maritime Delimitation and Territorial Questions between Qatar and Bahrain* (I.C.J., *Reports 1994*, p. 122).

[39] Paragraphs 4, 5 and 6 of Article 22 consider three types of Mandates.

> tional status for the Territory recognized by all the Members of the League of Nations, including the Union of South Africa"[40].

For these reasons, the fact that a Mandate had been confirmed by a resolution of the Council of the League of Nations does not imply a modification of its legal nature[41].

This international purpose – the sacred trust of civilization – implied a series of obligations that did not expire because the surveillance body – the League of Nations – had disappeared[42]. In the opinion of the Court, the right of the population to have the Territory administered in accordance with these rules did not depend on the existence of the League of Nations, and this view was confirmed by Article 80, paragraph 1 of the Charter.

Moreover, the declarations of the Government of the Union of South Africa constituted its recognition of the continuance of its obligations under the Mandate and not just a mere indication of the future conduct of that Government:

> "Interpretations placed upon legal instruments by the parties to them, though not conclusive as to their meaning, have considerable probative value when they contain recognition by a party of its own obligations under an instrument. In this case the declarations of the Union of South Africa support the conclusions already reached by the Court"[43].

With regard to the international supervision of the Mandate and the reception of the reports of the Mandatory, the I.C.J. states that the General Assembly has substituted the Assembly of the League of Nations, and that this competence derives "from the provisions of Article 10 of the Charter, which authorizes the General

---

[40] I.C.J., Advisory Opinion concerning the *International Status of South-West Africa, Reports 1950*, p. 132.

[41] Effectively:

> "It cannot be correctly regarded as embodying only an executive action in pursuance of the Covenant. The Mandate, in fact and in law, is an international agreement having the character of a treaty or convention. The Preamble of the Mandate itself shows this character" (I.C.J., *South-West Africa Cases Preliminary Objections*, *Reports 1962*, p. 330).

Along the same lines:

> "It is an instrument having the character of a treaty or convention and embodying international engagements for the Mandatory as defined by the Council and accepted by the Mandatory" (*ibid.*, p. 331).

[42] Obligations that "represent the very essence of the sacred trust of civilization" (Advisory Opinion concerning the *International Status of South West Africa, I.C.J., Reports 1950*, p. 133).

[43] *Ibid.*, p. 136.

Assembly to discuss any questions or any matters within the scope of the Charter and to make recommendations on these questions or matters to the Members of the United Nations"[44].

Later, in 1971, in its Advisory Opinion concerning the *Legal Consequences for States of the Continued Presence of South Africa in Namibia (South-West Africa) notwithstanding Security Council Resolution 276 (1970)*, the I.C.J. interprets the system of Mandates taking into account the historical evolution of International Law on the matter due to the Charter of the United Nations and stating that "mindful as it is of the primary necessity of interpreting an instrument in accordance with the intentions of the parties at the time of its conclusion, the Court is bound to take into account the evolution of the concepts embodied in Article 22 of the Covenant"[45].

The question of mandates has recently been addressed by the Court in its advisory opinions on the *Legality of the Threat or Use of Nuclear Weapons and on the Legal Consequences of the Construction of a Wall in the Occupied Palestinian Territory*, with regard to Palestine[46]. Here, the Court recalls its Advisory Opinion on the *International Status of South West Africa* where, speaking of mandates in general, it stated that "The Mandate was created, in the interest of the inhabitants of the territory, and of humanity in general, as an international institution with an international object – a sacred trust of civilization"[47]. It also recalls what was upheld in this regard on that occasion. This was the existence of two principles considered by the Court as of "paramount importance": the principle of non-annexation and the principle that the well-being and development of peoples not yet able to govern themselves formed that "sacred trust of civilization"[48].

---

44 *Ibid.*, p. 137.

45 Thus, the expressions contained in Article 22: "the strenuous conditions of the modern world" and "the well-being and development" of the peoples concerned,

> "were not static, but were by definition evolutionary, as also, therefore, was the concept of the 'sacred trust'. The parties to the Covenant must consequently be deemed to have accepted them as such" (I.C.J., *Reports 1971*, pages 31-32 et seq.).

46 As is known, Palestine was part of the Ottoman Empire. At the end of the First World War, a class "A" Mandate for Palestine was entrusted to Great Britain by the League of Nations, pursuant to paragraph 4 of Article 22 of the Covenant, according to which: "Certain communities, formerly belonging to the Turkish Empire have reached a stage of development where their existence as independent nations can be provisionally recognized subject to the rendering of administrative advice and assistance by a Mandatory until such time as they are able to stand alone".

47 I.C.J., *Reports 1950*, p. 132.

48 *Ibid.*, p. 131.

4 The right of self-determination of peoples

This right, enshrined in the Charter of the United Nations was subsequently developed by the General Assembly through a number of resolutions. The most important of these were the following: 1514 (XV), 1541 (XV) and 2625 (XXV). Pursuant to this last, "Every State has the duty to refrain from any forcible action which deprives peoples referred to [in that resolution] ... of their right to self-determination".

The same principle of self-determination of peoples is also reaffirmed by Article 1 common to the International Covenant on Economic, Social and Cultural Rights and the International Covenant on Civil and Political Rights, which lays upon the States parties the obligation to promote the realization of that right and to respect it, in conformity with the provisions of the United Nations Charter.

The I.C.J. takes account of this legal development stating that, as in other domains of International law, "the *corpus iuris gentium* has been considerably enriched, and this Court, if it is faithfully to discharge its functions, may not ignore this"[49].

In the legal context, it is Resolution 1514 (XV) which "provided the basis for the process of decolonisation", complemented in some of it aspects by Resolution 1541 (XV) and some of the provisions of the latter "give effect to the essential feature of the right of self-determination as established in resolution 1541 (XV)"[50]. It is the case of the situations of free association or integration as result of a "free and voluntary choice by the peoples of the territory concerned, expressed through informed and democratic processes"[51]. But the Court, relying on Resolution 2625 (XXV), states that there are possibilities other than independence, association or integration, although all of these have in common the necessity – described by the Court itself as fundamental" – to take into account the will of the population in question. Nevertheless, the General Assembly has not always considered such consultation as necessary. The I.C.J. reiterates this fact by stating that the validity of the principle of self-determination is not affected by the fact that in certain cases the General Assembly has dispensed with the requirement to consult the inhabitants of a given territory[52]. In the opinion of the Court, "those instances were based either on the consideration that a certain population did not constitute a 'people' entitled to self-determination or on the conviction that a consultation was totally unnecessary, in the light of special circumstances"[53].

---

49 I.C.J., *Reports 1971*, p. 32.

50 Case concerning the *Western Sahara* (I.C.J., *Reports 1975*, pages 32-33).

51 *Ibid.*, p. 33. The Court adds that paragraphs 2, 5 and 6 of Resolution 1514 (XV), "confirm and emphasize that the application of the right of self-determination requires a free and genuine expression of the will of the peoples concerned" (*ibid.*, p. 32).

52 Principle "defined as the need to pay regard to the freely expressed will of the peoples" (*ibid.*, p. 33).

53 *Ibid.*

In the opinion of the I.C.J., with regard to the Western Sahara, the decolonisation process will respect the right of the members of the population "to determine their future political status by their own freely expressed will"[54].

Related to mandates, in its Advisory Opinion on the *Legal Consequences of the Construction of a Wall in the Occupied Palestinian Territory*, the Court recalls that in 1971 it emphasized that current developments in "international law in regard to non-self-governing territories, as enshrined in the Charter of the United Nations, made the principle of self-determination applicable to all [such territories]" and that it went on to state that "These developments leave little doubt that the ultimate objective of the sacred trust" referred to in Article 22, paragraph 1, of the Covenant of the League of Nations "was the self-determination ... of the peoples concerned" *(Legal Consequences for States of the Continued Presence of South Africa in Namibia (South West Africa) notwithstanding Security Council Resolution 276 (1970), Advisory Opinion,* I.C.J., *Reports 1971*, p. 31, paras. 52-53)"[55]. It also recalls that it had referred to this principle on a number of occasions in its jurisprudence[56] and that it had made it clear that the right of peoples to self-determination is today a right *erga omnes*[57].

The nature of obligation *erga omnes* of the right of peoples to self-determination had been previously stressed by the I.C.J. in the case concerning *East Timor*. In our opinion, its statement in that case represents a clear example of a regressive attitude of the Court not only with regard to the right of self-determination but, also, to its construction concerning the existence of obligations *erga omnes*, which was made in the *Barcelona Traction* case.

As is known, in the *East Timor* case, the dispute concerns a Treaty made between Australia and Indonesia – which invaded the territory of East Timor on 7 December 1975 – concerning the "Timor Gap", that is, an international treaty for the joint exploration and exploitation of the resources of an area of the continental shelf of East Timor. In other words, resources which belonged neither to Australia nor to Indonesia.

East Timor, which had been a territory under the administration of Portugal, had – until the referendum of self-determination which took place in 1999 – the status of a non-self-governing territory, with the right to self-determination and, in accordance with some resolutions of the United Nations General Assembly, sovereign over its natural resources.

Due to the Treaty of 1989 between Australia and Indonesia, Portugal – which was the administering Power of East Timor before it was invaded by Indonesia – asked the I.C.J. to adjudge and declare, principally, that the rights of the people of

---

[54] *Ibid.*, p. 36.

[55] I.C.J., *Legal Consequences of the Construction of a Wall in the Occupied Palestinian Territory, Advisory Opinion*, para. 88.

[56] See I.C.J., *Western Sahara, Advisory Opinion,* I.C.J., *Reports 1975*, p. 68, para. 162.

[57] See I.C.J., *East Timor (Portugal v. Australia), Judgment*, I.C.J., *Reports 1995*, p. 102, para. 29.

East Timor to self-determination, to territorial integrity and unity and to permanent sovereignty over its wealth and natural resources are opposable to Australia, which is under an obligation not to disregard these, but to respect them. Also, that, Australia, inasmuch as it negotiated, concluded and initiated the performance of the Agreement of 11 December 1989, took internal legislative measures for the application thereof, and continued to negotiate with Indonesia the delimitation of the continental shelf in the area of the Timor Gap, it had infringed and was infringing the right of the people of East Timor to self-determination, to territorial integrity and unity and its permanent sovereignty over its natural wealth and resources, and was in breach of the obligation not to disregard but to respect this right, integrity and sovereignty.

On the other hand, Australia submitted that the Court lacked jurisdiction to decide.

The I.C.J. took advantage of the fact that Indonesia had not accepted its jurisdiction, gave priority to it based on the character of *jus cogens* of the right of self-determination. In the view of the Court:

> "Australia's behaviour cannot be assessed without first entering into the question why it is that Indonesia could not lawfully have concluded the 1989 Treaty, while Portugal allegedly could have done so; the very subject-matter of the Court's decision would necessarily be a determination whether, having regard to the circumstances in which Indonesia entered and remained in East Timor, it could or could not have acquired the power to enter into treaties on behalf of East Timor relating to the resources of its continental shelf. The Court could not make such a determination in the absence of the consent of Indonesia"[58].

Unfortunately, the Court did not follow the preceding judgements characterized by a progressive interpretation of International Law[59]. On the contrary, even accepting that the right of peoples to self-determination is of an *erga omnes* character,

> "the Court considers that the *erga omnes* character of a norm and the rule of consent to jurisdiction are two different things. Whatever the nature of the obligations invoked, the Court could not rule on the lawfulness of the conduct of a State when its judgement would imply an evaluation of the lawfulness of the conduct of another State which is not a party to the case. Where it is so, the Court cannot act, even if the right in question is a right *erga omnes*"[60].

[58] I.C.J., *Reports 1995*, p. 102.

[59] For example, its judgement in the case concerning *Military and Paramilitary Activities in and against Nicaragua* (I.C.J., *Reports 1986*), in which the difficulty of the presence of the reservation of the United States was surmounted by the interpretation of the Court concerning the application of customary International Law in order to have jurisdiction over the case.

[60] I.C.J., *Reports 1995*, p. 102.

Then, one can wonder about the practical consequences and effects of *jus cogens* and of obligations *erga omnes* affirmed by the I.C.J. in its judgement in the *Barcelona Traction* case and later codified in Articles 53 and 64 of the 1969 and 1986 Vienna Conventions on the Law of Treaties[61], as well as in Article 19 of the Draft Articles on the Origin of State Responsibility, this last concerning international crimes[62]. Effectively, the judgement of the I.C.J. concerning the case of *East Timor* is the opposite of what was stated in the judgement and international texts just quoted. In our opinion, it is a regressive contribution to International Law. Firstly, because the Court should have protected the right of the people of East Timor to self-determination as well as to sovereignty over its natural resources as a consequence of the former. If the Court had had the will to do so, this interpretation should have been made[63].Contrary to the case concerning *Military and Paramilitary Activities in and against Nicaragua*, in the *East Timor* case the I.C.J. had no will to exercise its jurisdiction. To justify its standing, the Court chose the argument of the absence of jurisdiction due to the lack of consent from Indonesia. In 1986, the reservation to the jurisdiction of the Court made by the United States of America was clearly in order to prevent the Court from judging the case. Nevertheless, the I.C.J. made a very intelligent interpretation – it was more a legal construction – to have jurisdiction. In 1995, the I.C.J. could have concluded its jurisdiction based on the fact of the existence of norms of *jus cogens* and obligations *erga omnes* applicable to the case prevailing over those other norms concerning its jurisdiction. But it did not do so.

Secondly, with its decision regarding its incapacity to exercise its jurisdiction, the I.C.J. made it impossible to protect the rights of peoples with the right to self-determination, and this, even when that protection is represented before the Court by the State which had been the administrating power of the territory concerned and when those rights are infringed by treaties concluded between other States. This is why one cannot accept the statement of the I.C.J concerning the fact that:

---

[61] Article 53 states:

> "A treaty is void if, at the time of its conclusion, it conflicts with a peremptory norm of general international law. For the purposes of the present Convention, a peremptory norm of general international law is a norm accepted and recognized by the international community of States as a whole as a norm from which no derogation is permitted and which can be modified only by a subsequent norm of general international law having the same character".

[62] Before its suppression from the Draft Article, this Article stated that an international crime might result, for example, from:

> "(b) a serious breach of an international obligation of essential importance for safeguarding the right of self-determination of peoples, such as that prohibiting the establishment or maintenance by force of colonial domination;".

[63] The Court recognises that "it is not necessarily prevented from adjudicating when the judgement it is asked to give might affect the legal interests of a State which is not a party to the case" and quotes the case concerning *Certain Phosphate Lands in Nauru (Nauru v. Australia)* (I.C.J., *Reports 1995*, p. 104).

> "it has taken note in the present Judgement (paragraph 31) that, for the two Parties, the Territory of East Timor remains a non-self-governing territory and its people has the right to self-determination"[64].

But such a conclusion is deprived of value – and of real consequences – after having eliminated the effects of the category of *jus cogens* as well as those of obligations *erga omnes* as a consequence of its decision not to have jurisdiction.

Finally, the interpretation of the I.C.J. concerning General Assembly resolutions on East Timor is also restrictive and negative. Firstly, because it voluntarily silences the binding nature of those resolutions[65]. And secondly, because it implicitly accepts the fact of the invasion of the territory of East Timor by Indonesia as well as the acts carried out by this State over a territory not belonging to it; acts which constitute serious breaches of International Law.

On the other hand, the facts and serious breaches of International Law which took place in East Timor after the referendum on self-determination showed that the question submitted to the I.C.J. by Portugal was not irrelevant and that, by its passivity, the Court lacked an opportunity to contribute to the assertion and the development of International Law. In other words, to the progression of international justice.

5 A joint communiqué can be an international agreement or the question of the form of international agreements

This question is dealt with by the I.C.J. and in two cases it is the starting point of its reasoning concerning both the definition of treaty contained in Article 2.1 a) of the 1969 Vienna Convention. Especially, at the end when it refers to the irrelevance of the designation given to the treaty by the Parties. Thus, the Court itself recalls that in International Law no rule exists banning the fact that a joint communiqué could constitute an international agreement[66].

The criteria to specify whether such an agreement has been concluded are twofold: the terms employed by the Parties in its drafting and the circumstances in

---

64 I.C.J., *Reports 1995*, pages 105-106.

65 So:

> "Without prejudice to the question whether the resolutions under discussion could be binding in nature, the Court considers as a result that they cannot be regarded as 'givens' which constitute a sufficient basis for determining the dispute between the Parties" (I.C.J., *Reports 1995*, p. 104).

66 See the cases concerning *Aegean Sea Continental Shelf* (I.C.J., *Reports 1978*, p. 39) and *Maritime Delimitation and Territorial Questions between Qatar and Bahrain* (I.C.J., *Reports 1994*, pages 120-121).

which the drafting of the communiqué took place. Its use in two cases leads to different results due to the circumstances of the case and of the proof. Thus, in the case of the *Maritime Delimitation and Territorial Questions between Qatar and Bahrain* the I.C.J. concludes that the joint communiqué of 1990 refers to the consultations between the Ministers for Foreign Affairs of Qatar and Bahrain in the presence of the Minister for Saudi Arabia, in the context of a mediation, sometimes referred to as "good offices" of the King of Saudi Arabia. The communiqué states what was agreed by the Parties and reaffirms previous obligations. So, in opinion of the Court, the communiqué listed the commitments to which the Parties consented. They thus create rights and obligations in International Law for the Parties. Consequently, they constitute an international agreement[67].

Nevertheless, in the case concerning the *Aegean Sea Continental Shelf* the I.C.J. responds negatively. In its opinion, in this case the context is given by the previously expressed willingness of Turkey jointly to submit the dispute to the Court, after negotiations and by a special agreement defining the matters to be decided. The Court considers that, in this context, the terms of the Communiqué do not appear to evidence any change in the position of the Turkish Government in regard to the conditions under which it was ready to agree to the submission of the dispute to the Court. This context is completed by the analysis of the terms of the Joint communiqué and of the circumstances in which it was established and published[68].

6 The exercise of consular functions relating to nationals of the sending State

The question concerning the obligations of the receiving State derived from article 36[69] of the Vienna Convention on Consular Relations of 24 April 1963 (hereinafter referred to as the "Vienna Convention") occurred in the *LaGrand* (Germany *v.* United States of America) and *Avena and other Mexican Nationals* (Mexico *v.* United States of America) cases[70]. According to paragraph 1 of Article 36:

---

67 See I.C.J., *Reports 1994*, p. 121. Moreover, the text of the Communiqué was signed by the Ministers for Foreign Affairs so Bahrain cannot maintain that it was no more than a simple record of negotiations (see *ibid.*).

68 Accordingly, the Joint Communiqué of Brussels does not furnish a valid basis for establishing the Court's jurisdiction to entertain the Application filed by Greece (see I.C.J., *Reports 1978*, pages 39-44).

69 Article 36 relates, according to its title, to "Communication and contact with nationals of the sending State".

70 The same question arose in the case concerning the *Vienna Convention on Consular Relations (Paraguay v. United States of America)*, I.C.J., *Reports 1998*. The dispute brought by Paraguay to the Court concerned alleged violations of the Vienna Convention on Consular Relations of 24 April 1963 with respect to the case of Mr. Angel Fran-

> "With a view toward facilitating the exercise of consular functions relating to nationals of the sending State:
>
> *(a)* consular officers shall be free to communicate with nationals of the sending State and to have access to them. Nationals of the sending State shall have the same freedom with respect to communication with and access to consular officers of the sending State;
>
> *(b)* if he so requests, the competent authorities of the receiving State shall, without delay, inform the consular post of the sending State if, within its consular district, a national of that State is arrested or committed to prison or to custody pending trial or is detained in any other manner. Any communication addressed to the consular post by the person arrested, in prison, custody or detention shall be forwarded by the said authorities without delay. The said authorities shall inform the person concerned without delay of his rights under this subparagraph;
>
> *(c)* consular officers shall have the right to visit a national of the sending State who is in prison, custody or detention, to converse and correspond with him and to arrange for his legal representation. They shall also have the right to visit any national of the sending State who is in prison, custody or detention in their district in pursuance of a judgment. Nevertheless, consular officers shall refrain from taking action on behalf of a national who is in prison, custody or detention if he expressly opposes such action."

In order to situate the interpretation of Article 36 in its context, it is useful to refer to the statements of the I.C.J. concerning *the nature of the Vienna Convention.* In the opinion of the Court, this Convention

> "lays down certain standards to be observed by all States parties, with a view to the 'unimpeded conduct of consular relations', which, as the Court observed in 1979, is important in present-day international law 'in promoting the development of friendly relations among nations, and ensuring protection and assistance for aliens resident in the territories of other States' (*United States Diplomatic and Consular Staff in Tehran (United States of America* v. *Iran), Order of 15 December 1979,* I.C.J., *Reports 1979*, pp. 19-20, para. 40)".

---

cisco Breard, a Paraguayan national convicted of murder in Virginia (United States), whose execution had been scheduled for 14 April 1998 and who was eventually executed on that date. By a letter of 2 November 1998, the Government of Paraguay informed the Court that, despite the fact that it had filed a Memorial on the merits of the case on 9 October last, it did not wish to go ahead with the proceedings and requested that the case be removed from the Court's List. On 10 November 1998 the Court made an Order recording the discontinuance of the proceedings and directing the removal of the case from the Court's List.

Concerning the interpretation of Article 36, paragraph 1, the Court underlines that it "establishes an interrelated régime designed to facilitate the implementation of the system of consular protection"[71]. Also, the necessity "to revisit the interrelationship of the three subparagraphs of Article 36, paragraph 1, in the light of the particular facts and circumstances"[72] of each case.

This interrelated regime "begins with the basic principle governing consular protection: the right of communication and access (Art. 36, para. 1 *(a)*). This clause is followed by the provision which spells out the modalities of consular notification (Art. 36, para. 1 *(b)*). Finally Article 36, paragraph 1 *(c)*, sets out the measures consular officers may take in rendering consular assistance to their nationals in the custody of the receiving State. It follows that when the sending State is unaware of the detention of its nationals due to the failure of the receiving State to provide the requisite consular notification without delay,..., the sending State has been prevented for all practical purposes from exercising its rights under Article 36, paragraph 1"[73]. And this, independently of whether the national of the sending State would have sought consular assistance from it, whether the sending State would have rendered such assistance, or whether a different verdict would have been rendered. It is the criterion of the I.C.J. that "it is sufficient that the Convention conferred these rights" and that the sending States as well as their nationals "were in effect prevented by the breach" of the receiving State "from exercising them, had they so chosen"[74].

In the case concerning *Avena and other Mexican Nationals* (Mexico *v.* United States of America), the I.C.J. describes more precisely the interpretation of Article 36, paragraph 1 (b) of the Vienna Convention:

> "It begins by noting that Article 36, paragraph 1 *(b)*, contains three separate but interrelated elements: the right of the individual concerned to be informed without delay of his rights under Article 36, paragraph 1 *(b)*; the right of the consular post to be notified without delay of the individual's detention, if he so requests; and the obligation of the receiving State to forward without delay any communication addressed to the consular post by the detained person."[75]

---

[71] I.C.J., *LaGrand* case (IC.J. *Reports 2001*, p. 492, para. 74); case concerning *Avena and other Mexican Nationals* (I.C.J., *Reports 2004*, p. 29, para. 50 and p. 41, para. 99).

[72] I.C.J., case concerning *Avena and other Mexican Nationals* (I.C.J., *Reports 2004*, p. 41, para. 100).

[73] I.C.J., *LaGrand* case (IC.J. *Reports 2001*, p. 492, para. 74).

[74] *Ibid.*

[75] I.C.J., case concerning *Avena and other Mexican Nationals* (I.C.J., *Reports 2004*, p. 33, para. 61).

6.1 Article 36, paragraph (b) creates individual rights

The Court notes that this Article spells out the obligations the receiving State has towards the detained person and the sending State. It is from the I.C.J. that this Article provides that,

> "at the request of the detained person, the receiving State must inform the consular post of the sending State of the individual's detention "without delay". It provides further that any communication by the detained person addressed to the consular post of the sending State must be forwarded to it by authorities of the receiving State "without delay". Significantly, this subparagraph ends with the following language: "The said authorities shall inform the person concerned without delay of *his rights* under this subparagraph" (emphasis added). Moreover, under Article 36, paragraph 1 *(c)*, the sending State's right to provide consular assistance to the detained person may not be exercised "if he expressly opposes such action". The clarity of these provisions, viewed in their context, admits of no doubt. It follows, as has been held on a number of occasions, that the Court must apply these as they stand (see *Acquisition of Polish Nationality, Advisory Opinion, 1923,* P.C.I.J., *Series B, No. 7*, p. 20; *Competence of the General Assembly for the Admission of a State to the United Nations, Advisory Opinion,* I.C.J., *Reports 1950*, p. 8; *Arbitral Award of 31 July 1989, Judgment,* I.C.J., *Reports 1991*, pp. 69-70, para. 48; *Territorial Dispute (Libyan Arab Jamahiriya/ Chad), Judgment,* I.C.J., *Reports 1994*, p. 25, para. 51)"[76].

Consequently, the Court concludes that, based on the text of these provisions, Article 36, paragraph 1, "creates individual rights, which, by virtue of Article I of the Optional Protocol, may be invoked in this Court by the national State of the detained person. These rights were violated in the present case"[77].

In relation to the rights under subparagraph 1 *(b)* of Article 36 of the Vienna Convention (the right, if requested by the national, to inform the consular post of the State of its nationality of its situation of arrest, commission to prison or to custody pending to trial or of detention in any other manner, and to do this without delay), the Court finds that they are individual rights which are to be asserted, at any rate in the first place, within the domestic legal system of the United States. Only when that process is completed and local remedies are exhausted would the sending State be entitled to espouse the individual claims of its nationals through the procedure of diplomatic protection[78].

---

[76] I.C.J., *LaGrand* case (IC.J. *Reports 2001*, p. 493, para. 77).

[77] *Ibid.*

[78] Cf. I.C.J., case concerning *Avena and other Mexican Nationals* (I.C.J., *Reports 2004*, p. 26, para. 40).

In both cases the Court recalls that violations of the rights of the individual under Article 36 "may entail a violation of the rights of the State, and that violations of the rights of the latter may entail a violation of the rights of the individual"[79]. In these special circumstances of interdependence of the rights of the State and of individual rights, the sending State may, in submitting a claim in its own name, request the Court to rule on the violation of rights which it claims to have suffered both directly and trough the violation of individual rights conferred on its nationals under Article 36, paragraph *(b)*. The I.C.J. concludes that in such situations "the duty to exhaust local remedies does not apply to such a request"[80].

But the right to consular notification and consular communication under the Vienna Convention is not a fundamental human right that constitutes part of due process in criminal proceedings and that should be guaranteed in the territory of each of the Contracting Parties to the Vienna Convention. The Court observes that "neither the text nor the object and purpose of the Convention, nor any indication in the *travaux préparatoires*, support the conclusion" drawn by Mexico from its contention in that regard[81].

6.2 The presence of two elements: The right to be informed (A) "without delay" (B)

As regards the terminology employed to designate the obligations incumbent upon the receiving State under Article 36, paragraph 1 *(b)*, in the *case concerning Avena and other Mexican Nationals,* the Court notes that the Parties have used the terms "inform" and "notify" in differing senses. This is why, "for the sake of clarity, the Court, when speaking in its own name in the present Judgment, will use the word "inform" when referring to an individual being made aware of his rights under that subparagraph and the word "notify" when referring to the giving of notice to the consular post"[82].

A. The right to be informed

The I.C.J. finds that the duty upon the detaining authorities to give Article 36, paragraph 1 (b) information to the individual *arises* once it is realized that the person is a foreign national, or once there are grounds to think that the person is probably a foreign national. It also states that "precisely when this may occur will vary with circumstances"[83]. This is why it suggests that "it would be desirable for enquiry routinely to be made of the individual as to his nationality upon his deten-

---

79 *Ibid.*

80 *Ibid.*

81 Cf. *ibid.*, p. 49, para. 124.

82 Cf. *ibid.*, p. 17, para. 18.

83 Cf. *ibid.* p. 33, para. 61.

tion, so that the obligations of the Vienna Convention may be complied with". And adds:

> "The United States has informed the Court that some of its law enforcement authorities do routinely ask persons taken into detention whether they are United States citizens. Indeed, were each individual to be told at that time that, should he be a foreign national, he is entitled to ask for his consular post to be contacted, compliance with this requirement under Article 36, paragraph 1 *(b)*, would be greatly enhanced. The provision of such information could parallel the reading of those rights of which any person taken into custody in connection with a criminal offence must be *informed* prior to interrogation by virtue of what in the United States is known as the "Miranda rule"; these rights include, *inter alia*, the right to remain silent, the right to have an attorney present during questioning, and the right to have an attorney appointed at government expense if the person cannot afford one. The Court notes that, according to the United States, such a practice in respect of the Vienna Convention rights is already being followed in some local jurisdictions"[84].

Concerning the *content of the obligation to inform*, the Court notes that "the clear duty to provide consular information under Article 36, paragraph 1 *(b)*, does not invite assumptions as to what the arrested person might prefer, as a ground for not informing him. It rather gives the arrested person, once informed, the right to say he nonetheless does not wish his consular post to be notified"[85].

Finally, the giving of information is relevant as regards satisfying the element in Article 36, paragraph *(b)*, on which the other two elements therein depend: to make possible the action of the sending State and to make it possible "without delay"[86].

B. *"Without delay"*

In the *Case concerning Avena and other Mexican Nationals* the I.C.J. begins by noting that "the precise meaning of 'without delay', as it is to be understood in Article 36, paragraph 1 (*b*), is not defined in the Convention. This phrase therefore requires interpretation according to the customary rules of treaty interpretation reflected in Articles 31 and 32 of the Vienna Convention on the Law of Treaties"[87].

In its process of interpretation the Court will pay attention to the following criteria: the object and purpose of the Vienna Convention and the preparatory works. But

[84] *Ibid.*, p. 34, para. 64.
[85] *Ibid.*, p. 36, para. 76.
[86] *Ibid.*, p. 39, para. 91.
[87] *Ibid.*, p. 38, para. 83.

its interpretation will begin with a general consideration of the meaning of the phrase "without delay" in the various languages of that Convention. Thus, it states:

> "Article 1 of the Vienna Convention on Consular Relations, which defines certain of the terms used in the Convention, offers no definition of the phrase "without delay". Moreover, in the different language versions of the Convention various terms are employed to render the phrases "without delay" in Article 36 and "immediately" in Article 14. The Court observes that dictionary definitions, in the various languages of the Vienna Convention, offer diverse meanings of the term "without delay" (and also of "immediately"). It is therefore necessary to look elsewhere for an understanding of this term"[88].

According to the *object and purpose* of the Vienna Convention, the Court observes that Article 36 provides "for consular officers to be free to communicate with nationals of the sending State, to have access to them, to visit and speak with them and to arrange for their legal representation". But it is not envisaged, "either in Article 36, paragraph 1, or elsewhere in the Convention, that consular functions entail a consular officer himself or herself acting as the legal representative or more directly engaging in the criminal justice process. Indeed, this is confirmed by the wording of Article 36, paragraph 2, of the Convention. Thus, neither the terms of the Convention as normally understood, nor its object and purpose, suggest that "without delay" is to be understood as "immediately upon arrest and before interrogation"[89].

The resort to the *preparatory works* of the Vienna Convention, notwithstanding the uncertainties they present, does not support such an interpretation. It is the opinion of the Court that

> "During the diplomatic conference, the conference's expert, former Special Rapporteur of the International Law Commission, explained to the delegates that the words "without undue delay" had been introduced by the Commission, after long discussion in both the plenary and drafting committee, to allow for special circumstances which might permit information as to consular notification not to be given at once. Germany, the only one of two States to present an amendment, proposed adding "but at latest within one month". There was an extended discussion by many different delegates as to what such outer time-limit would be acceptable. During that debate no delegate proposed "immediately". The shortest specific period suggested was by the United Kingdom, namely "promptly" and no later than "48 hours" afterwards. Eventually, in the absence of agreement on a precise time period, the United Kingdom's other proposal to delete the word "undue" was accepted as the position around which delegates could converge. It is also of interest that

88 *Ibid.*, p. 38, para. 84.

89 *Ibid.*, p. 38, para. 85.

> there is no suggestion in the *travaux* that the phrase "without delay" might have different meanings in each of the three sets of circumstances in which it is used in Article 36, paragraph 1 *(b)*"[90].

From the analysis of the preparatory works the Court thus finds that "without delay" is not necessarily to be interpreted as "immediately" upon arrest:

> "It further observes that during the Conference debates on this term, no delegate made any connection with the issue of interrogation. The Court considers that the provision in Article 36, paragraph 1 *(b)*, that the receiving State authorities "shall inform the person concerned without delay of his rights" cannot be interpreted to signify that the provision of such information must necessarily precede any interrogation, so that the commencement of interrogation before the information is given would be a breach of Article 36.
>
> 88. Although, by application of the usual rules of interpretation, "without delay" as regards the duty to inform an individual under Article 36, paragraph 1 *(b)*, is not to be understood as necessarily meaning "immediately upon arrest", there is nonetheless a duty upon the arresting authorities to give that information to an arrested person as soon as it is realized that the person is a foreign national, or once there are grounds to think that the person is probably a foreign national"[91].

7 The "centre of the main channel" as a criterion in order to determine the boundary of an international river

This question was present in the case concerning *Kasikili/Sedudu Island (Botswana/Namibia)*, where the Court was asked to determine, on the basis of the Anglo-German Treaty of 1 July 1890 and the rules and principles of International Law, the boundary between Namibia and Botswana around Kasikili/Sedudu Island and the legal status of the island.

As the interpretation of a treaty was the task of the Court, it notes that neither Botswana nor Namibia are parties to the Vienna Convention on the Law of Treaties of 23 May 1969, but both of them consider that Article 31 of the Vienna Convention is applicable inasmuch as it reflects customary International Law[92]. In

---

[90] *Ibid.*, pp. 38 and 39, para. 87 and 88.

[91] *Ibid.*, p. 39, para. 86.

[92] As we have seen in precedent pages of this work, the Court itself has had occasion in the past to hold that customary international law found expression in Article 31 of the Vienna Convention. As an example in recent cases, see *Territorial Dispute (Libyan Arab Jamahiriya/Chad), Judgment,* I.C.J., *Reports 1994*, p. 21, para. 41; *Oil Platforms (Islamic Republic of Iran* v. *United States of America), Preliminary Objections, Judgment,* I.C.J., *Reports 1996 (II)*, p. 812, para. 23).

addition, in this case the interpretation concerned a treaty dated 1890. Nevertheless, in the opinion of the I.C.J., Article 4 of the Vienna Convention on the Law of Treaties, which provides that it applies only to treaties which are concluded by States after the entry into force of that Convention with regard to such States, "does not, therefore, prevent the Court from interpreting the 1890 Treaty in accordance with the rules reflected in Article 31 of the Convention"[93].

The Court begins its task of interpretation by applying the rules of interpretation set forth in the 1969 Vienna Convention. Thus, it recalls the *general rule of interpretation* of Article 31:

> "a treaty must be interpreted in good faith, in accordance with the ordinary meaning to be given to its terms in their context and in the light of its object and purpose. Interpretation must be based above all upon the text of the treaty. As a supplementary measure recourse may be had to means of interpretation such as the preparatory work of the treaty." (*Territorial Dispute (Libyan Arab Jamahiriya/Chad), Judgment,* I.C.J., *Reports 1994*, pp. 21-22, para. 41)[94].

But, immediately, it makes clear that there is nothing that prevents it from taking into account the present-day state of scientific knowledge, "as reflected in the documentary material submitted to it by the Parties", in order "to illuminate the meaning of words agreed upon 1890"[95].

The Court begins with the examation of *the text* of Article III of the Treaty, which reads as follows:

> "In Southwest Africa the sphere in which the exercise of influence is reserved to Germany is bounded:
>
> 1. To the south by a line commencing at the mouth of the Orange river, and ascending the north bank of that river to the point of its intersection by the 20th degree of east longitude.
> 2. To the east by a line commencing at the above-named point, and following the 20th degree of east longitude to the point of its intersection by the 22nd parallel of south latitude; it runs eastward along that parallel to the point of its intersection by the 21st degree of east longitude; thence it follows that degree northward to the point of its intersection by the 18th parallel of south latitude;

93 I.C.J., case concerning *Kasikili/Sedudu Island*, para. 18.

94 *Ibid.*, para. 20.

95 The Court refers itself to the Arbitral Award concerning the "Controversia sobre el recorrido de la traza del límite entre el Hito 62 y el Monte Fitz Roy (Argentina/Chile) [Dispute concerning the course of the frontier between B.P. 62 and Mount Fitz Roy (Argentina/Chile)], also known as the "Laguna del desierto" case, Arbitral Award of 21 October 1994, International Law Reports (ILR), Vol. 113, p. 76, para. 157; Revue générale de droit international public (RGDIP), Vol. 2, 1996, p. 592, para. 157)" (*ibid.*).

> it runs eastward along that parallel till it reaches the river Chobe, and descends the centre of the main channel of that river to its junction with the Zambesi, where it terminates.
>
> It is understood that under this arrangement Germany shall have free access from her Protectorate to the Zambesi by a strip of territory which shall at no point be less than 20 English miles in width.
>
> The sphere in which the exercise of influence is reserved to Great Britain is bounded to the west and northwest by the above-mentioned line. It includes Lake Ngami.
>
> The course of the above boundary is traced in general accordance with a map officially prepared for the British Government in 1889."

It is the opinion of the Court that Article III "locates the diving line between the spheres of influence of the contracting parties in the 'main channel' of the River Chobe; however, neither this, nor any other provision of the Treaty, furnishes criteria enabling that 'main channel' to be identified. It must also be noted that the English version refers to the 'centre' of the main channel, while the German version uses the term 'thalweg' of that channel *(Thalweg des Hauptlaufes)*"[96].

In addition, the Parties (Botswana and Namibia) differed regarding the method to be applied for the purpose of interpreting these expressions. In the opinion of Botswana, in order to establish the line of the boundary around Kasikili/Sedudu Island, it is sufficient to determine the *thalweg* of the Chobe: "it is that which identifies the main channel of the river". For Botswana, the words *"des Hauptlaufes"* therefore add nothing to the text. For Namibia, however, the task of the Court is first to identify the main channel of the Chobe around Kasikili/Sedudu Island, and then to determine where the centre of this channel lies.

The Court notes that that various definitions of the term "thalweg" are found in treaties delimiting boundaries and that the concepts of the thalweg of a watercourse and the centre of a watercourse are not equivalent. It is of the Court that:

> "The word 'thalweg' has variously been taken to mean 'the most suitable channel for navigation' on the river, the line 'determined by the line of deepest soundings', or 'the median line of the main channel followed by boatmen travelling downstream'. Treaties or conventions which define boundaries in watercourses nowadays usually refer to the thalweg as the boundary when the watercourse is navigable and to the median line between the two banks when it is not, although it cannot be said that practice has been fully consistent"[97].

It notes, too, that at the time of the conclusion of the 1890 Treaty, it might have been that the terms "centre of the [main] channel" and *"Thalweg" des Hauptlaufes* were used interchangeably:

---

[96] *Ibid.*, para. 21.

[97] *Ibid.*, para 24.

> "In this respect, it is of interest to note that, some three years before the conclusion of the 1890 Treaty, the Institut de droit international stated the following in Article 3, paragraph 2, of the "Draft concerning the international regulation of fluvial navigation", adopted at Heidelberg on 9 September 1887: "The boundary of States separated by a river is indicated by the thalweg, that is to say, the median line of the channel" (*Annuaire de l'Institut de droit international*, 1887-1888, p. 182), the term "channel" being understood to refer to the passage open to navigation in the bed of the river, as is clear from the title of the draft. Indeed, the parties to the 1890 Treaty themselves used the terms "centre of the channel" and "thalweg" as synonyms, one being understood as the translation of the other (…)"[98].

Since both texts of the 1890 Treaty are authentic (one written in English, the other in German), the Court applies Article 33, paragraph 3 of the Vienna Convention on the Law of Treaties, under which "the terms of the treaty are presumed to have the same meaning in each authentic text". In connection with this, the Court observes that in the course of the proceedings Botswana and Namibia "did not themselves express any real difference of opinion on this subject". This is why the Court "treat the words "centre of the main channel" in Article III, paragraph 2, of the 1890 Treaty as having the same meaning as the words "Thalweg des Hauptlaufes"[99].

The Court adds that Botswana and Namibia have used the term "channel" to refer to each of the two branches of the river Chobe that ring Kasikili/Sedudu Island, and have not confined the term "channel" to the stricter usage meaning the navigable passage of a river or of one of its branches. In view of this fact, the Court itself, in its Judgment, employs the term "channel" in a broad sense.

In the Court's opinion, the real dispute between the Parties concerns the location of the main channel where the boundary lies[100]. Moreover, the Court observes that by introducing the term "main channel" into the draft treaty, "the contracting parties must be assumed to have intended that a precise meaning be given to it. For these reasons, the Court will therefore proceed first to determine the main channel. In so doing, it will seek to determine the ordinary meaning of the words "main channel" by reference to the most commonly used criteria in international law and practice, to which the Parties have referred"[101].

The Court notes that the Parties to the dispute have used several criteria for identifying the "main channel": channel capacity, flow velocity, volume of flow,

---

98 *Ibid.*, para 25.

99 *Ibid.*

100 "In Botswana's view, it is to be found "on the basis of the thalwegs in the northern and western channel of the Chobe", whereas in Namibia's view, it "lies in the centre (that is to say thalweg) of the southern channel of the Chobe River"." (*ibid.*, para. 27).

101 *Ibid.*

depth, velocity, discharge, sediment transport capacity, etc. But it finds that it cannot rely on one single criterion in order to identify the main channel of the river Chobe around Kasikili/Sedudu Island and decides to take into account all of these criteria. It also notes that the present hydrological situation of the Chobe around Kasikili/Sedudu Island "may be presumed the same as that which existed when the 1890 Treaty was concluded"[102].

After examining the criteria of the depth, width, flow (the volume of water carried), bed profile configuration and navigability, the Court concludes that "in accordance with the ordinary meaning of the terms that appear in the pertinent provision of the 1890 Treaty, the northern channel of the River Chobe around Kasikili/Sedudu Island must be regarded as its main channel"[103]. It adds that this conclusion is supported "by the results of various on-site investigations, as recorded in the reports drawn up on those occasions"[104].

Once that conclusion had been reached, the I.C.J. decides to consider how and to what extent the object and purpose of the treaty can clarify the meaning to be given to its terms. The Court considers that while the 1890 Treaty is not a boundary treaty proper but a treaty delimiting spheres of influence, "the Parties nonetheless accept it as the treaty determining the boundary between their territories. The major concern of each contracting party was to protect its sphere of influence against any intervention by the other party and to obviate any risk of future disputes"[105].

To show this, the Court analyses Article VII of the 1890 Treaty which is worded as follows:

> "The two Powers engage that neither will interfere with any sphere of influence assigned to the other by Articles I to IV. One Power will not in the sphere of the other make acquisitions, conclude Treaties, accept sovereign rights or Protectorates, nor hinder the extension of influence of the other.
>
> It is understood that no Companies nor individuals subject to one Power can exercise sovereign rights in a sphere assigned to the other, except with the assent of the latter."

It is the opinion of the Court that the contracting powers, by opting for the words "centre of the main channel", "intended to establish a boundary separating their spheres of influence even in the case of a river having more than one channel. They possessed only rudimentary information about the Chobe's channels. If they knew that such channels existed, their number, features, navigability, etc., and

[102] *Ibid.*, para. 31.
[103] *Ibid.*, para. 41.
[104] *Ibid.*, para. 42.
[105] *Ibid.*, para. 42.

their relative importance remained unknown to them. This situation explains the method adopted to define the southern boundary of the Caprivi Strip"[106].

In the opinion of the Court, the resort to the criteria of *the preparatory works* of the 1890 Treaty supports this reasoning[107].

Finally, the I.C.J. refers to *the subsequent practice* of the Parties to the 1890 Treaty; practice to which the Parties to the dispute have made abundant reference in the course of the proceedings. But, in this case, the Court notes that "while both Parties accept that interpretative agreements and subsequent practice do constitute elements of treaty interpretation under international law, they disagree on the consequences to be drawn from the facts in this case for purposes of the interpretation of the 1890 Treaty"[108].

After analysing this practice the Court concludes that

> "the subsequent practice of the parties to the 1890 Treaty did not result in any 'agreement between the parties regarding the interpretation of the treaty or the application of its provisions', within the meaning of Article 31, paragraph 3 *(a)*, of the 1969 Vienna Convention on the Law of Treaties, nor did it result in any 'practice in the application of the treaty which establishes the agreement of the parties regarding its interpretation', within the meaning of subparagraph *(b)* of that same provision.
>
> 80. However, the Court is bound to note that on at least three occasions, at different periods – in 1912, in 1948 and in 1985 – surveys carried out on the ground identified the channel of the Chobe to the north and west as the 'main channel' of the river around Kasikili/Sedudu Island. The factual findings that the parties concerned arrived at separately in 1948 were expressed in concurrent terms in a joint report. In addition, the survey made in 1985 was conducted jointly by the parties then concerned. The factual findings made on these occasions were not, as such, disputed at the time. The Court finds that these facts, while not constituting subsequent practice by the parties in the interpretation of the 1890 Treaty, nevertheless

---

[106] *Ibid.*, para. 43. The I.C.J. refers to the *Preah Vihear, (Merits)* case, where it stated that "there are boundary treaties which do no more than refer to a watershed line, or to a crest line, and which make no provision for any delimitation in addition." (I.C.J., *Reports 1962*, p. 34.)". Then, it adds: "in that Judgment the Court added that this was "an obvious and convenient way of describing a frontier line objectively, though in general terms" (*ibid.*, p. 35). In the present case, the contracting parties employed a similar approach" (*ibid.*, para. 43).

[107] It makes reference to the provisional agreement initialled on 17 June 1890, to the text subsequently prepared by the British and German negotiators, and transmitted to the British Foreign Office on 21 June 1890, as "a draft of the Articles of Agreement", as well as to the British proposal made on 25 June 1890.

[108] *Ibid.*, para. 51.

> support the conclusions which it has reached by interpreting Article III, paragraph 2, of the 1890 Treaty in accordance with the ordinary meaning to be given to its terms (…)"[109].

In conclusion, the foregoing interpretation of the relevant provisions of the 1890 Treaty leads the Court to state that the boundary between Botswana and Namibia around Kasikili/Sedudu Island provided for in that Treaty lies in the northern channel of the Chobe River. It adds that according to the English text of the Treaty, this boundary follows the "centre" of the main channel; the German text uses the word "thalweg". It also brings to mind that it had already stated that the parties to the 1890 Treaty intended these terms to be synonymous and that Botswana and Namibia had not themselves expressed any real difference of opinion on this subject.

Finally, resorting to the *travaux préparatoires*, the Court concludes that it is also clear from them that there was an expectation of navigation on the Chobe by both contracting parties as well as a common intention to exploit this possibility. In this sense, the Court underlines the fact that, in 1890, both parties used the terms "thalweg" and "centre of the channel" interchangeably, the former reflecting "more accurately the common intention to exploit navigation than does the latter. Accordingly, this is the term that the Court will consider determinative in Article III, paragraph 2"[110].

Consequently, the task of interpretation of the 1890 Treaty leads the I.C.J. to conclude that the boundary between Botswana and Namibia around Kasikili/Sedudu Island provided for in that Treaty lies in the northern channel of the Chobe River.

8 The application of international humanitarian law and international conventions of human rights to occupied territories

The question of the application of international humanitarian law and treaties of human rights to occupied territories has been analysed by the I.C.J. in its Advisory Opinion on the *Legal Consequences of the Construction of a Wall in the Occupied Palestinian Territory*. In relation to international humanitarian law, the law concerned was the Fourth Geneva Convention. With regard to human rights conventions, three were involved: the two International Covenants on Civil and Political Rights, and on Economic, Social and Cultural Rights, and the Convention on the Rights of the Child.

---

[109] *Ibid.*, para. 79-80.

[110] *Ibid.* And adds: "Inasmuch as Botswana and Namibia agreed, in their replies to a question put by a Member of the Court, that the thalweg was formed by the line of deepest soundings, the Court concludes that the boundary follows that line in the northern channel around Kasikili/Sedudu Island".

With regard to the application of the Fourth Geneva Convention to the Occupied Palestinian Territory, and since Israel was a party to that instrument, the Court had to address the argument invoked by Israel according to which that Convention is not applicable *de jure* within those territories because, under Article 2, paragraph 2, it applies only in the case of occupation of territories falling under the sovereignty of a High Contracting Party involved in an armed conflict, which is not the case here.

The answer of the I.C.J. is preceded by the interpretation of that Convention through the rules of Article 31 of the Vienna Convention on the Law of Treaties of 23 May 1969, which codify customary international law on the matter. Taking these rules into account, the Court notes that according to the first paragraph of Article 2 of the Fourth Geneva Convention, "that Convention is applicable when two conditions are fulfilled: that there exists an armed conflict (whether or not a state of war has been recognized); and that the conflict has arisen between two contracting parties. If those two conditions are satisfied, the Convention applies, in particular, in any territory occupied in the course of the conflict by one of the contracting parties"[111].

Moreover, in the opinion of the Court, the object of the second paragraph of Article 2 is not to restrict the scope of application of the Convention, as defined by the first paragraph, by excluding therefrom territories not falling under the sovereignty of one of the contracting parties: "It is directed simply to making it clear that, even if occupation effected during the conflict met no armed resistance, the Convention is still applicable"[112].

On the other hand, the Court founds that its interpretation reflects the intention of the drafters of the Fourth Geneva Convention to protect civilians who find themselves, in whatever way, in the hands of the occupying Power[113]. It also found that this interpretation is confirmed by the Convention's *travaux préparatoires*[114] and

[111] I.C.J., *Legal Consequences of the Construction of a Wall in the Occupied Palestinian Territory*, *Advisory Opinion*, para. 95.

[112] *Ibid.*

[113] Adding that "Whilst the drafters of the Hague Regulations of 1907 were as much concerned with protecting the rights of a State whose territory is occupied, as with protecting the inhabitants of that territory, the drafters of the Fourth Geneva Convention sought to guarantee the protection of civilians in time of war, regardless of the status of the occupied territories, as is shown by Article 47 of the Convention" (*ibid.*).

[114] In this sense: "The Conference of Government Experts convened by the International Committee of the Red Cross (hereinafter, 'ICRC') in the aftermath of the Second World War for the purpose of preparing the new Geneva Conventions recommended that these conventions be applicable to any armed conflict 'whether [it] is or is not recognized as a state of war by the parties' and 'in cases of occupation of territories in the absence of any state of war' *(Report on the Work of the Conference of Government Experts for the Study of the Conventions for the Protection of War Victims, Geneva, 14-26 April 1947*, p. 8). The drafters of the second paragraph of Article 2 thus had no intention, when they inserted that paragraph into the Convention, of restricting the latter's scope of application. They were merely seeking to provide for cases of occupation without combat, such as the occupation of Bohemia and Moravia by Germany in 1939" (*ibid.*).

that it was approved by the States parties to their Conference on 15 July 1999[115]. At least, it also reflects, the opinion of the ICRC[116], the General Assembly and the Security Council[117].

In view of the foregoing, the Court concludes the applicability of the Fourth Geneva Convention to "any occupied territory in the event of an armed conflict arising between two or more High Contracting Parties". As Israel and Jordan were parties to this Convention when the 1967 armed conflict broke out, the court finds that the "Convention is applicable in the Palestinian territories which before the conflict lay to the east of the Green Line and which, during that conflict, were occupied by Israel, there being no need for any enquiry into the precise prior status of those territories"[118].

The final question related to customary international law is that of the *applicability of international human rights conventions* to which Israel is party within the Occupied Palestinian Territory. In this regard, the Court takes into account the issue of the relationship between international humanitarian law and human rights concluding, as it did in its Advisory Opinion on the *Legality of the Threat or Use of Nuclear Weapons* in relation to the International Covenant on Civil and Political Rights, that:

> "the protection of the International Covenant of Civil and Political Rights does not cease in times of war, except by operation of Article 4 of the Covenant whereby certain provisions may be derogated from in a time of national emergency. Respect for the right to life is not, however, such a provision. In principle, the right not arbitrarily to be deprived of one's life applies also in hostilities. The test of what is an arbitrary deprivation of life, however, then falls to be determined by the applicable *lex specialis*, namely, the law applicable in armed conflict which is designed to regulate the conduct of hostilities." (*ibid.*, p. 240, para. 25.)

Therefore, for the Court, international humanitarian law constitutes *lex specialis* with regard to the branch of international law concerning human rights. But, in its

---

[115] Where they issued a statement "in which they 'reaffirmed the applicability of the Fourth Geneva Convention to the Occupied Palestinian Territory, including East Jerusalem'. Subsequently, on 5 December 2001, the High Contracting Parties, referring in particular to Article 1 of the Fourth Geneva Convention of 1949, once again reaffirmed the 'applicability of the Fourth Geneva Convention to the Occupied Palestinian Territory, including East Jerusalem'. They further reminded the Contracting Parties participating in the Conference, the parties to the conflict, and the State of Israel as occupying Power, of their respective obligations" (*ibid.*, para. 96).

[116] Which, in a declaration of 5 December 2001, recalled that "the ICRC has always affirmed the de jure applicability of the Fourth Geneva Convention to the territories occupied since 1967 by the State of Israel, including East Jerusalem" (*ibid.*).

[117] Cf. *ibid.*, paras. 98-100.

[118] *Ibid.*, para. 101.

Advisory Opinion on the *Legal Consequences of the Construction of a Wall in the Occupied Palestinian Territory,* it goes further stating that "the protection offered by human rights conventions does not cease in case of armed conflict, save through the effect of provisions for derogation of the kind to be found in Article 4 of the International Covenant on Civil and Political Rights"[119].

In its analysis, the I.C.J. undertakes three conventions to which Israel is party: the International Covenant on Civil and Political Rights, the International Covenant on Economic, Social and Cultural Rights, and the Convention on the Rights of the Child, and the Court concludes their applicability in the Occupied Palestinian Territory.

In the case of the International Covenant on Civil and Political Rights, the conclusion of the Court stating that this instrument "is applicable in respect of acts done by a State in the exercise of its jurisdiction outside its own territory" is based upon the *object* and *purpose* of this Covenant[120], upon the "constant practice" of the Human Rights Committee[121], as well as upon the *travaux préparatoires* of the Covenant[122] and upon the position taken by Israel in relation to the applicability of that instrument, in its communications to the Human Rights Committee, and the view of the Committee[123].

---

[119] *Ibid.*, para. 106.

[120] *Ibid.*, para. 109.

[121] Constant practice which the Court considers consistent with its conclusion concerning the applicability of the Covenant to the Occupied Palestinian Territory. It adds: "Thus, the Committee has found the Covenant applicable where the State exercises its jurisdiction on foreign territory. It has ruled on the legality of acts by Uruguay in cases of arrests carried out by Uruguayan agents in Brazil or Argentina (case No. 52/79, *López Burgos v. Uruguay*; case No. 56/79, *Lilian Celiberti de Casariego v. Uruguay*). It decided to the same effect in the case of the confiscation of a passport by a Uruguayan consulate in Germany (case No. 106/81, *Montero v. Uruguay*)" (*ibid.*).

[122] Which confirms the Committee's interpretation of Article 2 of the covenant: "These show that, in adopting the wording chosen, the drafters of the Covenant did not intend to allow States to escape from their obligations when they exercise jurisdiction outside their national territory. They only intended to prevent persons residing abroad from asserting, vis-à-vis their State of origin, rights that do not fall within the competence of that State, but of that of the State of residence (see the discussion of the preliminary draft in the Commission on Human Rights, E/CN.4/SR.194, para. 46; and United Nations, *Official Records of the General Assembly*, Tenth Session, Annexes, A/2929, Part II, Chap. V, para. 4 (1955))" (*ibid.*).

[123] The position of Israel is based on the non applicability of the Covenant in the occupied territories. The Committee has stated its applicability: "'in the current circumstances, the provisions of the Covenant apply to the benefit of the population of the Occupied Territories, for all conduct by the State party's authorities or agents in those territories that affect the enjoyment of rights enshrined in the Covenant and fall within the ambit of State responsibility of Israel under the principles of public international law' (CCPR/CO/78/ISR, para. 11)" (*ibid.*, para. 110).

With regard to the International Covenant on Economic, Social and Cultural Rights the Court places emphasis on the fact that no provision in its scope of application is present. In order to deal with the interpretation concerning its application to the occupied territories, it analyses the position taken by Israel in its reports to the Committee envisaged by that instrument. According to this position, the Covenant does not apply to areas which are not subject to its sovereign territory and jurisdiction. Nevertheless the Court, after considering the concern of the Committee in this regard[124], does not accept Israel's view and concludes that this State "is bound by the provisions of the International Covenant on Economic, Social and Cultural Rights. Furthermore, it is under an obligation not to raise any obstacle to the exercise of such rights in those fields where competence has been transferred to Palestinian authorities"[125].

Finally, as regards the Convention on the Rights of the child of 20 November 1989, the Court also concludes its applicability within the Occupied Palestinian Territory. In this case, its conclusion is raised upon Article 2 of this Convention according to which "States Parties shall respect and ensure the rights set forth in the … Convention to each child within their jurisdiction …"[126].

9 The competence of the General Assembly to make recommendations

The competence of the General Assembly to make recommendations was analysed by the I.C.J. in its advisory opinion concerning *Legal Consequences of the Construction of a Wall in the Occupied Palestinian Territory*[127]. The analysis took place in relationship with Article 12 of the Charter and the competence of the General Assembly to request the Court for an advisory opinion. According to Article 12, paragraph 1, of the Charter:

> "While the Security Council is exercising in respect of any dispute or situation the functions assigned to it in the present Charter, the General Assembly shall not make any recommendation with regard to that dispute or situation unless the Security Council so requests."

As the Court states, a request for an advisory opinion is not "in itself" a "recommendation" by the General Assembly "with regard to (a) dispute or situation"[128]

[124] According to which "'the State party's obligations under the Covenant apply to all territories and populations under its effective control' (E/C.12/1/Add.90, paras. 15 and 31)" (*ibid.*, para. 112).

[125] *Ibid.*

[126] *Ibid.*, para. 113.

[127] We will use the text published on www.icj-cij.org.

[128] *Ibid.*, para. *25*.

but, due to the fact of the argument that the General Assembly had acted *ultra vires* by taking the resolution requesting the advisory opinion of the Court, this one considers it appropriate for it to examine the significance of Article 12 of the Charter. In doing so, the Court has regard to the relevant texts as well as the practice of the United Nations.

The Court begins its task by taking into account Article 24 of the Charter. Under this Article, the Security Council has "primary responsibility for the maintenance of international peace and security". In that regard it can impose on States "an explicit obligation of compliance if for example it issues an order or command ... under Chapter VII" and can, to that end, "require enforcement by coercive action" (*Certain Expenses of the United Nations (Article 17, paragraph 2, of the Charter), Advisory Opinion of 20 July 1962,* I.C.J., *Reports 1962,* p. 163)"[129]. However, the Court emphasizes that Article 24 refers to a primary, but not necessarily exclusive, competence. In the words of the I.C.J.: "The General Assembly does have the power, inter alia, under Article 14 of the Charter, to 'recommend measures for the peaceful adjustment' of various situations (*Certain Expenses of the United Nations, ibid*., p. 163). '[T]he only limitation which Article 14 imposes on the General Assembly is the restriction found in Article 12, namely, that the Assembly should not recommend measures while the Security Council is dealing with the same matter unless the Council requests it to do so' (*ibid.*)"[130].

As regards the practice of the United Nations the Court underlines that, both the General Assembly and the Security Council initially interpreted and applied Article 12 to the effect that the Assembly could not make a recommendation on a question concerning the maintenance of international peace and security while the matter remained on the Council's agenda. Afterwards, it adds:

> "Thus the Assembly during its fourth session refused to recommend certain measures on the question of Indonesia, on the ground, *inter alia,* that the Council remained seised of the matter (*Official Records of the General Assembly, Fourth Session, Ad Hoc Political Committee, Summary Records of Meetings, 27 September – 7 December 1949*, 56th Meeting, 3 December 1949, p. 339, para. 118). As for the Council, on a number of occasions it deleted items from its agenda in order to enable the Assembly to deliberate on them (for example, in respect of the Spanish question (*Official Records of the Security Council, First Year: Second Series, No. 21*, 79th Meeting, 4 November 1946, p. 498), in connection with incidents on the Greek border (*Official Records of the Security Council, Second Year, No. 89*, 202nd Meeting, 15 September 1947, pp. 2404-2405) and in regard to the Island of Taiwan (Formosa) (*Official Records of the Security Council, Fifth Year, No. 48*, 506th Meeting, 29 September 1950,

[129] *Ibid*., para. 26.

[130] *Ibid.*

> p. 5). In the case of the Republic of Korea, the Council decided on 31 January 1951 to remove the relevant item from the list of matters of which it was seised in order to enable the Assembly to deliberate on the matter (*Official Records of the Security Council, Sixth Year*, S/PV.531, 531st Meeting, 31 January 1951, pp. 11-12, para. 57)"[131].

But it is the opinion of the Court that this interpretation of Article 12 of the Charter has subsequently evolved. Its statement is based on practice:

> "Thus the General Assembly deemed itself entitled in 1961 to adopt recommendations in the matter of the Congo (resolutions 1955 (XV) and 1600 (XVI)) and in 1963 in respect of the Portuguese colonies (resolution 1913 (XVIII)) while those cases still appeared on the Council's agenda, without the Council having adopted any recent resolution concerning them. In response to a question posed by Peru during the Twenty-third session of the General Assembly, the Legal Counsel of the United Nations confirmed that the Assembly interpreted the words "is exercising the functions" in Article 12 of the Charter as meaning "is exercising the functions at this moment" (Twenty-third General Assembly, Third Committee, 1637th meeting, A/C.3/SR.1637, para. 9). Indeed, the Court notes that there has been an increasing tendency over time for the General Assembly and the Security Council to deal in parallel with the same matter concerning the maintenance of international peace and security (see, for example, the matters involving Cyprus, South Africa, Angola, Southern Rhodesia and more recently Bosnia and Herzegovina and Somalia). It is often the case that, while the Security Council has tended to focus on the aspects of such matters related to international peace and security, the General Assembly has taken a broader view, considering also their humanitarian, social and economic aspects"[132].

This is why the Court considers that the accepted practice of the General Assembly, "as it has evolved", is consistent with Article 12, paragraph 1, of the Charter. This is also the reason why the Court concludes that the General Assembly, in adopting resolution ES-10/14, seeking an advisory opinion from the Court, did not contravene the provisions of Article 12, paragraph 1, of the Charter. According to this reasoning, it concludes that by submitting that request, the General Assembly did not exceed its competence.

---

[131] *Ibid.*, para. 27.

[132] *Ibid.*

CHAPTER IX:

Customary Norms

1 The general theory of custom

The work of the I.C.J. in relation to this normative sector of the international legal order can be classified as "creative": through its jurisprudence the Court, as we have seen in Chapter IV of this work, has specified the content, the elements and the characteristics of the customary norm. It has also modified some of these criteria. Thus, with regard to the time element and with practice (it is not necessary to have a lengthy duration and practice does not necessarily include all the States nor is it identical in its content). In its more recent jurisprudence the Court also gives fundamental importance to the "opinio iuris".

Its statement concerning the separate existence of conventional and customary norms even when they have the same content is along the same lines.

Due to the fact that these questions have been dealt with in the preceding pages, reference can be made to them[1].

2 Reservations to treaties

We include reservations to treaties in this Chapter dedicated to customary norms as, at the time when the Court analysed these, the 1969 Vienna Convention on the Law of Treaties did not exist. Consequently, this question was governed by customary International Law, and its systemisation was based on the principle of unanimity which had prevailed since the time of the League of Nations. In accordance with this, it was not possible to draw up a reservation without the unanimous consent of all the States Parties to the treaty. In its Advisory Opinion concerning *Reservations to the Convention on Genocide* the I.C.J. broke with this principle. As QUEL LOPEZ states, the refusal by the Court of the traditional principle is not only tacit, but the Court endeavours to demonstrate that the systematic application of the principle of unanimity was no longer possible[2]. After stating its comprehension with regard to the principle of unanimity, the Court specified:

---

1 See Chapter IV of the present work. See also, THIRLWAY, H., "The Law and Procedure of the International Court of Justice", *B.Y.I.L.* 1990, pages 31-110.

2 QUEL LOPEZ, F.J., *Las reservas a los tratados internacionales (Un examen de la práctica española), op. cit.*, p. 182. The change is due to the influence of the soviet block and of Latin American legal thought which, in the early years of the U.N.O., rejected the old League of Nations system.

> "A more general resort to reservations, a very great allowance made for tacit assent to reservations, the existence of practices which go so far as to admit that the author of reservations which have been rejected by certain contracting parties is, nevertheless, to be regarded as a party to the convention in relation to those contracting parties who have accepted the reservations, all these factors are manifestations of a new need for flexibility in the operation of multilateral conventions"[3].

This is why the I.C.J. provides a number of criteria to be taken into account in order to appraise whether reservations can or cannot be made in specific cases, as well as the effects, when nothing is mentioned in the treaty with regard to these. Such criteria are the following:

> "The character of a multilateral convention, its purpose, provisions, mode of preparation and adoption, are factors which must be considered in determining, in the absence of any express provision on the subject, the possibility of making reservations, as well as their validity and effect"[4].

Thus, "it is the compatibility of a reservation with the object and purpose of the Convention that must furnish the criterion for the attitude of a State making the reservation on accession as well as for the appraisal by a State objecting to the reservation. Such is the rule of conduct which must guide every State in the appraisal which it must make, individually and from its own standpoint, of the admissibility of any reservation,"[5].

The second principle established by the I.C.J. concerning reservations is the impossibility of making reservations with regard to general customary law. The question is addressed by the Court in the case concerning the *North Sea Continental Shelf*:

---

3 I.C.J., Advisory Opinion concerning *Reservations to the Convention on Genocide, Reports 1951*, pages 21-22.

4 *Ibid.*, p. 22. Besides the evolution of international practice, the I.C.J. also takes into account the fact that the conception of the absolute integrity of a convention had not been transformed into a rule of international law:

> "It does not appear, moreover, that the conception of the absolute integrity of a convention has been transformed into a rule of international law. The considerable part which tacit assent has always played in estimating the effect which is to be given to reservations scarcely permits one to state that such a rule exists, determining with sufficient precision the effect of objections made to reservations. In fact, the examples of objections made to reservations appear to be too rare in international law to have given rise to such a rule" (*ibid.*, pages 24-25).

Cf. QUEL LOPEZ, F.J., *Las reservas a los tratados ..., op. cit.*, pages 182-186.

5 *Ibid.*, p. 24.

> "... it is a characteristic of purely conventional rules and obligations that, in regard to them, some faculty of making unilateral reservations may, within certain limits, be admitted; whereas this cannot be so in the case of general or customary law rules and obligations which, by their very nature, must have equal force for all members of the international community, and cannot therefore be the subject of any right of unilateral exclusion exercisable at will by any one of them in its own favour"[6].

Consequently, the I.C.J. concludes that:

> "it is to be expected that when, for whatever reason, rules or obligations of this order are embodied, or are intended to be reflected in certain provisions of a convention, such provisions will figure amongst those in respect of which a right of unilateral reservation is not conferred, or is excluded"[7].

Finally, concerning the formulation of reservations to the conventions codifying customary norms, the Court has stated the separate applicability of conventional and customary norms. Consequently, the fact of having made a reservation to a conventional norm does not hinder the integral applicability of the customary norm with the same content[8].

3 The concept of "terra nullius"

In classical International Law there existed several ways to acquire territory. One of these was *occupation*. For occupation of a territory to become a legal title it was necessary that the territory be "terra nullius", that is to say, belonging to no one. The I.C.J. went back to the Law in force at that time, in the Advisory Opinion concerning *Western Sahara*, specifies that the expression "terra nullius" was "a technical legal term employed in connection with occupation as one of the accepted legal methods for acquiring sovereignty over territory"[9].

---

6 I.C.J., *Reports 1969*, pages 38-39.

7 *Ibid.*, p. 39. For a development of this question see QUEL LOPEZ, F.J., *op. cit.*, pages 286 et seq.

8 In the case concerning *Military and Paramilitary Activities in and against Nicaragua*, where it states:

> "this – the reservation of the United States – would not be a reason for the Court to take the view that the operation of the treaty process must necessarily deprive the customary norm of its separate applicability. Nor can the multilateral treaty reservation be interpreted as meaning that, once applicable to a given dispute, it would exclude the application of any rule of customary international law the content of which was the same as, or analogous to, that of the treaty-law rule which had caused the reservation to become effective" (I.C.J., *Reports 1986*, p. 94).

9 I.C.J., *Reports 1975*, p. 39, paragraph 79.

From an analysis of state practice in the XIX Century, in the opinion of the Court, it is clear that "territories inhabited by tribes or peoples with a social and political organization were not regarded as *terrae nullius*. It was generally considered that sovereignty in the case of such territories could not be acquired unilaterally by occupation of *terra nullius* through an original title but through agreements reached with local rulers"[10]. This is why the acquisition of sovereignty through agreements made between the authorities of the country was not considered to be occupation of "*terra nullius*" in the literal sense of such terms. On the contrary, "such agreements with local rulers, whether or not considered as an actual cession of the territory, were regarded as derivative roots of title, and not original titles obtained by occupation of *terrae nullius*"[11].

4 The principle of equidistance in the delimitation of continental shelves between two or more States

Since the starting point laid down by the 1958 Geneva Convention the case law of the I.C.J. has significantly developed this matter. Article 6 of that Convention takes two situations into account: on the one hand, the fact that the continental shelf is adjacent to the territories of States whose coasts are opposite each other. On the other, the fact that those States are bordering States. In both cases, according to Article 6,

> "the boundary of the continental shelf appertaining to such States shall be determined by agreement between them. In the absence of agreement, and unless another boundary line is justified by special circumstances, the boundary is the median line, every point of which is equidistant from the nearest point of the baselines from which the breadth of the territorial sea of each States is measured"[12].

---

[10] *Ibid.*, p. 39, paragraph 80.

[11] *Ibid.* This was the case of the Western Sahara when it was colonized by Spain:

> "(it) was inhabited by peoples which, if nomadic, were socially and politically organized in tribes and under chiefs competent to represent them", with which Spain concluded protection agreements (*ibid.*).

[12] The I.C.J. specifies that:

> "the Geneva Convention did not embody or crystallize any pre-existing or emergent rule of customary law, according to which the delimitation of continental shelf areas between adjacent States must, unless the Parties otherwise agree, be carried out on an equidistance-special circumstances basis. A rule was of course embodied in Article 6 of the Convention, but was a purely conventional rule" (I.C.J., case concerning the *North Sea Continental Shelf*, *Reports 1969*, p. 41).

This Article shows that the general principle on the matter is the agreement between the States concerned. In the case of the *North Sea Continental Shelf* the I.C.J. emphasizes that delimitation "must be the object of agreement between the States concerned, and that such agreement must be arrived at in accordance with equitable principles"[13]. Nevertheless, the I.C.J. itself stated that equidistance is only equitable in the case of regular and uniform coasts, but with other types of coasts this can lead to distorted results[14]. This is why in such cases States are under an obligation to enter into negotiations with a view to reaching an agreement and not merely in order to go through a formal process of negotiation for the application of a certain method of delimitation in the absence of agreement.

In conclusion, equidistance is one of the methods of delimitation and can be used, but only when the results are equitable and within the framework of the circumstances of each case, and are not of a general and absolute character[15].

---

[13] *Ibid.*, p. 46. As regards the differing content of the concept of "continental shelf" in International Law and in other disciplines the I.C.J. emphasizes "the lack of identity between the legal concept of the continental shelf and the physical phenomenon known to geographers by that name" (case concerning *Continental Shelf (Tunisia/Libyan Arab Jamahiriya)*, I.C.J., *Reports 1982*, p. 46).

[14] This was stated in the following terms:

> "The slightest irregularity in a coastline is automatically magnified by the equidistance line as regards the consequences for the delimitation of the continental shelf. Thus it has been seen in the case of concave or convex coastlines that if the equidistance method is employed, then the greater the irregularity and the further from the coastline the area to be delimited, the more unreasonable are the results produced. So great an exaggeration of the consequences of a natural geographical feature must be remedied or compensated for as far as possible, being of itself creative of inequity" (I.C.J, *Reports 1969*, p. 49).

[15] The recent jurisprudence of the I.C.J. confirms this conception: *Continental Shelf (Tunisia/Libyan Arab Jamahiriya* (I.C.J., *Reports 1982*, p. 92: "the delimitation must be carried out in accordance with equitable principles which take all the relevant circumstances into account"); *Delimitation of the Maritime Boundary in the Gulf of Maine Area* (I.C.J., *Reports 1984*, pages 100 et alt.); *Continental Shelf (Libyan Arab Jamahiriya/Malta)* (I.C.J., *Reports 1985*, pages 37 et alt.).

From the point of view of doctrine see BLECHER, M.D., "Equitable Delimitation of Continental Shelf", *A.J.I.L.*, 1979, pages 60 et alt.; GOURNAIS, E., "The delimitation of the continental shelf of islands. Some observations", *Revue Hellénique de Droit International (R.D.H.I.)*, 1980, pages 111 et alt.; RANGEL, V.M., "Le plateau continental dans la Convention de 1982 sur le Droit de la Mer", *R. des C.*, t. 194 (1985-V), pages 269-428; VILLANI, V., "La delimitazione della piattaforma continentale e della zona economica exclusiva si sensi della Convenzione delle Nazioni Unite sul diritto del mare", *Riv. Diritto Internazionale*, 1985/2, pages 261-298; JUSTE RUIZ, J., "Delimitaciones marinas en Africa Occidental. El Laudo arbitral sobre la delimitación de la frontera marítima entre Guinea y Guinea-Bissau", *R.E.D.I.*, 1990/1, pages 7-41; BEDJAOUI, M., "'L'énigme' des 'principes equitables' dans le droit des délimitations maritimes", *R.E.D.I.*, 1990/2, pages 367-389.

Moreover, this is the criterion adopted by Article 83 of the 1982 Convention on the Law of the Sea:

> "1. The delimitation of the continental shelf between States with opposite or adjacent coasts shall be effected by agreement on the basis of international law, as referred to in Article 38 of the Statute of the International Court of Justice, in order to achieve an equitable solution"

5 The principle of "uti possidetis juris"

This principle is addressed and applied for the first time by the I.C.J. in the case concerning the *Frontier Dispute* in which it substantially develops theory concerning its content, scope and significance[16].

As regards the construction made by a Chamber of the Court it should be stressed that its statement that it is a firmly established principle of International Law, of a general scope, connected with the decolonisation process with the intention of preventing disputes due to the challenging of frontiers when independence is achieved[17].

We agree with SANCHEZ RODRIGUEZ that the statement of the Court concerning the general or universal character of this principle is not assisted by specific reasons or data justifying it. In his opinion, it is evident that the Court was not obliged to do so but it should be recognized that statements of international doctrine do not seem to be so radical in their support of the generality of its recognition nor the universality of its application[18].

---

[16] See SANCHEZ RODRIGUEZ, L.I., "Uti possidetis: la reactualización jurisprudencial de un viejo principio (a propósito de la Sentencia del TIJ {Sala} en el asunto Burkina Fasso República de Mali)", *R.E.D.I.*, 1988/2, p. 123.

[17] I.C.J., *Reports 1986*, p. 565:

> "Nevertheless the principle is not a special rule which pertains solely to one specific system of international law. It is a general principle, which is logically connected with the phenomenon of the obtaining of independence, wherever it occurs. Its obvious purpose is to prevent the independence and stability of new States being endangered by fratricidal struggles provoked by the challenging of frontiers following the withdrawal of the administering power".

[18] See SANCHEZ RODRIGUEZ, L.I., "Uti possidetis ...", *op. cit.,* p. 129. From the statement of the I.C.J. which considers this principle to be a general principle of the international legal order, this author concludes that the Court raises the principle of *uti possidetis* to the category of the most important principles of International Law (see *Ibid.*, p. 144), and this is due to its link with structural principles such as the self-determination of peoples, because of its relationship with the intangibility of frontiers and, consequently, with that of the territorial integrity of States (cf. *ibid.*).

Secondly, the I.C.J. specifies the twofold content of this principle: on the one hand, the pre-eminence accorded to legal title over effective possession as a basis for sovereignty[19]. On the other, that the essence of the principle lies in its primary aim to secure respect for the territorial boundaries at the time when independence is achieved[20].

SANCHEZ RODRIGUEZ considers that the definition of this principle made by the I.C.J. is rather poor because it is very general. As it was the first time the Court had analysed this principle it should have examined it more thoroughly[21].

Finally, the I.C.J. also addresses the hypothetical conflict between this principle and the right to self-determination of peoples, stating that the principle of "uti possidetis":

> "has kept its place among the most important legal principles, despite the apparent contradiction which explained its coexistence alongside the new norms. Indeed it was by deliberate choice that African States selected, among all the classic principles, that of *uti possidetis*. This remains an undeniable fact."[22]

In subsequent cases, the I.C.J. repeats that the principle of *uti possidetis juris* is a rule of International Law applicable also in relation to maritime areas, islands and bays. Here considers that the effective interpretation given by the Parties to that principle in the years after independence is also evidence of its application[23].

---

19 This first element,

> "emphasized by the Latin genitive *juris*, is found in the pre-eminence accorded to legal title over effective possession as a basis of sovereignty. Its purpose, at the time of the achievement of independence by the former Spanish colonies of America, was to scotch any designs which non-American colonizing powers might have on regions which had been assigned by the former metropolitan State to one division or another, but which were still uninhabited or unexplored" (I.C.J., *Reports 1986*, pages 566).

20 In the words of the I.C.J.:

> "However, there is more to the principle of *uti possidetis* than this particular aspect. The essence of the principle lies in its primary aim of securing respect for the territorial boundaries at the moment when independence is achieved. Such territorial boundaries might be no more than delimitations between different administrative divisions or colonies all subject to the same sovereign. In that case, the application of the principle of *uti possidetis* resulted in administrative boundaries being transformed into international frontiers in the full sense of the term" (*ibid.*, p. 566).

21 And this because the I.C.J. does not pronounce on the *de facto* "uti possidetis", nor on the twofold nature (constitutional and international) of this principle in America (see SANCHEZ RODRIGUEZ, L.I., "Uti possidetis ...", *op. cit.,* pages 131-136).

22 I.C.J., *Reports 1986*, p. 567. Concerning this question see also our work *La frontera hispano-francesa y las relaciones de vecindad*, San Sebastian, 1990, pages 37-39, and the bibliography quoted in this work.

23 Thus, in the case concerning *Land, Island and Maritime Frontier Dispute (El Salvador/Honduras)*, (cf. I.C.J., *Reports 1992*, pages 565 et alt.).

In the doctrinal field, TORRES BERNARDEZ agrees with the customary nature of the principle which he considers to be applicable to all the cases of decolonisation, except when the Parties have expressly excluded it. It can also be employed in connection with the attribution of sovereign rights upon maritime and land areas and islands, as well as with land delimitations (rivers and lakes included) and maritime delimitations. However, he disagrees with the use of this principle in cases of separation or dissolution of States in which it can only be applicable if the Parties agree to it, but not as norm of International Law. Consequently, it is not directly applicable to territorial problems arising between new States which before were constituent territorial units of a sovereign State[24].

6 The legality of the threat or use of nuclear weapons

This question was analysed by the Court in its advisory opinion regarding the request of the United Nations General Assembly in the case concerning the *Legality of the Threat or Use of Nuclear Weapons*, dated 8 July 1996.

The question put to the I.C.J. was the following: “Is the threat or use of nuclear weapons in any circumstance permitted under international law?“

To answer it the Court, first, must decide, “after consideration of the great corpus of international law norms available to it, what might be the relevant applicable law”[25]. After excluding international norms relating to the right to life, the prohibition against genocide, as well as the safeguarding and protection of the environment, it concludes that

> “the most directly relevant applicable law governing the question of which it was seised, is that relating to the use of force enshrined in the United Nations Charter and the law applicable in armed conflict which regulates the conduct of hostilities, together with any specific treaties on nuclear weapons that the Court might determine to be relevant”[26].

With regard to the norm relating to the threat or use of force, in the view of the Court, the use of nuclear weapons in the exercise of the right of self-defence of

---

[24] Cf. TORRES BERNARDEZ, S., “The ‘Uti Possidetis Juris Principle’ in Historical Perspective”, in the collective work *Völkerrecht zwischen normativen Anspruch und politischer Realität. Festschrift für Karl Zemanek zum 65. Geburtstag*, Duncker & Humblot, Berlin, 1994, pages 417-437.Especially, pages 431 et alt.

[25] I.C.J., *Reports 1996*, p. 239.

[26] *Ibid.*, p. 242. And this, in the light

> “of the unique characteristics of nuclear weapons, and in particular their destructive capacity, their capacity to cause untold human suffering and their ability to cause damage to generations to come” (*ibid.*, p. 244).

Article 51 of the United Nations Charter as well as in the conduct of reprisals is governed by the principle of proportionality[27].

Concerning the law applicable in situations of armed conflict the I.C.J. states that international customary and treaty law does not contain any specific prescription authorizing the threat or use of nuclear weapons or any other weapon "in general or in certain circumstances, in particular those of the exercise of legitimate self-defence"[28]. The question is rather whether the illegality of the use of certain weapons as such is formulated in terms of prohibition. After analysing State practice, the Court concludes that the existing treaties cannot be considered as "amounting to a comprehensive and universal conventional prohibition on the use, or threat of use, of those weapons as such"[29].

With regard to customary International Law, and as result of the analysis of State practice, the I.C.J. concludes that it is not itself able to find that there is an *opinio juris* concerning such a prohibition[30]. On this point, although the existence of General Assembly resolutions adopted with substantial numbers of negative votes and abstentions – which is a clear sign of deep concern regarding the problem of nuclear weapons –, such resolutions "still fall short of establishing the existence of an *opinio juris* on the illegality of the use of such weapons"[31].

In conclusion, the Court does not find "a conventional rule with a general scope, nor a customary rule specifically proscribing the threat or use of nuclear weapons *per se*, …"[32].

The other point of view from which it will analyse the same question is that of *international humanitarian law applicable in armed conflict and the law of neutrality*. With regard to international humanitarian law, a great many rules of which

---

27 "The submission of the exercise of the right of self-defence to the conditions of necessity and proportionality is a rule of customary international law". And later: " … in any case any right of recourse to such reprisals would, like self-defence, be governed *inter alia* by the principle of proportionality" (I.C.J., *Reports 1996*, pages 245 and 246).

28 *Ibid.*, p. 247.

29 *Ibid.*, p. 253. As maximum,

> "these treaties could therefore be seen as foreshadowing a future general prohibition of the use of such weapons, but they do not constitute such a prohibition by themselves" (*ibid.*).

30 "Furthermore, the members of the international community are profoundly divided on the matter of whether non-recourse to nuclear weapons over the past 50 years constitutes the expression of an *opinio juris*" (*ibid.*, p. 254).

31 *Ibid.*, p, 255. In other words:

> "The emergence, as *lex lata*, of a customary rule specifically prohibiting the use of nuclear weapons as such is hampered by the continuing tensions between the nascent *opinio juris* on the one hand, and the still strong adherence to the practice of deterrence on the other" (*ibid.*).

32 *Ibid.*, p. 256.

constitute "intransgressible principles of international customary law"[33], the Court concludes its applicability to nuclear weapons[34]. Concerning the principle of neutrality, it also concludes its fundamental character similar to that of the humanitarian principles and rules as well as its applicability to all international armed conflict, whatever type of weapons might be used[35].

But at the time it responds to the advisory opinion requested, the I.C.J. shows its internal tensions. This can be seen in the following contradiction: the use of nuclear weapons seems scarcely reconcilable with the requirements derived from international humanitarian law – "at the heart of which is the overriding consideration of humanity"[36] –, but the Court, unfortunately, in our opinion, "considers that it does not have sufficient elements to enable it to conclude with certainty that the use of nuclear weapons would necessarily be at variance with the principles and rules of law applicable in armed conflict in any circumstance"[37].

It reaches such a conclusion because it gives priority to, in its own words, "the fundamental right of every State to survival, and thus its right to resort to self-defence, in accordance with Article 51 of the Charter, when its survival is at stake"[38].

Thus,

> "in view of the present state of international law viewed as a whole, as examined above by the Court, and of the elements of fact at its disposal, the Court is led to observe that it cannot reach a definitive conclusion as to the legality or illegality of the use of nuclear weapons by a State in an extreme circumstance of self-defence, in which its very survival would be at stake"[39].

The tensions and divisions between the different judges of the Court at the time this advisory opinion was given are also present in its most important conclusion. It was adopted by seven votes to seven, *with the President's casting vote*, and thus:

---

33 *Ibid.*

34 Its cardinal principles are the distinction between combatants and non-combatants (so States must never make civilians the object of attack and must consequently never use weapons that are incapable of distinguishing between civilian and military targets) and the prohibition to cause unnecessary suffering to combatants (according to this, it is prohibited to use weapons causing them such harm or uselessly aggravating their suffering), so States do not have unlimited freedom of choice of means in the weapon they use (cf. *ibid.*, p. 257).

35 Cf. *ibid.*, p. 261.

36 *Ibid.*, p. 262.

37 *Ibid.*, pages 262-263.

38 *Ibid.*, p. 263.

39 *Ibid.*

> "It follows from the above-mentioned requirements that the threat or use of nuclear weapons would generally be contrary to the rules of international law applicable in armed conflict, and in particular the principles and rules of humanitarian law;
>
> However, in view of the current state of international law, and of the elements of fact at its disposal, the Court cannot conclude definitively whether the threat or use of nuclear weapons would be lawful or unlawful in an extreme circumstance of self-defence, in which the very survival of a State would be at stake;"[40].

In any case, this advisory opinion of the I.C.J. will always have in its debit the division existing between the judges of the Court at the time of concluding the statement of International Law concerning the question put to it by the United Nations General Assembly. The fact that it was adopted by the President's casting vote shows the lack of a general opinion among the judges of the I.C.J. concerning this subject and the existence of varying interpretations concerning this point.

7 Immunity from criminal jurisdiction in other States and also inviolability of an incumbent Minister for Foreign Affairs

These questions are dealt with by the I.C.J. in the case concerning the *Arrest Warrant of 11 April 2000 (*Democratic Republic of the Congo *v.* Belgium) as a result of the issue by a Belgian investigating judge of "an international arrest warrant in absentia" against the incumbent Minister for Foreign Affairs of the Congo, alleging grave breaches of the Geneva Conventions of 1949 and of the Additional Protocols thereto and crimes against humanity. Consequently, an international circulation of arrest warrant through Interpol was issued.

The Democratic Republic of the Congo finds that the arrest warrant constitutes a breach of several international obligations. Particularly, those deriving from Article 2.1 of the Charter of the United Nations and from paragraph 2 of Article 41 of the Vienna Convention on Consular Relations of April 24, 1963 (concerning the diplomatic immunity of the Minister for Foreign Affairs of a sovereign State). Although the Application of the Congo originally put forward these two separate legal grounds, the submissions of the Congo in its Report and the final submissions which it presented at the end of the oral proceedings refer only to a violation in regard to the Congo of the rule of customary international law concerning the absolute inviolability and immunity from any criminal action of incumbent foreign ministers.

The Court observed that it is firmly established in international law that, like diplomatic and consular agents, certain holders of high-ranking office in a State, such as the Head of State, Head of Government and Minister for Foreign Affairs,

---

[40] *Ibid.*, p. 266.

enjoy immunities from both civil and criminal jurisdiction in other States. In the case concerning the *Arrest Warrant of 11 April 2000*, it is only immunity from criminal jurisdiction and the inviolability of an incumbent Minister for Foreign Affairs that are considered by the Court.

Regarding the tools the I.C.J. will use to deal with the questions put to it, it considers that even though the existing conventions provide useful guidance on certain aspects of the question of immunities[41], they do not, however, contain any provision specifically defining the immunities enjoyed by Ministers for Foreign Affairs. Thus, it is on the basis of customary international law that the Court decides to address the questions relating to the immunities of such Ministers raised in the present case.

7.1 Immunities in customary international law

The starting point for the interpretation of the I.C.J. is the finding that, in customary international law, the immunities accorded to Ministers for Foreign Affairs are not granted for their personal benefit, but to ensure the effective performance of their functions on behalf of their respective States.

In order to determine the extent of these immunities, the Court first considers the nature of the functions exercised by a Minister for Foreign Affairs and states:

> "He or she is in charge of his or her Government's diplomatic activities and generally acts as its representative in international negotiations and intergovernmental meetings. Ambassadors and other diplomatic agents carry out their duties under his or her authority. His or her acts may bind the State represented, and there is a presumption that a Minister for Foreign Affairs, simply by virtue of that office, has full powers to act on behalf of the State (see, e.g., Art. 7, para. 2 *(a)*, of the 1969 Vienna Convention on the Law of Treaties). In the performance of these functions, he or she is frequently required to travel internationally, and thus must be in a position freely to do so whenever the need should arise. He or she must also be in constant communication with the Government, and with its diplomatic missions around the world, and be capable at any time of communicating with representatives of other States"[42].

[41] These conventions are: the Vienna Convention on Diplomatic Relations (to which both the Congo and Belgium are parties) and the Vienna Convention on Consular Relations of 24 April 1963 (to which the Congo and Belgium are also parties), both reflecting customary international law. The Congo and Belgium further cite the New York Convention on Special Missions of December 8, 1969, to which they are not, however, parties.

[42] *I.C.J.*, case concerning the *Arrest Warrant of 11 April 2000*, p. 19, para. 53. About this case see SASSOLI, M., "L'arrrêt Yerodia: quelques remarques sur une affaire au point de colision entre les deux couches du droit international ", *R.G.D.I.P.*, Tome 106/2002/4, pp. 791-818; HENZELIN, M., "La compétence pénale universelle: une question non réso-

The Court further observes that a Minister for Foreign Affairs, "responsible for the conduct of his or her State's relations with all other States, occupies a position such that, like the Head of State or the Head of Government, he or she is recognized under international law as representative of the State solely by virtue of his or her office. He or she does not have to present letters of credence: on the contrary, it is generally the Minister who determines the authority to be conferred upon diplomatic agents and countersigns their letters of credence. Finally, it is to the Minister for Foreign Affairs that *chargés d'affaires* are accredited"[43].

In consequence the Court concludes that the functions "of a Minister for Foreign Affairs are such that, throughout the duration of his or her office, when abroad, he or she enjoys full immunity from criminal jurisdiction and inviolability. Such immunity and inviolability protect the individual concerned against any act of authority of another State which would hinder him or her in the performance of his or her duties"[44].

This immunity and inviolability are absolute and, unlike the immunity of jurisdiction of the State, no distinction can be drawn between the acts performed by a Minister for Foreign Affairs in an "official" capacity and those claimed to have been performed in a "private capacity", or, for that matter, between acts performed before the person concerned assumed office as Minister for Foreign Affairs and acts committed during the period of office:

> "Thus, if a Minister for Foreign Affairs is arrested in another State on a criminal charge, he or she is clearly thereby prevented from exercising the functions of his or her office. The consequences of such impediment to the exercise of those official functions are equally serious, regardless of whether the Minister for Foreign Affairs was, at the time of arrest, present in the territory of the arresting State on an "official" visit or a "private" visit, regardless of whether the arrest relates to acts allegedly performed before the person became the Minister for Foreign Affairs or to acts performed while in office, and regardless of whether the arrest relates to alleged acts performed in an "official" capacity or a "private" capacity. Furthermore, even

lue par l'arrêt Yerodia", *R.G.D.I.P.*, Tome 106/2002/4, pp. 819-854; HOPKINS, K., "The International Court of Justice and the question of sovereign immunity: why the Yerodia case is an unfortunate ruling for the development of public international law", *South African Yearbook of International Law*, 27 (2002), pp. 256-263; TOMUSCHAT, Ch., "L'immunité des Etats en cas de violations graves des droits de l'homme", *R.G.D.I.P.*, Tome 109/2005/1, pp. 51-74; BIANCHI, A., "L'immunité des Etats et les violations graves des droits de l'homme: la fonction de l'interprète dans la détermination du droit international ", *R.G.D.I.P*, 2004/1, pp. 63-101; and CAPLAN, L. M., "State immunity, human rights, and *jus cogens*: a critique of the normative hierarchy theory", *A.J.I.L.*, 2003, Vol. 97, No. 4, pp. 741-781.

43 *Ibid.*

44 *Ibid.*, p. 20, para. 54.

> the mere risk that, by travelling to or transiting another State a Minister for Foreign Affairs might be exposing himself or herself to legal proceedings could deter the Minister from travelling internationally when required to do so for the purposes of the performance of his or her official functions"[45].

Once the absolute character of the immunity and of the inviolability of the Minister for Foreign Affairs is established independently of the "official" or "private" nature of the acts performed by him, the I.C.J. deals with Belgium's argument that immunities accorded to incumbent Ministers for Foreign Affairs can in no case protect them when they are suspected of having committed war crimes or crimes against humanity. In support of this position, Belgium refers to various legal instruments creating international criminal tribunals, to examples from national legislation, and to the jurisprudence of national and international courts. Belgium also points out that certain provisions of the instruments creating international criminal tribunals expressly state that the official capacity of a person shall not be a bar to the exercise of their jurisdiction by such tribunals. It also places emphasis on certain decisions of national courts, and in particular on the judgments rendered on March 24, 1999 by the House of Lords in the United Kingdom and on March 13, 2001 by the Court of Cassation in France in the *Pinochet* and *Qaddafi* cases respectively.

After examining State practice, including national legislation and those few decisions of national higher courts, such as the House of Lords or the French Court of Cassation, the Court states that:

> "it has been unable to deduce from this practice that there exists under customary international law any form of exception to the rule according immunity from criminal jurisdiction and inviolability to incumbent Ministers for Foreign Affairs, where they are suspected of having committed war crimes or crimes against humanity"[46].

To arrive at that conclusion the Court has also examined the rules concerning the immunity or criminal responsibility of persons having an official capacity contained in the legal instruments creating international criminal tribunals, and which are specifically applicable to the latter (see Charter of the International Military Tribunal of Nuremberg, Art. 7; Charter of the International Military Tribunal of Tokyo, Art. 6; Statute of the International Criminal Tribunal for the former Yugoslavia, Art. 7, para. 2; Statute of the International Criminal Tribunal for Rwanda, Art. 6, para. 2; Statute of the International Criminal Court, Art. 27). It finds that these rules likewise do not enable it to conclude that any such exception exists in customary international law with regard to national courts.

---

[45] *Ibid.*

[46] *Ibid.*, p. 21, para. 58.

Finally, the Court adds that none of the decisions of the Nuremberg and Tokyo international military tribunals, or of the International Criminal Tribunal for the former Yugoslavia, cited by Belgium deal with the question of the immunities of incumbent Ministers for Foreign Affairs before national courts where they are accused of having committed war crimes or crimes against humanity and concludes that "those decisions are in no way at variance with the findings it has reached above"[47].

Nevertheless, the absolute immunity and the inviolability of incumbent Ministers for Foreign Affairs does not resolve the problem which consequently arises: the fact of the impunity inherent to the interpretation made above, and the I.C.J. is aware of this. This is why it states "that the *immunity* from jurisdiction enjoyed by incumbent Ministers for Foreign Affairs does not mean that they enjoy *impunity* in respect of any crimes they might have committed, irrespective of their gravity. Immunity from criminal jurisdiction and individual criminal responsibility are quite separate concepts. While jurisdictional immunity is procedural in nature, criminal responsibility is a question of substantive law. Jurisdictional immunity may well bar prosecution for a certain period or for certain offences; it cannot exonerate the person to whom it applies from all criminal responsibility"[48].

The distinction between jurisdictional immunity and criminal responsibility made by the Court does not resolve the problem of impunity. Especially since the interpretation made by the Court clearly excludes all acts committed during the period in which that person was acting in an official way from this kind of responsibility. Moreover, as these kinds of acts (war crimes, crimes against humanity, genocide, aggression) are generally planned and organized by public powers. This is why they are not usually done in a private capacity.

Once the distinction between jurisdictional immunity and criminal responsibility is made, the Court refer to the situations in which the immunities enjoyed under international law by an incumbent or former Minister for Foreign Affairs do not represent a bar to criminal prosecution. Following the Court, there are four such situations.

The first situation, obviously, "such persons enjoy no criminal immunity under international law in their own countries, and may thus be tried by those countries' courts in accordance with the relevant rules of domestic law"[49].

The second situation is also obvious, such persons will cease to enjoy immunity from foreign jurisdiction if the State which they represent or have represented decides to waive that immunity.

The third situation (and here the construction of the Court does not resolve the problem of *impunity* inherent to the interpretation made by it before when it states

[47] But it does not take into account the fact that these international courts are competent to judge "any" person accused of having committed war crimes, crimes against humanity, genocide or aggression. It also includes persons performing public functions.

[48] *Ibid.*, p. 22, para. 60.

[49] *Ibid.*, p. 22, para.60.

the difference between jurisdictional immunity and criminal responsibility) the I.C.J. finds that "after a person ceases to hold the office of Minister for Foreign Affairs, he or she will no longer enjoy all of the immunities accorded by international law in other States". Consequently, "provided that it has jurisdiction under international law, a court of one State may try a former Minister for Foreign Affairs of another State in respect of acts committed prior or subsequent to his or her period of office, as well as in respect of acts committed during that period of office in a private capacity"[50].

The fourth situation, an incumbent or former Minister for Foreign Affairs "may be subject to criminal proceedings before certain international criminal courts, where they have jurisdiction. Examples include the International Criminal Tribunal for the former Yugoslavia, and the International Criminal Tribunal for Rwanda, established pursuant to Security Council resolutions under Chapter VII of the United Nations Charter, and the future International Criminal Court created by the 1998 Rome Convention. The latter's Statute expressly provides, in Article 27, paragraph 2, that "[i]mmunities or special procedural rules which may attach to the official capacity of a person, whether under national or international law, shall not bar the Court from exercising its jurisdiction over such a person"[51].

Unfortunately, the efforts of the Court as regards construction do not resolve the problem of immunity which results from its interpretation because jurisdictional immunity and inviolability of Ministers or Heads of State have never been conceived by international law to protect the commission of war crimes, crimes against humanity, genocide and acts of aggression. Neither can such acts be considered to be committed in a private capacity by persons acting in a public capacity. Consequently, the interpretation of the Court distinguishes between jurisdictional immunity and criminal responsibility and states that "provided that it has jurisdiction under international law, a court of one State may try a former Minister for Foreign Affairs of another State in respect of acts committed prior or subsequent to his or her period of office, as well as in respect of acts committed during that period of office in a private capacity" (*but not acts committed during that period of office in a public capacity*), the I.C.J. concludes the impunity of such kind of persons during such periods.

The Court also forgets that war crimes, crimes against humanity, genocide and acts of aggression can never be considered as acts carried out by such persons in a private or in a public capacity. It also forgets that jurisdictional immunity and inviolability have never been conceived by international law to allow or to protect the commission of war crimes, crimes against humanity, genocide and acts of aggression by persons acting in a public capacity. Such kinds of acts can never be qualified as acts inherent to State sovereignty; sovereignty which constitutes the

---

[50] *Ibid.* Nevertheless, war crimes, crimes against humanity, genocide and aggression can never be considered as acts committed during the period of office of a Minister for Foreign Affairs in a private capacity.

[51] *Ibid.*

foundation of both institutions in international law: immunity of jurisdiction and inviolability.

In addition, the I.C.J. does not take into account the evolution that has taken place in this sector of international law, characterized by the absence of inviolability and of jurisdictional immunity in relation to the commission of acts constituting war crimes, crimes against humanity, genocide and acts of aggression. This is shown by the examples of Art. 7, para. 2 of the Statute of the International Criminal Tribunal for the former Yugoslavia, Art. 6, para. 2 of the Statute of the International Criminal Tribunal for Rwanda, and Art. 27 of the Statute of the International Criminal Court (quoted by the Court). The same answer is also in Art. VI of the Convention on genocide as well as in Arts. 8 and 9 of the Draft Code of Crimes against the Peace and Security of Mankind of 1996.

Finally, as war crimes, crimes against humanity, genocide and acts of aggression are the result of the breach of a norm of *jus cogens* it could not be concluded that customary international law protects the commission of such kinds of acts if they are committed in a public capacity.

This last conclusion as well the examples stating the non relevance of public capacity when such acts are committed should have guided the Court to an interpretation more adapted to the actual state of international law.

8 The concept of occupied territory and international obligations resulting for the occupying Power

This question has been dealt with recently by the I.C.J. in its advisory opinion on the *Legal Consequences of the Construction of a Wall in the Occupied Palestinian Territory*, with regard to the territories situated between the Green Line and the former eastern boundary of Palestine under the Mandate and which were occupied by Israel in 1967 during the armed conflict between Israel and Jordan.

It is the opinion of the Court that a territory is considered occupied "when it is actually placed under the authority of the hostile army, and the occupation extends only to the territory where such authority has been established and can be exercised"[52].

Consequently, several international obligations have derived from the status of occupied territory. Their sources are in several rules and principles of International Law contained in the Charter of the United Nations, in the relevant resolutions adopted pursuant to the Charter by the General Assembly and the Security Council, as well as in several international treaties. These international norms are determined by the Court and the Court considers that they reflect customary international law; customary international law applicable to occupied territories.

[52] I.C.J., *Legal Consequences of the Construction of a Wall in the Occupied Palestinian Territory, Advisory Opinion*, para. 78.

The first of these rules and principles concern the *interdiction from the threat or use of force against the territorial integrity or political independence of any State, or in any other manner inconsistent with the Purposes of the United Nations*, retained by Article 2, paragraph 4 of the United Nations Charter as well as by the General Assembly resolution 2625 (XXV), adopted on 24 October 1970 and entitled "Declaration on Principles of International Law concerning Friendly Relations and Co-operation among States", in which it is emphasized that "No territorial acquisition resulting from the threat or use of force shall be recognized as legal".

The Court, after recalling its statement in its Judgement in the case concerning *Military and Paramilitary Activities in and against Nicaragua (Nicaragua v. United States of America)*[53], underlines that the principles concerning the use of force incorporated into the Charter reflect customary international law. It also states that "the same is true of its corollary entailing the illegality of territorial acquisition resulting from the threat or use of force"[54].

The second rule and principle of International Law applicable to occupied territories is that of the *self-determination of peoples*. It is a principle that has been enshrined in the United Nations Charter and reaffirmed by the General Assembly in resolution 2625 (XXV). Pursuant to it "Every State has the duty to refrain from any forcible action which deprives peoples referred to [in that resolution] ... of their right to self-determination". The same principle of self-determination of peoples is also reaffirmed by Article 1 common to the International Covenant on Economic, Social and Cultural Rights and the International Covenant on Civil and Political Rights, which lays upon the signatory States the obligation to promote the realization of that right and to respect it, in conformity with the provisions of the United Nations Charter.

With regard to this principle, the Court recalls that in 1971 it emphasized that current developments in "international law in regard to non-self-governing territories, as enshrined in the Charter of the United Nations, made the principle of self-determination applicable to all [such territories]" and that it went on to state that "These developments leave little doubt that the ultimate objective of the sacred trust" referred to in Article 22, paragraph 1, of the Covenant of the League of Nations "was the self-determination ... of the peoples concerned" *(Legal Consequences for States of the Continued Presence of South Africa in Namibia (South West Africa) notwithstanding Security Council Resolution 276 (1970), Advisory Opinion*, I.C.J., *Reports 1971*, p. 31, paras. 52-53)"[55].

---

[53] See I.C.J., *Reports 1986*, pp. 98-101.

[54] I.C.J., *Legal Consequences of the Construction of a Wall in the Occupied Palestinian Territory, Advisory Opinion*, para. 87.

[55] *Ibid.*, para. 88.

It also recalls that it had referred to this principle on a number of occasions in its jurisprudence[56] and that it had made it clear that the right of peoples to self-determination is today a right *erga omnes*[57].

Unfortunately, the Court has never developed the consequences of such obligations. Even though it had occasion to do so. Consequently, the nature of the *erga omnes* obligation of this principle and its consideration as a norm of *ius cogens* do not take effect in practice. The Court has never taken advantage of the cases before they went further. This was what occurred in the case of *East Timor*, where the Court did not give priority to the fact that there were norms of *ius cogens* as well as *erga omnes* obligations. Consequently, the rule contained in Article 53 of the 1969 Vienna Convention on the Law on Treaties which states that a treaty is void if, at the time of its conclusion, it conflicts with a peremptory norm of general international law remained without effect. In that case, the rule of consent to its jurisdiction prevailed over the *erga omnes* character of the norm to be applied. In the opinion of the Court, these are two different things. The consequences of this construction are obvious: *ius cogens* and *erga omnes* obligations are deprived of effect.

The third group of rules and principles concerns *International Humanitarian Law*. Due to the fact that Israel is not a party to the Fourth Hague Convention of 1907 the Court analyses its customary nature and its application to occupied territories. Concerning the first question, the Court observes that, in the words of the Convention, "those Regulations were prepared 'to revise the general laws and customs of war' existing at that time. Also that the International Military Tribunal of Nuremberg has found that the 'rules laid down in the Convention were recognised by all civilised nations, and were regarded as being declaratory of the laws and customs of war' (Judgment of the International Military Tribunal of Nuremberg, 30 September and 1 October 1946, page 65)"[58]. The Court finally recalls that it reached the same conclusion when examining the rights and duties of belligerents in their conduct of military operations on the occasion of its advisory opinion on the *Legality of the Threat or Use of Nuclear Weapons*[59]. It concludes that the provisions of the Hague Regulations "have become part of customary law, as is in fact recognized by all the participants in the proceedings before the Court"[60].

---

[56] See I.C.J., *Western Sahara, Advisory Opinion,* I.C.J., *Reports 1975*, p. 68, para. 162.

[57] See I.C.J., *East Timor (Portugal v. Australia), Judgment*, I.C.J., *Reports 1995*, p. 102, para. 29.

[58] I.C.J., *Legal Consequences of the Construction of a Wall in the Occupied Palestinian Territory, Advisory Opinion*, para. 89.

[59] See I.C.J., *Reports 1996 (I)*, p. 256, para. 75.

[60] *Ibid.*

9 Legal consequences of the commission of an internationally wrongful act

This question has been dealt with recently by the I.C.J. in the following cases: *LaGrand*, *Avena and other Mexican Nationals*, and the advisory opinion concerning *Legal Consequences of the Construction of a Wall in the Occupied Palestinian Territory*. In the two first cases as a consequence of the execution of Karl and Walter LaGrand (nationals of Germany) as wells as of Avena and other Mexican nationals. In the latter case, as a consequence of the construction, by Israel, of a wall in Occupied Palestinian Territory, including in and around East Jerusalem.

The legal consequences of the commission of an internationally wrongful act vary depending on the kind of obligations violated: if obligations derived from international norms other than norms of *jus cogens* or obligations *erga omnes*.

Those derived from the violation of the first kind of obligations are envisaged by the Court in the three cases quoted above. Those of obligations *erga omnes*, in its advisory opinion on the *Legal Consequences of the Construction of a Wall in the Occupied Palestinian Territory*.

The construction of the Court is based on several steps. Firstly, it takes into account that the general principle on the legal consequences of the commission of an internationally wrongful act is well established in Public International Law since the statement of the Permanent Court of International Justice in the *Factory at Chorzów* case, according to which: "It is a principle of international law that the breach of an engagement involves an obligation to make reparation in an adequate form"[61].

Thus, it faces the legal consequences of the commission of an internationally wrongful act and recalls the terms of its precedent Court in the case just quoted:

> "The essential principle contained in the actual notion of an illegal act – a principle which seems to be established by international practice and in particular by the decisions of arbitral tribunals – is that reparation must, as far as possible, wipe out all the consequences of the illegal act and reestablish the situation which would, in all probability, have existed if that act had not been committed"[62].

Concerning the forms of reparation in customary law, the Permanent Court of International Justice also states briefly,

> "What constitutes 'reparation in an adequate form' clearly varies depending upon the concrete circumstances surrounding each case and the precise nature and scope of the injury, since the question has

---

[61] P.C.I.J., *Series A, No. 9*, p. 21.

[62] I.C.J., *Legal Consequences of the Construction of a Wall in the Occupied Palestinian Territory, Advisory Opinion*, para. 152.

> to be examined from the viewpoint of what is the 'reparation in an adequate form' that corresponds to the injury"[63].

It goes further and gives several examples of forms of reparation:

> "Restitution in kind, or, if this is not possible, payment of a sum corresponding to the value which a restitution in kind would bear; the award, if need be, of damages for loss sustained which would not be covered by restitution in kind or payment in place of it – such are the principles which should serve to determine the amount of compensation due for an act contrary to international law (*Factory at Chorzów, Merits, Judgment No. 13, 1928,* P.C.I.J., *Series A, No. 17*, p. 47.)"[64].

In its Advisory Opinion on the *Legal Consequences of the Construction of a Wall in the Occupied Palestinian Territory* the I.C.J. refers to other consequences of the commission of an international wrongful act. As regards the State acting wrongfully, this is the case of the obligation to comply with the international obligations breached as well as the obligation to put an end to the violation of its international obligations[65].

In the *LaGrand* case as well in the case concerning *Avena and other Mexican nationals* the violation of the international obligation (contained in Article 36 of the Vienna Convention on Consular Relations) was due to a domestic law of the United States of America. The Court states that it is of its competence to determine the existence of a violation of an international obligation and that it can also hold that a domestic law has been the cause of this violation. But in both cases it concludes that the violation of Article 36 paragraph 2, of the Vienna Convention was caused by the circumstances in which the procedural default rule was applied, and not by the rule as such[66].

Concerning reparation as the legal consequence of the violation of an international obligation, the Court considers that as both cases are of the kind in which the individuals concerned have been subjected to prolonged detention or convicted and sentenced to severe penalties, "an apology would not suffice"[67]. So, it is the opinion of the Court that in these cases it would be incumbent upon the United States to allow the review and reconsideration of the conviction and sentence by

---

[63] I.C.J., case concerning *Avena and other Mexican nationals, Reports 2004*, para. 48.

[64] I.C.J., *Legal Consequences of the Construction of a Wall in the Occupied Palestinian Territory, Advisory Opinion*, para. 152.

[65] Concerning the several obligations relate to Israel see *ibid.*, paras. 149-153. About this questions see GOMEZ-ROBLEDO, J., "L'avis de la C.I.J. sur les conséquences juridiques de l'édification d'un mur dans le territoire palestinien occupé : timidité ou prudence?", *R.G.D.I.P.*, tome 109/2005/3, pp. 521-537.

[66] Cf. I.C.J., *LaGrand* case, *Reports 2001*, pp. 513-514, para. 125.

[67] *Ibid.*

taking account of the violation of the rights set forth in the Convention. It adds that this obligation can be carried out in various ways and that the choice of means for such review and reconsideration must be left to the United States[68].

In the case concerning *Avena and other Mexican nationals* the Court goes further stating that, however, this freedom in the choice of means for such review and reconsideration is not without qualification: "such review and reconsideration has to be carried out by taking account of the violation of the rights set forth in the Convention' (I.C.J., *Reports 2001*, p. 514, para. 125), including, in particular, the question of the legal consequences of the violation upon the criminal proceedings that have followed the violation"[69].

As the I.C.J. underlines, the current situation in the United States criminal procedure, as explained by the Agent at the hearings, is that "if the defendant alleged at trial that *a failure of consular information resulted in harm to a particular right essential to a fair trial*, an appeals court can review how the lower court handled that claim of prejudice", but that 'If the foreign national did not raise his Article 36 claim at trial, he may face procedural constraints [i.e., the application of the procedural default rule] on raising that particular claim in direct or collateral judicial appeals' (emphasis added). As a result, a claim based on the violation of Article 36, paragraph 1, of the Vienna Convention, however meritorious in itself, could be barred in the courts of the United States by the operation of the procedural default rule"[70].

This is why the Court does not consider sufficient for the United States to argue that "[w]hatever label [the Mexican defendant] places on his claim, his right ... must and will be vindicated if it is raised *in some form at trial" (emphasis added*), and that 'In that way, even though a failure to label the complaint as a breach of the Vienna Convention may mean that he has technically speaking forfeited his right to raise this issue as a Vienna Convention claim, on appeal that failure would not bar him from independently asserting a *claim that he was prejudiced because he lacked this critical protection needed for a fair trial' (Emphasis added.)*"[71].

As the Court points out, the question is that "by the operation of the procedural default rule as it is applied at present, the defendant is effectively barred from raising the issue of the violation of his rights under Article 36 of the Vienna Convention and is limited to seeking the vindication of his rights under the United States Constitution"[72]. It recalls that in the *LaGrand* case it left the choice of means

---

[68] Cf. *ibid.* Such review and reconsideration has to be carried out "by taking account of the violation of the rights set forth in the Convention -of Vienna on Consular Relations-" (I.C.J. *LaGrand* case, *Reports 2001*, p. 514, para. 125), including, in particular, the question of the legal consequences of the violation upon the criminal proceedings that have followed the violation (cf. case concerning *Avena and other Mexican nationals*, *Reports 2004*, para. 131.

[69] IC.J., case concerning *Avena and other Mexican nationals, Reports 2004*, para. 131.

[70] *Ibid.*, para. 133.

[71] *Ibid.*, para. 134.

[72] *Ibid.*

as to how review and reconsideration should be achieved to the United States, especially in the light of the procedural default rule. Nevertheless, the premise on which the Court proceeded in that case was that the process of review and reconsideration should occur within the overall judicial proceedings relating to the individual defendant concerned.

As regards the clemency procedure, the Court notes that this performs an important function in the administration of criminal justice in the United States and is "the historic remedy for preventing miscarriages of justice where judicial process has been exhausted" *(Herrera v. Collins, 506 U.S. 390 (1993) at pp. 411-412).* The Court accepts that executive clemency, while not judicial, is an integral part of the overall scheme for ensuring justice and fairness in the legal process within the United States criminal justice system. Nevertheless, it points out that what was at issue in that case was not whether executive clemency as an institution is or is not an integral part of the existing laws and regulations of the United States, but whether the clemency process as practised within the criminal justice systems of different states in the United States can, in and of itself, qualify as an appropriate means for undertaking the effective review and reconsideration of the conviction and sentence by taking account of the violation of the rights set forth in the Vienna Convention on Consular Relations, as the Court prescribed in the *LaGrand* Judgment[73].

The I.C.J. notes, however, that the clemency process, as currently practised within the United States criminal justice system, does not appear to meet the requirements described by it and that it is therefore not sufficient in itself to serve as an appropriate means of review and reconsideration as envisaged by the Court in the *LaGrand* case[74].

The standard fixed by the I.C.J. is that the review and reconsideration prescribed by it shall be effective. That means that it shall take account of the violation of the rights set forth in the Vienna Convention on Consular Relations as well as guarantee that the violation and the possible prejudice caused by the violation will be fully examined and taken into account in the review and reconsideration process. Lastly, review and reconsideration shall be both of the sentence and of the conviction[75].

Finally, the Court underlines that in a situation of the violation of rights under Article 36, paragraph 1, of the Vienna Convention, the defendant raises his claim in this respect "not as a case of 'harm to a particular right essential to a fair trial' – a concept relevant to the enjoyment of due process rights under the United States Constitution – but as a case involving the infringement of his rights under Article

[73] Cf. *LaGrand* case, (I.C.J., *Reports 2001*, p. 514, para. 125).

[74] Cf. case concerning *Avena and other Mexican nationals*, *Reports 2004*, para. 143. It adds that appropriate clemency procedures can supplement judicial review and reconsideration, "in particular where the judicial system has failed to take due account of the violation of the rights set forth in the Vienna Convention, as has occurred in the case of the three Mexican nationals referred to in paragraph 114 above" (*ibid.*, para.143).

[75] Cf. *ibid.*, para.138.

36, paragraph 1. The rights guaranteed under the Vienna Convention are treaty rights which the United States has undertaken to comply with in relation to the individual concerned, irrespective of the due process rights under United States constitutional law"[76].

In this regard, the Court also points out that what is crucial in the review and reconsideration process is the existence of a procedure which guarantees that full weight is given to the violation of the rights set forth in the Vienna Convention, "whatever may be the actual outcome of such review and reconsideration"[77].

As we have pointed out above, in its Advisory Opinion on the *Legal Consequences of the Construction of a Wall in the Occupied Palestinian Territory,* the Court also faces the consequences of the violation of *erga omnes* obligations. These are obligations that by their very nature concern all States and, in view of the importance of the rights involved, all States "can be held to have a legal interest in their protection"[78]. In that case, those derived from the violation of the obligation to respect the right of the Palestinian people to self-determination and as well as certain obligations under international humanitarian law.

The consequences for all other States derived from the violation by Israel of those *erga omnes* obligations are, in the opinion of the I.C.J., the following:

– They are under an obligation not to recognize the illegal situation resulting from the construction of the wall in the Occupied Palestinian Territory, including in and around East Jerusalem.

– They are under an obligation not to render aid or assistance in maintaining the situation created by such a construction.

– They shall act in order to bring to an end any impediment, resulting from the construction of the wall, to the exercise by the Palestinian people of its right to self-determination.

– They are under an obligation to ensure compliance by Israel with international humanitarian law as this is embodied in the Geneva Convention relative to the Protection of Civilian Persons in Time of War of 12 August 1949[79].

But there are also obligations for the United Nations. It is the opinion of the Court that the United Nations, "and specially General Assembly and the Security Council, should consider what further action is required to bring to an end the illegal situation resulting from the construction of the wall and the associated régime, taking due account"[80] of its Advisory Opinion on the matter.

---

[76] *Ibid.*, para. 139.

[77] *Ibid.*

[78] I.C.J., *Legal Consequences of the Construction of a Wall in the Occupied Palestinian Territory, Advisory Opinion*, para. 155.

[79] See *ibid.*, para. 159.

[80] *Ibid.*, para. 160.

CHAPTER X:

Institutional Norms of the United Nations

1 Resolutions of the General Assembly

As we have seen in the preceding pages, the I.C.J. has also addressed questions concerning United Nations General Assembly resolutions[1], both from the perspective of their legal effects and the language employed. We refer the reader to Chapter III of the present work, and we recall the essential aspects of the interpretation of the I.C.J.

Firstly, the fact that the Charter of the United Nations states that the General Assembly can adopt "recommendations" in certain cases within its competence, this does not mean that it can not adopt resolutions which make determinations or have an operative design. The same occurs with the "decisions" the General Assembly can take under Article 18 of the Charter: these do indeed include certain recommendations, but others have the force and effect of provisions[2].

Secondly, the effect of consent to the text of a resolution concerning obligations of the Charter cannot be understood as merely that of a reiteration or elucidation of the treaty commitment undertaken in the Charter, but as an acceptance of the validity of the rule or set of rules declared by the resolution in themselves[3].

Thirdly, the drafting employed by States can be evidence of the recognition that the content of the resolution in question is customary law[4].

Fourthly, the abstention of a state from voting on a General Assembly resolution cannot be interpreted as implying that it has consented to its content[5].

---

[1] Cf. the case concerning *Legal Consequences for States of the Continued Presence of South Africa in Namibia (South West Africa) notwithstanding Security Council Resolution 276 (1970)* (I.C.J., *Reports 1971*, p. 50).

[2] Cf. the case concerning *Certain Expenses of the United Nations* (I.C.J., *Reports 1962*, p. 163).

[3] Cf. the case concerning *Military and Paramilitary Activities in and against Nicaragua* (I.C.J., *Reports 1986*, p. 100).

[4] Cf. *ibid.*, p. 102 et seq.

[5] In the Advisory Opinion concerning the *Western Sahara*:

> "In view of Spain's persistent objections to the questions formulated in resolution 3292 (XXIX), the fact that it abstained and did not vote against the resolution cannot be interpreted as implying its consent to the adjudication of those questions by the Court.

Fifthly, the attitude of a State towards the resolution in question can be the expression of an *opinio juris* regarding such rule or set of rules and be thenceforth treated separately from the provisions, especially those of an institutional kind, to which it is subject on the treaty-law plane of the Charter[6]. On this point, in its advisory opinion concerning the *Legality of the Threat or Use of Nuclear Weapons*, the I.C.J. notes that General Assembly resolutions, "even if they are not binding, may sometimes have normative value. They can, in certain circumstances, provide evidence important for establishing the existence of a rule or the emergence of an *opinio juris*"[7].

Finally, in order to interpret a resolution of the General Assembly the proceedings of this Assembly previous to the adoption of that resolution shall be taken into account[8]. Also, in order to establish the existence of a rule or the emergence of an *opinio juris*. In both cases,

> "it is necessary to look at its content and the conditions of its adoption; it is also necessary to see whether an *opinio juris* exists as to its normative character. Or a series of resolutions may show the gradual evolution of the *opinio juris* required for the establishment of a new rule"[9].

More recently, in its advisory opinion concerning *Legal Consequences of the Construction of a Wall in the Occupied Palestinian Territory*, the I.C.J. recalls its statements on the question. Thus,

> "As the Court stated in its Advisory Opinion of 21 June 1971 concerning the Legal Consequences for States of the Continued Presence of South Africa in Namibia (South West Africa) notwithstanding Security Council Resolution 276 (1970), a 'resolution of a properly constituted organ of the United Nations which is passed in accordance with that organ's rules of procedure, and is declared by its President to have been so passed, must be presumed to have been validly adopted' (I.C.J., *Reports 1971,* p. 22, para. 20)"[10].

Moreover, its participation in the Court's proceedings cannot be understood as implying that it has consented to the adjudication of the questions posed in resolution 3292 (XXIX), for it has persistently maintained its objections throughout" (I.C.J., *Reports 1975*, p. 23).

6 Cf. the case concerning *Military and Paramilitary Activities in and against Nicaragua* (I.C.J., *Reports 1986*, p. 99).

7 I.C.J., *Reports 1996*, pages 254-255.

8 Cf. the Advisory Opinion concerning *Certain Expenses of the United Nations* (I.C.J., *Reports 1962*, p. 156). Concerning this question cf. SLOAN, B., "General Assembly Resolutions revisited (forty years later)", *B.Y.I.L.*, 1987, pages 39-150.

9 I.C.J., case concerning the *Legality of the Threat or Use of Nuclear Weapons, Reports 1996*, pages 254-255.

10 We will use the text published on www.icj-cij.org. The quotation corresponds to para. 35.

2 Resolutions of the Security Council

Concerning this type of institutional norm, Article 25 of the Charter provides that the Members of the United Nations "agree to accept and carry out the decisions of the Security Council" accordingly.

The I.C.J. addressed this question in the case concerning the *Legal Consequences for States of the Continued Presence of South Africa in Namibia (South West Africa) notwithstanding Security Council Resolution 276 (1970)*, and derived the following consequences. First, the importance of carefully analysing the language of a resolution of the Security Council before a conclusion can be made as to its binding effect. Starting from Article 25 of the Charter, and in view of the nature of the powers deriving from it, the Court states that the question whether they have in fact been exercised is to be determined in each case "having regard to the terms of the resolution to be interpreted, the discussion leading to it, the Charter provisions invoked and, in general, all circumstances that might assist in determining the legal consequences of the resolution of the Security Council"[11]. In short, the interpretative criteria employed by the I.C.J. with respect to the resolutions of the Security Council can be summed up as follows: the analysis of the terms of the resolution in question, the debates preceding its adoption, in order to determine whether the resolution in question has been adopted within the framework of the competence of the Security Council, the provisions of the Charter invoked, and all the elements that could help to specify the legal consequences of the resolution in question.

Secondly, as concerns the *obligatory character* of the decisions of the Security Council, the Court recalls its statement in the Advisory Opinion concerning *Reparation for Injuries Suffered in the Service of the United Nations*, that "the Charter has not been content to make the Organization created by it merely a centre 'for harmonizing the actions of nations in the attainment of these commons ends' (Article I, para. 4). It has equipped that centre with organs, and has given it special tasks. It has defined the position of the Members in relation to the Organization by requiring them to give it every assistance in any action undertaken by it (Article 2, para. 5), and to accept and carry out the decisions of the Security Council"[12].

Thus, when the Security Council adopts decisions under Article 25 of the Charter, it is for Member States to comply with those decisions, including those Members of the Security Council who voted against it and those Members of the United Nations who are not members of the Council. In the opinion of the I.C.J., "to hold otherwise would be to deprive this principal organ of its essential functions and powers under the Charter"[13].

---

[11] I.C.J., *Reports 1971*, p. 53.

[12] I.C.J., *Reports 1949*, p. 178.

[13] I.C.J., *Reports 1971*, p. 54.

Another aspect of the resolutions of the Security Council addressed by the Court concerns that of those decisions of that organ which obligatorily specify the *illegality of a situation*. In its reasoning, the I.C.J. begins by stating that it is inherent to its judicial functions to declare the existence of an obligation, particularly for the Members of the United Nations, to put an end to the illegal situation. This statement constitutes a reiteration of its preceding jurisprudence[14]. For these reasons the Member States are under "obligation to recognize the illegality and invalidity" of the act in question[15]. This declaration of illegality has, moreover, effects *erga omnes*. It is applicable to all States (U.N non-member States included) and transforms a situation "which is maintained in violation of international law" into an illegal situation[16].

After the changes that took place in the International Community since the beginning of the Nineties, the jurisprudential interpretation we have examined could have been further developed by the I.C.J. in the light of those changes and the questions resulting from them. For example, in the *Lockerbie* case in which the questions concerning the legality of resolution 748 (1992) of the Security Council and the excess of power of the Security Council in the exercise of its competences under the Charter of the United Nations were present. Unfortunately, the majority of the judges of the Court chose an interpretation protecting the Security Council and ignored the contribution they should have made as members of the principal judicial organ of the United Nations and the fact that the Security Council is also submitted to the Charter and to International Law. Due to the statement of the Court in that case, the dangers deriving from the discretion the Charter grants to the Security Council in order to classify the situations arising and to supply the legal grounds continues to persist and has increased owing to the interpretation made by the I.C.J and supported by article 103 of the Charter.

---

[14] Thus, in the *Haya de la Torre* case, in which it is stated that the I.C.J. decision "entails a legal consequence, namely that of putting an end to an illegal situation: …" (I.C.J., *Reports 1951*, p. 82).

[15] In this case, the presence of South Africa in Namibia (cf. I.C.J., *Reports 1971*, p. 54).

[16] *Ibid.* In this case, the illegal presence of South Africa in Namibia which harms "a people which must look to the international community for assistance in its progress towards the goals for which the sacred trust was instituted " (*ibid.*).

CHAPTER XI:

Unilateral Declarations

1 Unilateral declarations *stricto sensu*

As we have seen in Chapter V of this work, in the case of the *Nuclear Tests*, it was the I.C.J. which stated the possibility of creating legal obligations through the declaration of a single State. This is because it is possible to presume that such declarations are not made *in vacuo* but in relation to specific *de facto* or *de iure* situations. This presumption is completed with the analysis of the intention of the Parties to assume a legal obligation.

As has been done with regard to conventional and customary norms, we refer to what we have already expounded in this work concerning the case law construction relating to unilateral declarations[1].

2 Declarations of acceptance of the jurisdiction of the I.C.J.

With respect to the *declarations of acceptance of the jurisdiction of the I.C.J.*, the Court itself classifies them as "unilateral engagements" that States are absolutely free to make or not to make. This freedom includes the power either to do so unconditionally and with no time limit, or to qualify this with conditions or reservations. In this case, States can limit its effect to the disputes arising after a certain date or can specify how long the declaration itself shall remain in force, or what notice, if any, will be required to terminate it[2].

The criteria employed by the Court in order to appraise the intention of the author are similar to those of unilateral declarations *stricto sensu*, the starting point is the examination of the text of the declaration in order to specify whether

---

1 See Chapter V of this work. In the opinion of THIRLWAY, H., the Court had stated the principle in a dangerously wide formulation so that "in any future development of the law of the unilateral acts as a source of obligation, it may however be expected that some of the characteristics stated in *Nuclear Tests* will be tempered and modified" (*op. cit.*, *B.Y.I.L.*, 1989, p. 17).

2 See the case concerning *Military and Paramilitary Activities in and against Nicaragua*, (I.C.J., *Reports 1984*, p. 418).

the drafting employed in the declaration in question clearly reveals the intention of its author[3].

But, despite its parallelism, they are different declarations because those concerning the acceptance of the jurisdiction of the I.C.J., "even though they are unilateral acts, establish a series of bilateral engagements with other States accepting the same obligation of compulsory jurisdiction, in which the conditions, reservations and time-limit clauses are taken into consideration"[4]. This is why, although there is freedom to make it, it does not signify that the State making the declaration is free to amend the scope and contents of the commitments it has acquired[5].

With respect to the form, the only formality required is the deposit of acceptance with the Secretary-General of the United Nations under paragraph 4 of Article 36 of the Statute[6].

A recent example of the bilateral links deriving from declarations of acceptance of the compulsory jurisdiction of the Court is, from the point of view of Spain, the case concerning *Fisheries Jurisdiction* (Spain/Canada). The declarations of acceptance of both States contain exceptions concerning the types of disputes the Court is competent for. So, previous to the discussion concerning the merits of the case, Canada had invoked the non jurisdiction of the Court because it considered that the dispute was one of those covered by the exceptions contained in its declaration

---

3 See the cases concerning the *Temple of Preah Vihear* (I.C.J., *Reports 1961*, p. 32) and *Military and Paramilitary Activities in and against Nicaragua* (I.C.J., *Reports 1984*, p. 418. It can be deduced, consequently, that in the case of verbal statements that intention shall be derived from the terms employed in the declaration. See Chapter V of this work.

4 The principle of good faith plays "an essential role" (the case concerning *Military and Paramilitary Activities in and against Nicaragua*, I.C.J., *Reports 1984*, p. 418).

5 See the cases of the *Temple of Preah Vihear* (I.C.J., *Reports 1961*, p. 32) and *Military and Paramilitary Activities in and agianst Nicaragua* (I.C.J., *Reports 1984*, p. 418). In this latter case the I.C.J. states that: "Although the United States retained the right to modify the contents of the 1946 Declaration or to terminate it, a power which is inherent in any unilateral act of a State, it has, nevertheless assumed an inescapable obligation towards other States accepting the Optional Clause, by stating formally and solemnly that any such change should take effect only after six months have elapsed as from the date of notice" (*ibid.*, p. 419).

6 See *ibid.*, pages 31-32. About this question the I.C.J. stated that: "The precise form and language in which they do this is left to them, and there is no suggestion that any particular form is required, or that any declarations not in such form will be invalid", although "custom and tradition have brought it about that a certain pattern of terminology is normally, as a matter of fact and convenience, employed by countries accepting the compulsory jurisdiction of the Court; but there is nothing mandatory about the employment of this language" (*ibid.*, p. 32). See also the case concerning *Military and Paramilitary Activities in and against Nicaragua* (I.C.J., *Reports 1984*, p. 412).

of acceptance of the jurisdiction of the Court. In order to answer this question, the Court analysed Canada's declaration[7].

[7] See the Declaration of Canadá in I.C.J., *Yearbook 1993-1994*, No. 48, pages 91-92. That of Spain in *B.O.E.*, No. 275, of 16 November 1990. See also I.C.J., *Reports 1995*, pages 87-88.

The reasoning of Canada is based on paragraph 2 of its declaration of acceptance of the jurisdiction of the Court, according to which the Court has a compulsory jurisdiction "over all disputes … other than … disputes arising out of or concerning conservation and management measures taken by Canada with respect to vessels fishing in the NAFO Regulatory Area … and the enforcement of such measures" (I.C.J., *Yearbook 1993-1994*, No. 48, p. 91). See also pp. 259-261 of the present work.

CHAPTER XII:

Procedural Instruments, Facts Alleged and Exercise of the Jurisdiction Attributed to the I.C.J.

1 Access to the Court in the light of Article 35, paragraph 2, of the Statute of the I.C.J.

This question is addressed by the Court in the case concerning *Legality of Use of Force* (*Serbia and Montenegro v. Belgium*)[1] in order to determine whether the Court was open to Serbia and Montenegro through this provision.

According to paragraph 2 of Article 35 of the Statute of the Court:

> "The conditions under which the Court shall be open to other States [i.e. States not parties to the Statute] shall, subject to the special provisions contained in treaties in force, be laid down by the Security Council, but in no case shall such conditions place the parties in a position of inequality before the Court."

Before beginning the interpretation of this Article, the Court advances that it will proceed in accordance with customary international law, as "reflected in Article 31 of the 1969 Vienna Convention on the Law of Treaties. According to paragraph 1 of Article 31, a treaty must be interpreted in good faith in accordance with the ordinary meaning to be given to its terms in their context and in the light of the treaty's object and purpose. Interpretation must be based above all upon the text of the treaty. As a supplementary measure recourse may be had to means of interpretation such as the preparatory work of the treaty and the circumstances of its conclusion"[2].

It first analyses the meaning of the expression "the special provisions contained in treaties in force", present in Article 35, paragraph 2, in the context of the question of access to the Court. It divides its analysis into two parts. The first concerns the words "*special provisions*". The second, the words "*treaties in force*". But the interpretation of both is carried out by taking the words in their "natural and ordinary meaning"[3].

---

1 I.C.J., *Reports 2004*.

2 *Ibid.*, para. 100.

3 *Ibid.*, para. 101.

It is of the Court that taking the natural and ordinary meaning of the words "*special provisions*", in the view of the Court the reference must be to treaties which make "special provision" in relation to the Court, "and this can hardly be anything other than provision for the settlement of disputes between the parties to the treaty by reference of the matter to the Court"[4]. As for the words "*treaties in force*" it states that, in their natural and ordinary meaning, they do not indicate at what date the treaties considered are to be in force, and thus, they may lend themselves to different interpretations. And adds:

> "One can construe those words as referring to treaties which were in force at the time that the Statute itself came into force, as was contended by certain Respondents; or to those which were in force on the date of the institution of proceedings in a case in which such treaties are invoked. In favour of this latter interpretation, it may be observed that the similar expression "treaties and conventions in force" is found in Article 36, paragraph 1, of the Statute, and the Court has interpreted it in this sense (for example, *Questions of Interpretation and Application of the 1971 Montreal Convention arising from the Aerial Incident at Lockerbie, (Libyan Arab Jamahiriya* v. *United Kingdom), Preliminary Objections, Judgment,* I.C.J., *Reports 1998*, p. 16, para. 19). The expression "treaty or convention in force" in Article 37 of the Statute has also been read as meaning in force at the date proceedings were instituted (*Barcelona Traction, Light and Power Company, Limited, Preliminary Objections, Judgment,* I.C.J., *Reports 1964*, p. 27)"[5].

After taking the words in their natural and ordinary meaning, the Court makes reference to the *object and purpose* of Article 35 of the Statute. It is the opinion of the Court that the object and purpose of that provision is to define the conditions of access to the Court:

> "While paragraph 1 of that Article opens it to the States parties to the Statute, paragraph 2 is intended to regulate access to the Court by States which are not parties to the Statute. The conditions of access of such States are, "subject to the special provisions contained in treaties in force", to be determined by the Security Council, with the proviso that in no case shall such conditions place the parties in a position of inequality before the Court. The Court considers that it was natural to reserve the position in relation to any relevant treaty provisions that might then exist; moreover, it would have been inconsistent with the main thrust of the text to make it possible in the future for States to obtain access to the Court simply by the conclusion between themselves of a special treaty, multilateral or bilateral, containing a provision to that effect"[6].

4 *Ibid.*

5 *Ibid.*

6 *Ibid.*, para. 102.

In the opinion of the Court, the first interpretation holds that Article 35, paragraph 2, refers to treaties in force at the time that the Statute came into force is, in fact, reinforced by an examination of the *travaux préparatoires* of the text. In order to prove this, the Court analyses the Statute of the Permanent Court of International Justice which contained substantially the same provision; a provision which was used as a model when the Statute of the I.C.J. was drafted. That is why the Court considers it necessary to examine the history of the drafting of both Statutes.

The first step in this history of drafting was the text proposed by the 1920 Committee of Jurists (as Article 32 of its draft), according to which:

> "The Court shall be open of right to the States mentioned in the Annex to the Covenant, and to such others as shall subsequently enter the League of Nations.
>
> Other States may have access to it.
>
> The conditions under which the Court shall be open of right or accessible to States which are not Members of the League of Nations shall be determined by the Council, in accordance with Article 17 of the Covenant." (League of Nations, Permanent Court of International Justice, *Documents concerning the action taken by the Council of the League of Nations under Article 14 of the Covenant and the adoption by the Assembly of the Statute of the Permanent Court*, p. 78.)"[7]

The second step was the consideration of this text by the Sub-Committee of the Third-Committee of the First Assembly Meeting of the League of Nations, where it was pointed out "that under the Treaties of Peace the Central Powers would often be Parties before the Court" and that "[t]he text of the draft does not take sufficient account of this fact" and it was proposed to suppress the first two paragraphs of the Article.

At this point the question was raised regarding "whether the Council might place conditions on the admission of Germany before the Court, for example in the case mentioned in Article 380 of the Treaty of Versailles" to which a negative response was given. Then the Chairman proposed to entrust a small committee with the task of drafting a new formula for Article 32 which "should act upon the three following principles, upon which the Sub-Committee was agreed:

> "1. The Council shall have the power to determine conditions for the admission of States which are not Members of the League of Nations before the Court.
>
> 2. The rights of the Parties before the Court are equal.
>
> 3. Account shall be taken of *Parties who may present themselves before the Court by virtue of the Treaties of Peace*."[8]

---

[7] *Ibid.*, para. 103.

[8] Cf. *ibid.*, para. 104.

According to this task the Sub-Committee received a proposal for a new text of Article 32from the three delegates entrusted with this. This text was as follows:

> "1st paragraph: No change.
> The conditions under which the Court shall be open to other States shall, subject to special provisions contained in treaties in force, be laid down by the Council.
> When a State which is not a Member of the League of Nations is a party to a dispute, the Court will fix the amount which that party shall contribute towards the expenses of the Court."

The Court notes that "it is here, that for the first time in the legislative history of what later became Article 35, paragraph 2, the phrase "subject to the special provisions contained in treaties in force" appeared. It may safely be assumed that this phrase was inserted into the text as a response to principle 3 referred to above"[9].

The third step was the presentation of the text to the Sub-Committee. Here, "the Chairman recalled the proposal made at the previous meeting, to add to Article 32 a provision stating that, as far as party rights are concerned, all States are equal before the Court. In order to meet this objection of the Chairman and of the author of that proposal, one of the three co-authors of the proposed text of Article 32 suggested making the following addition to the second paragraph of Article 32: "The conditions under which the Court shall be open to other States shall, subject to the special provisions contained in treaties in force, be laid down by the Council, but in no case shall such provision place the parties in a position of inequality before the Court" (*ibid.*, p. 144). The second paragraph thus amended was adopted without any further discussion"[10].

Finally, in the report presented to the Assembly by the Third Committee, it was stated that:

> "The wording of this Article [i.e. the original draft Article 32] seemed lacking in clearness, and the Sub-Committee has re-cast it in an effort to express clearly [that]
> ...
> The access of other States to the Court will depend either on the special provisions of the Treaties in force (for example the provisions of the Treaty of Peace concerning the right of minorities, labour, etc.) or else on a resolution of the Council (*ibid.* p. 210.)"[11].

Once the history of the drafting of Article 32 of the Statute of the Permanent Court of International Justice was examined, the I.C.J. made reference to cases coming before it concerning the issue. This took place on two occasions. The first, in the

[9] *Ibid.*, para. 105.

[10] *Ibid.*, para. 107.

[11] *Ibid.*, para. 108.

S.S. "Wimbledon" case[12]. The second, in the case concerning *Certain German Interests in Polish Upper Silesia*[13].

In the *S.S. "Wimbledon"* case the jurisdiction of the Court was founded on Article 386 of the Treaty of Versailles of 28 June 1919. When the proceedings were brought in that case against Germany, that State was not a Member of the League of Nations nor was it mentioned in the Annex to the Covenant. A declaration by Germany accepting the jurisdiction of the Court was not considered as necessary, in the light of the reservation contained in Article 35, paragraph 2, of the Statute which was intended, as shown above, to cover special provisions in the Peace Treaties.

In the case concerning *Certain German Interests in Polish Upper Silesia*, the proceedings were instituted by Germany, before its admission to the League of Nations, against Poland on the basis of Article 23 of the Convention relating to Upper Silesia of 15 May 1922 and brought into force on 3 June 1922. The Court noted that Poland "[did] not dispute the fact that the suit has been duly submitted to the Court in accordance with Articles 35 and 40 of the Statute"[14]. Before rendering its judgment, the Permanent Court of International Justice considered the issue and

> "was of the opinion that the relevant instruments when correctly interpreted (more especially in the light of a report made by M. Hagerup at the First Assembly of the League of Nations) authorized it in accepting the German Government's application without requiring the special declaration provided for in the Council Resolution"[15].

Nevertheless, the I.C.J. notes that "when the Court was discussing amendments of its Rules of Court a year later, two judges expressed the view that the exception in Article 35 "could only be intended to cover situations provided for by the treaties of peace"[16]. One of them explained that, in the case concerning *Certain German Interests in Polish Upper Silesia*,

> "the question then related to a treaty – the Upper Silesian Convention – drawn up under the auspices of the League of Nations which was to be considered as supplementary to the Treaty of Versailles. It was therefore possible to include the case in regard to which the Court had then to decide in the general expression 'subject to treaties in force', whilst construing that expression as referring to the peace treaties ..." (*ibid.*, p. 105.)".

---

[12] Cf. P.C.I.J., *1923, Series A*, No. 1, p. 6.

[13] Cf. P.C.I.J., *1925, Series A*, No. 6.

[14] P.C.I.J., *1925, Series A*, No. 6, p. 11.

[15] *P.C.I.J.*, Annual Report of the Permanent Court of International Justice (1 January 1922-15 June 1925), *Series E*, No. 1, p. 261.

[16] P.C.I.J., *Acts and Documents (1926), Series D, No. 2, Add.*, p. 106.

And concludes that no other interpretation of the phrase at issue was advanced by any Member of the Court when in 1926 it discussed the amendment of its Rules.

When the Charter of the United Nations and the Statute of the Court were under preparation, the issue was first discussed by the United Nations Committee of Jurists. The I.C.J. recalls that, in the debate, "some confusion apparently arose regarding the difference between a non-Member State which may become party to the Statute and one which may become party to a case before the Court. Some delegates did not make a clear distinction between adherence to the Statute and access to the Court. The debate mostly concentrated on the respective roles of the General Assembly and the Security Council in that context: there was some criticism that the Assembly was excluded from action under paragraph 2 of Article 35 (*Documents of the United Nations Conference on International Organization*, Vol. XIV, pp. 141-145)"[17].

It also recalls that a proposal was made to adopt paragraph 2 as it stood, but some delegates continued to argue for a role of the Assembly to be recognized in that paragraph. It was the case of the United Kingdom which suggested that there in paragraph 2, after the words "Security Council", the phrase "in accordance with any principles which may have been laid down by the General Assembly"[18] might be inserted.

A new proposal was then made to adopt the Article as contained in the draft. Thereupon the delegate of France observed that "it lay within the power of the Council to determine conditions in particular cases but the actual practice had not given cause for criticism". He then continued:

> "The Council could not restrict access to the Court when the Assembly permitted it, but the Council could be more liberal in particular cases. The decision of the Assembly was actually the more important, and the Council could not go against it. The Council furthermore would have to take into account any existing treaties, and it could not prevent access to the Court when a State had a treaty providing for compulsory jurisdiction"[19].

The report on the draft of the Statute of an International Court of Justice was submitted by the United Nations Committee of Jurists to the United Nations Conference on International Organization at San Francisco. In respect of Article 35 it noted that:

> "Aside from the purely formal changes necessitated by references to The United Nations Organization instead of to the Covenant of the League of Nations, Article 35 is amended only in that, in the English

---

[17] I.C.J., case concerning *Legality of Use of Force (Serbia and Montenegro v. Belgium), Reports 2004,* para. 110.

[18] *Ibid.*

[19] *Ibid.* The I.C.J. adds: "He then proposed that Article 35 be adopted as it stood; no further substantive discussion followed, and Article 35 was adopted".

> text of paragraph 2, the word 'conditions' is substituted for the word 'provisions' and in paragraph 3, the word 'case' is substituted for the word 'dispute' which will assure better agreement with the French text" (*ibid.*, p. 839).

However, since the draft Statute of the I.C.J. was based on the Statute of the Permanent Court of International Justice, the report did not state any change in respect of the scope of the applicability of Article 35, paragraph 2.

At the San Francisco Conference, the question examined here was not touched upon; the discussion of draft Article 35 focused mainly on a proposal by Egypt to insert a new paragraph 2 stating "[t]he conditions under which states not members may become parties to the Statute of the Court shall be determined in each case by the General Assembly upon recommendation of the Security Council" (*ibid.*, Vol. XIII, p. 484). In the debate in Committee IV/I of the Conference,

> "[i]t was pointed out that the question as to what states are to be parties to the Statute should be decided in the Charter, while the question as to what states may appear before the Court in the case, once the Court is established, should be determined by the Statute"[20].

After this analysis the I.C.J. considers that the legislative history of Article 35, paragraph 2, of the Statute of the Permanent Court demonstrates that it was intended as an exception to the principle stated in paragraph 1, in order to cover cases taken into account in agreements concluded in the aftermath of the First World War before the Statute entered into force. However, in the opinion of the Court

> "the *travaux préparatoires* of the Statute of the present Court are less illuminating. The discussion of Article 35 was provisional and somewhat cursory; it took place at a stage in the planning of the future international organization when it was not yet settled whether the Permanent Court would be preserved or replaced by a new court. Indeed, the records quoted in paragraphs 110 to 112 above do not include any discussion which would suggest that Article 35, paragraph 2, of the Statute should be given a different meaning from the corresponding provision in the Statute of the Permanent Court. It would rather seem that the text was reproduced from the Statute of the Permanent Court; there is no indication that any extension of access to the Court was intended"[21].

This is why, in the opinion of the I.C.J., Article 35, paragraph 2, of its Statute

> "must be interpreted, *mutatis mutandis*, in the same way as the equivalent text in the Statute of the Permanent Court, namely as

---

[20] The Egyptian proposal was not pursued but the essence of it was reflected in Article 93, paragraph 2, of the Charter (cf. *ibid.* para. 112).

[21] *Ibid.* para. 113.

> intended to refer to treaties in force at the date of the entry into force of the new Statute, and providing for the jurisdiction of the new Court. In fact, no such prior treaties, referring to the jurisdiction of the present Court, have been brought to the attention of the Court, and it may be that none existed. In the view of the Court, however, neither this circumstance, nor any consideration of the object and purpose of the text, nor the *travaux préparatoires*, offer support to the alternative interpretation that the provision was intended as granting access to the Court to States not parties to the Statute without any condition other than the existence of a treaty, containing a clause conferring jurisdiction on the Court, which might be concluded any time subsequently to the entry into force of the Statute. As noted above (paragraph 102), this interpretation would lead to a result quite incompatible with the object and purpose of Article 35, paragraph 2, namely the regulation of access to the Court by States non-parties to the Statute. In the view of the Court therefore, the reference in Article 35, paragraph 2, of the Statute to "the special provisions contained in treaties in force" applies only to treaties in force at the date of the entry into force of the Statute, and not to any treaties concluded since that date"[22].

The Court thus concludes that, even assuming that Serbia and Montenegro was a party to the Genocide Convention at the time, Article 35, paragraph 2, of the Statute does not provide it with a basis to have access to the Court under Article IX of that Convention as the Convention only came into force on 12 January 1951, after the entry into force of the Statute. This is why the I.C.J. does not consider it necessary to decide whether Serbia and Montenegro was or was not a party to the Genocide Convention on 29 April 1999 when the current proceedings were instituted[23].

2 The liberty of the I.C.J. to interpret the request and the conclusions of the Parties

On several occasions the Court has stated its competence to interpret the request, and provides that it is its duty to isolate the real issue in the case and to identify the object of the claim and recalls that it has never been contested that the Court is entitled to interpret the submissions of the parties as this is one of the attributes of its judicial functions. Acting in such a way, what the Court does is to reformulate the questions submitted to it by the Parties.

The most significant example of such conduct, in our opinion, is the case concerning *Nuclear Tests*, in which it also states that it is the Court that must ascertain

---

22 *Ibid.*

23 Cf. *ibid.* para. 114.

the true object and purpose of the claim and in doing so it cannot confine itself to the ordinary meaning of the words used, but must take a number of factors into account: the Application as a whole, the arguments of the Applicant before the Court, the diplomatic exchanges brought to the Court's attention as well as public statements made on behalf of the defending Government[24].

As is known, the consequence of this reasoning in this case is an interpretation of the I.C.J. of the declarations made by the representatives of the French Republic which led the Court to refrain from pronouncing on the petitions submitted by New Zealand and Australia. This is why, in the *Request for an Examination of the Situation in Accordance with Paragraph 63 of the Court's Judgement of 20 December 1974 in the Nuclear Tests*, the I.C.J. concluded that the basis of the Judgement delivered on 20 December 1974 was France's undertaking not to conduct any further atmospheric nuclear tests; "whereas it was only, therefore, in the event of a resumption of nuclear tests in the atmosphere that that basis of the Judgement would have been affected; and whereas that hypothesis has not materialized"[25].

Another example is the case concerning the *Land, Island and Maritime Frontier Dispute* in which the Chamber of the I.C.J. stated that, although Honduras, in its submissions, has not formally requested that its sovereignty over El Tigre be decided on by the Chamber, the Chamber "considers that it should, consistently with its interpretation of its task under the Special Agreement, define the legal situation of El Tigre"[26].

In 1998, in the case concerning *Fisheries Jurisdiction (Spain v. Canada)*, the I.C.J. went beyond its competence to interpret the request: it changed its object so that it might subsequently be able to reject its jurisdiction over the case.

In this case, in accordance with Article 40 of the Statute of the I.C.J. and Article 38.1 of its Rules, the object was clearly established by Spain to the effect that Canada had no right under International Law to act on the high seas against ships flying the flag of a foreign State, and more specifically, against ships flying the Spanish flag, as it did in March 1995. Also, that the actions of Canada, which occurred on the high seas outside Canada's Exclusive Economic Zone, violated fundamental principles of International Law relating, *inter alia*, to the freedom of the high seas, the sovereign rights of Spain, safety at sea, and the prohibition of the use of force; this last, a principle enshrined in the United Nations Charter. Canada contended that its actions fell within the ambit of its reservation to the

---

[24] See *Reports 1974*, p. 263. To support its reasoning the I.C.J. quotes jurisprudence of the P.I.C.J. as well as its own jurisprudence (see *ibid.*). Another example is given by the *Minquiers and Ecrehous* case in which, starting from the interpretation the Court made of the petitions of the Parties it concluded that these excluded the statute of *res nullius* as well as that of *condominium* (cf. I.C.J., *Reports 1953*, p. 52). Similarly, but more recently, see the case concerning the *Frontier Dispute* (I.C.J., *Reports 1986*, p. 573).

[25] I.C.J., *Reports 1995*, pages 305-306.

[26] The Chamber judged that sovereignty over the island belongs to Honduras (Cf. I.C.J., *Reports 1992*, p. 570).

compulsory jurisdiction of the Court and were thus not subject to scrutiny by it: the measures adopted by Canada would be conservation and management measures as well as the enforcement of such measures, even on the high seas[27].

In the opinion of Spain, in spite of Canada's reservation, the I.C.J. had jurisdiction. Canada alleged the contrary. Previously, in paragraph 30 of its judgement, the Court prepared the field in which it would play an active role – and not as a judicial body – because it would change the object of the dispute submitted to it by Spain in order to subsequently conclude its lack of jurisdiction. In fact, as one can see, the I.C.J. did not examine the applicant's submission. On the contrary, it substituted it with the application of Canada. In order to have grounds for its decision, the Court quoted its judgement in the *Nuclear Tests* case. Curiously a case in which the I.C.J. also reformulated the submissions of the Parties.

Continuing with its reasoning, the Court repeated what it usually employs to justify its line of argument, that

> "it is for the Court itself, while giving particular attention to the formulation of the dispute chosen by the Applicant, to determine on an objective basis the dispute dividing the parties, by examining the position of both Parties"[28].

This was in order to pronounce on the previous question concerning its jurisdiction[29].

Finally, in order to complete its work, it defined the subject of the dispute so that it could subsequently conclude that it had no jurisdiction:

> "The specific acts (…) which gave rise to the present dispute are the Canadian activities on the high seas in relation to the pursuit of the *Estai*, the means used to accomplish its arrest and the fact of its arrest, and the detention of the vessel and arrest of its master, arising from Canada's amended Coastal Fisheries Protection Act and implement-

---

[27] In accordance with the reservation of Canada, the jurisdiction of the Court is relieved of

> "disputes arising out of or concerning conservation and management measures taken by Canada with respect to vessels fishing in the NAFO Regulatory Area, as defined in the Convention on Future Multilateral Co-operation in the Northwest Atlantic Fisheries, 1978, and the enforcement of such measures".

[28] I.C.J., *Reports 1998*, paragraph 30. See also paragraphs 30 and 31 where it states that the Court will not confine itself to the formulation by the Applicant when determining the subject of the dispute and that the Court will itself determine the real dispute that has been submitted to it. This is stated quoting its case law.

[29] In paragraph 33:

> "In order to decide on the preliminary issue of jurisdiction which arises in the present case, the Court will ascertain the dispute between Spain and Canada, taking account of Spain's Application, as well as the various written and oral pleadings placed before the Court by the Parties".

> ing regulations. The essence of the dispute between the Parties is whether these acts violated Spain's rights under international law and require reparation. The Court must now decide whether the Parties have conferred upon it jurisdiction in respect of that dispute"[30].

The last thing it should have done was to position itself on the field on which it wanted to play, that is to say on whether or not it had jurisdiction, which implies the analysis of Canada's reservation, in such a way that it would be able to conclude that it did not have jurisdiction. This underlies its judgement concerning the case in question. The consequences are obvious: acceptance of several breaches of International Law by Canada; acceptance of the exercise of Canada's jurisdiction on the high seas; acceptance of Canada's use of force; no analysis of the way in which Canada's reservation was made and whether or not it was in accordance with International Law[31]; no analysis of the subject of the dispute submitted by Spain (the applicant!).

In our opinion, the judgement of the I.C.J. in the case concerning *Fisheries Jurisdiction (Spain v. Canada)* is, like that of the *Nuclear Tests,* a good example to prove the way in which the Court sometimes acts: unconnected with the interpretation and application of International Law. Moreover, it shows how it sometimes uses the liberty it has due to the fact that the Parties involved in a dispute accept its compulsory jurisdiction.

The same attitude with regard to the interpretation of requests appears when *advisory opinions* appear. Thus, in the case concerning the *Interpretation of the Agreement of 25 March 1951 between the WHO and Egypt*, in which it considers this to be inherent to its judicial function. In its own words: "The Court points out that, if it is to remain faithful to the requirements of its judicial character in the exercise of its advisory jurisdiction, it must ascertain what the legal questions really at issue in questions formulated in a request are "[32].

To provide grounds for its reasoning, the I.C.J. uses the case law of the P.C.I.J. which, in reply to a request for an advisory opinion, likewise found it necessary in some cases first to ascertain "what the legal questions really at issue in the questions raised in the request were"[33].

In short, the examples we have quoted show the power the Court has and exercises in order to interpret the requests and submissions of the Parties in specific disputes. It is one of the attributes of its judicial function and another sign of the liberty it has as a consequence of the acceptance of its jurisdiction or of a request

---

30 *Ibid.*, paragraph 35.

31 As Judge VERESHCHETIN states, the Court, in fact, gives effect to a reservation which expressly exempts from its jurisdiction the examination of conducts manifestly inconsistent with different norms of International Law (cf. paragraph 11 of his Dissenting Opinion).

32 I.C.J., *Reports 1980*, p. 88.

33 *Ibid.*, p. 89. The cases of the P.I.C.J. quoted by the I.C.J. are: *Jaworzina* (P.C.I.J., *Series B* No. 8, p. 282); *Interpretation of the Greco-Turkish Agreement of 1 December 1926* (P.C.I.J., *Series B* No. 16, pages 5-16).

for an advisory opinion. Although the latter have no compulsory character, they do have substantial importance because they make up part of the Court's case law and are subsequently repeated and developed by the Court, and now contribute to making International Law "a much more elaborated, developed and complete system of law than many people realize"[34].

But liberty to interpret the request and the conclusions of the Parties does not mean the power to change the submissions made by the Parties or the object of the dispute as defined by them. Nevertheless, in practice, this is the real problem. Effectively, what are the limits within which the I.C.J. shall act? Is it omnipotent? In other words, as we will see later, the problem is the discretion the Court has not only to interpret the applications and the conclusions of the Parties, but also to decide the exercise of the jurisdiction attributed to it by the Parties who have previously accepted this.

3 Appraisal of the facts alleged and their proof

From the analysis of the case law of the I.C.J. it can be seen that the appraisal of the facts alleged by the Parties and their proof is inherent to the autonomy of its judicial function. The most relevant example is, once again that of the *Nuclear Tests*, in which that autonomy appears in the fact that "it is especially incumbent upon the Court to satisfy itself that it is in possession of all the available facts" as well as "to form its own view of the meaning and scope intended by the author of a unilateral declaration which may create a legal obligation"[35]. Consequently, it is the Court itself which specifies the facts the Parties present to it, appraises these facts and decides the meaning and scope intended by the author of the unilateral declaration. Thus, on the occasion of the interpretation of the unilateral declaration in the *Nuclear Tests* case, the intervention of the Court led to the substitution of the intention supported by the French Republic with the conclusion of the Court itself (which did not coincide with the intention of France).

This reasoning which, as we have seen above, makes it possible for the Court to refrain from pronouncing on the specific petitions of the Applicants in the *Nuclear Tests* case and also demonstrates the extent of the margin of its appraisal once a dispute has been submitted to it. This has been criticized by its own judges in their dissenting opinions. Thus, in the aforementioned case, some of them remind the Court that although it has the power to interpret the submissions of the Parties, it is not authorized to reformulate these[36]. This criticism becomes more acute when

[34] JENNINGS, R., "The role and functioning of the Court", I.C.J., *Yearbook 1991-1992*, No. 46, The Hague, 1992, p. 209.

[35] I.C.J., *Reports 1974*, pages 262 and 269.

[36] "If, however, the Court lacks the power to reformulate inadequate submissions, *a fortiori* it cannot reformulate submissions as clear and specific as those in this case" (*ibid.*, p. 316). It is the dissident opinion common to judges ONYEAMA, DILLARD, JIMENEZ DE ARECHAGA and WALDOCK.

they state that, in their opinion, in the interpretation made by the Court, it has not interpreted the text, the submissions of Australia and New Zealand, but has revised and eliminated the text in order to conclude what the Applicant had stated was "the main prayer in the Application", that is to say, the request for a declaration of the illegality of atmospheric nuclear tests in the South Pacific Ocean. In their opinion, "a radical alteration or mutilation of an applicant's submission under the guise of interpretation has serious consequences because it constitutes a frustration of a party's legitimate expectations that the case which it has put before the Court will be examined and decided"[37].

This case law criteria is also stated by the Court with regard to advisory opinions. This is involved in the case concerning *Certain Expenses of the United Nations* in which it states that it must have full liberty to consider all relevant data available to it "in forming an opinion on a question put to it for an advisory opinion"[38].

4 Has the I.C.J. discretional powers to decide the exercise of the jurisdiction attributed to it?

At the material level, *ratione materiae*, the jurisdiction of the I.C.J. is unlimited insofar as it can know of any question of International Law[39]. Article 36 of the Statute of the Court retains this conception which is present in the various cases where the consent of the State at the time its jurisdiction is accepted arises. Consequently, it is in the framework of the consent of the parties with regard to the acceptance of the jurisdiction of the Court that the Court exercises its judicial function[40]. This is why, on occasions, before the grounds for the case are known, the Court must analyse and interpret the declarations of acceptance of its jurisdiction made by the Parties in the specific case, in order to establish its jurisdiction; jurisdiction which is sometimes also initially disputed by the Parties.

---

[37] *Ibid.*, p. 317. And they add

> "In this instance the serious consequences have an irrevocable character because the Applicant is now prevented from resubmitting its Application and seizing the Court again by reason of France's denunciation of the instruments on which it is sought to base the Court's jurisdiction in the present dispute" (*ibid.*).

[38] I.C.J., *Reports 1962*, p. 157.

[39] On this question see the report of the I.C.J.' President at the 44th meeting of the forty-sixth session of the General Assembly, held on 8 November 1991 (I.C.J., *Yearbook 1991-1992*, No. 46, The Hague 1992, pages 205-212).

[40] The Court stated that neither its Statute nor its Rules require that this consent shall be expressed in a certain form. Consequently, the Court cannot hold it to be irregular "a proceeding which is not precluded by any provision in these texts" (*The Corfu Channel Case*, I.C.J., *Reports 1947-48*, p. 28. Cf. also p. 26). In this case, the proceeding was the letter of the Minister of Foreign Affairs of Albania of 2 July 1947.

The Court has addressed this question since its earliest cases. Thus, in the *Nottebohm Case*, in which it states that paragraph 6 of Article 36 of its Statute merely adopts a rule consistently accepted by general international law in the matter of international arbitration. In fact, since the *Alabama Case*, following the earlier precedents and in the absence of any agreement to the contrary, it has been generally recognized that an international tribunal "has the right to decide as to its own jurisdiction and has the power to interpret for this purpose the instruments which govern that jurisdiction"[41]. Moreover, this principle, which is accepted by general International Law in the matter of arbitration, assumes particular force when the international tribunal "is no longer an arbitral tribunal constituted by virtue of special agreement between the parties for the purpose of adjudicating on a particular dispute, but is an institution which has been pre-established by an international instrument defining its jurisdiction and regulating its operation and – that is –, in the present case, the principal judicial organ of the United Nations"[42].

The fact that it is the Court that decides on its jurisdiction in the specific case leads to the fact that, in this area, the same problems arise which we have already examined with regard to its duty concerning interpretation and the way in which it exercises the liberty it has to interpret the application and the conclusions of the Parties. Now, this is the way in which the Court exercises the jurisdiction concerning its own jurisdiction. At present, in order to decide, the Court has the liberty inherent to the acceptance of its jurisdiction by the Parties. It is the Court which appraises and decides, while being aware that its decision on this previous question will be imposed upon the Parties and will subsequently allow it to know the grounds of the case (except if it declares that it does not have jurisdiction).

An example of this is given by one of its first cases, the *Corfu Channel* Case, on which the Court will base its jurisdiction regarding the interpretation of the letter of the Minister of Foreign Affairs of Albania of 2 July 1947, considering that this letter constitutes "a voluntary acceptance of its jurisdiction"[43].Along the same lines, in 1986, we have the example of the case concerning *Military and Paramilitary Activities in and against Nicaragua* in which the Court rejects the reasoning of the United States based on its reservation concerning the acceptance of the jurisdiction of the Court. In this case, the Court had an interest in exercising its jurisdiction. This is why it grounds this on its intention to know the dispute and to resolve it by the application of customary International Law. It did so and built up a very interesting theory concerning the relations between conventional and customary International Law.

---

41 I.C.J., *Reports 1953*, p. 119. Cf. also the case law of the I.C.J. in the following cases: *Reparation for Injuries Suffered in the Service of the United Nations* (I.C.J., *Reports 1949*, p. 178); *Anglo-Iranian Oil Company* (I.C.J., *Reports 1952*, pages 102-103); and *Monetary Gold Removed from Rome* (I.C.J., *Reports 1954*, p. 32).

42 *Ibid.*

43 I.C.J., *Reports 1947-48*, p. 26. Afterwards, it states that it is for the Court "to decide, with binding force as between the parties, what the interpretation of the letter of July 2nd, 1947 is" (*ibid.*, p. 28).

An example of the contrary is the *Lockerbie* case, already examined in several parts of this work, in which the Court initially declared its jurisdiction to subsequently state that it had no jurisdiction to adopt the provisional measures requested by Libya. This was done through an interpretation which is doubtfully in accord with International Law. We do not agree with this.

But, the best example to show the problems related to the discretional powers the I.C.J. has to decide the exercise of jurisdiction attributed to it is given by its judgement in the case concerning *Fisheries Jurisdiction (Spain v. Canada)*. Here, it concludes its lack of jurisdiction after having substituted the applicant's submission by that of the defendant in order to be able to give effect to Canada's reservation to its jurisdiction. This does not take into account the way in which this reservation was conceived and made to substitute Canada's preceding reservation and does not contrast it with International Law. In the case concerning *Fisheries Jurisdiction* we can conclude that the discretional powers of the I.C.J. have been used in a way which is not in accord with International Law.

These examples show the importance of the action of the I.C.J. and the problems that can arise. It is the Court which appraises, interprets and decides based on the consent to its jurisdiction given by the Parties concerned and the liberty it has can lead to several results such as those quoted in the present section. In a way, we are faced with the same problem already examined with respect to certain resolutions of the Security Council: that of the discretion it has in the exercise of its own competences.

5 Value and legal effects of an order stating provisional measures

The question of the binding character of orders indicating provisional measures was dealt with by the I.C.J. in the *LaGrand case*. It was the first time. Previously, it had been "extensively discussed in the literature"[44].

In the *LaGrand case* the question concerns the existence of an international legal obligation to comply with the Order on Provisional Measures issued by the Court on 3 March 1999 according to which the United States of America "should take all measures at its disposal to ensure that Walter LaGrand is not executed pending the final decision in these proceedings, and should inform the Court of all the measures which it has taken in implementation of this Order".

It is the opinion of the Court that the dispute concerns the interpretation of Article 41, "which is worded in identical terms in the Statute of each Court (apart from the respective references to the Council of the League of Nations and the Security Council). This interpretation has been the subject of extensive controversy in the literature. The Court will therefore now proceed to the interpretation

[44] *I.C.J.*, p. 33, para. 116.

of Article 41 of the Statute. It will do so in accordance with customary international law, reflected in Article 31 of the 1969 Vienna Convention on the Law of Treaties. According to paragraph 1 of Article 31, a treaty must be interpreted in good faith in accordance with the ordinary meaning to be given to its terms in their context and in the light of the treaty's object and purpose"[45].

In its analysis the Court concludes that both texts (the French and the English) are not in total harmony. According to the French text, Article 41 reads as follows:

> "1. La Cour a le pouvoir *d'indiquer*, si elle estime que les circonstances l'exigent, quelles mesures conservatoires due droit de chacun *doivent* être prises à titre provisoire.
>
> 2. En attendant l'arrêt définitif, *l'indication* de ces mesures est immédiatement notifiée aux parties et au Conseil de Sécurité."[46]

The Court observes that in this text, "the terms 'indiquer' and 'l'indication' may be deemed to be neutral as to the mandatory character of the measure concerned; by contrast the words "doivent être prises" have an imperative character"[47].

For its part, the English version of Article 41 reads as follows:

> "1. The Court shall have the power to *indicate*, if it considers that circumstances so require, any provisional measures which *ought* to be taken to preserve the respective rights of either party.
>
> 2. Pending the final decision, notice of the measures *suggested* shall forthwith be given to the parties and to the Security Council"[48].

Concerning the English version of Article 41, the interpretation of this article made by the United States concluded the lack of mandatory effect[49].

The Court finds that both texts are not in total harmony and it makes reference to the relationship existing between the Charter of the United Nations and the Statute of the Court. So, it notes ("first of all") that "according to Article 92 of the Charter, the Statute forms an integral part of the present Charter" and that "under Article 111 of the Charter, the French and English texts of the latter are "equally authentic" and that "the same is equally true of the Statute"[50].

---

[45] *Ibid.*, p. 27, para. 99.

[46] *Ibid.*, p. 28, para. 100. Emphasis added by the Court.

[47] *Ibid.*

[48] *Ibid.* Emphasis also added by the Court.

[49] According to the United States, "the use in the English version of "indicate" instead of "order", of "ought" instead of "must" or "shall", and of "suggested" instead of "ordered", is to be understood as implying that decisions under Article 41 lack mandatory effect". Nevertheless the Court added that, having regard to the fact that in 1920 the French text was the original version, "such terms as "indicate" and "ought" have a meaning equivalent to "order" and "must" or "shall"" (*ibid.*).

[50] *Ibid.*, p. 28, para. 101.

After taking into account the fact that neither the Statute nor the Charter states how to proceed in cases of divergence between the equally authentic versions of the Statute (and due to the absence of agreement between the parties in this respect), the Court considers it appropriate to refer to paragraph 4 of Article 33 of the Vienna Convention on the Law of Treaties, "which in the view of the Court again reflects customary international law"[51].

In its task of interpretation of Article 41 the Court first makes use of the *object and purpose* of the Statute *together with the context* of Article 41. Concerning the *object and purpose*, the I.C.J. states:

> "The object and purpose of the Statute is to enable the Court to fulfil the functions provided for therein, and in particular, the basic function of judicial settlement of international disputes by binding decisions in accordance with Article 59 of the Statute"[52].

Regarding the *context*, it manifests:

> "The context in which Article 41 has to be seen within the Statute is to prevent the Court from being hampered in the exercise of its functions because the respective rights of the parties to a dispute before the Court are not preserved".

Finally, it concludes:

> "It follows from the object and purpose of the Statute, as well as from the terms of Article 41 when read in their context, that the power to indicate provisional measures entails that such measures should be binding, inasmuch as the power in question is based on the necessity, when the circumstances call for it, to safeguard, and to avoid prejudice to, the rights of the parties as determined by the final judgment of the Court. The contention that provisional measures indicated under Article 41 might not be binding would be contrary to the object and purpose of that Article"[53].

After concluding the binding character of orders made under Article 41 (a question that was clear to public international law scholars) the I.C.J. develops its statement. It makes reference to the existing principle according to which the parties to a case must abstain from any measure capable of exercising a prejudicial effect in regard to the execution of the decision to be given, and, in general, not

[51] *Ibid.* This provision reads:

> "when a comparison of the authentic texts discloses a difference of meaning which the application of Articles 31 and 32 does not remove the meaning which best reconciles the texts, having regard to the object and purpose of the treaty, shall be adopted".

[52] *Ibid.*, para. 102.

[53] *Ibid.*

allow any step of any kind to be taken which might aggravate or extend the dispute. This principle was recognized by the Permanent Court of International Justice in the *case of the Electricity Company of Sofia and Bulgaria, Order of 5 December 1939*[54] and was also confirmed by the I.C.J. in several cases where it ordered such kinds of measures to be implemented[55].

Due to the conclusions reached in interpreting the text of Article 41 of the Statute in the light of its object and purpose, the Court considers that it is not necessary to resort to the *preparatory work* of the Statute in order to determine the meaning of Article 41. It is the opinion of the Court that the preparatory work of the Statute does not preclude the conclusion that orders under Article 41 have binding force. However, it analyses the initial preliminary draft of the Statute of the Permanent Court of International Justice as prepared by the Committee of Jurists established by the Council of the League of Nations and concludes that it made no mention of provisional measures. It also notes that a provision to that effect was inserted only at a later stage in the draft prepared by the Committee, following a proposal from the Brazilian jurist Raul Fernandes. After a brief study of these works[56] the Court concludes that:

> "The preparatory work of Article 41 shows that the preference given in the French text to "*indiquer*" over "*ordonner*" was motivated by the consideration that the Court did not have the means to assure the execution of its decisions. However, the lack of means of execution and the lack of binding force are two different matters. Hence, the fact that the Court does not itself have the means to ensure the execution of orders made pursuant to Article 41 is not an argument against the binding nature of such orders"[57].

---

[54] *P.C.I.J, Series A/B, No. 79*, p. 199.

[55] The Court quotes the followings: *Nuclear Tests (Australia* v. *France), Interim Protection, Order of 22 June 1973,* I.C.J., *Reports 1973*, p. 106; *Nuclear Tests (New Zealand* v. *France), Interim Protection, Order of 22 June 1973,* I.C.J., *Reports 1973*, p. 142; *Frontier Dispute, Provisional Measures, Order of 10 January 1986,* I.C.J., *Reports 1986*, p. 9, para. 18, and p. 11, para. 32, point 1 A; *Application of the Convention on the Prevention and Punishment of the Crime of Genocide, Provisional Measures, Order of 8 April 1993,* I.C.J., *Reports 1993*, p. 23, para. 48, and p. 24, para. 52 B; *Application of the Convention on the Prevention and Punishment of the Crime of Genocide, Provisional Measures, Order of 13 September 1993,* I.C.J., *Reports 1993*, p. 349, para. 57, and p. 350, para. 61 (3); *Land and Maritime Boundary between Cameroon and Nigeria, Provisional Measures, Order of 15 March 1996,* I.C.J., *Reports 1996 (I)*, pp. 22-23, para. 41, and p. 24, para. 49 (1), (*ibid.*, p. 29, para. 103).

[56] What includes the proposal of Fernandes as well as the works of the Drafting Committee, the Committee of Jurists and the Sub-Committee of the Third Committee of the first Assembly of the League of Nations (cf. *ibid.*, pp. 29-30, para. 105-106).

[57] *Ibid.*, p. 30, para. 107.

The Court finally considers Article 94 of the United Nations Charter in order to determine whether it precludes attributing binding effect to orders stating provisional measures. This Article reads as follows:

> "1. Each Member of the United Nations undertakes to comply with the decision of the International Court of Justice in any case to which it is a party.
>
> 2. If any party to a case fails to perform the obligations incumbent upon it under a judgment rendered by the Court, the other party may have recourse to the Security Council, which may, if it deems necessary, make recommendations or decide upon measures to be taken to give effect to the judgment."

In the opinion of the I.C.J. the question arises as to the meaning to be attributed to the words "the decision of the International Court of Justice" in paragraph 1 of this Article:

> "This wording could be understood as referring not merely to the Court's judgments but to any decision rendered by it, thus including orders indicating provisional measures. It could also be interpreted to mean only judgments rendered by the Court as provided in paragraph 2 of Article 94. In this regard, the fact that in Articles 56 to 60 of the Court's Statute, both the word "decision" and the word "judgment" are used does little to clarify the matter"[58].

It is the opinion of the Court that "under the first interpretation of paragraph 1 of Article 94, the text of the paragraph would confirm the binding nature of provisional measures; whereas the second interpretation would in no way preclude their being accorded binding force under Article 41 of the Statute. The Court accordingly concludes that Article 94 of the Charter does not prevent orders made under Article 41 from having a binding character"[59].

Finally, it underlines its conclusion concerning the binding character of orders on provisional measures by referring to the rules of interpretation it had used before and states:

> "In short, it is clear that none of the sources of interpretation referred to in the relevant Articles of the Vienna Convention on the Law of Treaties, including the preparatory works, contradict the conclusions drawn from the terms of Article 41 read in their context and in the light of the object and purpose of the Statute. Thus, the Court has reached the conclusion that orders on provisional measures under Article 41 have binding effect"[60].

---

[58] *Ibid.*, p. 31, para. 108.

[59] *Ibid.*

[60] *Ibid.*, p. 31, para. 109.

Once the interpretation of Article 41 of the Statute of the Court is made, according to which orders on provisional measures have binding effect, the Court considers its Order of 3 March 1999. This Order stated provisional measures charging the United States of America in the following terms:

> "*(a)* The United States of America should take all measures at its disposal to ensure that Walter LaGrand is not executed pending the final decision in these proceedings, and should inform the Court of all the measures which it has taken in implementation of this Order;
>
> *(b)* The Government of the United States of America should transmit this Order to the Governor of the State of Arizona"[61]

The Court highlights the fact that this Order "was not a mere exhortation" because it was adopted pursuant to Article 41 of the Statute. Consequently, the Order was of a binding nature and created a legal obligation for the United States[62]. However, the United States of America did not take the necessary measures to comply with it. Effectively, the "mere transmission" of the Order to the Governor of Arizona was not sufficient. Such a transmission,

> "without any comment, particularly without even so much as a plea for a temporary stay and an explanation that there is no general agreement on the position of the United States that orders of the International Court of Justice on provisional measures are non-binding, was certainly less than could have been done even in the short time available"[63].

The Court concludes that the various competent United States authorities failed to take all the steps they could have taken to give effect to the Court Order. It stresses that the Order did not require the United States to exercise powers it did not have; but it did impose an obligation: the obligation to "take all measures at its disposal to ensure"[64] that Walter LaGrand would not be executed pending the final decision in those proceedings. Consequently, the Court finds that the United States did not discharge that obligation and that under those circumstances the United States had not complied with the Order of 3 March 1999.

---

[61] *Ibid.*, p. 12, para. 32.

[62] Cf. *ibid.*, p. 31, para. 110.

[63] In opinion of the Court the same is also true of the United States Solicitor General's categorical statement in his brief letter to the United States Supreme Court (cf. *ibid.*, p. 32, para. 112).

[64] *Ibid.*, p. 32, para. 115.

6 The jurisdiction of the Court to give advisory opinions

Unlike the jurisdiction in contentious matter, in which the basis is constituted by the consent of the Parties, its jurisdiction to give advisory opinions is restricted to the organs of the United Nations already examined, and the decision of the Court is of an advisory nature. This is why, in the case concerning the *Interpretation of Peace Treaties with Bulgaria, Hungary and Romania*, the I.C.J. itself stated that "it follows that no State, whether a Member of the United Nations or not, can prevent the giving of an Advisory Opinion which the United Nations considers to be desirable in order to obtain enlightenment as to the course of action it should take. The Court's Opinion is given not to the States, but to the organ which is entitled to request it; the reply of the Court, itself an 'organ of the United Nations', represents its participation in the activities of the Organization, and, in principle, should not be refused"[65].

The grounds for this assertion is in Article 65 of the Statute, considered permissive by the Court because it gives it "the power to examine whether the circumstances of the case are of such a character as should lead it to decline to answer the Request"[66]. In short, as in the case of its jurisdiction in contentious matter, it is the Court itself which decides[67]. Consequently, it can decide that the organ of the United Nations concerned is not entitled to request an advisory opinion. A recent example: the case concerning *Legality of the Use by a State of Nuclear Weapons in Armed Conflict*, in which the request was made by the World Health Assembly through resolution WHA46.40, dated 14 May 1993[68].

Duly authorized, in accordance with Article 96, paragraph 2, of the Charter, the World Health Assembly, requests the I.C.J. to rule on whether:

> "in view of the health and environmental effects, ... the use of nuclear weapons by a State in war or other armed conflict (would) be a breach of its obligations under international law including the WHO Constitution"[69].

Nevertheless, the Court will seek to determine whether the advisory opinion requested by the WHO relates to a question arising "within the scope of the activities" of that Organization. This search will imply the analysis of the relevant rules

65 I.C.J., *Reports 1950*, p. 71.

66 *Ibid.*, p. 72.

67 This jurisprudence is repeated by the I.C.J. in more recent cases, in which it underlines the discretional character of its jurisdiction and specifies that it is for it to maintain it "unimpaired", and there are no restrictions to the discretionary power of the Court to give advisory opinions. So, for example, in its Advisory Opinion concerning *Application for Review of Judgement No. 273 of the United Nations Administrative Tribunal* from Article 65 of the Statute of the I.C.J. (cf. I.C.J, *Reports 1982*, p. 347). Cf. *ibid.*, pages 337 and 347.

68 I.C.J., *Reports 1996*, pages 66-85.

69 *Ibid.*, p. 73.

of the WHO – its constitution, a multilateral treaty –, in order to specify the field of activity or the area of competence of this International Organization. The instrument will be "the well-established rules of treaty interpretation" because "from a formal standpoint, the constituent instruments of international organizations are multilateral treaties"[70]. But the Court is more specific: the constituent instruments of international organizations are also treaties "of a particular type; their object is to create new subjects of law endowed with a certain autonomy, to which the parties entrust the task of realizing common goals"[71]. They can raise specific problems of interpretation that shall be resolved by the application of Article 31 of the 1969 Vienna Convention on the Law of Treaties. Consequently the I.C.J.:

> "will also apply it in this case for the purpose of determining whether, according to the WHO Constitution, the question to which it has been asked to reply arises 'within the scope of (the) activities' of that Organization"[72].

The Court resorts to the interpretative canons of the general rule of interpretation contained in Article 31: the ordinary meaning of the terms, in the context, in the light of the object and purpose of the WHO Constitution, as well as the practice followed by that Organization. The result of such interpretation is that:

> "the provisions of its Article 2 may be read as authorizing the Organization to deal with the effects on health of the use of nuclear weapons, or of any other hazardous activity, and to take preventive measures aimed at protecting the health of (the) population in the event of such weapons being used or such activities engaged in"[73].

But, immediately, the Court adds that the question put to it related not to the effects of the use of nuclear weapons on health, "but to the *legality* of the use of such weapons *in view of their health and environmental effects*"[74]. Consequently,

> "Whatever those effects might be, the competence of the WHO to deal with them is not dependent on the legality of the acts that caused them. Accordingly, it does not seem to the Court that the provisions of Article 2 of the WHO Constitution, interpreted in accordance with the criteria referred to above, can be understood as conferring upon the Organization a competence to address the legality of the use of nuclear weapons, and thus in turn a competence to ask the Court about that"[75].

---

70 I.C.J., *Reports 1996*, p. 74.

71 *Ibid.*

72 *Ibid.*, p. 75.

73 *Ibid.*, p. 76.

74 *Ibid.*

75 *Ibid.*

The I.C.J. will conclude that the WHO was not entitled to request such an advisory opinion and that, as a consequence of this, the Court lacked jurisdiction in that case. Effectively, in the opinion of the I.C.J., the WHO could only be competent to take those actions "of primary prevention" which fall "within the functions of the Organization as defined in Article 2 of its Constitution. In consequence, the references to this type of prevention which are made in the Preamble to resolution WHA46.40 and the link there suggested with the question of the legality of the use of nuclear weapons" do not affect the conclusions of the Court in the sense of not making the question fall within the functions of the WHO[76].

In the opinion of the I.C.J. the causes of the deterioration in human health are numerous and varied, and the legality or illegality of the use of nuclear weapons in no way determines the specific measures, regarding health or otherwise which could be necessary in order to seek to prevent or cure some of their effects. This reasoning of the Court does not take into account that the answer to the question on the legality or the illegality of the use of nuclear weapons, in the event that the answer was that it was illegal, could have been grounds for warning the State in question not only about the effects of such use but, especially, that such use constitutes a breach of International Law which could be responded to by (individual or collective) measures taken by other States or International Organizations. In any case, the answer to this question, which is, unfortunately, not progressive, is given by the I.C.J. in its advisory opinion to the request made by the United Nations General Assembly in the case concerning the *Legality of the Threat or Use of Nuclear Weapons*[77]. Here, the Court concluded that it had the authority to deliver an opinion on the question put by the General Assembly and that there existed no compelling reasons which would lead the Court to exercise its discretion not to do so.

The answer of the I.C.J. to the Advisory Opinion requested by the WHO Organization is also interesting from the point of view of the interpretation of the I.C.J. concerning the *subjectivity* of International Organizations. It begins by recalling that these types of Organizations "are subjects of international law which do not, unlike States, possess a general competence", the Court adds that they are governed by the "principle of speciality":

> "they are invested by the States which create them with powers, the limits of which are a function of the common interests whose promotion those States entrust to them"[78].

But they can also exercise powers called "implied powers". That is to say, those not expressly provided for in their constituent instruments but conferred upon them by

---

[76] *Ibid.*, p. 77.

[77] I.C.J., *Reports 1996*, pages 226-267. See AKANDE, D., "The Competence of International Organizations and the Advisory Jurisdiction of the International Court of Justice", *E.J.I.L.*, Vol. 9 (1998) No. 3, pp. 437-467.

[78] *Ibid.*, p. 78. The Court also says: "The powers conferred on international organizations are normally the subject of an express statement in their constituent instruments" (*ibid.*, p. 79).

necessary implication as being essential to the performance of their duties[79]. In fact the necessities "of international life may point to the need for organizations, in order to achieve their objectives, to possess subsidiary powers which are not expressly provided for in the basic instruments which govern their activities"[80].

In the present case, in the light of the purposes assigned to the WHO by its member States, this organization has no competence to address the legality of the use of nuclear weapons, even in view of their health and environmental effects. The contrary "would be tantamount to disregarding the principle of speciality"[81]. Moreover, the WHO is an international organization of a particular kind. So, as is seen in the Preamble as well as in Article 69 of its Constitution, the WHO is one of the specialized agencies referred to in Article 57 of the Charter of the United Nations. Articles 57, 58 and 63 of this Charter demonstrates that this "laid the basis of a 'system' designed to organize international co-operation in a coherent fashion by bringing the United Nations, invested with powers of a general scope, into relationship with several autonomous and complementary organizations, invested with sectorial powers"[82]. The exercise of these powers by the organizations belonging to the "United Nations system" is generally co-ordinated by the relationship agreements reached by the United Nations and each of the specialized agencies. In the present case through the agreement of 10 July 1948. Consequently, in the opinion of the I.C.J., it follows from the different instruments mentioned above that the WHO Constitution

> "can only be interpreted, as far as the powers conferred upon that Organization are concerned, by taking due account, not only of the general principle of speciality, but also of the logic of the overall system contemplated by the Charter"[83].

The Court considers that the WHO has, by virtue of Article 57 of the Charter, wide international responsibilities necessarily restricted to the sphere of public health and "cannot encroach on the responsibilities of other parts of the United Nations system", and concludes:

> "And there is no doubt that questions concerning the use of force, the regulation of armament and disarmament are within the competence of the United Nations and lie outside that of the specialized

---

[79] Principle applied before to the International Labour Organization and to the United Nations (see *Reparation for Injuries Suffered in the Service of the United Nations, Advisory Opinion*, I.C.J., *Reports 1949, pages 182-183*, and the *Effect of Awards of Compensation Made by the United Nations Administrative Tribunal, Advisory Opinion*, I.C.J., *Reports 1954*, p. 57).

[80] *Ibid.*, p. 79.

[81] *Ibid.*

[82] *Ibid.*, p. 80.

[83] *Ibid.*

> agencies. Besides, any other conclusion would render virtually meaningless the notion of a specialized agency; …"[84].

In order to confirm its interpretation, the I.C.J. takes into consideration the practice of the WHO manifested in its resolutions, paying special attention to the World Health Assembly resolution WHA46.40, in order to conclude that it could not be taken to express or to amount by itself "to a practice establishing an agreement between the members of the Organization to interpret its Constitution as empowering it to address the question of the legality of the use of nuclear weapons" and "nowhere else does the Court find any practice of this kind"[85]. Furthermore, the fact that the resolution in question had been adopted by the required majority only proves that it had been duly adopted from a procedural point of view but it could not suffice to remedy hypothetical fundamental defects. Nor was the argument that the General Assembly of the United Nations had, by its resolution 49/75 K, confirmed the competence of the WHO to request an opinion of the I.C.J. concerning the legality of the use of nuclear weapons, accepted by the Court:

> "In expressing this opinion, the General Assembly clearly reflected the wish of a majority of States that the Assembly should lend its political support to the action taken by the WHO, which it welcomed. However, the Court does not consider that, in doing so, the General Assembly meant to pass upon the competence of the WHO to request an opinion on the question raised. Moreover, the General Assembly could evidently not have intended to disregard the limits within which Article 96, paragraph 2, of the Charter allows it to authorize the specialized agencies to request opinions from the Court – limits which were reaffirmed in Article X of the relationship agreement of 10 July 1948"[86].

This conclusion implies that the Court had previously interpreted the Constitution of the WHO in order to determine the competence of this Organization as regards requesting such an opinion. Starting from the fact that it corresponds to the World Health Assembly to decide on its own competence to submit a request to the Court, this Court adds that "through the reference made, respectively, by Article 96, paragraph 2, of the Charter to the 'scope of (the) activities' of the Organization and by Article X, paragraph 2, of the Agreement of 10 July 1948 to its 'competence', the Court also finds itself obliged, in the present case, to interpret the Constitution of the WHO"[87]. With this interpretation, the Court reaches different con-

---

84 *Ibid.* "For all these reasons, the Court considers that the question raised in the request for an advisory opinion submitted to it by the WHO does not arise 'within the scope of (the) activities' of that Organization as defined by its Constitution" (*ibid.*, p. 81).

85 *Ibid.*

86 *Ibid.*, pages 83-84.

87 *Ibid.*, p. 83.

clusions from those reached by the World Health Assembly when it adopted resolution WHA46.40.

Only in the case of the existence of what the I.C.J. calls "compelling reasons" can a request for an advisory opinion be rejected. This is the case of the irregularities which feature throughout the proceedings and that "could well be regarded as constituting 'compelling reasons' for a refusal by the Court to entertain the request". Nevertheless, the stability and efficiency of the international organizations – the advisory opinion was requested by the U.N.O. – are, however, of such paramount importance to world order "that the Court should not fail to assist a subsidiary body of the United Nations General Assembly in putting its operation upon a firm and secure foundation"[88].

Another example of a "compelling reason" justifying making it inappropriate for the Court to entertain a request is that its judicial role would be endangered or discredited[89]. But it is not the case in the situation in question, and the Court states that it does not find that considerations of judicial restraint should prevent it from pronouncing the advisory opinion requested[90].

In any case, the I.C.J. should not forget that the trust States have in its jurisdiction depends on the way it exercises this jurisdiction. If liberty and discretion are used with political purposes and not in compliance with its judicial function, both the Court and International Law will suffer the consequences.

This question of the jurisdiction of the I.C.J. to give advisory opinions has been recently addressed by the Court on the occasion of the advisory opinion requested by the General Assembly on the *Legal Consequences of the Construction of a Wall in the Occupied Palestinian Territory*, where it examines several aspects related to its advisory jurisdiction.

The starting point of the reasoning of the Court is clear: it is the Court's mission to decide whether it has jurisdiction to give the opinion requested. Also, if there is any reason why it should decline to exercise any such jurisdiction:

> "When seised of a request for an advisory opinion, the Court must first consider whether it has jurisdiction to give the opinion requested and whether, should the answer be in the affirmative, there is any reason why it should decline to exercise any such jurisdiction (see *Legality of the Threat or Use of Nuclear Weapons, Advisory Opinion,* I.C.J., *Reports 1996 (I)*, p. 232, para. 10)"[91].

---

88 *Ibid.*, p. 347.

89 Cf. *ibid.*

90 Cf. *ibid.* Moreover, in this case, this refusal "would leave in suspense a very serious allegation against the Administrative Tribunal, that it had in effect challenged the authority of the General Assembly" (*ibid.*).

91 *Ibid.*, para. 13.

This statement is followed by the reference to Article 65, paragraph 1, of the Statute of the Court on which the competence of the I.C.J. is based. According to this, the Court

> "may give an advisory opinion on any legal question at the request of whatever body may be authorized by or in accordance with the Charter of the United Nations to make such a request".

Related to Article 65, paragraph 1, of its Statute, the Court first stresses the word *may*[92] (give an advisory opinion) and immediately recalls its jurisprudence on the matter. According to this, the words "The Court may give an advisory opinion…"

> "should be interpreted to mean that the Court has a discretionary power to decline to give an advisory opinion even if the conditions of jurisdiction are met *(Legality of the Threat or Use of Nuclear Weapons, Advisory Opinion,* I.C.J., *Reports 1996 (I)*, p. 234, para. 14). The Court however is mindful of the fact that its answer to a request for an advisory opinion 'represents its participation in the activities of the Organization, and, in principle, should not be refused' *(Interpretation of Peace Treaties with Bulgaria, Hungary and Romania, First Phase, Advisory Opinion,* I.C.J., *Reports 1950*, p. 71; see also, for example, *Difference Relating to Immunity from Legal Process of a Special Rapporteur of the Commission of Human Rights, Advisory Opinion,* I.C.J., *Reports 1999 (I)*, pp. 78-79, para. 29.) Given its responsibilities as the 'principal judicial organ of the United Nations' (Article 92 of the Charter), the Court should in principle not decline to give an advisory opinion. In accordance with its consistent jurisprudence, only 'compelling reasons' should lead the Court to refuse its opinion *(Certain Expenses of the United Nations (Article 17, paragraph 2, of the Charter), Advisory Opinion,* I.C.J., *Reports 1962,* p. 155; see also, for example, *Difference Relating to Immunity from Legal Process of a Special Rapporteur of the Commission of Human Rights, Advisory Opinion,* I.C.J., *Reports 1999 (I)*, pp. 78-79, para. 29)"[93].

Nevertheless, even thought the power of the Court to decline to give an advisory opinion is discretionary, it recalls that it has never declined to respond to a request for an advisory opinion. In this sense, it explains that its decision not to give the advisory opinion on the *Legality of the Use by a State of Nuclear Weapons in Armed Conflict* requested by the World Health Organization was based on the

---

[92] Emphasis added.

[93] I.C.J., advisory *Opinion on the Legal Consequences of the Construction of a Wall in the Occupied Palestinian Territory*, para. 44.

Court's lack of jurisdiction, and not on considerations of judicial propriety[94]. Likewise, it makes reference to the only occasion on which the Court's predecessor, the Permanent Court of International Justice, did take the view that it should not reply to a question put to it. It was in the advisory opinion concerning the *Status of Eastern Carelia*[95] but in the opinion of the I.C.J. this was due to

> "the very particular circumstances of the case, among which were that the question directly concerned an already existing dispute, one of the States parties to which was neither a party to the Statute of the Permanent Court nor a Member of the League of Nations, objected to the proceedings, and refused to take part in any way" (*Legality of the Threat or Use of Nuclear Weapons,* I.C.J., *Reports 1996 (I)*, pp. 235-236, para. 14)"[96].

In any case, as the I.C.J. states, the foregoing considerations "do not release the Court from the duty to satisfy itself, each time it is seised of a request for an opinion, as to the propriety of the exercise of its judicial function, by reference to the criterion of 'compelling reasons' as cited above"[97].

Consequently, according to Article 65, paragraph 1, of the Statute of the I.C.J., three conditions must be fulfilled so that the Court might become competent. Firstly, the advisory opinion shall be requested by an organ duly authorized to seek it under the Charter. Secondly, it shall be requested on a legal question. Finally, except in the case of the General Assembly or the Security Council[98], this question shall be one arising within the scope of the activities of the requesting organ[99]. Consequently, it is for the Court to satisfy itself that the request for an advisory opinion comes from an organ or agency having competence to make it.

---

[94] See I.C.J., *Reports 1996 (I)*, p. 235, para. 14.

[95] See P.C.I.J., *Series B*, No. 5.

[96] I.C.J., advisory opinion on the *Legal Consequences of the Construction of a Wall in the Occupied Palestinian Territory*, para. 44.

[97] *Ibid.*, para. 45.

[98] Concerning both organs Article 96, paragraph 1, of the Charter provides: "The General Assembly or the Security Council may request the International Court of Justice to give an advisory opinion on any legal question".

[99] In the words of the I.C.J.: "It is … a precondition of the Court's competence that the advisory opinion be requested by an organ duly authorized to seek it under the Charter, that it be requested on a legal question, and that, except in the case of the General Assembly or the Security Council, that question should be one arising within the scope of the activities of the requesting organ'. *(Application for Review of Judgement No. 273 of the United Nations Administrative Tribunal, Advisory Opinion,* I.C.J., *Reports 1982*, pp. 333-334, para. 21.)" (*ibid.*, para. 14).

6.1 The "legal question" as object of the advisory opinion requested

Another question addressed by the Court in its advisory opinion on the *Legal Consequences of the Construction of a Wall in the Occupied Palestinian Territory* was that of the "legal question" which, according to Article 96, paragraph 1, of the Charter and Article 65, paragraph 1, of the Statute of the Court, constitutes the object of the advisory opinion requested.

However, what is a "legal question"? Concerning this aspect, in its advisory opinion concerning *Legal Consequences of the Construction of a Wall in the Occupied Palestinian Territory*, the Court highlights that it has "sometimes in the past" given certain indications as to the relationship between the question which was the subject of a request for an advisory opinion and the activities of the General Assembly[100]. In the present case, the Court observes that the question referred to it is directed to the *legal consequences arising from a given factual situation*. Moreover, using its phrase in its Advisory Opinion on Western Sahara, it states that the question posed by the General Assembly has "been framed *in terms of law and raise[s] problems of international law*[101]"; it is by its very nature susceptible of a reply based on law; indeed it is scarcely susceptible of a reply otherwise than on the basis of law. In the view of the Court, it is indeed a question of a legal character"[102].

6.2 The lack of clarity of the terms of the request and its effects on the "legal nature" of the question referred to the Court

The lack of clarity of the terms of the request was alleged in the case concerning *Legal Consequences of the Construction of a Wall in the Occupied Palestinian Territory*. The Court, after stating that this question is directed to the legal consequences arising from a given factual situation considering the rules and principles of international law, recalls its statement in its Advisory Opinion on *Western Sahara*, and adds that the question submitted by the General Assembly has been framed "'in terms of law and raise[s] problems of international law'; it is by its very nature susceptible of a reply based on law; indeed it is scarcely susceptible of a reply otherwise than on the basis of law. In the view of the Court, it is indeed a question of a legal character (see *Western Sahara, Advisory Opinion,* I.C.J., *Reports 1975*, p. 18, para. 15)"[103].

---

[100] It was so in the following cases: *Interpretation of Peace Treaties with Bulgaria, Hungary and Romania*, I.C.J., *Reports 1950*, p. 70; *Legality of the Threat or Use of Nuclear Weapons*, I.C.J., *Reports 1996* (I), pp. 232 and 233, paras. 11 and 12).

[101] Emphasis added.

[102] See *Western Sahara*, Advisory Opinion, I.C.J., *Reports 1975*, p. 18, para. 15. See also the advisory opinion about the *Difference relating to immunity from legal process of a Special Rapporteur of the Commission on Human Rights* (I.C.J., *Reports 1999*, paras. 26 and 27).

[103] I.C.J., *Legal Consequences of the Construction of a Wall in the Occupied Palestinian Territory, Advisory Opinion,* para. 37.

Consequently, a "legal question" is a question of a legal nature, framed in terms of law and raising problems of International Law. By its very nature it is also a question susceptible of a reply based on law even if it is also susceptible of a reply otherwise than on the basis of law.

In any case, and this assertion is important, it is the opinion of the Court that the lack of clarity in the drafting of a question does not deprive the Court of jurisdiction. If this arises, "such uncertainty will require clarification in interpretation, and such necessary clarifications of interpretation have frequently been given by the Court"[104].

The problem is not new. The proof is that it has been dealt with both by the Permanent Court and by the I.C.J. The latter distinguishes three situations. The one, constituted by cases were the wording of a request for an advisory opinion did not accurately state the question on which the Court's opinion was being sought[105]. The second, formed by cases where the wording of a request for an advisory opinion did not correspond to the "true legal question" under consideration[106]. The third, concerns one case in which the Court noted that "the question put to the Court is, on the face of it, at once infelicitously expressed and vague"[107].

This is why the I.C.J. "has often been required to broaden, interpret and even reformulate the questions put"[108]. And this is what it also does in its advisory opinion on the *Legal Consequences of the Construction of a Wall in the Occupied Palestinian Territory*. That is, "identify the existing principles and rules, interpret them and apply them ..., thus offering a reply to the question posed based on law"[109].

---

[104] *Ibid.*, para. 38.

[105] See P.C.I.J., *Interpretation of the Greco-Turkish Agreement of 1 December 1926 (Final Protocol, Article IV)*, Advisory Opinion (P.C.I.J., *Series B*, No. 16 (I), 1928, pp. 14-16).

[106] See I.C.J., *Interpretation of the Agreement of 25 March 1951 between the WHO and Egypt*, Advisory Opinion, I.C.J., *Reports 1980*, pp. 87-89, paras. 34-36).

[107] I.C.J., *Application for Review of Judgement No. 273 of the United Nations Administrative Tribunal, Advisory Opinion,* I.C.J., *Reports 1982*, p. 348, para. 46).

[108] I.C.J., *Legal Consequences of the Construction of a Wall in the Occupied Palestinian Territory*, Advisory Opinion, para. 38. And that, in the following Opinions: *Interpretation of the Greco-Turkish Agreement of 1 December 1926 (Final Protocol, Article IV)*, Advisory Opinion (P.C.I.J., *Series B*, No. 16 (I), 1928; *Interpretation of the Agreement of 25 March 1951 between the WHO and Egypt*, Advisory Opinion, I.C.J., *Reports 1980*; *Application for Review of Judgement No. 273 of the United Nations Administrative Tribunal*, Advisory Opinion, I.C.J., *Reports 1982*; Jaworzina, Advisory Opinion, 1923, P.C.I.J., *Series B*, No. 8; *Admissibility of Hearings of Petitioners by the Committee on South West Africa*, Advisory Opinion, I.C.J., *Reports 1956*, p. 25; *Certain Expenses of the United Nations (Article 17, paragraph 2, of the Charter)*, Advisory Opinion, I.C.J., *Reports 1962*, pp. 157-162.

[109] Like it stated in its advisory opinion on the *Legality of the Threat or Use of Nuclear Weapons,* I.C.J., *Reports 1996 (I)*, p. 234, para. 13). Cf. also *Legal Consequences of the Construction of a Wall in the Occupied Palestinian Territory, Advisory Opinion*, para. 38.

But, in this case, due to the request of the General Assembly concerning the statement of the "legal consequences" arising from the construction of the wall,

> "the use of these terms necessarily encompasses an assessment of whether that construction is or is not in breach of certain rules and principles of international law. Thus, the Court is first called upon to determine whether such rules and principles have been and are still being breached by the construction of the wall along the planned route"[110].

6.3 The "abstract nature" of the question posed to the Court

In its advisory opinion on the *Legal Consequences of the Construction of a Wall in the Occupied Palestinian Territory* the Court also faces the argument related to the "abstract nature" of the question posed to it. Accordingly to this argument, the "abstract nature" of the question raised an issue of jurisdiction. The Court answers that the statement that it should not deal with a question couched in abstract terms is "a mere affirmation devoid of any justification" and that "the Court may give an advisory opinion on any legal question, abstract or otherwise"[111].

6.4 The lack of jurisdiction because of the "political" character of the question posed to the Court

This argument is invoked in the advisory opinion on the *Legal Consequences of the Construction of a Wall in the Occupied Palestinian Territory*. The Court, once more, recalls its "clear" and "long-standing" jurisprudence on this point[112]. According to this, the fact that a legal question also has political aspects:

> "as, in the nature of things, is the case with so many questions which arise in international life, does not suffice to deprive it of its character as a 'legal question' and to 'deprive the Court of a competence expressly conferred on it by its Statute'(*Application for Review of Judgement No. 158 of the United Nations Administrative Tribunal,*

[110] I.C.J., *Legal Consequences of the Construction of a Wall in the Occupied Palestinian Territory, Advisory Opinion*, para. 39.

[111] I.C.J., case *concerning the Legality of the Threat or Use of Nuclear Weapons (Reports 1996 (I)*, p. 236, para. 15. The Court also recalls its jurisprudence on the matter: *Conditions of Admission of a State to Membership in the United Nations (Article 4 of the Charter), Advisory Opinion, 1948,* I.C.J., *Reports 1947-1948*, p. 61; *Effect of Awards of Compensation Made by the United Nations Administrative Tribunal, Advisory Opinion,* I.C.J., *Reports 1954*, p. 51; and *Legal Consequences for States of the Continued Presence of South Africa in Namibia (South West Africa) notwithstanding Security Council Resolution 276 (1970), Advisory Opinion,* I.C.J., *Reports 1971*, p. 27, para. 40).

[112] I.C.J., *Legal Consequences of the Construction of a Wall in the Occupied Palestinian Territory, Advisory Opinion*, para. 41.

> *Advisory Opinion, I.C.J, Reports 1973*, p. 172, para. 14). Whatever its political aspects, the Court cannot refuse to admit the legal character of a question which invites it to discharge an essentially judicial task, namely, an assessment of the legality of the possible conduct of States with regard to the obligations imposed upon them by international law (cf. *Conditions of Admission of a State to Membership in the United Nations (Article 4 of the Charter), Advisory Opinion, 1948,* I.C.J., *Reports 1947-1948*, pp. 61-62; *Competence of the General Assembly for the Admission of a State to the United Nations, Advisory Opinion,* I.C.J., *Reports 1950*, pp. 6-7; *Certain Expenses of the United Nations (Article 17, paragraph 2, of the Charter), Advisory Opinion,* I.C.J., *Reports 1962*, p. 155)." (*Legality of the Threat or Use of Nuclear Weapons,* I.C.J., *Reports 1996 (I)*, p. 234, para. 13)"[113].

In the same advisory opinion, the Court goes further and takes into account the importance of its advisory opinions for an international organization as regards the legal principles applicable with respect to the matter concerning the request. In thisrespect, it recalls its statement in its Opinion concerning the *Interpretation of the Agreement of 25 March 1951 between the WHO and Egypt*, where it indeed emphasized that,

> "in situations in which political considerations are prominent it may be particularly necessary for an international organization to obtain an advisory opinion from the Court as to the legal principles applicable with respect to the matter under debate ..." (I.C.J., *Reports 1980*, p. 87, para. 33). Moreover, the Court has affirmed in its Opinion on the Legality of the Threat or Use of Nuclear Weapons that "the political nature of the motives which may be said to have inspired the request and the political implications that the opinion given might have are of no relevance in the establishment of its jurisdiction to give such an opinion" (I.C.J., *Reports 1996 (I)*, p. 234, para. 13)"[114].

6.5 The question of the lack of consent to the Court's jurisdiction by interested States and its consequences on the Court's jurisdiction to give an advisory opinion

This question is developed by the Court in its advisory opinion on the *Legal Consequences of the Construction of a Wall in the Occupied Palestinian Territory*. The analysis of the Court starts from the statement that the lack of consent to the Court's contentious jurisdiction by States concerned has no bearing on the Court's jurisdiction to give an advisory opinion. It is founded on its advisory opinion of

---

[113] *Ibid.*, para. 41.

[114] *Ibid.*

1950 concerning *Interpretation of Peace Treaties with Bulgaria, Hungary and Romania, First Phase*, where the Court took into account the differences between its jurisdiction in contentious cases and its jurisdiction with regard to advisory proceedings. As the Court explained on that occasion:

> "The consent of States, parties to a dispute, is the basis of the Court's jurisdiction in contentious cases. The situation is different in regard to advisory proceedings even where the Request for an Opinion relates to a legal question actually pending between States. The Court's reply is only of an advisory character: as such, it has no binding force. It follows that no State, whether a Member of the United Nations or not, can prevent the giving of an Advisory Opinion which the United Nations considers to be desirable in order to obtain enlightenment as to the course of action it should take. The Court's Opinion is given not to the States, but to the organ which is entitled to request it; the reply of the Court, itself an 'organ of the United Nations', represents its participation in the activities of the Organization, and, in principle, should not be refused"[115].

Thus, the Court recalls that, in those proceedings, it did not refuse to respond to the request for an advisory opinion on the grounds that, in the particular circumstances, it lacked jurisdiction. However, it did examine the opposition of certain interested States to the request by the General Assembly in the context of issues of judicial property. For example, "commenting on its 1950 decision, the Court explained in its Advisory Opinion on *Western Sahara* that it had 'Thus ... recognized that lack of consent might constitute a ground for declining to give the opinion requested if, in the circumstances of a given case, considerations of judicial propriety should oblige the Court to refuse an opinion'"[116].

However, the I.C.J. recognizes that "in certain circumstances" the lack of consent of an interested State may render the giving of an advisory opinion incompatible with the Court's judicial character. It is of the Court that:

> "An instance of this would be when the circumstances disclose that to give a reply would have the effect of circumventing the principle that a State is not obliged to allow its disputes to be submitted to judicial settlement without its consent." (*Western Sahara,* I.C.J., *Reports 1975*, p. 25, paras. 32-33.)"[117].

[115] I.C.J., *Interpretation of Peace Treaties with Bulgaria, Hungary and Romania, First Phase*, Advisory Opinion, *Reports 1950*, p. 71; see also *Western Sahara*, I.C.J., *Reports 1975*, p. 24, para. 31.

[116] I.C.J., *Legal Consequences of the Construction of a Wall in the Occupied Palestinian Territory, Advisory Opinion*, para. 47.

[117] *Ibid.* The Court adds: "In applying that principle to the request concerning Western Sahara, the Court found that a legal controversy did indeed exist, but one which had arisen during the proceedings of the General Assembly and in relation to matters with which the Assembly was dealing. It had not arisen independently in bilateral relations (*ibid.*, p. 25, para. 34).

Nevertheless, it is not the case of the request for the advisory opinion on the *Legal Consequences of the Construction of a Wall in the Occupied Palestinian Territory*. In the opinion of the Court, in this case the subject-matter of the General Assembly's request can not be regarded as only a bilateral matter between Israel and Palestine but, given the powers and responsibilities of the United Nations in questions relating to international peace and security, the construction of the wall concerns the United Nations directly[118].

6.6 The question of the purpose of advisory opinions

This question has been recently addressed by the Court. Specifically, in its advisory opinion on the *Legal Consequences of the Construction of a Wall in the Occupied Palestinian Territory*, where it recalls its jurisprudence on the matter. Briefly, from the Court's jurisprudence it is clear that advisory opinions "have the purpose of furnishing to the requesting organs the elements of law necessary for them in their action"[119].

According to the jurisprudence of the I.C.J. on the matter:

- "The object of this request for an Opinion is to guide the United Nations in respect of its own action"[120];
- "The request is put forward by a United Nations organ with reference to its own decisions and it seeks legal advice from the Court on the consequences and implications of these decisions"[121];
- The advisory opinion it was to give would "furnish the General Assembly with elements of a legal character relevant to its further treatment of the decolonization of Western Sahara"[122].

6.7 The use the General Assembly would make of an advisory opinion

This question has been analyzed by the Court in its advisory opinions on the Legality of the Threat or Use of Nuclear Weapons and on the *Legal Consequences of the Construction of a Wall in the Occupied Palestinian Territory*. In this last, and with regard to the argument that the General Assembly had not made it clear what

[118] Cf. *ibid.* paras. 49-50.

[119] *Ibid.*

[120] I.C.J., *Opinion concerning Reservations to the Convention on the Prevention and Punishment of the Crime of Genocide* (I.C.J., *Reports 1951*, p. 19).

[121] I.C.J., opinion on the *Legal Consequences for States of the Continued Presence of South Africa in Namibia (South West Africa) notwithstanding Security Council Resolution 276 (1970)* (I.C.J., *Reports 1971*, p. 24, para. 32).

[122] I.C.J., *Western Sahara,* (*Reports 1975*, p. 37, para. 72).

use it would make of an advisory opinion on the wall, the Court recalls what it stated in its Opinion on the Legality of the Threat or Use of Nuclear Weapons:

> "Certain States have observed that the General Assembly has not explained to the Court for what precise purposes it seeks the advisory opinion. Nevertheless, it is not for the Court itself to purport to decide whether or not an advisory opinion is needed by the Assembly for the performance of its functions. The General Assembly has the right to decide for itself on the usefulness of an opinion in the light of its own needs"[123]

Consequently, it follows from the jurisprudence of the Court that it "cannot decline to answer the question posed based on the grounds that its opinion would lack any useful purpose. The Court cannot substitute its assessment of the usefulness of the opinion requested for that of the organ that seeks such opinion, namely the General Assembly. Furthermore, and in any event, the Court considers that the General Assembly has not yet determined all the possible consequences of its own resolution. The Court's task would be to determine in a comprehensive manner the legal consequences of the construction of the wall, while the General Assembly and the Security Council may then draw conclusions from the Court's findings"[124].

[123] I.C.J., *Legality of the Threat or Use of Nuclear Weapons* (I.C.J., *Reports 1996 (I)*, p. 237, para. 16. Also quoted in opinion on the *Legal Consequences for States of the Continued Presence of South Africa in Namibia (South West Africa) notwithstanding Security Council Resolution 276 (1970)*, I.C.J., *Reports 1971*, p. 24, para. 61.

[124] I.C.J., opinion on the *Legal Consequences for States of the Continued Presence of South Africa in Namibia (South West Africa) notwithstanding Security Council Resolution 276 (1970)*, I.C.J., *Reports 1971*, p. 24, para. 62.

CHAPTER XIII:

Conclusions

1. Contrary to what might be thought, interpretation of any legal instrument remains a question of immediate interest for international as well as national practice. Concerning the first, the International Community remains a community composed preferably of sovereign States and is characterized by the decentralization of political power. Consequently, the sovereignty of a State affects the process of law-making as well as its application. This sovereignty materialises in the autonomy and liberty of States to make and to interpret norms, although both steps are governed by principles, such as that of good faith, which must guide their conduct. But these principles do not prevent problems as it is difficult to make them more specific.

Liberty and autonomy inherent to state sovereignty become greater due to the inexistence of compulsory methods for the peaceful settlement of disputes, as well as for the identical value which the divergent interpretations of States have. This is why, except for the cases in which the Parties agree to a specific method of peace settlement for the dispute in question or if this is imposed by a treaty which they are Parties to, the dispute on interpretation does not disappear. The consequence is then, the inapplicability of the controversial norm. This is why it can be said that States have discretional competence for interpretation.

State sovereignty is expressed through language, and this is the instrument through which their will is materialised in the text of the norm which manifests their understanding. To make this possible, on occasions, States voluntarily employ general, discretional terms, or draft the obligations with a wide margin for discretion for their debtors and this language is a fertile field for discrepancies. But it is also true that the problems of interpretation can also arise with regard to norms drafted in compulsory and specific terms. Definitively, problems of interpretation appear in relation to conventional and institutional norms, as well as unilateral declarations. With regard to customary norms, problems are greater due to the inexistence of a text manifesting the will of the State and the necessity to analyse and interpret the conduct of the State in order to be able to conclude the existence of the obligation, its content and its application to the specific case.

Interpretation has also another dimension within the framework of the exercise of the international judicial or arbitral function, where it can take place previous to the exercise of such a function (with regard to the declaration of acceptance of the jurisdiction of the body in question), on the occasion of its exercise, or subsequently on the occasion of a request for the interpretation of the judgement, in the case of the I.C.J., or of the advisory opinion which has been given.

2. The discretional competence of States to interpret any legal instrument is modulated by principles that must guide them in this task. It is the case of the principle of good faith. This obligation as regards conduct clearly has a fundamental or structural character, and the difficulty is the determination of its content. So, practice gives examples of divergent interpretations of the same norm protected by the discretional competence of interpretation and based on the principle of good faith even in cases in which what is defended is in contradiction with the obligation expressed in the text. Such situations are a consequence of state sovereignty, and lead to the inapplicability of the norm and the persistence of the dispute until the time that the Parties concerned decide to submit it to a third party. This is why the principle of good faith, which is present in the process of law making as well as in its application, is no more than a principle with serious limitations. One of these is that its content is appraised and evaluated by the Parties from the point of view of their interests in the dispute. The consequence is that this principle is only effective when the Parties concerned agree to submit it to a third party who can appraise and apply it.

3. The existence of problems derived from state sovereignty as well as from the insufficiency of the principle of good faith is confirmed by the fact that, first customarily and later conventionally, a number of criteria had been made in order to permit the interpretation of treaties. These criteria, codified in the Vienna Conventions of 23 May 1969 and 21 March 1986 on the Law of Treaties, consist of a general rule (the ordinary meaning to be given to the terms in their context and in the light of the object and purpose), supplementary means of interpretation (preparatory works of the treaty and the circumstances of its conclusion) and some principles relating to the interpretation of treaties authenticated in two or more languages. They have been conceived by the I.L.C. in order to be employed in a unitary and combined manner. The elements of the general rule were structured by the I.L.C. without any hierarchy. The interpreter, then, must use them jointly and not as autonomous elements lacking any relationship between them. These elements constitute an attempt to legally delimitate a process widely dependent on the autonomy of the will of a State and characterized by the employment of specific legal methods but limited to conventional norms.

Nevertheless, in spite of the existence of these rules, the interpretation of treaties by States continues to be conditioned by sovereignty because, in spite of these rules and of the principle of good faith guiding the whole interpretative process, the interpretation defended by the Parties in the dispute usually has as its object the protection of the respective interests, and the result of this process is divergent interpretations of the specific norm. Consequently, the dispute will only be resolved if a third party intervenes. It will apply the same rules and its decision will be imposed upon the Parties. In this hypothesis, the third party has the benefit of the liberty inherent in the acceptance of its jurisdiction by the Parties and that liberty focuses its attention on the appreciation and application of the rules and principles just quoted.

Once the jurisdiction of the I.C.J. has been accepted, the liberty this acceptance implies for the benefit of the international judicial body is materialised in its power to interpret the request and the conclusions of the Parties, to specify its object as well as the facts, and to appraise them. This way of working, a consequence of the autonomy it has in the exercise of its judicial function, can lead on occasions to interpretations of the Court moving away from the requests made by the Parties (*Nuclear Tests Case* and *Fisheries Jurisdiction*). The problem derives from the way in which the I.C.J. exercises its jurisdiction as well as from the manner in which it specifies its jurisdiction in the light of the declarations made by the States which having accepted this jurisdiction. It is clear that "ratione materiae" the jurisdiction of the Court has no limits. But whether the liberty inherent to the exercise of its judicial function has no limits is quite a different question. In practice, the Court exercises this without any kind of control, and is aware of the fact that its judgement is definitive and that it will be imposed upon the Parties (both as regards its decision on the grounds as well as the decision on its jurisdiction). That liberty makes it possible to have judgements like those in the following cases: *Nuclear Tests*, *Military and Paramilitary Activities in and against Nicaragua*, *Lockerbie* and *East Timor*, all these are good examples of what we are stating and of the contradictory way in which the Court acts. In the first two cases, it states its jurisdiction in spite of the failure of one of the Parties to appear before the Court (and in the *Nuclear Tests Case*, the resolution was made ignoring the petition of the Parties). In the third case, it affirms its jurisdiction to state subsequently that it cannot take the provisional measures requested by Libya due to the resolution of the United Nations Security Council. By this interpretation the Court submits itself to the Security Council. Finally, in the *East Timor Case* the I.C.J. concludes that it cannot exercise its jurisdiction because, in order to decide the claims of Portugal, it would have to rule, as a prerequisite, on the lawfulness of the conduct of Indonesia in the absence of the consent of Portugal. With such an interpretation, the Court waives giving effect to the construction as it did in the *Barcelona Traction Case* concerning the existence of obligations "erga omnes". Furthermore, it also waives giving effect to the right of self determination and the protection of the rights of the people of East Timor, fundamentally with regard to its sovereignty over its natural resources, damaged by the treaty concluded between Indonesia and Australia concerning the continental shelf of East Timor.

But in International Law there is no compulsory jurisdiction. Consequently, the intervention of this third party will only be possible if the previous understanding of the Parties concerned exists or because it is imposed by a treaty to which they are Parties. If one or other of these hypotheses is not carried out, the dispute will continue and will not be resolved due to the divergent interpretations of the Parties.

4. The analysis of the interpretation of the I.C.J. previous to the 1969 Vienna Convention on the Law of Treaties shows that this Court continues with the tradition

of its predecessor, the P.C.I.J., using as *interpretative canons* those canons subsequently codified by that Convention in articles 31 to 33. Among these rules, the resort to the natural and ordinary meaning of the terms, classified by the Court since the first cases (the *Corfu Channel* case, in 1949) as "generally accepted rules", prevails. At the same time, it states that the resort to other methods such as the preparatory work is only justified when, with the natural and ordinary meaning of the terms, it is not possible to achieve a satisfactory result in the interpretation. Only in this case must the Court resort to other methods in order to specify the intention of the Parties.

Together with the general rule of interpretation, the I.C.J. employs other interpretative criteria such as the intention of the Parties and the principle of effectiveness.

Since the case concerning the *Aerial Incident*, in 1959, the Court also began to use as interpretative canons the "context", the "subsequent practice" (in 1960, in its advisory opinion concerning the *Constitution of the Maritime Safety Committee of the Inter-Governmental Maritime Consultative Organization)* and "equity" (in the *South West Africa* case, in 1966).

Since the codification made by the 1969 Vienna Convention on the Law of Treaties, in addition to referring to its constant case law regarding interpretation, the I.C.J. already expressly mentions the Convention, sometimes using the general rule as it was conceived by the I.L.C. in order to avoid an exclusively textual interpretation. That is to say, combining the different elements of the rule in a logical, and not in a hierarchical way (cases concerning the *Arbitral Award of 31 July 1989* and the *Aegean Sea Continental Shelf*). Nevertheless, this conduct is not usual in the Court because it generally gives priority to the textual element without combining this with the other elements of the general rule (case concerning *Land, Island and Maritime Frontier Dispute)*, and employs the context, the subsequent practice and the object and purpose of the treaty to confirm or reinforce the interpretation made starting from the analysis of the text. Acting in such a way, the I.C.J. employs the elements of the general rule with a complementary character that they do not have. In fact, only the preparatory works of the treaty and the circumstances of its signing were conceived by the I.C.L. with this end in view. On the contrary, the Court makes a correct use of the complementary means of interpretation of article 32. That is to say, in order to specify the scope and object of the treaty, to confirm the interpretation made or to reinforce it, and states that resort to these is not possible if the text of the treaty is clear.

5. The process of institutionalisation of the International Community has also impinged upon the process of formation of international norms as well as upon its process of application. Concerning the former, the traditional methods used by States to make International Law have been modified by the influence of International Organizations in the process of the formation of treaties and international custom. Furthermore, the crystallization of individual consent and the consensus of the state within International Organizations have acquired a form which is dif-

ferent from treaty and custom: the institutional norm. This is why it is not possible to answer the question of the value or legal force of institutional norms starting from the simple analysis of the constituent treaty of the Organization in question, excluding such effects when the constituent treaty does not affirm them expressly or classify them as "recommendations" (this is the case of the acts of the United Nations General Assembly).

This is why, in opposition to doctrinal opinions taking this analytical approach, we consider it to be more interesting and more in accord with the reality of the problem that there be an examination of the attitude of the State in the process of the formation of the institutional norm manifested in the language employed in its drafting, its content, the procedure taken to approve it and the way in which it was adopted, as well as at the time of its application (for example, through the subsequent practice of States). Through the resort to such criteria it will be possible to conclude the value or the legal force of the institutional norm because they specify the two stages inherent to the process of formation of every international norm: the individual consent of the State (the initial moment) and the consensus of the plurality of States (the final moment representing the birth of the norm), as stated by the I.C.J. in the cases concerning the *North Sea Continental Shelf* and the *Fisheries Jurisdiction*.

The conception we defend is coherent with the institutional dimension of the International Community in which the relational, the sovereignty, has been moved to the institutional. The consequences of this fact have been the creation of new ways for the production of consensus (a clear example of this is given by the way in which the United Nations General Assembly resolutions are made, that is to say, in a very similar manner to the way in which multilateral treaties are also made) and the effect that the institutional has upon the process of formation of customary norms (declaring an international custom, crystallizing a customary norm in the process of formation or constituting the institutional norm as the starting point of an international custom).

Both aspects have been emphasized by the jurisprudence of the I.C.J. The first in the advisory opinions concerning the *Reparation for Injuries Suffered in the Service of the United Nations*, *Legal Consequences for States of the Continued Presence of South Africa in Namibia (South West Africa) notwithstanding Security Council Resolution 276 (1970)*, *Western Sahara* and *Legal Consequences of the Construction of a Wall in the Occupied Palestinian Territory*. The second, in the case concerning *Military and Paramilitary Activities in and against Nicaragua*.

6. As regards the interpretation of customary norms it is the conduct of the State, the expression of the will of the State, which constitutes the object of the discrepancy, the same problems concerning the sovereignty of the state and the principle of good faith, just quoted, are also present. But in the case of customary norms difficulties become greater due to the absence of a written text. The object of interpretation is the conduct of the State (active or passive) and there are no rules guiding the interpreter in his task nor limiting the discretional competence of the

state. At the same time, it is a field where the role of the third party called on by the Parties to interpret acquires great importance because once this party's jurisdiction is accepted, this third party will specify whether the norm exists or not, its content, its applicability or not to the specific case, as well as the way in which it must be applied, and his decision is imposed upon the Parties.

In order to carry out this task, the I.C.J. has equipped itself with a number of elements or criteria. First, *practice* which, according to I.C.J. case law must be generalised, constant, uniform and effective; although since 1969 (in the case concerning the *North Sea Continental Shelf*) and in 1986 (in the case concerning *Military and Paramilitary Activities in and against Nicaragua)* the Court specified that for a rule to be established as customary it is not necessary that the corresponding practice be in absolutely rigorous conformity with the rule, but that practice should correspond to the States concerned in order to be considered as being sufficiently representative.

Second, the *time element*, as regards this, since 1969 the I.C.J., in the same case just quoted, stated that it is not necessary for there to be a considerable period of time for a custom to be built up due to the rapidity of the transmission of information in the contemporary International Community.

Finally, the *opinio iuris* or the legal feeling concerning the binding character of the norm. It is the Court, starting from its own perception of the case, which specifies the presence or absence of this element in the case in question.

The application of these three elements to the specific case allows the Court to specify the existence of the norm, its content and whether it shall be applied or not in order to resolve the dispute. Initially, with immediate effect upon the Parties concerned but, subsequently, it is projected to the whole International Community since it is repeated, developed or specified by the same body by which the decision was given. This means that, on occasions, the I.C.J. becomes an organ for law-making. Especially, when it makes statements about sectors of International Law which are not sufficiently developed or lack regulation, or concerning problems not ruled by international order.

Concerning the process of international custom, three phases can be distinguished: the determination of its existence, the classification of behaviour and attitudes as customary practice and the specification of the content of the norm, which are appraised by the interpreter. At first, this task will be carried out by the States involved in the dispute and only after its jurisdiction has been accepted will an international judicial or arbitral body intervene. Once this choice has been made, the Parties are submitted to the decision of that third party who, in the performance of his task, enjoys the liberty derived from the acceptance of his jurisdiction by the Parties. This third party will specify whether or not there are elements of the customary norm (in particular, the *opinio iuris*) and will also carry out his own evaluation of the specific case. It is in such a way, that the Parties place themselves in a relationship of dependence with regard to the interpreter because the latter will impose his conception. In order to achieve this, and due to the lack of rules such as those for the interpretation of treaties, the third party will use what has been quoted above and these elements will be evaluated starting from the practice of the States concerned, as well as from the particular perspective the third party will build up regarding the same case.

7. The interpretation of *unilateral declarations* also shows the dependence of State on the interpreter because it is from the time when the intervention of the interpreter is accepted that he interprets the intention of the State as well as the effect of the declaration (even if one of the Parties does not act before the Court). As with customary norms, with regard to unilateral declarations the I.C.J. acts as a law making body. It is the Court which, from the analysis of the text and the conduct of the State, specifies the effects of the unilateral declaration. The general theory of custom as well as the theory concerning unilateral declarations have in common the fact of being conceptions built up by the I.C.J.

From the study we have made it turns out that the intention extracted from the unilateral declarations does not always coincide with the intention that the same declarations have for their authors. The statements of the I.C.J. in the cases concerning the *Nuclear Tests Case*, the *Minquiers and Ecrehos Case* and the *Border Dispute* (Mali-Chad) are good examples of this. Thus, what happens is that the will of the author of the declarations is substituted by the interpretation of that declaration made by the I.C.J. This conclusion is accepted by the Court when, in the cases concerning *Nuclear Tests* and the *Border Dispute,* it states that it is for the Court to form its own view of the meaning and scope intended by the author of a unilateral declaration.

Unlike the interpretation of treaties, in the interpretation of unilateral declarations it is the I.C.J. which gives content to the principle of good faith, and its task is facilitated by the previous acceptance of its jurisdiction. The same occurs with regard to the declarations of acceptance of its compulsory jurisdiction, classified by the Court as obligatory, unilateral engagements establishing a series of bilateral commitments within a conventional frame governed by the principles of reciprocity and mutuality. Thus, the I.C.J. remains confined within the limits of the declarations of acceptance of its jurisdiction made by the States, but this fact has no significant effect upon the discretion the Court has at the time it appraises the declarations in order to rely on its competence in the case in question.

The principle of good faith, the text of the declaration and the intention of its authors to be bound by a legal commitment (an intention specified by the Court starting from the content of the act and from the circumstances of fact in which that act has taken place) are the interpretative canons used by the Court but whose employment leads it to different conclusions in the specific case (sometimes, giving legal effects to the declaration, and at other times, denying these effects).

8. The interpretation made by the I.C.J. since 1945 up to now has had as object a plurality of categories of norms or international instruments. Within the *conventional instruments or those of a statutory nature*, besides the interpretation of treaties *stricto sensu*, the Court has interpreted the Charter of the United Nations, the system of Mandates, the right of self-determination of peoples and the question of

the form of international agreements in relation to joint communiqués, the exercise of consular functions relating to nationals of the sending State, the "centre of the main channel" as a criterion in order to determine the boundary of an international river, the application of international humanitarian law and international conventions of human rights to occupied territories and the competence of the General Assembly to make recommendations.

With regard to the *Charter*, the case law of the I.C.J. has specified its legal nature and declared itself competent to interpret it, the conditions a State shall comply with in order to become a member of the U.N.O., the obligation Member States have to bear the expenses of the Organization as apportioned by the General Assembly, the relationships between the Organization and its functionaries, the compulsory character of the judgements of the Administrative Tribunal of the United Nations, the relationships between the different organs of the Organization and its consequences upon the way the I.C.J. acts, as well as the institutional balance between the Security Council and the Court itself (giving primacy to the power of the Security Council to the detriment of the rule of law which the I.C.J. must ensure and does not address the question of the legality of the resolution of the Security Council adopted in the case in question: *Lockerbie*).

Concerning the *Mandates*, the I.C.J. states the validity of the obligations inherent to this system in spite of the disappearance of the League of Nations, as the General Assembly of the United Nations is its substitute. It also recalls that mandates were created, in the interest of the inhabitants of the territory, and of humanity in general, as an international institution with an international object: a "sacred trust of civilization". Finally, the Court underlines the existence of two principles considered by it as of "paramount importance": the principle of non-annexation and the principle that the well-being and development of peoples not yet able to govern themselves formed that "sacred trust of civilization".

The *right of self-determination of peoples*, present in the Charter, is interpreted by the I.C.J. in the light of General Assembly Resolutions and it states the existence of different ways to exercise this: independence, association or integration. All of these have in common the essential necessity of taking into account the will of the population and the validity of this right is not diminished because on some occasions – and depending on certain circumstances – the General Assembly has not considered it necessary to consult the population (this is not the case of the Western Sahara).

It is of the Court that this right is today a right *erga omnes* but, unfortunately, such a conclusion is deprived of value and of real consequences in practice because the I.C.J. has never gone further when it has had the opportunity to do so. The *East Timor* case is the best example of this.

In order to specify whether a *joint communiqué* is or is not an international agreement, the I.C.J. uses two canons: the terms employed by the Parties in its drafting and the circumstances in which the drafting of the communiqué have taken place. Based on both criteria, the Court will conclude whether the Parties have consented to the creation of rights and obligations.

The *exercise of consular functions relating to nationals* of the sending State and the obligations of the receiving State derived from Article 36 of the Vienna Convention on Consular Relations of 24 April 1963. After the interpretation of the Court, Article 36 contains three separate but interrelated elements: the right of the individual concerned to be informed without delay of his rights under this Article; the right of the consular post to be notified without delay of the individual's detention, if he so requests; and the obligation of the receiving State to forward without delay any communication addressed to the consular post by the detained person. Consequently, Article 36, paragraph 1, creates individual rights which are to be asserted, at any rate and in the first place, within the domestic legal system. Only when that process is completed and local remedies are exhausted would the sending State be entitled to espouse the individual claims of its nationals through the procedure of diplomatic protection. This is why violations of the rights of the individual under Article 36 may entail violation of rights of the State, and violations of the rights of the latter may entail a violation of the rights of the individual. In any case, the right to consular notification and consular communication under the Vienna Convention is not a fundamental human right that constitutes part of due process in criminal proceedings and that should be guaranteed in the territory of each of the Contracting Parties to the Vienna Convention.

Related to *boundaries of international rivers*, the I.C.J. has stated the "centre of the main channel" as a criterion to be used in order to determine the boundary of an international river. In the specific case both parties used the terms "Thalweg" and "centre of the channel" interchangeably. But in the opinion of the Court, the former reflects more accurately the common intention to exploit navigation than does the latter. This is why it considers the former determinative.

According to the Court, *international humanitarian law and international conventions of human rights are applicable to occupied territories*. Concerning International humanitarian law, interpretation of Article 2 of the Fourth Geneva Convention lays down that this Convention is applicable when two conditions are fulfilled: the existence of an armed conflict (whether or not a state of war has been recognized) and that the conflict has arisen between two contracting parties. After the Court, if those two conditions are satisfied, the Convention applies, in particular, in any territory occupied in the course of the conflict by one of the contracting parties. Finally, for the Court, international humanitarian law also constitutes *lex specialis* with regard to the branch of international law concerning human rights.

International conventions of human rights are also applicable to occupied territories because they are applicable in respect of acts carried out by a State in the exercise of its jurisdiction outside its own territory. This conclusion of the Court is based upon the constant practice of the Human Rights Committee, as well as upon the *travaux préparatoires* of the Covenant (both with regard to the International Covenant on Civil and Political Rights). But the same conclusion is applicable to the Covenant on Economic, Social and Cultural Rights in regard to which States Parties are under an obligation not to raise any obstacle to the exercise of such rights in those fields where competence has been transferred to the authorities of the occupied territory.

A similar conclusion derives from Article 2 of the Convention on the Rights of the child of 20 November 1989, according to which States Parties shall respect and ensure the rights set forth in the Convention to each child within their jurisdictions.

Finally, with regard to the *competence of the General Assembly to make recommendations* the Court considers that the interpretation of Article 12 of the Charter (initially interpreted and applied to the effect that the Assembly could not make a recommendation on a question concerning the maintenance of international peace and security while the matter remained on the Council's agenda) has subsequently evolved to the extreme of an increasing tendency over time for the General Assembly and the Security Council to deal in parallel with the same matter concerning the maintenance of international peace and security. Consequently, the accepted practice of the General Assembly as it has evolved is consistent with Article 12, paragraph 1, of the Charter.

9. The importance of the interpretative work of the I.C.J. with regard to *customary norms* has been specified in several sectors of the international legal order. In this field, the interpretation of the I.C.J. has addressed the following sectors of International Law. The *formation process of international custom*, whose general theory with its different elements has been created by the Court itself. It is also the case concerning the *recognition of the existence of regional and local customs or the interaction between custom and treaty*, as well as the statement concerning the separate existence of both kinds of norms even when they have the same content. Also, reservations to treaties before the 1969 Vienna Convention on the Law of Treaties (breaking the principle of unanimity governing this question in customary International Law before that Convention, specifying the criteria that should be taken into account in order to appreciate the possibility of making reservations regarding a multilateral treaty, the impossibility of making reservations regarding general customary norms, as well as the separate existence of conventional and customary norms so that a reservation concerning a conventional norm does not hinder the integral application of the customary norm which has the same content).

Third, as regards the *concept of "terra nullius"*, it stated that it was a technical legal term employed in connection with occupation as one of the accepted legal methods for acquiring sovereignty over a territory, but not valid in the XIX Century with regard to territories inhabited by tribes or peoples having a social and political organization (the case of the *Western Sahara*), and considered that the agreements reached with the authorities of these countries were not original titles obtained by occupation of a "terra nullius" but derivative roots of title.

The interpretation of international customary norms has also involved the *Law of the Sea*, where the Court has pronounced on the system of straight baselines as a method for the delimitation of bays when geographical characteristics are present, as well as the non-existence of an international obligation, from a customary point of view, to resort to the principle of equidistance-special principles for the delimitation of continental shelves between two or more States. In these cases, the Court has stated that it is a method of delimitation to be used only when the results of its application are equitable, in the circumstances of each case and not with a general and absolute character (criteria adopted by article 83 of the 1982 Convention on the Law of the Sea).

Another principle interpreted by the Court has been the principle of "*uti possidetis*" with regard to which the I.C.J. states that it is a firmly established principle of International Law, of a general scope, connected with the phenomenon of decolonisation, compatible with the right of self determination of peoples, whose purpose is to prevent disputes provoked by the challenging of frontiers on the occasion of the obtaining of independence, also applicable in the delimitation of maritime areas, islands and bays, and it has a twofold content: on the one hand, the pre-eminence accorded to legal title over effective possession as a basis of sovereignty. On the other, its primary aim to secure respect for the territorial boundaries at the time when independence is achieved.

With regard to the *legality of the threat or use of nuclear weapons* the Court does not find a conventional rule with a general scope, nor a customary rule specifically proscribing the threat or use of nuclear weapons *per se*. Nevertheless, international humanitarian law (a great many rules of which constitute inviolable principles of international customary law) is applicable to nuclear weapons. The principle of neutrality has also a fundamental character and is also applicable to all international armed conflicts, regardless of the type of weapons which might be used. The conclusions of the Court are raised giving priority to, in the words of the Court, "the fundamental right of every State to survival, and thus its right to self-defence, in accordance with Article 51 of the Charter, when its survival is at stake".

Concerning *immunity from criminal jurisdiction in other States and also inviolability of an incumbent Minister for Foreign Affairs*, in customary international law the immunities accorded to Ministers for Foreign Affairs are not granted for their personal benefit, but to ensure the effective performance of their functions on behalf of their respective States. The functions of a Minister for Foreign Affairs are such that, throughout the duration of his or her office, when abroad, he or she enjoys full immunity from criminal jurisdiction and inviolability. Such immunity and inviolability protect the individual concerned against any act of authority of another State which would hinder him or her in the performance of his or her duties. Consequently, this immunity and inviolability are absolute and, unlike the immunity of jurisdiction of the State, no distinction can be drawn between the acts performed by a Minister for Foreign Affairs in an "official" capacity and those claimed to have been performed in a "private capacity", or, for that matter, between acts performed before the person concerned assumed office as Minister for Foreign Affairs and acts committed during the period of office.

The consequence of this interpretation is impunity. Even the Court states that immunity from jurisdiction does not mean impunity in respect of any crimes incumbent Ministers for Foreign Affairs or Ministers or Heads of State, its interpretation does not resolve the problem of impunity. Especially since the interpretation made by the Court clearly excludes all acts committed during the period in which that person was acting in an official way with this kind of responsibility. Moreover, as these kinds of acts (war crimes, crimes against humanity, genocide, aggression) are generally planned and organized by public powers.

In any case, immunity of jurisdiction and inviolability of Ministers or Heads of State have never been conceived by International Law to protect the commission of war crimes, crimes against humanity, genocide and acts of aggression. Neither can such acts be considered to be committed in a private capacity by persons acting in a public capacity. Furthermore, as war crimes, crimes against humanity, genocide and acts of aggression are the result of the breach of a norm of *ius cogens* it could not be concluded that customary International Law protects the commission of such kinds of acts if they are committed in a public capacity. This last conclusion as well the examples stating the non relevance of public capacity when such acts are committed should have guided the Court to an interpretation more adapted to the current state of international law.

Another question interpreted by the I.C.J. has been the *concept of occupied territory and international obligations resulting for the occupying Power*. According to the Court a territory is occupied when it is actually placed under the authority of the hostile army, and the occupation extends only to the territory where such authority has been established and can be exercised. Consequently, several international obligations derived from this status; obligations which reflect customary international law applicable to those territories. They are the following: no territorial acquisition resulting from the threat or use of force shall be recognized as legal; the illegality of territorial acquisition resulting from the threat or use of force; the principle of self-determination of peoples, as well as rules and principles of international humanitarian law such those contained in the Fourth Hague Convention of 1907 which have a customary nature.

Another category interpreted by the Court has been that of the *legal consequences of the commission of an internationally wrongful act.* The legal consequences of the commission of an internationally wrongful act vary depending on the kind of obligations violated: if obligations derived from international norms other than norms of *ius cogens* or obligations *erga omnes*.

The general principle on the legal consequences of the commission of an internationally wrongful act is well established in Public International Law since the statement of the Permanent Court of International Justice in the *Factory at Chorzów* case, according to which the breach of an engagement involves an obligation to make reparation in an adequate form. Concerning reparation this must, as far as possible, wipe out all the consequences of the illegal act and re-establish the situation which would, in all probability, have existed if that act had not been committed. To achieve this, several forms are admitted but, as the P.C.I.L. stated in the past, what constitutes reparation in an adequate form clearly varies depending upon the specific circumstances surrounding each case and the precise nature and scope of the injury. This is why the question has to be examined from the viewpoint of what the reparation in an adequate form which corresponds to the injury is. According to this principle, violation of international obligations in the *LaGrand* case and in the case concerning *Avena and other Mexican nationals*, in which the individuals concerned were subjected to prolonged detention or convicted and sentenced to severe penalties, an apology would not suffice and it would be incumbent upon the State concerned to allow the review and reconsideration of the conviction and sentence by taking account of the violation of the rights set forth in the Convention. The ways in which this obligation can be carried out and the choice of the means for such review and reconsideration must be left to the State concerned. The Court states that it should occur within the overall judicial proceedings relating to the individual defendant concerned and that it shall be effective. That means that it shall take account of the violation of the rights set forth in the Vienna Convention on Consular Relations as well as guarantee that the violation and the possible prejudice caused by the violation will be fully examined and taken into account in the review and reconsideration process. Lastly, review and reconsideration shall include both the sentence and the conviction.

In other internationally wrongful acts restitution in kind, payment of a sum corresponding to the value which a restitution in kind would bear, the award, if need be, of damages for loss sustained which would not be covered by restitution in kind or payment in place of this, constitute forms of reparation.

When the internationally wrongful act takes place by violation of *erga omnes* obligations all States can be held to have a legal interest in their protection because these are obligations that by their very nature concern all States. The consequences for all other States derived from the violation by a State of *erga omnes* obligations are the following. They are under an obligation not to recognize the illegal situation resulting from that violation. They are also under an obligation not to render aid or assistance in maintaining the situation created by such violation. Third, they shall act in order to bring to an end any impediment, resulting from the violation of the *erga omnes* obligation. Finally, they are under an obligation to ensure compliance with international law by the State concerned.

In its Advisory Opinion on the *Legal Consequences of the Construction of a Wall in the Occupied Palestinian Territory* the Court states that there are also obligations for the United Nations. It is of the Court that the United Nations, and specially General Assembly and the Security Council, should consider what further action is required to bring to an end the illegal situation resulting from the violation of *erga omnes* obligations, taking due account of its Advisory Opinion on the matter.

10. With regard to *institutional norms*, besides the aspects just quoted in the conclusion concerning such norms, the I.C.J. interpretation of the *resolutions of the United Nations Security Council* deserves special consideration. The Court underlines the importance of a careful analysis of the language employed, the discussions preceding its adoption as well as all the elements which are useful in order to conclude whether the resolution has or does not have binding effects. It shall be specified whether the Security Council has exercised the powers conferred upon it

by article 25 of the Charter and this must be checked case by case. The interpretation of the I.C.J. has also affected other aspects related to institutional norms, specifying the character of abstention in the adoption of United Nations Security Council Resolutions and recognizing the legal effects of the acceptance of institutional norms.

11. With regard to *arbitral case law* the study we have made shows the use as interpretative canons, in cases concerning interpretation of treaties, those that were in force from the customary point of view before the 1969 Vienna Convention on the Law of Treaties would be codified by that Convention and subsequently by the 1986 Vienna Convention on the Law of Treaties between States and International Organizations or between International Organizations. That is to say, the natural and ordinary meaning of the terms (the canon most applied), the object and purpose of the treaty, the context, the principle of effectiveness, the preparatory works and the subsequent practice. With regard to treaties authenticated in two or more languages, the arbitral jurisprudence employs as principal canon that of giving priority to the clear text in order to interpret the obscure text. Nevertheless, in cases subsequent to 1969, that interpretative canon was substituted by the one contained in article 33.4 of the Vienna Convention on the Law of Treaties. In other words, interpretation of such kinds of treaties shall be made "having regard to the object and purpose of the treaty".

Unlike the I.C.J., the arbitral jurisprudence subsequent to 1969 applies the rules and canons codified by the Vienna Convention correctly. That is to say, as they were conceived by the I.L.C. This fact is especially important because, unlike the I.C.J., arbitral jurisprudence does not proceed from a single body (which could mean practice of this case law with less uniformity).

12. From the study we have made it can be seen that there are different *types of interpretation* in the international order: interpretation depending on the interpreter (States, International Organizations, international jurisdictions and municipal organs of the State), its content (abstract or concrete), its legal scope (authentic, quasi-authentic, unilateral, bilateral, multi-lateral, collective, executive or institutional), the degree of liberty of the interpreter, as well as the kinds of legal instruments to be interpreted (treaties, customary norms, institutional norms, unilateral declarations, declarations of acceptance of the jurisdiction of the I.C.J., international judicial or arbitral judgements), or its effects (compulsory and non-compulsory).

In addition, there are a number of *methods* depending on the interpretative rules employed by the interpreter: grammatical, textual or objective, teleological or functional, logical-systematic, subjective and historical-evolutionary.

13. Concerning *jurisdiction* the Court has stated its competence to interpret the request, and provides that it is its duty to isolate the real issue in the case and to identify the object of the claim and recalls that it has never been contested that the Court is entitled to interpret the submissions of the parties as this is one of the

attributes of its judicial functions. But, as analysis of its jurisprudence shows, acting in such a way what the Court does is to reformulate the questions submitted to it by the Parties. This is why it may be remembered that the liberty the Court has to interpret the request and the conclusions of the Parties does not mean the power to change the submissions made by the Parties or the object of the dispute as defined by them.

Inherent to its jurisdictional function the *appraisal of the facts alleged* by the Parties and *their proof* corresponds to the Court. It is also the Court itself which decides the *meaning* and *scope* intended by the author of the unilateral declaration.

According to Article 36 of the Statute of the Court at the material level, *ratione materiae*, its jurisdiction is unlimited insofar as it can know of any question of international law. This is why, on occasions, before the grounds for the case are known, the Court must analyse and interpret the declarations of acceptance of its jurisdiction made by the Parties in the specific case, in order to establish its jurisdiction; jurisdiction which is sometimes also initially disputed by the Parties. In doing so the Court acts in complete liberty, fulfilling its right to decide as to its own jurisdiction and the power to interpret for this purpose the instruments which govern that jurisdiction. This leads to the question of the way in which the Court exercises the jurisdiction concerning its own jurisdiction. In other words, the discretion it has in the exercise of its own competences.

With regard to the *value and legal effects of an order stating provisional measures*, Article 41 leads to the conclusion that the power to indicate provisional measures entails that such measures should be binding, inasmuch as the power in question is based on the necessity, when the circumstances call for it, to safeguard, and to avoid prejudice to, the rights of the parties as determined by the final judgment of the Court. Consequently, they are not mere exhortations.

According to article 65 of its Statute the Court has also jurisdiction to give *advisory opinions* to the requests restricted to the organs of the United Nations. Even thought the power of the Court to decline to give an advisory opinion is discretionary, it has recalled that it has never declined to respond to a request for an advisory opinion. Nevertheless, the conditions of Article 65, paragraph 1, of the Statute of the Court must be fulfilled. Firstly, the advisory opinion shall be requested by an organ duly authorized to seek it under the Charter. Secondly, it shall be requested on a legal question. Finally, except in the case of the General Assembly or the Security Council, this question shall be one arising within the scope of the activities of the requesting organ. Consequently, it is for the Court to satisfy itself that the request for an advisory opinion comes from an organ or agency having competence to make it.

Legal questions constitute the object of the contentious and of the advisory jurisdiction of the Court, a legal question being a question of legal nature framed in terms of law and raising problems of International Law. But by its very nature it is also a question susceptible of a reply based on law even if it is also susceptible of a reply otherwise than on the basis of law.

Legal questions have also political aspects but this fact does not suffice to deprive them of their character as legal questions and to deprive the Court of the competence expressly conferred on it by its Statute.

It shall be added that even the lack of clarity in the drafting of a question does not deprive the Court of jurisdiction. If this arises, such uncertainty will require clarification in interpretation, and such necessary clarifications of interpretation have frequently been given by the Court.

Related to advisory opinions the Court has also stated that it may give an advisory opinion on any legal question, abstract or otherwise. It is also of the Court that the lack of consent to its contentious jurisdiction by States concerned has no bearing on its jurisdiction to give an advisory opinion. Only in certain circumstances the lack of consent of an interested State would render the giving of an advisory opinion incompatible with the Court's judicial character. This would be the case when the circumstances disclose that to give a reply would have the effect of circumventing the principle that a State is not obliged to allow its disputes to be submitted to judicial settlement without its consent.

Finally, with regard to the purpose of advisory opinions the Court has stated that advisory opinions have the purpose of furnishing to the requesting organs the elements of law necessary for them in their action. That is, to guide the United Nations in respect of its own action. But the use the General Assembly would make of the advisory opinion is not of the concern of the Court. Briefly, it is not for the Court itself to purport to decide whether or not an advisory opinion is needed by the Assembly for the performance of its functions. Moreover, it is the General Assembly which has the right to decide for itself on the usefulness of an opinion in the light of its own needs.

Bibliography and International Case Law

Bibliography

ABRAHAM, R., *Droit international, droit communautaire et droit français*, Hachette, Paris, 1989.

AKANDE, D., "The Competence of International Organizations and the Advisory Jurisdiction of the International Court of Justice", *E.J.I.L.*, Vol. 9 (1998) No. 3, pp. 437-467.

AKEHURST, M., "Custom as a Source of International Law", *BYIL*, 1974-75, pp. 1-53.

ARANGIO RUIZ, G., "On the Security Council's 'Law-Making'", *R.D.I.*, 2000, vol. LXXXIII, nº 3, pp. 609-725.

BARATI, H., "La règle d'interprétation *contra proferentem* en droit international", *R.G.D.I.P.*, 1999, tome 103 nº 4, pp. 891-926.

BEDJAOUI, M., "'L'énigme' des 'principes équitables' dans le droit des délimitations maritimes", *R.E.D.I.*, 1990/2, pp. 367-389.

BEDJAOUI, M., *Droit International. Bilan et perspectives*, vols. 1 and 2, Pedone, Paris, 1991.

BERGER, V., *Jurisprudence de la Cour européenne des droits de l'homme*, 2ª ed., Sirey, Paris, 1989.

BERLIA, G., "Contribution à l'interprétation des traités", *R. des C.*, t. 114 (1965-I), pp. 283-333.

BERMAN, F., "Treaty 'interpretation' in a judicial context ", *The Yale Journal of International Law*, 29 (2004) 2, pp. 315-322.

BERNHARDT, R., *Die Auslegung völkerrechtlicher Verträge insbesondere in der neuen Rechtsprechung internationaler Gerichte*, C. Heymanns Verlag, Köln-Berlin, 1963.

BERNHARDT, R., "Evolutive Treaty Interpretation, Especially of the European Convention on Human Rights", *G.Y.I.L.*, 1999, vol. 42, pp. 11-25.

BIANCHI, A., "L'immunité des Etats et les violations graves des droits de l'homme: la fonction de l'interprète dans la détermination du droit international ", *R.G.D.I.P,* 2004/1, pp. 63-101.

BLECHER, M.D., "Equitable Delimitation of continental Shelf", *A.J.I.L.*, 1979, pp. 60-79.

BLOKKER, N., "Decisions of International Organizations: the Case of the European Union", *N.Y.I.L.*, 1999, vol. XXX, pp. 45-74.

BOS, M., "Theory and practice of treaty interpretation", *Netherlands International Law Review*, 1980/3, pp. 11-50.

BOS, M., "The interpretation of international judicial decisions", *R.E.D.I.*, 1981/1, pp. 11-50.

BOULOIS, J., "La fonction normative de la jurisprudence", *Droit Social*, 1989, nº 7/8, juillet-août, pp. 524-525.

BOULOIS, J., "A propos de la fonction normative de la jurisprudence. Remarques sur l'oeuvre jurisprudentielle de la Cour de Justice des Communautés Européennes", in *Mélanges Marcel Waline*, vol. I, Paris, 1974, pp. 149-171.

BOYLE, A.F., "Some Reflections on the Relationship of Treaties and Soft Law", *I.C.L.Q.*, 1999, vol. 48, nº 4, pp. 901-913.

BREDIMAS, A., "Comparative Law in the Court of Justice of the European Communities", *The Yearbook of World Affairs*, 1978, pp. 320-333.

BREDIMAS, A., *Methods of Interpretation and Community Law*, North-Holland Pub., Amsterdam, 1978.

BROWNLIE, I., *Principles of Public International Law*, 6ª ed., Clarendon Press, Oxford, 2003.

BROWNLIE, I., "Some problems in the evaluation of the practice of status as an element of custom", in *Studi di diritto internazionale in onnore di Gaetano Arangio Ruiz*, 2004, vol. I, pp. 313-318.

BUFFET-TCHAKALOFF, M.F., "L'interprétation des traités internationaux par le Conseil d'Etat", *R.G.D.I.P.*, 1991/1, pp. 109-124.

CAHIER, P., "Le droit interne des Organisations Internationales", *R.G.D.I.P.*, 1963, pp. 563-582.

CAHIER, P., "Cours général de droit international public", *R. des C.*, t. 195 (1985-VI), pp. 9- 374.

CAPLAN, L. M., "State immunity, human rights, and *jus cogens*: a critique of the normative hierarchy theory", *A.J.I.L.*, 2003, Vol. 97, No. 4, pp. 741-781.

CAPOTORTI, F., "Sul valore della prasi applicativa dei trattati secondo la convenzione di Vienna", en la obra colectiva *Le Droit International à l'heure de sa codification. Etudes en l'honneur de Roberto Ago*, vol. I, Giuffrè ed., Milano 1987, pp. 197-218.

CARREAU, D., *Droit International*, 3ª. ed., Pedone, Paris, 1991.

CARRILLO SALCEDO, J.A., *Curso de Derecho Internacional Público*, Tecnos, Madrid, 1991.

CARRILLO SALCEDO, J.A., "Algunas reflexiones sobre el valor jurídico de la Declaración Universal de Derechos Humanos", in *Hacia un nuevo orden internacional y europeo. Homenaje al Profesor M. Díez de Velasco*, Tecnos, Madrid, 1993, pp. 167-178.

CASTAÑEDA, J., "Valeur juridique des résolutions des Nations Unies", *R. des C.*, t. 129 (1970-I), pp. 205-232.

CASTILLO, L. De, "Comentarios sobre el derecho internacional de los actos jurídicos unilaterales", in *Estudios de derecho internacional en homenaje al profesor Ernesto Rey Caro*, Zlata Drnas de Clément ed., 2002, vol. I, pp. 23-57.

CHINKIN, C.M., "The challenge of soft law: development and change in International Law", *I.C.L.Q.*, 1989/3, pp. 850-866.

CHUECA SANCHO, A., & DIEZ-HOCHTLEITNER, J., "La admisión de la tesis restrictiva de las inmunidades del Estado extranjero en la reciente práctica española", *R.E.D.I.*, 1988/2, pp. 7-54.

COHEN-JONATHAN, G., *La Convention européenne des Droits de l'Homme*, Economica, Paris, 1989.

CONDORELLI, L., "Interpretazione giurisprudenziale ed interpretazione autentica di trattati internazionali nell'ordinamento italiano", *Riv. Dir. Int.*, 1973/2, pp. 224-251.

CONFORTI, B., "Hummanité et renouveau de la production normative", in *Hummanité et Droit International ...*, *op. cit.*, pp. 113-120.

CONFORTI, B., *Diritto Internazionale*, 6ª ed., Ed. Scientifica, Napoli, 2002.

COT, J.P., "L'interprétation de l'accord franco-américain relatif au transport aérien international (Sentence arbitrale du 22 décembre 1963)", *A.F.D.I.*, 1964, pp. 352-383.

COT, "La conduite subséquente des parties à un traité", *R.G.D.I.P.*, 1966, vol. 70, pp. 632-666.

CORRIENTE CORDOBA, J.A., *Valoración jurídica de los preámbulos de los tratados internacionales*, EUNSA, Pamplona, 1973.

D'AMATO, A., "Trashing Customary International Law", *A.J.I.L.*, 1987/1, pp. 101-105.

DANILENKO, G.M., "The Theory of International Customary Law", *G.Y.I.L.*, 19xx, pp. 11-47.

DEGAN, V., "Procédés d'interprétation tirés de la jurisprudence de la Cour de Justice des Communautés Européennes", *Rev. Trimestrielle de Droit Européen*, 1966, pp. 189-209.

DIEZ DE VELASCO, M., *Instituciones de Derecho Internacional Público*, 15 ed., Tecnos, Madrid, 2005.

DUPUY, P.M., "Le Droit international de l'Environnement et la souveraineté des Etats. Bilan et perspectives", in *L'Avenir du Droit International de l'Environnement*, Colloque Workshop, La Haye, 1985, pp. 29-50.

DUPUY, P.M., "Le juge et la règle générale", *R.G.D.I.P.*, 1989/3, pp. 569-598.

DUPUY, P.M., "Hummanité, communauté et efficacité du droit", in *Hummanité et Droit International. Mélanges René-Jean DUPUY*, Paris, Pedone, 1991, pp. 133-148.

DUPUY, P.M., *Droit international public*, Dalloz, Paris, 1992.

DUPUY, R.J., "Droit déclaratoire et Droit programmatoire: de la coutume sauvage à la soft law", in *L'élaboration du droit international public*, ed. A. Pedone, Paris, 1975, pp. 132-148.

DUPUY, R.J., "Communauté internationale et disparités de développement", *R. des C.*, t. 165, (1979-IV), pp. 9-232.

ECONOMIDES, C., "Les actes institutionnels internationaux et les sources du Droit international", *A.F.D.I.*, 1988, pp. 131-145.

FAVRE, A., "L'interprétation objectiviste des traités internationaux", *Annuaire Suisse de Droit International*, 1960, pp. 75-99.

FERNANDEZ DE CASADEVANTE ROMANI, C., *La interpretación de las normas internacionales*, Aranzadi, Pamplona, 1996.

FERNANDEZ DE CASADEVANTE ROMANI, C., "Lenguaje y Derecho Internacional", in *Homenaje al Profesor D. Juan Manuel Castro Rial y Canos*, Madrid, Trotta, 2002, pp. 299-318.

FERRARI BRAVO, L., "Méthodes de recherche de la coutume internationale dans la pratique des Etats", *R. des C.*, t. 192 (1985-III), pp. 233-330.

FITZMAURICE, G., "The law and procedure of the I.C.J. 1951-1954: treaty interpretation and other treaty points", *British Yearbook of International Law*, 1957, pp. 203-293.

FOCSANEANU, L., "Les langues comme moyen d'expression du droit international", *A.F.D.I.*, 1970, pp. 257-274.

FROWEIN, J.A., "The internal and external effects of resolutions by international organisations", *Z.a.ö.R.V.*, 1989/4, pp. 778-790.

FURET, M.-F., "L'interprétation des traités par le législateur", *R.G.D.I.P.*, 1977, pp. 5-14.

GANSHOF VAN DER MEERSCH, W.J., "Les méthodes d'interprétation de la Cour Européenne des Droits de l'Homme", in *Perspectives canadiennes et européennes des droits de la personne*, Eds. Y. Balis, Quebec, 1986, p. 190.

GIRAUD, E., "Le droit international public et la politique", *R. des C.*, t. 110 (1963-III), pp. 731-763.

GOURNAIS, E., "The delimitation of the continental shelf of islands. Some observations", *Revue Hellénique de Droit International (R.H.D.I.)*, 1980, pp. 111-125.

GEORGOPULOS, T.G., "Le droit intertemporel et les dispositions conventionnelles évolutives: Quelle thérapie contre la vieillesse des traités? ", *R.G.D.I.P.*, 2004/1, pp. 123-148.

GOMEZ-ROBLEDO, J., "L'avis de la C.I.J. sur les conséquences juridiques de l'édification d'un mur dans le territoire palestinien occupé: timidité ou prudence?", *R.G.D.I.P.*, tome 109/2005/3, pp. 521-537.

GIULIANO, M., SCOVAZZI, T., TREVES, T., *Diritto Internazionale. Parte Generale*, Giuffrè ed., 1991.

GONZALEZ CAMPOS, J.D., SANCHEZ RODRIGUEZ, L.I., ANDRES SAENZ DE SANTA MARIA, Mª.P., *Curso de Derecho Internacional Público*, vol. I, 5ª ed., Servicio de Publicaciones de la Facultad de Derecho de la Universidad Complutense, Madrid, 1992. Also, 8th ed. and 3rd ed. revisited, Civitas, Madrid, 2003.

GUTIERREZ ESPADA, C., *Derecho Internacional Público*, Trotta, Madrid, 1995.

GUGGENHEIM, P., *Traité de droit international public*, 2ª. ed., vol. I, Genève, 1967.

HAGGENMACHER, R., "La doctrine du droit coutumier dans la pratique de la Cour internationale", *R.G.D.I.P.*, 1986/1, pp. 5-126.

HARDY, J., "The interpretation of plurilingual treaties by international Courts and Tribunals", *British Yearbook of International Law*, 1961, pp. 72-83.

HENKIN, L., "International Law: politics, values and functions", *R. des C.*, t. 216 (1989-IV), pp. 9-416.

HENZELIN, M., "La compétence pénale universelle: une question non résolue par l'arrêt Yerodia", *R.G.D.I.P.*, Tome 106/2002/4, pp. 819-854.

HOPKINS, K., "The International Court of Justice and the question of sovereign immunity: why the Yerodia case is an unfortunate ruling for the development of public international law", *South African Yearbook of International Law*, 27 (2002), pp. 256-263

HUESA VINAIXA, R., *El nuevo alcance de la "opinio iuris" en el Derecho Internacional contemporáneo*, Tirant lo Blanch, Valencia, 1991.

INTERNATIONAL LAW COMMISSION, "Draft Articles on the La won Treaties", *Yearbook of the I.L.C.*, 1966, vol. II, pp. 240-247.

JACQUE, J.-P., "Acte et norme en Droit International Public", *R. des C.*, t. 227 (1991-II), pp. 361-417.

JACQUE, J.-P., *Eléments pour une théorie de l'acte juridique en droit international public*, Paris, L.G.D.J., 1972.

JENNINGS, R., "The internal judicial practice of the International Court of Justice", *B.Y.I.L.*, 1988, pp. 31-47.

JIMENEZ DE ARECHAGA, E., "The work and jurisprudence of the International Court of Justice", *B.Y.I.L.*, 1987, pp. 1-38.

JUSTE RUIZ, J., CASTILLO, M., *Derecho internacional público*, Valencia, 2000.

JUSTE RUIZ, J., "Delimitaciones marinas en África Occidental. El Laudo arbitral sobre la delimitación de la frontera marítima entre Guinea y Guinea-Bissau", *R.E.D.I.*, 1990/2, pp. 367-389.

KAMMERHOFER, J., "Uncertainty in the formal sources of international law: customary international law and some of its problems", *European Journal of International Law*, 15 (2004) 3, pp. 523-553.

KISS, A.Ch., *Répertoire Français de Droit International Public*, tomo I, CNRS, Paris, 1962, pp. 399-496.

KOLB, R., "La bonne foi en droit international public", *R.B.D.I.*, 1998, vol. XXXI, nº 2, pp. 661-732.

KOZLOWSKI, A., "Interpretation of treaties inn the light of the relationship between international law and the law of the European Communities (European Union)", *The Polish yearbook of international law*, 26 (2002-2003), pp. 115-133.

KUNER, Ch. B., "The interpretation of multilingual treaties: comparison of texts versus the presumption of similar meaning", *I.C.L.Q.*, 1991/4, pp. 953-964.

KUTSCHER, H., "Alcune tesi sui metodi d'interpretazione del diritto comunitario dal punto di vista d'un giudice", *Riv. di Diritto Europeo*, 1976, pp. 283-314.

LAUTERPACHT, H., "La théorie des différends non justiciables en droit international", *R. des C.*, t. 34 (1930-IV), pp. 499-653.

LEIBIGER, M., *Die souveränitätsfreundliche Auslegung im Völkerrecht*, Frankfurt am Main, Berlin, Bern, Wien, Lang, 2005.

LERCHE, C., "Die Kompetenz des französischen Conseil d'Etat zur Auslegung völkerrechtlicher Verträge", *Z.a.ö.R.V.*, 1990, nº 50/4, pp. 869-890.

LIACOURAS, P., "The International Court of Justice and Development of Useful 'Rules of Interpretation' in the Process of Treaty Interpretation", *Proceedings of the American Society of International Law*, 1965, pp. 161-169.

LUKASHUK, I.I., "The principle *Pacta Sunt Servanda* and the Nature of Obligation Under International Law", *A.J.I.L.*, 1989/3, pp. 513-518.

MACGIBBON, I., "Means for the identification of International Law. General Assembly Resolutions: Custom. Practice and Mistaken Identity", in CHENG, B., *International Law: Teaching and Practice*, Stevens, London, 1982, pp. 10-26.

MACLACHIAN, C., "The principle of systematic integration and Article 31(3)(C) of the Vienna Convention", *The international and comparative law quarterly*, 54 (2005), 2, pp. 279-320.

MAKAROV, A.N., "Zur Auslegung mehrsprachiger Staatsverträge", en la obra colectiva *Hommage Paul Guggenheim*, Genève, 1968, pp. 403-428.

MALUWA, T., "Treaty interpretation and the exercise of prudential discretion by the International Court of Justice: some reflections on the PLO Mission Case", *N.I.L.R.*, 1990, pp. 330-346.

MALUWA, T., "International Law-Making in the Organization of African Unity: An Overview", *Rev. Afr. D.I. & Comp.*, 2000, vol. 12, nº 2, pp. 201-225.

MARIÑO MENENDEZ, F., *Nociones de Derecho Internacional Público*, Servicio de Publicaciones de la Universidad de Zaragoza, Zaragoza, 1990.

MARIÑO MENENDEZ, F., *Derecho Internacional Público (Parte General)*, 3rd ed. revisited, Trotta, Madrid, 1999.

MCWHINNEY, E., *Les Nations Unies et la formation du droit*, Pedone/Unesco, Paris, 1986.

MENDELSON, M.H., "The Formation of Customary International Law", *R.C.A.D.I.*, 1998, vol. 272, pp. 155-410.

MERTENS DE WILMARS, J., "Réflexions sur les méthodes d'interprétation de la Cour de Justice des Communautés Européennes", *Cahiers de Droit Européen*, 1986, pp. 1-20.

MIAJA DE LA MUELA, A., "Los actos unilaterales en las relaciones internacionales", *R.E.D.I.*, vol. 20, 1967, pp. 429-464;

MILLAN MORO, L., *La opinio iuris en el Derecho Internacional contemporáneo*, ed. Centro de Estudios de Ramón Areces S.A., Madrid, 1990.

MONACO, R., "Les principes d'interprétation suivis par la Cour de Justice des Communautés Européennes", in *Mélanges Rolin*, Pedone, Paris, 1964, pp. 217-227.

MOSLER, H., "Remarques sur la superposition du droit des Organisations Internationales au droit des gens interétatiques", in *Estudios de Derecho Internacional. Homenaje al profesor Miaja de la Muela*, Tecnos, Madrid, 1979, vol. I, pp. 429-442.

MULLERSON, R.A., "Sources of International Law: New Tendencies in Soviet Thinking", *A.J.I.L.*, 1989/3, pp. 494-512.

O'CONNOR, J.F., *Good Faith in International Law*, Dartmouth, Aldershot, 1991.

ORAKHELASHVILI, A., "The Impact of Peremptory Norms on the Interpretation and Application of United Nations Security Council Resolutions", *E.J.I.L*, Vol. 16, Nr. 1, February 2005, pp. 59-88.

ORMAND, R., "L'utilisation particulière de la méthode d'interprétation des traités selon leur 'effet utile' par la Cour de Justice des Communautés Européennes", *Rev. Trim. Droit Européen*, 1976, pp. 624-634.

ORTEGA CARCELEN, M.C., "Análisis del valor de la jurisprudencia en el Derecho Internacional", *R.E.D.I.*, 1988/2, pp. 55-87.

OST, F., "Originalité des méthodes d'interprétation de la Convention européenne des droits de l'homme", in *Raissoner la raison d'Etat. Vers une Europe des droits de l'homme*, P.U.F., Paris, 1989.

PALMISANO, G., "Les garanties de non-répétition entre codification et réalisation juridictionnelle du droit: à propos de l'affaire LaGrand ", *R.G.D.I.P.*, Tome 106/2002/4, pp. 753-790.

PAMBOU TCHIVOUNDA, G., "Le droit international de l'interprétation des traités à l'épreuve de la jurisprudence", *Journal de Droit International*, 1986/3, pp. 627-650.

PASTOR RIDRUEJO, J.A., *Curso de Derecho Internacional Público y Organizaciones Internacionales*, 9ª. ed., Tecnos, Madrid, 2003.

PEÑARANDA, A., *La costumbre en el Derecho Internacional*, ed. de la Universidad Complutense, Madrid, 1988.

QUOC DINH, N., DAILLIER, P., PELLET, A., *Droit International Public*, 4ª ed., L.G.D.J., Paris, 1992.

RANGEL, V.M., "Le plateau continental dans la Convention de 1982 sur le Droit de la Mer", *R. des C.*, t. 194 (1985-V), pp. 269-428.

REMIRO BROTONS, A., *Derecho Internacional Público. 2 Derecho de los Tratados*, Tecnos, Madrid, 1987.

REMIRO BROTONS, A., RIQUELME, R.M., ORIHUELA, E., DIEZ-HOCHLEITNER, J., *Derecho Internacional Público*, McGraw Hill, Madrid, 1997.

REUTER, P., *Introduction au Droit des Traités*, P.U.F., Paris, 1985.

REUTER, P., "Quelques réflexions sur le vocabulaire du droit international", in *Mélanges en l'honneur de M. le Doyen Trotabas*, Pedone, Paris, 1970, pp. 423-445.

RIDEAU, J., "Les accords internationaux dans la jurisprudence de la Cour de Justice des Communautés Européennes: réflexions sur les relations entre les ordres juridiques international, communautaire et nationaux", *R.G.D.I.P.*, 1990/2, pp. 289-418.

RÖBEN, V., "Le précédent dans la jurisprudence de la Cour internationale", *German Yearbook of International Law*, 1989, vol. 32, pp. 382-407.

ROLLAND, P., "L'interprétation de la Convention", *R.U.D.H.*, 1991, pp. 280-288.

RODRIGUEZ CARRION, A., *Lecciones de Derecho Internacional Público*, 5 ed., Tecnos, Madrid, 2002.

ROSENNE, S., "Conceptualism as a Guide to Treaty-Interpretation", in *Le Droit International à l'heure de sa codification. Etudes en l'honneur de Roberto Ago*, vol. I, Giuffrè ed., Milano 1987, pp. 417-432.

RUDOLF, W., "Posibilidades de la redacción del texto de los tratados internacionales en distintas lenguas", *R.E.D.I.*, 1977, vol. XXX, pp. 257-264.

ROBERTS, A.E., "Traditional and Modern Approaches to Customary International Law – A Reconciliation", *A.J.I.L.*, 2001, nº 4, pp. 757-791.

RODRIGUEZ CARRION, A., *Lecciones de Derecho Internacional Público*, 5th. ed., Tecnos, Madrid, 2002.

SALMON, J., "Le fait dans l'application du droit international", *R. des C.*, t. 175 (1982-II), pp. 257-414.

SANCHEZ RODRIGUEZ, L.I., "'Uti possidetis': la reactualización jurisprudencial de un viejo principio. (A propósito de la Sentencia del TIJ (Sala) en el asunto Burkina Fasso/República de Mali", *R.E.D.I.*, 1988/2, pp. 121-151.

SANCHEZ RODRIGUEZ, L.I., *Las inmunidades de los Estados extranjeros ante los Tribunales españoles*, Universidad de Alcalá/Civitas, Madrid, 1990.

SAPIENZA, R., "Les déclarations interprétatives unilaterales et l'interprétation des traités", *R.G.D.I.P.*, 1999, tome 103 nº 3, pp. 601-629.

SASSOLI, M., "L'arrrêt Yerodia: quelques remarques sur une affaire au point de colision entre les deux couches du droit international ", *R.G.D.I.P.*, Tome 106/2002/4, pp. 791-818.

SCHERMERS, H.G., "International Organizations and the Law of Treaties", *G.Y.I.L.*, 1999, vol. 42, pp. 56-65.

SCHREUER, H., "The interpretation of treaties by domestic Courts", *B.Y.I.L.*, 1971, pp. 255-301.

SEPULVEDA, C., "Methods and procedures for the creation of legal norms in the International System of States: an inquiry into the progressive development of International Law in the present Era", *German Y.I.L.*, 1990, vol. 33, pp. 432-459.

SICAULT, J., "Du caractère obligatoire des engagements unilatéraux en Droit international public", *R.G.D.I.P.*, 1979, pp. 633-688.

SIMON, D., *L'interprétation judiciaire des traités d'Organisations Internationales*, Pedone, Paris, 1981.

SIMMA, B., "Consent: Strains in the Treaty System", in MACDONALD, R.St.J./JOHNSTON, D.M., *The structure and process of International Law*, M. Nijhoff, 2ª ed., Dordrecht, 1986, pp. 485-511.

SKUBISZEWSKI, K., "L'élaboration des grandes conventions multilatérales et des instruments non conventionnels à fonction ou à vocation normative", *Yearbook of the Institute of International Law*, vol. 61-I, A. Pedone, Paris, 1985, pp. 29-249 and 305-358; and vol. 61-II, A. Pedone, Paris, 1986, pp. 257-276.

SKUBISZEWSKI, K., "Les actes unilatéraux des Etats", in BEDJAOUI, M., *Droit International. Bilan et perspectives*, t. I, Paris, 1991, pp. 231-250.

SLOAN, B., "General Assembly Resolutions revisited (forty years later)", *B.Y.I.L.*, 1987, pp. 39-150.

SUR, S. *L'interprétation en droit international public*, L.G.D.J., Paris, 1974.

SUY, E., *Les actes juridiques unilatéraux en Droit international public*, L.G.D.J., Paris, 1962.

TEBOUL, G., "Le droit international non écrit devant le juge administratif. Quelques reflexions", *R.G.D.I.P.*, 1991/2, pp. 321-370.

TETLEY, W., "Interpretation and construction of The Hague", *The Journal of International Maritime Law*, 10 (2004), 1, pp. 30-70.

THIERRY, H., "L'évolution du Droit International. Cours général de droit international public", (*R. des C.*, t. 222 (1990-III), pp. 9-186.

THIRLWAY, H., "The law and procedure of the International Court of Justice", *B.Y.I.L.*, 1989, pp. 1-157.

THIRLWAY, H., "The law and procedure of the International Court of Justice", *B.Y.I.L.*, 1990, pp. 1-133.

TOMUSCHAT, Ch., "L'immunité des Etats en cas de violations graves des droits de l'homme", *R.G.D.I.P.*, Tome 109/2005/1, pp. 51-74.

TORRIONE, H., *L'influence des conventions de codification sur la coutume en droit international public*, eds. Universitaires, Fribourg, 1989.

TOUSCOZ, J., *Le principe d'effectivité dans l'ordre international*, L.G.D.J., Paris, 1964.

TRINIDADE, A.A.C., "La interpretación de tratados en el derecho internacional y la especificidad de los tratados de derechos humanos", in *Estudios de derecho internacional en homenaje al profesor Ernesto rey Caro*, Zlata Drnas de Clément ed., 2002, vol. I, pp. 747-776.

VALLAT, F.A., "The competence of the United Nations General Assembly", *R. des C.*, t. 97 (1959-II), pp. 203-292.

VENTURINI, G., "La portée et les effets juridiques des attitudes et des actes unilatéraux des Etats", *R. des C.*, t. 112 (1964-II), pp. 369-466

VILLANI, U., "La delimitazione della piattaforma continentale e della zona economica exclusiva si sensi della Convenzione delle Nazioni Unite sul diritto del mare", *Riv. Diritto Internazionale*, 1985/2, pp. 261-298.

VIRALLY, M., "La distinction entre textes internationaux de portée juridique et textes internationaux dépourvus de portée juridique", *Yearbook of the Institute of International Law*, vol. 60-I, A. Pedone, Paris, 1985, pp. 166-257.

VIRALLY, M., "The sources of International Law", in SORENSEN, M., *Manual of Public International Law*, Londres, 1968, pp. 116-174.

VIRALLY, M., "Résolution et accord international", en la obra colectiva *Essays in International Law in honour of judge Manfred Lachs*, Nijhoff, The Hague, 1984, pp. 299-306.

VIRALLY, M., *Le Droit International en devenir. Essais écrits au fil des ans*, P.U.F., Paris, 1990, pp. 119-122.

VISMARA, F., "La prova di una pratica generale acettata come diritto nella prassi della Corte internazionale di giustizia", *Comunità Internazionale*, 2000, vol. LV, nº 3, pp. 439-463.

VISSCHER, Ch. de, *Problèmes d'interprétation judiciaire en droit international public*, L.G.D.J., Paris, 1963.

WEIL, P., "Vers une normativité relative en Droit International", *R.G.D.I.P.*, 1982/1, pp. 5-47.

YASSEEN, M.K., "L'interprétation des traités d'après la Convention de Vienne sur le droit des traités", *R. des C.*, t. 151 (1976-III), pp. 1-114.

YEE, S., "The News that Opinio Juris 'Is not a Necessary Element of Customary (International) Law' Is Greatly Exaggerated", *G.Y.I.L.*, 2000, vol. 43, pp. 227-238.

ZOLLER, E., "Art. 2.2", in COT, J.-P. and PELLET, A., *La Charte des Nations Unies*, Economica, Paris, 1985, pp. 98-100.

International Case Law

1 Arbitral

- Case concerning *William E. and William Barron v. U.S.A. (n° 633)*, (Mexico/United States of America) decision of 16 August 1871 (COUSSIRAT-COUSTERE, V., & EISEMAN, P.M., *Repertory of International Arbitral Jurisprudence*, vol. I, p. 30).
- Case concerning the *Treaty of Limits of 1858* (Costa Rica /Nicaragua), decision of 26 July 1899 (*ibid.*, p. 31).
- Case concerning the *Frontier in the area of the Manica plateau*, (Portugal/United Kingdom), decision of 30 January 1897 (COUSSIRAT-COUSTERE, V., & EISEMAN, P.M., *op. cit.*, vol. I, p. 41-42).
- Case concerning the *Heirs of Jean Maninat* (France/Venezuela), decision of 31 July 1905 (*Recueil of International Arbitral Awards (R.I.A.A.)*, vol. X, p. 78).
- Case concerning the *Walfish Bay boundary* (Germany/United Kingdom), Arbitral Award of 23 May 1911 (*R.I.A.A.*, vol. XI, pp. 267-308; COUSSIRAT-COUSTERE, V., & EISEMAN, P.M., *op. cit.*, vol. I, pp. 31-32).
- Case concening the *Timor island* (Netherlands/Portugal), Judgement of 25 June 1914 (*R.I.A.A.*, vol. IX, pp. 490-509; COUSSIRAT-COUSTERE, V., & EISEMAN, P.M., *op. cit.*, vol. I, p. 34).
- Case concerning *German reparations (art. 260 of the Treaty of Versailles* (Germany/Reparation Commission), decision of the 3rd September 1924 (*R.I.A.A.*, vol. I, pp. 431-528).
- Case concerning *Cayuga Indians v. United States* (United Kingdom/United States of America), Judgement of 22 January 1926 (*R.I.A.A.*, vol. VI, pp. 175-190; COUSSIRAT-COUSTERE, V., & EISEMAN, P.M., *op. cit.*, vol. I, p. 35ff.).
- Case concerning *Paula Mendel et alt. v. Germany* (Germany/United States of america), decision of 13 August 1926 (*R.I.A.A.*, vol. VII, pp. 380-389; COUSSIRAT-COUSTERE, V. & EISEMAN, P.M., *op. cit.*, vol. II, p. 24).
- Case concerning *Banque d'Orient v. Gouvernment turc*, Judgement of 9 February 1928 (COUSSIRAT-COUSTERE, V., & EISEMAN, P.M., *op. cit.*, vol. II, p. 36).

– Case concerning *Asunto Dampfschiffahrtsgesellschaft "Argo" v. The Hanseatic Maritime Agency Ldt.in Liq.*, Judgement of 21 June 1928 (COUSSIRAT-COUSTERE, V., & EISEMAN, P.M., *op. cit.*, vol. II, p. 35).

– Case concerning *Interpretation of the Tardieu-Jaspar agreement of January 12, 1930* (Belgium/France), Judgement of 12 January 1930 (*R.I.A.A.*, vol. III, pp. 1703-1716; COUSSIRAT-COUSTERE, V., & EISEMAN, P.M., *op. cit.*, vol. II, p. 35).

– Case concerning the *Pensions of officials of the Saar Territory* (Germany/Governing Commission of the Saar Territory), decision of 4 September 1934 (*R.I.A.A.*, vol. III, pp. 1564-1565; COUSSIRAT-COUSTERE, V., & EISEMAN, P.M., *op. cit.*, vol. II, p. 36).

– Case concerning *Maison Hermann Schlessiger* (Germany/Rumania), decision of 15 April 1935 (*R.I.A.A.*, vol. III, pp. 1641-1655; COUSSIRAT- COUSTERE, V., & EISEMAN, P.M., *op. cit.*, vol. II, p. 25).

– Case concerning *Special capital levy dutie (No. 32)* (France/Italy), decision of 29 August 1949 (*R.I.A.A.*, vol. XIII, p. 122; COUSSIRAT-COUSTERE, V., & EISEMAN, P.M., *op. cit.*, vol. III, t. 1, p. 167).

– Case concerning *Interpretation of article V of the Constitution of the United Nations Educational, Scientific and Cultural Organization*, Judgement of 19 September 1949 (COUSSIRAT-COUSTERE, V., & EISEMAN, P.M., op. cit., vol. III, t. 1, pp. 135-136).

– Case concerning *Società Mineraria e Metallurgica di Pertusola (n° 95)*, decision of the French-Italian Conciliation Commision of 8 March 1951 (*R.I.A.A.*, vol. XIII, pp. 179-197; COUSSIRAT-COUSTERE, V., & EISEMAN, P.M., *op. cit.*, vol. III, t. 1, p. 116).

– Case concerning the *Gold of the National Bank of Albania* (France, Italy, United Kingdom, United States of America), decision of 20 February 1953 (*R.I.A.A.*, vol. XII, pp. 19-52).

– Case concerning the *Agreement on German External Debts*, Judgement of 27 February 1953 (COUSSIRAT-COUSTERE, V., & EISEMAN, P.M., *op. cit.*, vol. III, t. 1, p. 112).

– Case concerning *German External Debts*, Judgement of 27 February 1953 (*I.L.R.*, 1958-I, vol. XXV, pp. 33-70; COUSSIRAT-COUSTERE, V., & EISEMAN, P.M., *op. cit.*, vol. III, t. 1, p. 136).

– Case concerning *Interpretation and application of the provisions of article 78, paragraph 7, of the Peace Treaty to Ethiopian territory (No. 201)* (France/Italy), decision of 16 March 1956 (R.I.A.A., vol. XIII, pp. 636-658; COUSSIRAT-COUSTERE, V., & EISEMAN, P.M., op. cit., vol. III, t. 1, p. 116-117).

– Case concerning *Albert Flegenheimer (No. 182)* (Italy/United States of America), decision of 20 September 1958 (*R.I.A.A.*, vol. XIV, pp. 328-390).

- Case concerning *Property, Rights and Interests in Germany* (Italian Republic v. Federal Republic if Germany) Judgement of 14 November 1959 (COUSIRAT-COUSTERE, V., & EISEMAN, P.M., *op. cit.*, vol. III, t. 1, p. 137).
- Case concerning *Eugenio Fubini et alt. (No. 201)* (Italy/United States of America), decision of 12 December de 1959, (*R.I.A.A.*, vol. XIV, pp. 421-434).
- Case concerning *Mary De Pascale et alt. (No. MD/1018)* (Italy/United States of America), decision of 24 June 1961 (*R.I.A.A.*, vol. XVI, p. 234; COUSSIRAT-COUSTERE, V., & EISEMAN, P.M., *op. cit.*, vol. III, t. 1, p. 132).
- Case concerning the *Société des Comptoirs Dufay et Gigandet et alt. (n. 284)* (France(Italy), decision of 9 July 1962 (*R.I.A.A.*, vol. XVI, pp. 199-219; COUSSIRAT-COUSTERE, V., & EISEMAN, P.M., *op. cit.*, vol. III, t. 1, p. 120).
- Case concerning *Asunto de la Krankenversorgung der Bundesbahnbeamten v. República Austriaca*, binding No. 37 of the Austro-German Arbitral Tribunal of 14 November 1962 (COUSSIRAT-COUSTERE, V., & EISEMAN, P.M., *op. cit.*, vol. III, t. 1, p. 171).
- Case concerning *Interpretation of the Air Transport Services Agreement dated March 27, 1946* (France/United States of America), Judgement of 22 December 1963 (*R.I.A.A.*, vol. XVI, pp. 11-71; COUSSIRAT-COUSTERE, V., & EISEMAN, P.M., *op. cit.*, vol. III, t. 1, pp. 147-148).
- Case *Compagnie du Katanga v. Colonie du Congo Belge*, (*B.Y.I.L.*, 1964, pp. 184-194; COUSSIRAT-COUSTERE, V., & EISEMAN, P.M., *op. cit.*, vol. II, p. 35).
- Case concerning *Interpretation of the Air Transport Services Agreement dated February 6, 1948* (Italy/United States of America), Advisory opinion of 17 July 1965 (*R.I.A.A.*, vol. XVI, pp. 81-102; *R.G.D.I.P.*, 1968, vol. LXXII, pp. 461-486; COUSSIRAT-COUSTERE, V., & EISEMAN, P.M., *op. cit.*, vol. III, t. 1, p. 158.159).
- Case concerning the *Legality of a system for the selective adjustment of quotas (International Coffee Agreement, 1962)* decision of 30 November 1965 (*I.L.R.*, 1965, vol. LXII, p. 427 & s.; COUSSIRAT-COUSTERE, V., & EISEMAN, P.M., *op. cit.*, vol. III, t. 1, p. 128).
- Case concerning *Dr. René Springer V. Federal Republic if Germany*, decision of 26 May 1966 (COUSSIRAT-COUSTERE, V., & EISEMAN, P.M., *op. cit.*, vol. III, t. 1, p. 162-163).
- Case concerning the *Agreement on German External Debts* (Kingdom of Greece v. Federal Republic of Germany), Judgement on the merits of 26 January 1972 (*R.I.A.A.*, vol. XLVII, pp. 423-462; COUSSIRAT-COUSTERE, V., & EISEMAN, P.M., *op. cit.*, vol. III, t. 1, p. 126).
- Case of the *Delimitation of the continental shelf between Great Britain and France* (*R.I.A.A.*, vol. XVIII, p. 366).

- Case concerning the *Beagle Channel*, (*I.L.R.*, 1978, vol. LII, pp. 97-228; COUSSIRAT-COUSTERE, V., & EISEMAN, P.M., *op. cit.*, vol. III, t. 1. p. 109).
- Case concerning the *Young Plan (No. 6-10)* (Kingdom of Belgium, French Republic, Swiss Confederation, United Kingdom and United States of america v. Federal Republic of Germany), Judgement of 16 May 1980 (*I.L.R.*, 1980, vol. LIX, pp. 529-530; *R.G.D.I.P.*, 1980/4, pp. 1158-1206; COUSSIRAT-COUSTERE, V., & EISEMAN, P.M., *op. cit.*, vol. III, t. 1, p. 174).
- Case concerning the *Agreement on German External Debts*, Judgement of 16 May 1980 (*I.L.R.*, 1980, vol. LIX, pp. 502-550; COUSSIRAT-COUSTERE, V., & EISEMAN, P.M., *op. cit.*, vol. III, t. 1, p. 151; *R.G.D.I.P.*, 1980/4, pp. 1158-1206).
- Case concerning *United States-Iran, Case No. A 17 (DEC 37-A 17-FT*, Interim Judgement of 13 May 1985 (COUSSIRAT-COUSTERE, V., & EISEMAN, P.M., *op. cit.*, vol. III, t. 1, p. 109).
- Case concerning *Fileting within the Gulf of St. Lawrence* (Canada/France), decision of 17 July 1986 (*R.G.D.I.P.*, 1986, pp. 734-735; COUSSIRAT-COUSTERE, V., & EISEMAN, P.M., *op. cit.*, vol. III, t. 1, p. 129).
- Case concerning *The Islamic Republic of Iran v. The United States of America (ITL 63-A 15-FT)*, Interlocutory award of 20 August 1986 (COUSSIRAT-COUSTERE, V., & EISEMAN, P.M., *op. cit.*, vol. III, t. 1, p. 127).
- Case of the *Dispute concerning the course of the frontier between B.P. 62 and Mount Fitz Roy (Argentina/Chile)*, Decision of 21 October 1994 (*R.I.A.A.*, vol. XXII, pp. 3-152) and Decision of the Tribunal with respect to the application for revision and subsidiary interpretation of the Award of 21 October 1994, submitted by Chile, decision of 13 October 1995 (*R.I.A.A.*, vol. XXII, pp. 153-207).
- Case concerning *Territorial Sovereignty and Scope of the Dispute* (Eritrea/Yemen), Award of the Arbitral Tribunal in the first stage of the proceedings, of 9 October 1998 (*R.I.A.A.*, vol. XXII, pp. 209-331) and Award of the Arbitral Tribunal in the second stage of the proceedings between Eritrea and Yemen (Maritime Delimitation), of 17 December 1999) (*R.I.A.A.*, vol. XXII, pp. 333-410).

2 P.C.I.J.

- Case concerning the *Competence of the ILO in regard to International Regulation of the Conditions of Labour of Persons Employed in Agriculture (*P.C.I.J., *Serie B No. 2*, pp. 39).
- Case concerning *Interpretation of Article 3, Paragraph 2, of the Treaty of Lausanne* (P.C.I.J., *Serie B No. 12*, p. 24).
- Case concerning the *Serbian Loans* (P.C.I.J., *Serie A No. 21*, p. 119).

- *Lotus* case (P.C.I.J., *Serie A No. 10*, pp. 16-18).
- Case concerning *Free Zones of Upper Savoy and the District of Gex (*P.C.I.J., *Serie A No. 22*, p. 13).
- Case concerning *Polish Postal Service in Danzig* (P.C.I.J., *Serie B No. 11*, p. 39).

3 I.C.J.

- Advisory Opinion concerning *Conditions of Admission of a State to Membership in the United Nations (Article 4 of the Charter)* (I.C.J., *Reports 1948*, p. 61).
- *Corfu Channel* case (I.C.J., *Reports 1949*, p. 24).
- Advisory Opinion concerning *Interpretation of Peace Treaties with Bulgaria, Hungary and Romania* (I.C.J., *Reports 1950,* p. 74 and pp. 227-229).
- Advisory Opinion concerning the *International Status of South West Africa* (I.C.J., *Reports 1950*, p. 132).
- *Asylum* case (I.C.J., *Reports 1950*, p. 275).
- *Request for Interpretation of the Judgement of 20 November 1950 in the Asylum Case (Columbia-Peru)*, (I.C.J., *Reports 1950*).
- Advisory Opinion concerning the *Competence of the General Assembly for the Admission of a State to the United Nations* (I.C.J., *Reports 1950,* p. 8).
- *Fisheries* case (I.C.J., *Reports 1951*, p. 131).
- Advisory Opinion concerning *Reservations to the Convention on the Prevention and Punishment of the Crime of Genocide* (I.C.J., *Reports 1951,* p. 23).
- *Haya de la Torre* case (I.C.J., *Reports 1951*, p. 81).
- Case concerning *Rights of Nationals of the United States of America in Morocco* (I.C.J., *Reports 1952*, p. 189).
- *Ambatielos* case (I.C.J., *Reports 1952*, p. 41).
- *Anglo-Iranian Oil Co.* case (I.C.J., *Reports 1952*, p. 104).
- Advisory Opinion concerning *Admissibility of Hearings of Petitioners by the Committee on South West Africa* (I.C.J., *Reports 1956,* p. 28).
- Advisory Opinion concerning *Judgements of the Administrative Tribunal of the ILO upon Complainst Made against Unesco* (I.C.J., *Reports 1956,* p. 77.
- Case concerning the *Right of Passage over Indian Territory* (I.C.J., *Reports 1957,* p. 141).
- *Interhandel* case (I.C.J., *Reports 1959*, p. 27).
- Case concerning *Sovereignty over Certain Frontier Land* (I.C.J., *Reports 1959,* p. 221).

- Case concerning the *Aerial Incident of 27 July 1955* (I.C.J., *Reports 1959,* p. 142).
- Advisory Opinion concerning *Composition of the Maritime Safety Committee of the Inter-Governmental Maritime Consultative Organization* (I.C.J., *Reports 1960,* p. 158).
- Case concerning the *Arbitral Award Made by the King of Spain on 23 December 1906* (I.C.J., *Reports 1960,* p. 209).
- Case concerning the *Right of Passage over Indian Territory* (I.C.J., *Reports 1960,* p. 38).
- Case concerning the *Temple of Preah Vihear* (I.C.J., *Reports 1961*, p. 32).
- Advisory Opinion concerning *Certain Expenses of the United Nations (Article 17, paragraph 2, of the Charter)* (I.C.J., *Reports 1962,* p. 155).
- Case concerning *South-West Africa, Preliminary Objections* (I.C.J., *Reports 1962,* p. 330).
- Case concerning the *Temple of Preah Vihear, Merits* (I.C.J., *Reports 1962,* p. 32).
- Case concerning *South-West Africa, Second Phase* (I.C.J., *Reports 1966,* p. 48).
- *North Sea Continental Shelf* case (I.C.J., *Reports 1969,* p. 38).
- Advisory Opinion concerning the *Legal Consequences for States of the Continued Presence of South Africa in Namibia (Sout West Africa) notwithstanding Security Council Resolution 276 (1970)* (I.C.J., *Reports 1971,* p. 31).
- *Nuclear Tests* case (I.C.J., *Reports 1974*, p. 267).
- Advisory Opinion concerning the *Western Sahara* (I.C.J., *Reports 1975*, p. 11).
- *Aegean Sea Continental Shelf* case (I.C.J., *Reports 1978,* p. 22).
- Case concerning *United States Diplomatic and Consular Staff un Tehran* (I.C.J., *Reports 1980,* p. 3).
- *Continental Shelf (Tunisia/Libyan Arab Jamahiriya case)* (I.C.J., *Reports 1982,* p. 45).
- Case concerning *Delimitation of the Maritime Boundary in the Gulf of Maine Area* (I.C.J., *Reports 1984,* p. 264).
- *Continental Shelf (Libyan Arab Jamahiriya/Malta case)* (I.C.J., *Reports 1985,* p. 29).
- *Application for Revision and Interpretation of the Judgement of 24 February 1982 in the case concerning the Continental Shelf (Tunisia/Libyan Arab Jamahiriya) (Tunisia v. Libyan Arab Jamahiriya)*, (I.C.J., *Reports 1985*).
- Case concerning *Military and Paramilitary Activities in and against Nicaragua* (I.C.J., *Reports 1986,* p. 33).

- Case concerning the *Frontier Dispute* (I.C.J., *Reports 1986*, p. 567).
- Case concerning *Elettronica Sicula S.p.A. (ELSI),* (I.C.J., *Reports 1989,* p. 42).
- Case concerning *Applicability of Article VI, Section 22, of the Convention on the Privileges and Immunities of the United Nations*, Advisory Opinion (I.C.J., *Reports 1989,* p. 177).
- Case concerning the *Arbitral Award of 31 July 1989* (I.C.J., *Reports 1991,* p. 67).
- Case concerning *Questions of Interpretation and Application of the 1971 Montreal Convention arising from the Aerial Incident at Lockerbie* (I.C.J., *Reports 1992,* p. 3).
- Case concerning *Land, Island and Maritime Frontier Dispute (El Salvador/Honduras: Nicaragua intervening)* (I.C.J., *Reports 1992,* p. 351).
- Case concerning *Maritime Delimitation in the Area between Greenland and Jan Mayen* (I.C.J., *Reports 1993,* p. 38).
- Case concerning *Territorial Dispute* (Lybian Arab Jamahiriya/Chad) (I.C.J., *Reports 1994,* p. 6).
- Case concerning *Maritime Delimitation and Territorial Questions between Qatar and Bahrain* (I.C.J., *Reports 1995,* p. 6).
- Case concerning *East Timor* (Portugal v. Australia) (I.C.J., *Reports 1995,* p. 90).
- Advisory Opinion concerning the *Legality of the Use by a State of Nuclear Weapons in Armed Conflict* (I.C.J., *Reports 1996,* p. 66).
- Advisory Opinion concerning the *Legality of the Threat or Use of Nuclear Weapons* (I.C.J., *Reports 1996,* p. 226).
- *Fisheries Jurisdiction* case (Spain v. Canada) (I.C.J., *Reports 1998,* p. 3).
- Request for the interpretation of the judgement of 11 June 1998 in the *case concerning the land and maritime boundary between Cameroon and Nigeria* (Cameroon v. Nigeria), Preliminary Objections (Nigeria v. Cameroon), (I.C.J., *Reports 1999*).
- Case concerning *Kasikili/Sedudu Island* (Botswana/Namibia) (I.C.J., *Reports 1999*).
- Advisory Opinion on the *Difference relating immunity from legal process of a Special Rapporteur of the Commission on Human Rights*, (I.C.J., *Reports 1999*).
- Case concerning *Maritime Delimitation and Territorial Questions between Qatar and Bahrain* (Qatar v. Bahrain), (I.C.J., *Reports 2001*).
- *LaGrand* case (Germany v. United States of America), (I.C.J., *Reports 2001*)
- Case concerning the *Arrest Warrant of 11 April 2000* (Democratic Republic of the Congo v. Belgium), (I.C.J., *Reports 2002*)

- Case concerning *Sovereignty over Pulau Ligitan and Pulau Sipadan* (Indonesia/Malaysia), (I.C.J., *Reports 2002*).
- Case concerning the *Land and Maritime Boundary between Cameroon and Nigeria* (Cameroon v. Nigeria: Equatorial Guinea intervening), (I.C.J., *Reports 2002*).
- Case concerning *Oil Platforms* (Islamic Republic of Iran v. United States of America), (I.C.J., *Reports 2003*)
- Application for Revision of the Judgement of 11 September 1992 in the *Case concerning the Land, Island and Maritime Frontier Dispute (El Salvador/Honduras: Nicaragua intervening)* (El Salvador v. Honduras), (I.C.J., *Reports 2003*).
- Case concerning *Avena and other Mexican Nationals* (Mexico v. United States of America) (I.C.J., *Reports 2004*).
- *Case concerning legality of use of force* (Serbia and Montenegro v. Belgium), I.C.J., *Reports 2004*).
- Advisory Opinion on the *Legal Consequences of the Cosntruction of a Wall in the Occupied Palestinian Territory*, (I.C.J., *Reports 2004*).
- *Frontier Dispute* (Benin/Niger), (I.C.J., *Reports 2005*).
- Case concerning *Certain Property (Liechtenstein v. Germany)*, (I.C.J., *Reports 2005*).